AF361593

Eastward of Good Hope

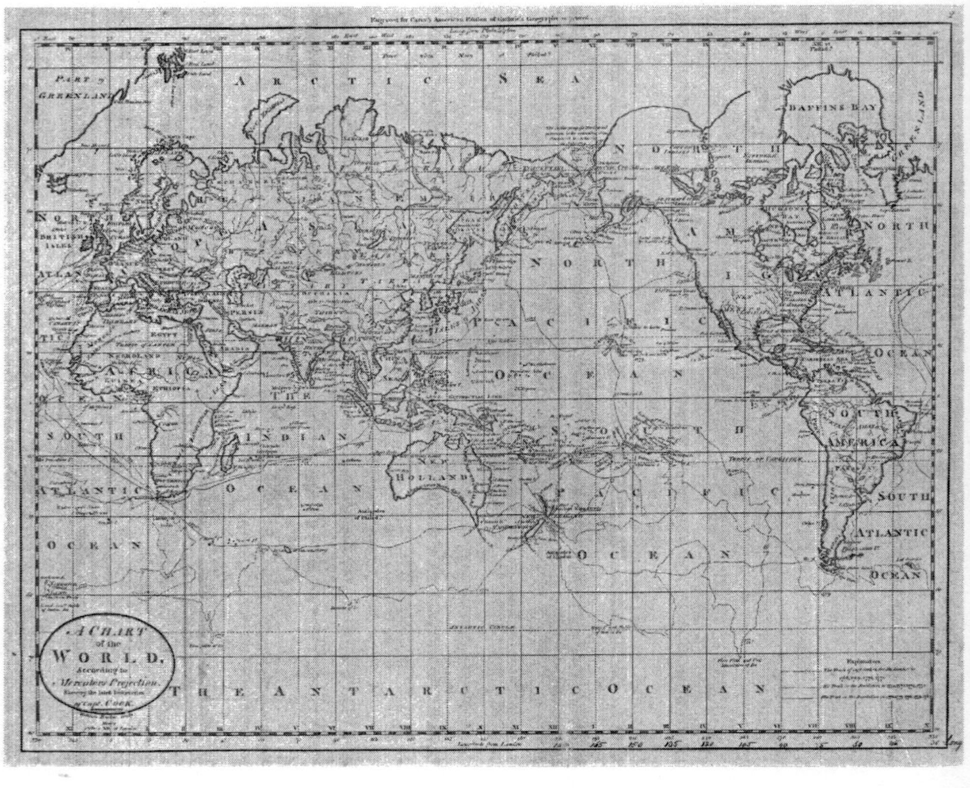
Engraved for Carey's American Edition of Guthrie's Geography improved.
Longitude from Philadelphia
ARCTIC SEA
PART of GREENLAND
BAFFINS BAY
GREENLAND
NORTH
NORTH AMERICA
NORTH ATLANTIC OCEAN
ATLANTIC OCEAN
AFRICA
EGYPT
PERSIA
NEGROLAND
ETHIOPIA
THE INDIAN OCEAN
PACIFIC OCEAN
NORTH PACIFIC OCEAN
SOUTH PACIFIC OCEAN
NEW HOLLAND
SOUTH AMERICA
SOUTH ATLANTIC OCEAN
SOUTH ATLANTIC OCEAN
Tropic of Capricorn
Antarctic Circle
THE ANTARCTIC OCEAN
A CHART of the WORLD, According to Mercators Projection. Shewing the latest Discoveries of Capt. Cook.
Explanation
Longitude from London

EASTWARD OF GOOD HOPE

Early America in a Dangerous World

Dane A. Morrison

Johns Hopkins University Press

Baltimore

© 2021 Johns Hopkins University Press
All rights reserved. Published 2021
Printed in the United States of America on acid-free paper
2   4   6   8   9   7   5   3   1

Johns Hopkins University Press
2715 North Charles Street
Baltimore, Maryland 21218-4363
www.press.jhu.edu

Library of Congress Cataloging-in-Publication Data

Names: Morrison, Dane Anthony, author.
Title: Eastward of Good Hope : early America in a dangerous world /
Dane A. Morrison.
Description: Baltimore : Johns Hopkins University Press, 2021. |
Includes bibliographical references and index.
Identifiers: LCCN 2020057646 | ISBN 9781421442365 (hardcover) |
ISBN 9781421442372 (ebook)
Subjects: LCSH: Americans—Travel—Asia—History—19th century. |
Americans—Travel—Oceania—History—19th century. | Asia—Description
and travel. | Oceania—Description and travel. | Asia—Foreign public
opinion, American. | Oceania—Foreign public opinion, American. |
Asia—Foreign relations—United States. | United States—Foreign
relations—Asia. | Oceania—Foreign relations—United States. |
United States—Foreign relations—Oceania.
Classification: LCC DS8 .M77 2021 | DDC 915.0409/034—dc23
LC record available at https://lccn.loc.gov/2020057646

A catalog record for this book is available from the British Library.

Frontispiece: William Barker, "A Chart of the World, according to Mercators
Projection, shewing the latest Discoveries of Capt. Cook" (Philadelphia:
Mathew Carey, 1796), folio 150, 1978. Courtesy of Beinecke Rare Book and
Manuscript Library, Yale University Library.

*Special discounts are available for bulk purchases of this book. For more
information, please contact Special Sales at specialsales@jh.edu.*

CONTENTS

In the autumn of 1806, American newspapers were filled with the horrific news of the loss of the ship *Essex*. This was not the famous, ill-fated barque that had been "stove by a whale" in 1820, later transformed into an American icon through the pen of Herman Melville, although the reports of this *Essex*, a merchant ship out of Salem, Massachusetts, were, in fact, as lurid and terrifying:

> News is received here that Captain Joseph Orne in the ship *Essex* had arrived at Mocha, with $60,000 to purchase coffee, and that Mahomet Ikle, commander of an armed ship, persuaded him to trade at Hadidido, and to take on board 30 of his Arabs to help navigate her thither while his vessel kept her company; that on the approach of night, and at a concerted signal, the Arabs attacked the crew of the *Essex*, . . . and that the result was the slaughter of Captain Orne, and all his men. . . . The headless corpse of Capt. Orne and the mutilated remains of a merchant floated on shore and were decently buried. It was soon after ascertained that the faithless Mahomet was a notorious pirate of that country.[1]

It would have been difficult for Americans in the early republic to escape this tragedy and the thousands of similar reports from around the globe that depicted the world beyond their shores in such dire terms. News of similar assaults on their countrymen aboard the *Boston* off Nootka Sound in 1803, the *Putnam* in 1805, and the *Friendship* off Sumatra in 1831; the murders of Captain James Cook in 1779 and the men of the US Exploring Expedition in the South Seas in the 1830s; the loss of explorers and traders such as Joseph Ingraham and Isaac Pendleton and the mysterious disappearances of the US Navy sloop *Wasp* (October 9, 1814) and countless other Yankee vessels; and the loss of voyagers such as Samuel Shaw and William Henry Low to "tropical fever" assaulted American readers. Even before stepping onto a global stage in the 1780s, Americans had imagined the world as disordered and dangerous, deranged by tyranny or steeped in chaos, often deadly, always uncertain, unpredictable, and unstable, and their encounters after independence reinforced their assumptions. As historians assert, "seasons of misery" confronted early Americans in their "barbarous years" and particularly in distant lands among "dangerous neighbors." This vision of the world, more than anything else, shaped Americans' ideas of their place in the world. It has been a view shared by Puritans who carried a reformist sense of "a city upon a hill" to American shores, Yankee voyagers who freighted a mission of bringing order to a world that they found "in a constant state of flux" in the early republic, and Americans today who feel inundated with news reports of foreign wars, terrorism, massacres, and refugee crises.

Focusing on four representative arenas—the Ottoman Empire, China, India, and the Great South Sea (collectively, the East Indies, Oceania, and the American continent's Northwest coast)—this book recasts the relationship between America and the world by examining the early years of the republic, when its national character was particularly pliable and its foundational posture in the world was forming.[2] Freed from restrictions of British mercantilism, Yankee merchants sent "voyages of commerce and discovery" into distant seas. Through the "news from the East," carried in mariners' news reports, ships' logs, journals, and correspondence, Americans at home imagined the world as a congeries of dangerous and incoherent sites, distinct from their own values, yet amenable to their molding.

In this book, I reconsider American ideas about the world through three questions: (1) How did British Americans imagine the world before independence allowed them to travel "eastward of Good Hope"? (2) What were the signal encounters that filled the public sphere in their early years of global encounter? And (3) how did Americans' contacts with other peoples inflect their ideas about the world and their place in it? This study draws on scholarship from global history and early American print culture, in particular, to describe the connected vision through which Americans forged their relationships with the world. The book identifies a dominant theme that emerges in the travelogues of Americans who voyaged to distant lands—the sense of threat to Americans and to their culture and interests across the globe.[3]

I may be accused of contributing to what Beth Fowkes Tobin describes as a "colonialist historiography" in which "the historian retells the history of the colonizers, not the colonized nation."[4] That is not my intent. I hope to avoid re-inscribing a colonialist narrative by interrogating the texts deeply and bringing to the surface the victimhood that American travelers described even as they imposed their power on other peoples. However, I do want to explore these encounters deeply, in the moment, to understand what travelers experienced and how these experiences fostered a canon of literary impressions. As Bronwen Douglas observes, "voyagers' representations of Oceanian people should be read not merely as reflections of received knowledge derived from dominant metropolitan discourses or literary and artistic conventions but also as personal productions generated in the flux, stress, high emotion and uncertainty of meetings with actual people in the vulnerable settings of voyages under sail."[5]

A number of historians have wrestled with the contradiction between a national narrative whose arc is one of upward liberal progress, confidently strutting across the continent carrying republican values and institutions, and the more fragmented collections of an "anxious republic," steeped in the violence of racism and exploitation. The former is a twice-told tale, invented through selected materials by amateur historians in the nineteenth century and repeated at county fairs and business-club dinners, imposed through rote in public schools on children who learn to hate history without ever having learned it.

Studies that directly address the issues that are raised in this project appear to be rare. The closest example is perhaps Kathleen Donegan's *Seasons of Misery: Catastrophe and Colonial Settlement in Early America*, which explores the existential colonial American experience as one of suffering, disorientation, and incoherence. Likewise, in *Our Savage Neighbors: How Indian War Transformed Early America*, Peter Silver examines "how fear and horror" along the colonial American frontier, "with suitable repackaging, can remake whole societies and their political landscapes." Linda Colley has examined a related issue for British national identity in her *Captives: Britain, Empire, and the World, 1600–1850*. A recent trend, the history of emotions, has begun to delve into American responses to encounters abroad. The collected essays in Lauric Henneton and L. H. Roper, *Fear and the Shaping of Early American Societies*, for instance, explore fear in Brazil and the Caribbean, yet elide the broader global encounters that *Eastward of Good Hope* proposes to investigate. Historians of slavery and the Atlantic slave trade have touched on the idea of terror as an impellent for holding human beings in bondage. Alan Taylor is one who recalls Jefferson's admonition that slaveholders did not dare free their slaves for fear of retaliation in his excellent *The Civil War of 1812: American Citizens, British Subjects, Irish Rebels, and Indian Allies.* Holger Hoock carries this idea further in his *Scars of Independence: America's Violent Birth*, a narrative in which he "writes the violence back into the story of the Revolution."[6]

The book begins with chapter 1, "Coffeehouse Chatter," which sets the stage in the world of Thomas Boylston, an eighteenth-century Boston merchant, and re-creates the early American world of global information. The chapter identifies the many forms of media that brought news to British America—such as newspapers and periodicals, private journals and diaries, ships' logs, diplomatic correspondence and private letters, and maps and globes—examines the particular kinds of information each brought, and reveals how these distinct carriers of knowledge interacted to foster a view of the world as a dangerous and disordered domain.

Americans encountered the Ottoman Empire earlier than they did other parts of the globe. As we see in chapter 2, "Unholy Lands," the Ottoman Empire figured prominently in the American imagination, and early impressions flavored American ideas about the world at large. American encounters along the Barbary Coast and in the Levant yielded two of the most influential tropes of early America—that of "Turkish tyranny" and a "False God."

In chapter 3, "'Unfeeling Mandarins' in Canton and Macao," we see how China, too, figured prominently in the American imagination, and these impressions likewise flavored American ideas about the world at large. Yankee encounters in Canton and Macao supported a vision of China as a corrupt, backward, and oppressive place, as they imagined the Ottoman Empire. For one thing, they were localized, confined to the tiny commercial spaces of Canton and Macao. They were commercial, as a careless captain could lose the value of voyage. The pervasive dishonesty, the inefficiency of commerce, the corruption of officials, the arbitrary and baffling regulations—all could be laid at the doorstep of the imperial government.

A voyage to India brought its own particular dangers, as chapter 4, "Hindoos and Fakirs in India," relates. Nature presented its challenges, as mariners sailed through "the notoriously turbulent Bay of Bengal, terror of mariners past," still and flat in the winter monsoons, raging when the summer monsoons riled the waters with silt and storm.[7] Here, Oriental tyranny was framed in more subtle hues, in the economic disparities between the few who lived in opulence and luxury and the many who eked out bare subsistence in grinding poverty. Somehow, the news from "eastward of Good Hope" reported, encounters in the Indian Ocean could carry contagions back to America, and the fanaticism revealed in Indian religions, the submissiveness exhibited before British conquest, and the fatalism before nature might induce a cultural contamination that would infect Yankee values.

Chapter 5, "Cannibal Isles," explores American encounters in the Great South Sea, comprising the Pacific Ocean and the East Indies. For early Americans, the Ottomans represented the dangers of exposure to "Turkish tyranny," China epitomized the hazards of dealing with an imperious court and conniving subjects, and India exposed the vulnerabilities of division and unbridled luxury; the Great South Sea, that vast expanse of water that covered the earth from the Cape of Good Hope to America's Northwest coast, unfolded yet another kind of peril. The news from the East brought accounts of savage peoples who delighted in barbaric ceremonies and cannibal rituals, lurking in tropical coves to pounce on unsuspecting voyagers.

The legacies described in chapter 6, "Echoes," recount that the history of American expansion that we associate with manifest destiny, an "empire of liberty," filibusters, the Monroe and Truman Doctrines, the "opening of Japan," "fire when ready," and the "new world order" has its roots in the early republic, when Americans imagined the world as a place of disorder and danger.[8] In its relationship with the wider world, the new nation was as much a republic of fear as it was a republic of letters.

ACKNOWLEDGMENTS

This project received generous support from several sources, including seed grants from the Salem State University School of Graduate Studies, which sustained the research and writing phases of the book. Department chairs Donna Seger and Andrew Darien, as well as my History Department colleagues, have been staunch supporters.

In a time when international travel allowed participation at conferences and meetings, I was fortunate to share ideas—and meals—with brilliant scholars whose observations challenged me to hone my analysis and whose generous spirit led me to important sources. World History Association conferences, and those of its regional affiliate, the New England Regional World History Association, were both exciting and cordial. From Boston to Costa Rica, Al Andrea, Michael Feener, Katrina Gulliver, Roland Higgins, Angela Lee, Suzanne M. Litrel, Gwenn Miller, David Northrup, and Lincoln Paine shared penetrating insights and graceful conversation. At a meeting of the Society for Historians of American Foreign Relations, the work of Konstantin Dierks, Jason Smith, Michael Verney, and Kariann Yokota complemented my own in unexpected ways. Just prior to the global pandemic shutdown, an excellent conference in Paris on Captain Cook's legacy offered a remarkable opportunity to share insights from colleagues at the Hakluyt Society and SELVA, including Anna Agnarsdóttir, Pierre Lurbé, Ladan Niayesh, Emmanuelle Peraldo, and Pierre-François Peirano; they were most charming hosts. And other colleagues contributed to this book in ways they might not imagine, but I will never forget their influence: John Brooke, Don Carlton, Abby Chandler, Thomas Doherty, Ronan Donahoe, Lige Gould, Isaac Land, and Lincoln Paine.

A number of museums, archives, and libraries opened their collections to my perusal, and their respective staffs were generous with their time and expertise. At the Forbes House Museum in Milton, Massachusetts, Heidi Vaughn and Barbara Silberman displayed the "opium chair" and opium pipes of Robert Bennet Forbes, among stashes of elegant tea tables and porcelain. At the Massachusetts Historical Society, the indomitable Anne Bentley acquainted me with a human-bone hook from Hawai'i and other remarkable goods, and Anna J. Clutterbuck-Cook and Daniel Hinchin procured seemingly endless amounts of archival materials. Boston's Museum of Fine Arts offers a treasure trove of materials, from Copley's portraits to South Seas tapa cloth and spears, that helped to frame the first chapter. At Harvard University's outstanding Peabody Museum of Ethology and Ethnography, sideshow posters, maps, war clubs, and a "feegee mermaid" frame the ways in which Americans have imagined the South Seas. The National Park Service is one of the gems of our republic, and experts such as Emily Murphy, at the Salem Maritime National Historic Site, who situated letters from Calcutta within the provenance of place, make connections that I would not otherwise have gleaned. For scholars who are interested in early American global trade, Thomas Hardiman, Keeper of the Portsmouth Athenaeum, and Jean Marie Procious, Executive Director of the Salem Athenaeum, watch over indispensable collections of books and papers, and they generously granted me the freedom to explore their realms. Where would scholars be without the careful guidance of research librarians and archivists?

At the Peabody Essex Museum's Phillips Library, Jennifer Hornsby was an invaluable pilot through its boundless collections. Several other staff members and curators at the Peabody Essex Museum were of inestimable help, and I am especially appreciative of the support I received from Daniel Finamore, Karina Corrigan, Lynn Francis-Lunn, and George Schwartz. Paintings, portraits, and maps from Yale's Beinecke Library, Historic Deerfield (Massachusetts), and the Woodman Museum (Dover, New Hampshire) augmented the essential material culture of early American global encounters. In this curious age of shrinking research budgets and pandemic restrictions, I have also been grateful for the digital archives that have allowed me to transcend boundaries of time and distance, particularly Hathi Trust, Internet Archives, and William Reese catalogues.

I have never enjoyed working with a publisher as much as I have with Johns Hopkins University Press. The people at JHUP managed this disorganized and often forgetful author with both remarkable professionalism and laudable grace. Acquisitions editors Elizabeth Demers and Laura Davulis shepherded the project into the JHUP fold. Press employees Catherine Goldstead,

Kyle Kretzer, Hilary Jacqmin, Kathryn Marguy, Juliana McCarthy, Katie Feild, Jennifer Paulson, and Esther Rodriguez were instrumental in the preparation, production, and publicity of the final book, and copyeditor Plaegian Alexander guided the manuscript into a readable form. Important in this regard, also, was the guidance of anonymous readers for JHUP.

As most readers know, a book project is an exciting, challenging, and, at times, daunting affair. My brilliant wife, Kimberly Alexander, and darling child, Gray, inspire and sustain my spirits every day, and to them I dedicate the book.

Eastward of Good Hope

CHAPTER ONE

Coffeehouse Chatter

In one of the world's most refined cities, in one of that city's most distinguished institutions, in one of that museum's most stately galleries, hangs a portrait of one of the city's most eminent gentlemen. The representation of Boston merchant Nicholas Boylston (1716–1771), painted ca. 1769 by the rising young artist John Singleton Copley (1738–1815), now hangs in the Art of the Americas gallery in Boston's Museum of Fine Arts. Staring out from the walls of the Americana gallery, Boylston's gaze pierces directly into the viewer, as if taking stock of a potential investor.[1] A closer examination reveals traits that complicate the self-satisfied, even smug image of a wealthy, comfortable colonial merchant.[2] Even among Georgian Boston's most fashionable parvenus, Nicholas Boylston stood out as something of an exotic peacock (we are blocks away from Boylston Street and the transit's Boylston Station).

True to his reputation for extravagant living, Boylston, in Copley's painting, is sumptuously adorned in a sea of silk, a voluminous Indian *banyan*, or dressing gown, woven of lustrous brown silk damask, and capped with an Arabian-style *tam*, or turban.[3] This study conforms to similar portraits that Copley painted of Boylston's younger brother Thomas (1721–1798) *à la turk* and sister Rebecca Boylston Gill, similarly adorned in "a Turkish-style costume distinguished by gold embroidery, a silk turban laced with pearls, and a rose-colored mantle draped across one arm."

About the time that Copley produced the paintings, the brothers had formed a partnership, with warehouses on Griffin's Wharf, and, as the Harvard University Galleries observe, "Copley composed the paintings to reinforce their connection. The men's poses mirror one another, and all three portraits share the same scale and have matching elaborately carved rococo frames." The three portraits do not, however, conform to our idea of provincial

Americans, as in Copley's other paintings of Paul Revere, Samuel Adams, or Joseph Warren.[4]

Someone made the decision to cast both brothers in banyans and turbans. Was it the sitters or the artist? Boylston or Copley?[5] The Boylston brothers were not the only sitters whom Copley rendered in Oriental costume. Margaret Kemble Gage, wife of the general who imposed martial law on Boston in 1774, sat for Copley in fanciful Turkish garb in 1771.[6] Did each of these patrons come with their own wardrobe? Did Copley have a stock of costumes? Whatever the answer, what does this tell us about British Americans, on the edge of empire, on the peripheries of the world they called civilized?[7]

What we do know is that they were participants in an early modern fantasy known as *turquoiserie*, an aesthetic fascination with the Ottoman Empire, the Muslim domain that ranged along the Mediterranean in uneasy concordance with Europe's Christian states and, often, with itself. Ottoman armies had threatened Europe throughout the seventeenth century, even accosting Vienna in the 1680s, but well before the Boylstons' day, conflict had waned to guarded appreciation. A number of texts claiming to depict Turkish culture circulated widely throughout the colonies, including William Bradshaw's translation of Marana's *Turkish Letters* and John Ozell's 1722 translation of Montesquieu's *Persian Letters*, and, after 1763, American readers could explore Constantinople, if vicariously, through Lady Mary Wortley Montague's letters from her travels in the Ottoman Empire.[8] By 1766, these texts and more filled the shelves of libraries, associations, taverns, and coffeehouses, and one volume attested itself as "Nancy Peck's Book, Presented her by her Father."[9] Ottoman paintings circulated throughout Europe and European artists such as Rembrandt in the Netherlands and Jonathan Richardson in England were caught up in the enchantment of *turquoiserie* and "collected oriental paintings and drew studies of Ottoman figures," awakening British American talent.[10] German-born Johan Zoffany (1733–1810), Genevan Jean-Étienne Liotard (1702–1789), and the English artist George Chinnery (1774–1852) lived in Ottoman lands or India or China for decades, drawing on an expatriate gaze for inspiration.[11] Consequently, the Boylston sitters certainly could have found inspiration in Charles-Amédée-Philippe van Loo's influential seraglio representations of *Le Costume turc*, exhibited in France during the 1770s. Any number of eminent Europeans sought portraits *à la turk* during Boylston's lifetime, including Richard Collins's *A Family of Three at Tea* (1727) and Antoine de Favray's *Comtesse de Vergennes in Turkish Dress* (1766).

Imaginings

The Boylstons' Boston was a domain of global penetration. As boys growing up in a seaport linked, if indirectly, to Smyrna, Calcutta, and Canton, their consciousness was bathed in the fashions and fancies of the wider world. A global sensibility intruded into their lives in an essay on truth and tolerance in Boston's *Weekly Rehearsal* for February 28, 1732, observing: "Look around the habitable World, not to mention those Countries remote and little known. . . . The crowded *Christian* Countries point out Rome; The spacious *Ottoman* Empire turn their Eyes to *Mecca*; and the *Chinese* to the School of their *Confucius*. Every People have a Name peculiar to themselves, whom all the World, the say, are bound to worship."

Global awareness likewise intervened in the poetry that young gentlemen in Boston would read in the literary-oriented *Massachusetts Gazette and Boston News-Letter*, such as in a charming piece printed for September 1, 1763, titled "On a Young Lady's Dress":

> Fair Chloe's dress (which Venus self might wear)
> From various Climes is cull'd with happy Care.
> To grace the well-shap'd Foot, in Turky's Soil,
> Thro' Life's short Span laborious Silkworms toil.
> The Whale in Zembla's frozen Regions found,
> That forms the swelling Hoops capacious Round.
> The Belgian Nymphs, a nice industrious Race,
> Weave the fine Texture of the curious Lace.
> Peruvian Mines the rich Brocade bestow,
> in Guiney's Treasures in her Bucle glow.
> Afric the Tribute of its Ivory pays,
> On polish'd Sticks the spreading Fan to raise.
> The Phrygian Swans there down the Plumage shed,
> and from the scorching Sun defend her head.
> The Bear's warm Furr the Russian Desarts yield
> from falling Snow her whiter Breast to shield.
> The blest Arabia sends from balmy Air,
> Essence, less fragrant then the breathing Fair.
> India's rich Coasts the sparkling Gem supply,
> Less sparkling than the Lustre of her Eye.
> How oft the Merchant glows beneath the Line,
> Chloe all accomplish'd thus may shine![12]

Contravening our modern, compartmentalized mythologies that make no connection between American colonial development and awareness of the world beyond the Atlantic Ocean, over the course of the seventeenth and eighteenth centuries, British American travelers' experiences in distant lands reached their countrymen and countrywomen, fostering what historian Mukhtar Ali Isani has called "the general Puritan awareness of the Orient" in New England and, indeed, well beyond. Illustrating this broader colonial view, John Winthrop Jr. had intended to sail to Salem with a Puritan fleet in 1629, but perhaps from a dislike of erstwhile governor John Endecott of Massachusetts Bay Colony, instead voyaged through the Mediterranean, eventually reaching Constantinople.[13] Adam Smith appreciated the connections between old worlds and new in his declaration of economic independence, *An Inquiry into the Nature and Causes of the Wealth of Nations* (1776), writing:

> The discovery of America, and that of a passage to the East Indies by the Cape of Good Hope, are the two greatest and most important events recorded in the history of mankind. Their consequences have already been very great: but, in the short period of between two and three centuries which has elapsed since these discoveries were made, it is impossible that the whole extent of their consequences can have been seen. What benefits, or what misfortunes to mankind may hereafter result from those great events, no human wisdom can foresee. By uniting, in some measure, the most distant parts of the world, by enabling them to relieve one another's wants, to increase one another's enjoyments, and to encourage one another's industry, their general tendency would seem to be beneficial.[14]

This early global consciousness ensured that at the beginning of the eighteenth century, "Americans were actively and independently engaging with a Far Eastern aesthetic . . . and that they understood China and Chinese art with much the same level of sophisticated prejudice as any Londoner."[15]

Yet beneath the surface of Nicholas and Thomas Boylstons' placid expressions lay a world of worry.[16] Along with the calicoes and boheas, ships from abroad carried word of clashes, conflicts, and catastrophes that disturbed their impressions of a world of bounty. Consequently, the world they imagined was a dangerous, troubling place that might threaten not only their access to exotic goods but also the very foundations of their own stable culture. Consider Nicholas Boylston making his daily rounds in the provincial town of Boston, about the time that Copley rendered him in oils, some three thousand miles from what he imagined to be the centers of "civilization" in London,

Paris, and Amsterdam. Commonly, he would begin the day at his sumptuous home on School Street, a structure so elegantly appointed that it became known as the Mansion House, and awed men of the "middling sort," such as John Adams, who described the furnishings as "the most magnificent of any Thing I have ever seen."[17] In the morning, Boylston awakened in a room filled with the things that he may have imported from across the globe—perhaps in an English-made bed crafted of rosewood from China or mahogany from Brazil, ornamented with "crimson Damask Curtains and Counterpins (counterpanes)." Behind a coromandel screen crafted in Madras (actually, of Japanese origin), he might have donned the brown banyan depicted in Copley's painting, woven in India of fine silk from China, and nankeen leggings from China.[18] The room would have been wallpapered, perhaps with scenes of pagodas and peacocks, and layered with "Turkey" carpets to warm the feet.[19]

In Boylston's colonial America, one could not but have had a global consciousness. Yet the hierarchical thinking of the eighteenth-century provinces determined that this perspective would not be culturally neutral. Even the small world of Boylston's bedroom invoked this contradiction between the parochial and the cosmopolitan. The global goods that made up the room's furnishings distinguished their owner from more modest Bostonians, just as, ironically, they distinguished him from the "barbaric" peoples who produced them. Consequently, the goods that he imported from Asia, Africa, and South America, which ornamented his home and which his family consumed in elegantly appointed rooms, were tokens of his imagined superiority as a civilized man and of the decided inferiority of the people who produced these same goods.[20]

Boylston would likely have commenced his day with a Bible passage populated by other peoples—Hebrews, Chaldeans, Pharisees, Egyptians, and Greeks. Stories of epic battles and tribal tragedies, enslavements, and sufferings, both felt and imposed by the same peoples, framed his understanding of humanity. It was a selective reading, however, that confirmed a belief that he was not like either the Egyptians, who oppressed the Jews and whose civilization now lay in ruins, or the Romans, who had crucified the Savior of Mankind and whose civilization likewise paid the price.

Even amid the bountiful prosperity that global trade brought him, there was much to pray for.[21] Certainly, there were abundant dangers in early America, and these constituted what we might call the "ordinary" or "normal" dangers of everyday life. Mortal men—and women—faced the calamities of everyday life from many directions. In a world of farms and fishing, there were many ways to die: a man could fall from an apple tree, leaving a pregnant widow and six orphans; catch his head between a beam and a post at a house-raising; drown in a sinking canoe; or succumb during a "very sickly and dying time"—incidents that became more common with the increase in population and expansion of trade.[22] Earthquakes were remarkably common, frightening a superstitious populace and leaving them to cry in unison: "Lord, our Flesh trembleth for fear of thee."[23] More worrisome were lightning strikes and, particularly for women, childbirth and fire at the hearth. A 1769 map titled "A New Plan of the Town of Boston in New England" recorded nine outbreaks of "General Small Pox"—1640, 1666, 1677, 1678, 1680, 1690, 1702, 1721, and 1730—and nine "Great Fires"—1653, 1676, 1679, 1683, 1690, 1691, 1702, 1711, 1759—culminating in a "Tenth Terrible Fire" in 1760.[24]

Fire struck with regularity in the winter months, destroying metropolises such as London and minor seaports such as Boston, built from wood and using wood for fuel. In almost biblical terms, whole towns could be consumed in flames, or nearly so. On March 20, 1760, conflagration destroyed nearly 350 properties in Boston, and, again in the cruel year of 1764, fire leveled Harvard Hall at the colony's seat of higher learning, and five thousand books turned to ash.[25] Disease stalked towns, as well, particularly market towns, and the roads and sea routes that brought the latest fashions and fresh thoughts also carried vicious pathogens. Smallpox swept away victims and scarred survivors repeatedly in Boylston's lifetime, beginning with the 1721 plague that led his uncle, apothecary Zabdiel Boylston (1679–1766), and minister Cotton Mather to experiment with inoculation. As a member of London's renowned Royal Society, Mather had access to unparalleled scientific archives. He used his access to peruse two important essays in the group's publication, *Transactions*, which described the remedy for smallpox commonly used in the Ottoman Empire, a strategy validated by his West African slave, Onesimus.[26]

These were the "ordinary" terrors that stalked everyday life in early America. Some rose and fell with the seasons—"seasons of misery," Kathleen Donegan has called them—others returned every few years, and, as the sad tidings that filled colonial newspapers and sermons remind us, many occurred every single day.[27] All brought grief and trepidation.[28] The regularity that rendered some calamities "ordinary," that made them part of the routine of everyday life, made it possible for victims and survivors to find remedies to alleviate these problems. Marblehead, Massachusetts, presented an example of such commonplace tragedy. In June 1770, the town applied to the General Court for relief. Over the previous two and a half years, the town had lost twenty-four fishing and merchant vessels and 170 men and boys and left 70 widows and 150 orphans.[29] Throughout colonial America (as in the rest of the world), midwives mixed potions and poultices, following traditional folk recipes and incorporating the herbs they found in the natural world around them. In seaport towns such as Boston, New York, and Philadelphia, citizens formed associations, clubs, and juntos; paved streets; laid wooden water pipes; formed volunteer fire departments; and replaced wood construction with brick. For smallpox, there was the possibility of inoculation, especially after Zabdiel Boylston's experiments proved successful. Even after an earthquake damaged steeples and rattled windows, one could rebuild and replace. In the occasional food riots that struck during times of scarcity, especially during decades of war, stores could be replenished, as a congregation of one hundred women reminded Thomas Boylston in July 1777, when they broke open his storehouse to distribute the grain and coffee he had been hoarding.[30]

But the Boylstons and their neighbors had scant remedies to address the "extraordinary" crises in distant lands that haunted their sermons and newspapers. As men and women of the age knew too well, "No certain and known danger can so powerfull arouse us, as when uncertain and unlimited."[31] Paraphrasing Peter Silver, confronting exotic dangers was central to the stories Americans told about themselves and their nation—the dangers of the frontier environment, the dangers of "savage" peoples, the dangers of the unknown.[32] Scale and scope made some dangers catastrophic, as the great earthquake that struck Lisbon on All Saints' Day 1755, washing away somewhere between ten and one hundred thousand souls and destroying most of the city. Other catastrophes, such as hurricanes that fell "like the very hand of God," devastated coastal communities, although on a smaller scale, but coming with disturbing regularity. From August through October, hurricane season in the West Indies reduced the number of voyages merchants such as the Boylstons sent southward.[33]

Threats from abroad, from other peoples, carried a particularly nefarious resonance. As Jack P. Greene observes, "the long-standing tendency of Europeans to view the world beyond Europe as a collection of essentially lawless and chaotic zones" was deeply embedded in the Western psyche.[34] This is perhaps a paradox, as distant threats were less likely to present themselves. There was scant chance that a Muslim army would invade Connecticut or Virginia. Yet recollections of Barbary corsairs pillaging the coasts of the British Isles lingered in historical memory, striking Cornwall in 1625 and 1645 and the "stolen village" of Baltimore, Ireland, in 1631, and carrying hundreds of men, women, and children into slavery. Taverns and coffeehouses were filled with such chatter into the next century, no doubt echoing an entry of February 8, 1661, in Samuel Pepys's diary:

> went to the Fleece Tavern to drink; and there we spent till four o'clock, telling stories of Algiers, and the manner of the life of slaves there! And truly Captn. Mootham and Mr. Dawes (who have been both slaves there) did make me fully acquainted with their condition there: as, how they eat nothing but bread and water. . . . How they are beat upon the soles of their feet and bellies at the liberty of their pardon. How they are all, at night, called into their master's Bagnard; and there they lie. How the poorest men do use their slaves best. How some rogues do live well, if they do invent to bring their masters in so much a week by their industry or theft; and then they are put to no other work at all. And theft there is counted no great crime at all.[35]

Boylston pulled his knowledge of the world from many sources, and his first steps of the morning likely carried him into a modest but well-ordered room that opened the wider world to him. His personal library graced the first floor of the Mansion House, perhaps wainscoted in mahogany, with Turkey carpets, and papered walls adorned with maps that brought him the "Great South Sea," the "Pacifick Ocean," the "Western Ocean," "Afric," and India. Here, he might comfortably peruse Moroccan-bound titles such as *Citizen of the World* and *Persian Tales* and journey vicariously through *Travels into the Inland Parts of Africa* and Commodore George Anson's *Voyages*. In an age when a "steadily expanding literature attracted a vast and varied audience to the romance or the science of maritime exploration in the South Seas," as well as China, India, the East Indies, and the Ottoman world, Boylston might hope to acquire in these travelogues the knowledge that would fill in the blanks and bring order to the world or, at least, to the mental maps that filled his head.[36] Here, he could grasp the contours of the Great South Sea, the Indian Ocean, the Red Sea, and beyond. Safely ensconced within his private library, amid books, maps, sketches, and drawings imported from Europe, he could mark the differences between people like himself, who imagined themselves civilized by virtue of the homes they kept, the clothes they wore, and the books they read, and the naked, illiterate, unwashed "savages" of the world.[37]

Boylston's seaport library might have counted among its holdings many of the titles held on the inland plantations of the eminent Byrd family of Westover, Virginia. The first William Byrd requested his London agents to send him copies of Giovanni Paolo Marana's *Letters Writ by a Turkish Spy.* The second

Byrd wrote to ask the naturalist Sir Hans Sloane to send "your account of Jamaica, and if there be any other good voyages published since I left England." Byrd's correspondence shows that he understood the context for Robert Beverly's discovery of ginseng in the Virginia mountains; he had read Father Jartoux's *Travels of the Jésuites into China and Tartary* and the volume of the *Philosophical Transactions* that described the root. He owned, as well, *The Travels of Several Learned Missioners of the Society of Jesus, into Divers Parts of the Archipelago, India, China, and America* (London, 1714).[38]

Similarly, the Mansion House study might have encompassed titles held in Harvard's library, such as those saved from the 1764 fire. Perhaps Boylston could peruse the two-volume folio of John Harris's *Voyages*, Henry's *Explorations*, or Robert Wood's *The Ruins of Athens, Balbec, Palmyra*.[39] To satisfy his curiosity about human nature and character, in an age when the psychology of Freud could not be imagined, histories must answer, and Boylston could learn much from Basnage's *History of the Jews*, Dupin's *Historical Library*, Lope's six-volume octavo of *Homer* and his five volumes of *The Odyssey*, Francis's *Horace*, or Campbell's four-volume *Lives of the British Admirals*. Perhaps Boylston purchased and perused gentility guides, such as *Gentleman's Calling*, Wilkin's *Real Character*, *The Whole Duty of Man*, or the five-volume folio of *Biographia Britannica*. For literary escape, he might have subscribed to the *American Magazine*, the *Royal American*, the *Gentleman's Magazine*, *The Spectator*, or *The Tatler*.[40] The wider world came to his door through *Dionysiri's Geography* by Wells, Moll's *Geography*, Bosman's *Description of Guineau*, Hughes's *Natural History of Barbadoes*, or Henry Moore's popular *Travels into the Inland Parts of Africa*, published in multiple volumes throughout the century.[41]

What did it all mean, these waves of knowledge washing into Boston harbor. The books available to a Boylston or a Byrd or on the shelves of a coffeehouse or tavern included histories, geographies, and travelogues whose wisdom had been rediscovered by generations of writers and readers alike from the time of Marco Polo and into the Age of Discovery.[42] Some private libraries included sacred tracts, others showed a more secular orientation. Taken together, they constructed an idea of the world as an inherently disordered place, and enabled British Americans to imagine the peoples of India, China, Africa, and the Ottoman East as backward and needing their own guiding hand to make manifest the Biblical injunction to make the world productive.[43] Central to this construction were ideas of race, although these ideas, like the world they purported to represent, were in flux, complicated by an "ambiguous intersection of civilisation and race in the differentiation and ranking of colonial subject," as Douglas and Ballard describe.[44]

Ideas of difference had not yet hardened into the scientific racism that characterized the nineteenth century, as in an 1848 geography that depicted four stages of societal development from Savage (American Indian) to Barbarous (Arab) to Half-civilized (Chinese and Muslim) to Enlightened (American or European). Yet the seeds of a profound intolerance had been planted in Europe, especially in Protestantism's ongoing wars against Catholics and Muslims. Captain John Smith's own several captivities themselves captured the fetid atmosphere of hate in his 1630 text, part travelogue, part captivity narrative, part polemic, *True Travels*, in which he castigated Catholics, Moors, their European allies, and, for good measure, the seduction of Asian luxuries. By the mid-eighteenth century, philosophers clutched onto a stadial theory of human development that foregrounded the scientific racism of a century later. Smith, for instance, proposed "four distinct states which mankind pass thro: 1st, the Age of Hunters; 2ndly, the Age of Shepherds; 3rdly, the Age of Agriculture; and 4thly, the Age of Commerce."[45]

Later that morning, Boylston might settle in his parlor, meeting potential investors around a japanned table where tea was served in a silver service. They might have imagined they were following a ritual they associated with China. For these affairs, a gentleman or lady knew to serve a green tea, such as "bing," "hyson," or "imperial," rather than the harsher red or brown "bohea" (what we know today as oolong).[46] A lacquered coromandel screen, produced in southern China rather than India, as its name implied, and transshipped on East India Company ships from Madras or another port along India's southeastern coast, would provide an Oriental backdrop.[47]

The impression of the East that these Asian goods presented would have been complicated indeed. Yet, Asian goods complicated early American impressions of the East, seen, for instance, in a series of wall panels in the Vernon house in Newport, Rhode Island. The Vernon screens feature wall panels, probably painted by erstwhile owner William Gibbs in the early 1700s.[48] Carolyn Frank speculates that Gibbs might have procured coromandel screens from China and that scenes from these shaped the artist's geographical imagination.[49] These were not impressions of willow trees and pagodas serenely set along gently flowing rivers. Instead, they are disturbing scenes that depict various forms of Chinese torture and punishment. Quite popular in Europe from the earliest days of contact with China, such images likely fostered a selective perception of the East that emphasized cruelty.[50]

Significantly, these goods were not the monopoly of a merchant elite, as earlier historians asserted. James Walvin, for instance, observes that tea and its equipage flowed down to the "middling sort" and working classes, as some 215 million pieces of China were imported into England alone, and prices dropped over the course of the eighteenth century. In 1712, a teacup imported into England cost 1½d., but this cost decreased dramatically by the time Nicholas Boylston was serving tea to partners and investors. Furthermore, wealthy consumers often passed their chipped pieces onto servants. As Frank observes:

> By the second decade of the eighteenth century, colonial Americans residing in the northeast had a much richer exposure to the material arts of Asia than historians or curators have traditionally acknowledged. Colonial seaports welcomed a continual stream of immigrants and visitors from European cities, where orientalism in all its finest Eastern trappings was moving to the forefront of popular fashion. A deluge of Chinese objects poured into the North Atlantic basin in the seventeenth and eighteenth centuries, including some 70 million pieces of porcelain.[51]

A visit to his counting house was Boylston's next order of business. His passeggiata from Mansion House to Griffin's Wharf took him toward the harbor, where ships unloaded the goods of the world—opium from Smyrna, bohea tea from Canton, pepper from Sumatra or India. As Boylston walked down to Central Wharf, he would take in the sights and senses of a busy waterfront that served the ports of the Atlantic and Caribbean waters. But Boylston's vision encompassed a geography that necessarily transcended the Atlantic Ocean.[52] Along the wharves and quays, the rumble of cartwheels over cobblestone would be mixed with the language of global commerce. His uncle, Zabdiel, sold the world's spices at his apothecary shop in Dock-Square.[53] By 1800, a Bostonian might overhear a mother say to her son: "Well, young master. Pray, run to the bazaar [Arabian] for a chow [Chinese] of goods. I need a chow of bandanna and calico [Indian], nankeen [Chinese], coffee [Arabian], Turkey rug [Ottoman]. I give you 5 pounds [using the Indian notation for numbers]. If you run chop-chop [Chinese], you will receive a cumshaw [Chinese]." Boylston might overhear seaport denizens describe a dinghy as a "hawpoo-boat" (Chinese), an overbearing first mate as a "mandarin" (Chinese), and an auctioneer as a "banyan" or "dubash" (Indian).

A tour of Boylston's establishment would have revealed a spectacle of efficiency. Here, he oversaw his adolescent clerks "booking" waste books, balancing ledgers, reproducing the multiple copies that needed to cross the Atlantic, and whisking off or returning with messages. Beneath the routine lay an underlying current, a tense struggle to master the dangers of uncertainty. The merchant's enemy was ignorance. A dearth of information from abroad would upend the order that Boylston sought to impose on the world and threaten his livelihood, his ships, his cargoes, and his crews.

Boylston's counting house might have held the maps that traced sea routes. But what did a merchant see when he gazed upon a map? Not likely the same things that a schoolmaster or philosopher saw. His eye would have taken in currents and winds, invisible on the chart, but quite clear to him. Perhaps he recognized sites of wrecks or shoals where ships had gone down. Here, he learned of the world, its bounty of goods and the many dangers it presented even to Bostonians, perched on the edge of that world, so distant from India's monsoons and the South Seas' volcanoes.

An accumulation of images would have populated Boylston's view of the world as a menagerie of exotic goods and savage peoples. Of particular prominence was a map's cartouche—a corner of the print that displayed the title and tropes—revealing the conventional emblems thought to represent each part of the globe. Henry Popple's 1733 *Map of the British Empire in America* typified these provocative images that suggested both profit and peril. The cartouche set the South Sea against three imagined Indians, dressed only in loincloths and feathered headdresses, each carrying a quiver of arrows. Juxtaposed against two monkeys, a parrot, and palm trees, one bare-breasted native woman caresses a child sitting atop a crocodile or alligator, one foot resting on the severed head of a European man, an arrow embedded in his forehead. To the right of another naked woman and child, further symbols of fecundity, sit barrels of tobacco and a chest of treasure. Beyond, the background view depicts a panel of European traders chatting as crewmen batten casks and tighten bales, and, in the distance, a ship lays at anchor, with three more sailing to the New World to accept its bounty.[54]

In the same year, and likewise to be found in merchants' libraries or on tavern walls for generations after, was printed the *Penisula Indiae citra Gangem*, guiding the mind's eye to a distinctly Western impression of the perils and profits of the Indian subcontinent. Boylston's eye would have settled on the cartouche in the chart's lower left corner. Here, astride a magnificent elephant, the animal draped in an exquisite rug, sits an imagined Indian ruler, sword in hand. At the feet of the pachyderm, the viewer takes in a scene that depicts a trade negotiation. What appear to be African and European traders, dressed in the striped costumes of the region, and their slaves, clad only in loincloth, lay around a cornucopia of goods: a chest of gold, ivory tusks, and a repast of foods and spices.

Matthew Seutter's 1741 copper-plate map, *India Orientalis,* surveyed the area from India through Southeast Asia and into the Oceanus Chinensis, the South China Sea. Its splendidly detailed cartouche offered a magisterial scene of humanity and geography. Scampering atop a pediment, mischievous monkeys chase parrots; at the base, a feast of exotic delicacies is laid out. To the left of the column, against a background of mountains and fecund date palms, we see a conventicle of worshippers paying obeisance to Mohammed, who receives sustenance and wisdom from two cherubs. To the right, half-naked peoples from various nations carry their bounty to a goddess, while Neptune in the background points to a fleet of European Indiamen carrying commerce to her domain.

De Vaugondy's engraved map of China, *L'Empire de la Chine*, printed in 1751, presented another set piece of stock images: a family reclines beneath a parasol, as a man clangs gongs, the scene embraced by peonies and pomegranates. A porcelain teacup and vase sit amid various edibles, offset by a lattice-work villa and a gently inclining stairway.

A cartouche in *The Western Coast of Africa from Cape Blanco to Cape Virga*, engraved by Thomas Jefferys in 1789, presents an African man dressed in loincloth, the ubiquitous trope that signified a "backward" civilization in eighteenth-century imagery. He is seated virtually astride a very angry lion, surrounded by a menagerie of exotic creatures: an ostrich, a camel, a cobra, and a lizard. A pyramid in the background recalls Egypt, and suggests the ancient civilization had fallen into decadence.

Together, cartouches and the maps they deciphered formed an accumulated vision, imagined though it was. Like Copley's portraits of the Boylston family, beneath the placid images of contentment lay contradictions within the nature of these global encounters that would trouble the country—and the world—for generations to come. The places and their peoples represented in these gracefully illustrated panels produced the exotic goods that filled the warehouses of Long Wharf and Griffin Wharf in Boston, Derby Wharf and Turner Wharf in Salem, and Samuel Carpenter's Wharf or Fishbourn's Wharf in Philadelphia. The artists meant to direct a colonial gaze toward them as commercial entities, but the lions, the snakes, and the armed and naked "savages" who represented Africa, Asia, and South America depicted dangers that someone had to confront in order to equip the counting house and tearoom. One kind of danger is missing in the images, one that threatened the rest of the creatures and peoples who populate the cartouches. We see no interaction *between* Western traders and indigenous Africans and Arabs—no greetings, no conversations, no engagement at all. Instead, the panels illustrate an idea of exploitation. They represent an expectation of cultural separation that distinguishes the emerging idea of free trade. The Western trader would sail to distant lands, exchange goods, but foster no bonds with the peoples he encountered. These panels insinuated in Boylston's mind a clear distinction between the community of civilized nations and the barbaric people of the rest of the world. These panels convey a form of globalization that was to be culturally and personally sterile, and a form of trade that was to be free of human connection. This disengaged commerce made it more possible to exploit other peoples as well as the environment in ways that would ultimately threaten their ways of life.

As the sixteenth century flowed into the seventeenth, and the seventeenth into the eighteenth, colonial merchants could imagine the world as presenting sites of great opportunity and greater danger. As Jonathan D. Spence writes, this quintessential oppositional fantasy of the East can be seen in Christopher Columbus's notes on his 1496 edition of Marco Polo's *Travels*, which detailed both the sources of precious commodities and the terrors that might await a traveler.[55] This was not isolated knowledge, however. Although these impressions registered deepest in the mental maps of merchants, they were transferred in conversation, advertisements, and imagery to nearly everyone else—sailors who carried goods homeward, auctioneers who sold them, housewives who made the purchases, schoolchildren, and the like. They were the "tastemakers and information hubs, people whose opinions circulated widely in clubs and coffeehouses and in print."[56]

During the early decades of the sixteenth century, the scope of the world and the nature of human experience began to alter. The early modern world presented new opportunities, new wonders, and new experiences, even for those who sat on the edge of civilization.[57] A new world of goods beckoned from the Indies, East and West. From the "Oriental Indies" came drugs that healed the ill and altered experience, as Garcia de Orta observed in his 1563 treatise, *Colóquios*, announcing its subject matter as "medicinal simples, and drugs [*drogas*], and other medical things of the Oriental Indies."[58] Modern drugs were one benefit, as Benjamin Breen describes: "New varieties of mental and physical experience [introduced] a defining feature [of] what we mean by early modernity."[59] But they posed hazards of their own. The "innocent sleep" induced by opium could be intoxicating, but also addictive. And as they pressed into the world, they met greater dangers.

By late morning, Boylston's steps would take him to a coffeehouse, such as the Bunch of Grapes, the Crown, the Green Dragon, or the British Coffee House in Boston. His colleagues in other colonial towns—there were no real cities—trod a similar path, to the London Coffee House in Salem, Carpenter's in Philadelphia, the Merchant's in New York.[60] All modeled themselves on the urbane establishments of London, where the "liquor of the urn" and cosmopolitan conversation flowed in abundance and lubricated "gentlemanly conversation."[61] Indeed, if Boylston traveled, he could find "London" coffeehouses in Philadelphia, Salem, and, of course, London, England, and Exchange coffeehouses in Charleston, New York, Annapolis, and Norfolk.[62] Coffee, as a bean and a process, had emigrated from the Ottoman domain, carried to England by the overseas merchants of the Levant Company (initially chartered in 1581), diplomats, and travelers such as Lady Mary Wortley Montague.[63] The first advertisements for coffee appeared in London newspapers in 1652, describing "the Grain or Berry called Coffee [that] groweth upon little Trees, only in the Deserts of Arabia," connecting consumption and culture to a distinct part of the world accessed by commerce and global consciousness.[64] Coffeehouses had proliferated in Restoration England; one could peer into any of the 550 in London by 1740 to watch merchants gulping bowls of strong black coffee and where the fashion was to drink it as the Turks did.[65] With coffeehouses came the exotic consumables of the world, bringing tea from China, tobacco from the Chesapeake, tea's "inseparable companion" sugar from the Caribbean (both tea and sugar being produced by enslaved men, women, and children from Africa), and drinks from the tropics, many of them served in Chinese and Japanese porcelain.[66] Drawing together the alluring aromas and intriguing flavors from across the globe, distant lands bearing exotic names such as Mocha, Ceylon, Bencoolen, and Celebes, the coffeehouse was a sensory pleasure palace. New foods made their way. Here, one could enjoy coffees from Africa, green and black teas from China, sugar cut from Jamaican cane and formed in cones; from India, cinnamon; from the East Indies, nutmeg and mace. By 1771, it was possible to sample pineapple (a tuppence in Boston).[67]

Promoters of the goods parleyed in Europe's coffeehouses touted not only the benefits but also the associations with the lands from which these goods were procured. Thus, Richard Bradley, in *The Virtue and Use of Coffee; with Regard to the Plague, and Other Infectious Distempers* (London, 1772, p. 12), observed that, in the Ottoman lands, it was imbibed "in little China Dishes, as hot as they can suffer it; black as Soot and tasting not unlike it."[68] An advertisement for tea in a 1660 handbill described it as "of such known virtues, that those very Nations famous for Antiquity, Knowledge, and Wisdom, do frequently sell it among themselves for twice its weight in silver."[69] A surviving board for The Turk's Head tavern in inland Chester, Pennsylvania, reminiscent of Bellini's magnificent portrait of the Ottoman sultan Mehmet II (1480), is evidence to the penetration this idea of the world made. He might spice "liquor of the urn" with cinnamon from India or nutmeg, mace, and allspice from the South Seas. After the 1660s, he might imbibe an increasingly popular concoction—green or black teas from China.[70] A chest of porcelain held more than six hundred pieces of porcelain, some five hundred pounds. More merchants seem to have brought in special orders of porcelain in boxes containing four to five dozen pieces.[71] This was not the primary cargo, bringing in less money, hence profit, than tea or cloth. Rather, porcelain's real worth was as ballast that served to keep a ship's hull steady and as a platform to support the cloth and tea that would otherwise be discolored or contaminated by bilge water. Here, it was unrecorded in customs records, a private adventure.[72] Here, too, were carried teapots made of silver mined in the Andes, perhaps molded by Revere, to steep the fragrant million pounds of tea that colonists imported through London or smuggled through Amsterdam.[73]

Denizens of coffeehouses and even taverns could read and experience the wider world through the sum of their senses. Colonial newspapers provided a cornucopia of the world's cultivated offerings. If Boylston had perused the *Boston Post-Boy* for May 4, 1767, about the time that Copley would paint the first of three portraits for him, the eminent merchant could find advertised by his neighbor Gilbert DeBlois "a complete fashionable Assortment of English & India Piece Goods" that signified a well-ordered world: hyson and bohea teas from China, "best large Turkey Figs," black pepper from India's Malabar coast, and "China ware."

Merchants were discovering what these products were and how they worked.[74] One source of knowledge was inchoate groups such as Britain's Royal Society, whose imprimatur stamped a seal of authority. Because Richard Bradley bore the stamp of Fellow of the Royal Society, a reader might trust, for instance, his *Virtue and Use of Coffee*, a six-pence octavo published in London in 1721. Coffee, tea, and chocolate, which came to Europe about the mid-sixteenth century, were mysteries. How should they be prepared? What were their benefits? Soon, they challenged everyday rituals and even conventional medical wisdom. The idea of balancing the body's humors, or fluids, advanced by Hippocrates and Galen, was destabilized by the use of the exotic new liquids carried from China, North Africa, and South America.

But more than goods were imbibed here. They were "penny universities," and Boylston would have met and conversed with other aspiring merchants and tradesmen (but not women), and could catch the gossip and read up on the latest "curiosities of the British World."[75] As a writer identified only as "C" essayed in the *Boston Weekly News-Letter* in October 1727, "I have observed in all the Companies I have been in, from the *Caravan-Lodge* in *China*, to the *Crown Coffee-House* upon the *Long Wharffe*, that all Conversation is built upon Equality; Title and Distinction must be laid aside in order to talk and act socially."[76] Here, Boylston participated in "its role in enhancing and promoting certain sorts of sociability and social discourse that were intrinsic to the emergence of what Habermas famously identified as the public sphere."[77]

Coffeehouses were information clearinghouses: they held transatlantic mail, housing libraries of newspapers, books, and poetry. As Andrew Pettigrew describes, the world was hungry for news. By 1700, as simple newssheets evolved into newspapers, there was a news revolution.[78] News journals, in particular, brought the world and its variant parts into a manageable focus by organizing categories based on an account's region of origin. As Kathleen Wilson observes, early modern newspapers "functioned like imaginative literature in reproducing and refracting world events into socially meaningful categories and hierarchies."[79] Especially after the Restoration, Nat Cutter demonstrates, English newsprint provided an increasingly accurate picture of political and social life in regions such as North Africa "to a vast and socially diverse group of readers."[80]

Bad news poured in from the beginning, a point sometimes missed by historians, even specialists in print culture.[81] The news carried to merchants and tradesmen in coffeehouses and to sailors in taverns accounts of boarding parties, confiscated ships, and impressed crews, of Caribbean hurricanes and North Atlantic gales, of ships wrecked along coasts or simply vanished on oceans.[82] News of disturbances in Constantinople also crept into Boylston's world, and these had a particular resonance. Most disturbing were threats that emanated from the western frontier and from beyond the coast, reducing white populations there to the "slavish fears . . . those People are so much addicted to."[83]

Terror and mayhem stalked the western frontier, of course, and Americans then were all too familiar with the horrors of Indian attack. Boylston could read in the *Boston Evening-Post* of a gruesome rampage, only a few hundred miles to the west, along the Pennsylvania wilderness: "From Carlisle we hear the following melancholy intelligence, that on the 25th ult. a woman named Cunningham, big with child, was met with by the Indians a little way from her own bouse, who murdered, scalped, and otherwise most horribly abused her."[84] Word of "great consternation" followed Indian assaults at Augusta, Georgia,[85] and warnings of "Invasions and Devastations of the French, and their Indians" from Governor William Shirley likewise left New England in a panic.[86] Conflicts along the Appalachian frontier fed colonial America's original literary genre, the Indian captivity narrative, resonant at least from the time of Mary Rowlandson's *Narrative of Captivity and Restoration* in Metacomet's War up through the mid-nineteenth century.[87]

No one represented the ambiguities of exotic dangers more than did pirates. Buccaneers posed a risk as great as a hurricane, threatening the entirety of a venture, swallowing cargoes of sugar and rum, the crew, and the ship itself. At times, Boylston's eyes would rest upon a common waterfront sight in the early eighteenth century, crows picking at the rotting corpses of pirates, swinging from gallows beneath pennants of a grimacing Jolly Roger. He may well have joined the throngs to gape upon the victims as they offered their last, likely scripted words of admonition to the gathered crowd to avoid their own errant paths "as a Spectacle for the Warning of others, especially Sea faring Men." As Marcus Rediker observes, Boylston would have been an observer of "a dialectic of terror": between threats from outlaws of the sea against the lives and property of law-abiding subjects and sentences imposed by elites, invoking Jehovah as "the king of terrors," to maintain the social order.[88]

Yet, when the winds of war blew, they altered the rules of commerce, and a peacetime merchant could purchase a *letter of marque* and transform himself into a wartime privateer. "Turning pirate" was not always authorized, however, and Boylston's Boston had built its profits on buccaneering forays into the Indian Ocean and Red Sea in the seventeenth century.[89]

The topic of piracy came up frequently and epitomized the complexities of the world. In whispered conversations, men invested in buccaneering, especially as the targets shifted away from the British American trade routes. The ships of Catholic enemies were prized, and especially also were those of the "Musselmen" in the Indian Ocean and Red Sea.[90] The emerging British

Empire had a long history of piracy—supporting and opposing it—and many colonial ports continued this ambivalent participation in various forms of buccaneering.[91]

The general instability of conditions also threatened businesses whose connections were scattered across the globe. The vicissitudes of war and weather could trigger bankruptcies in London or Seville that demanded an immediate response, which, in turn, required up-to-date information.[92] But how was one to respond to fragments of news, rumor, and gossip farther afield? What was Boylston to make of a report in the *Boston Gazette* for November 7, 1768, that "we have just now received the news of the failure of two considerable trading-houses at Smyrna"? How would "letters from the confines of Turkey," printed in the *Pennsylvania Gazette* in August 1742 and bringing word of "a great Revolution at Constantinople [in which] the Grand Vizier has been given up to and massacred by the Janissaries" have shaped his understanding of the world beyond Boston's Long Wharf?

A subscription to the genteel *Gentleman's Magazine* or a chance fragment of newsprint found in the Bunch of Grapes tavern carried reports of extraordinary and volatile events in distant lands that could trigger a butterfly effect, endangering trade, the safety of the colonies, and matters of empire. Perusing the *Boston Evening Post* in June 1744, Boylston would have noted these ties under the byline "From the *London Gazette*, June 16," which reprinted an "Extract of a Letter from George Anson, Esq, Commander of a Squadron lately employed in the South Sea, who arrived Yesterday at St. Helens, in his Majesty's Ship the Centurion, from Canton in China, to his Grace the Duke of Newcastle, dated from on board his Majesty's Ship the Centurion, at St. Helen's, June 14. 1744."

What would our provincial reader learn from Anson's passage through the South China Sea and capture of the Manila Galleon? That the "South West Monsoon being set in on the Coast of *China*" prevented ships from returning to Europe before October. That even so experienced a commander as Anson was "under great Difficulty in navigating two such large Ships in a dangerous and unknown Sea." That sailing conditions during the summer were "very tempestuous." That upon entering the Canton River, a ship master would treat with a "Mandarine," who would sell "a Licence for supplying me with Provisions from Day to Day" and explain "the Payment of the Duties and Measurage, which . . . by the Emperor's Orders, were to be demanded from all ships."

How does one make sense out of this barrage of bad news from the East? There is much that we do not know about eighteenth- and nineteenth-century reactions to news.[93] Still, even at this preliminary stage of investigation, it is possible to discern certain general characteristics that distinguished an early American sense of the world: (1) it was dangerous, both the natural and social worlds; (2) it was confusing, paradoxically chaotic and tyrannical; (3) it was constantly in flux. David Shields discerns "the cultural associations they evoked for Americans and transatlantic clienteles."[94]

There were authorities that might help to make sense of a chaotic world. Scanning the advertisements further could transport the consciousness of a well-read provincial, making him a citizen of the world. Boylston, for instance, would happen upon an offering from the bookseller David Hall, for texts "just imported from London" that included, alongside the *Voyages* of Anson and Smollett, Alexander Drummond's *Travels*; the popular, if fantastical, histories of *Mahomet*; *James Fraser's History of Nadir Shah*; Pope's *Iliad* and *Odyssey*; and the immensely popular *Arabian Nights Entertainment*.[95] He might have had access to George Abbot's *A Briefe Description of the Whole World* (published between 1617 and 1699).[96] By 1769, the *New Hampshire Gazette* was announcing a large inventory of books at William Appleton's store in Portsmouth that included four volumes of *The History of the Arabians*, *The Turkish Spy*, *The Adventures of a Guinea*, *Persian Tales*, *Smollett's Travels*, *Lady Montague's Letters* in four volumes, *The Travels of the Jesuits* in two volumes, *The Trader's Sure Guide*, *The West Indies Pilots*, "and all sorts of books of navigation." Plays, travelers' accounts, and fictional letters drew on a long European tradition of writing about the East and Africa. Many of the most influential accounts that were published in England had been translated from French and Italian sources.[97] Yet a number documented authentic journeys. An early and influential piece was by Johannes Nieuhof, *An Embassy from the East-India Company of the United Provinces, to the Grand Tartar Cham Emperor of China*, first published in the Netherlands in 1665, then translated by Johns Ogilby and published in London in 1669, 1673, and repeatedly after.

Here, a colonial merchant could read the latest newspapers and almanacs and talk with well-informed gentlemen. Zabdiel Boylston could have idled his hours in a coffeehouse in the autumn of 1727 perusing "A History of the Late Revolution in Persia," continued in several issues of the *American Weekly Mercury*.[98] And, in their day, his grandsons Nicholas and Thomas Jr. could pass their time in the London Coffee House, perusing an extended essay reprinted from *Rivington's New-York Gazetteer*, October 12, 1775, on the "Present State of Algiers."[99] Newspapers were another source, keeping Americans aware of events, if at a lag. Newspapers began in Boston in 1704 and immediately filled their columns with news from the East, a feature that only increased over the decades.[100] The *Boston News-Letter* of April 20, 1713, for instance, reported from Constantinople that the sultan "in a Council held at the Seraglio . . . resolved to declare War against the Czar" and from Venice: "Several Venetian Vessels are come in from the Levant, and bring an account, that a great Fire hath happen'd at Galata, near Constantinople, which burnt down above Eighteen hundred Houses." The *Boston Gazette*, on October 3, 1720, for instance, reported: "We have great expectations here from the magnitude of the trade to India, which they have begun to carry on with such expedition, that the like has never been heard of, and they tell us they have already settled three considerable factories, one on the Malabar coast, and two in the bay of Bengal, or, as it is more properly called the gulf of India. They talk of settling factories and several other places, but the particulars are too great to speak of them with any insurance, till we see them go on a little farther." Reports such as these were repeated throughout the colonies. But reading this required a sophisticated knowledge of geography, commerce, and risk.[101]

By the time the *Empress of China* sailed for the East, American libraries had accumulated a rich archive of readings on the Orient. This knowledge came slowly. In 1720, the *Boston News-Letter* complained, "We have very seldom any Advices from the Indies, for there being no Intercourse of Communication by Post with those Countries, by reason of the Tyrannical Governments in the East, the knowledge of several remarkable Events, that happened in those Countries, does very seldom come to us."[102] Ten years later, an irate reader groused to the editor of the *New-England Weekly Journal* about the clergy's ignorance of the world. The occasion was the death of Samuel Sewell—Boston merchant, Salem Witch Trials judge, and sincere Puritan confessor—and the sermon delivered at his funeral. T. P. was incredulous that the Rev. Thomas Prince of Boston's South Church identified the location of the Land of Canaan incorrectly, and evidenced his complaint by identifying the correct locations of various parts of the world: "That a North East Line passes thro' the Orkney Islands, Poland, and the Mouth of the Persian Gulph, Northeast by North thro' Iceland, the Eastern Part of Persia, and the Ile of Ceylon in the East Indian Ocean, North North East thro' Greenland, Muscovy, the Mogul's Empire, and the Island of Sumatra which cuts the Equintoctal Line itself; and lastly, when I point due North, I point both towards the North Pole of the Earth, Tartary, China, and the Ilands of Borneo and Java in the East Indies." T. P. was adamant and urged his countrymen, especially "our rising Gentry," to avail themselves of a globe.[103]

About the same time, in England, Bishop George Berkeley was likewise grappling with the many confusions that the wider world presented. In 1726, Berkeley penned an ode to the idea that civilization's eventual apex would settle in the West, *Translatio studii*, in the proper Latin. Finally published in 1752, his "On the Prospect of Planting Arts and Learning in America" inspired many, and his generosity helped young artists such as Tobias Smibert and John Singleton Copley.[104] Such verses laid out a binary distinction in their imagined geographies, as in a purported inscription on a Plymouth, Massachusetts stone: "The Eastern World enslav'd, its Glory ends / And Empire rises where the Sun descends."[105]

Consequently, it would have been difficult for most people to avoid the fact that Philadelphia or Boston or New York, and their surrounding environs, sat within a global context. This was especially the case after 1720, just before the consumer revolution. As noted above, in 1721 Parliament passed the Calico Act, or, "An Act to preserve and encourage the Woollen and Silk Manufactures of this Kingdom, and for more effectual employing the Poor, by prohibiting the Use and Wear of all printed, painted, stained or dyed Callicoes in Apparel, Houshold Stuff, Furniture, or otherwise."[106] The legislation redirected the Indies cloth trade to North America, where American consumers could acquire calico and nankeen more easily than could Britons. About 1720, also, another East India Company policy redirected porcelain to America. Company letters advised merchants not to itemize porcelain and ordered "China where must be overall useful sorts."[107] The following year, the Company officially separated the direct trade from Asia to the West Indies and prohibited Company vessels from carrying African slaves into American waters "for fear of filling the plantations with India goods." So, from this date, we find not in customs records but in colonial newspapers advertisements for porcelain from the Indies.[108] The supply was there, as European traders flowed into Asia from 1717, with entries from the Darien Company (Scotland), the Prussian Bengal Company, and the Danish, Swedish, and Imperial (Austrian, based in Trieste) East India Companies. France got into the act in 1718, when King Louis XV consolidated trade to both East and West under a reorganized East India Company.[109]

What do we make of the news? Modern historians who delve into colonial newspapers may see the news as a congeries of discrete, disconnected, virtually free-floating elements. But to appreciate how colonials took in the news, we need to imagine how it was read: the setting, the goods, the company around a reader, all influenced how he took in the news. But, even more so, did the pattern that one saw, weaving the pieces together in constellations of meaning. A reader did not simply sample pieces, as historians do today. Rather, the daily, monthly, yearly reading created an accumulated experience. And, as it is today, the news was selective. Yet certain themes stood out for colonial Americans. The "news from the East" presented a set of consistent themes that reinforced the idea of the world as dangerous and disordered.

The news from the western frontier presented the western edge of the colonies with grim reminders of violence and chaos virtually every week. Algonquian and Iroquois adoption of European technology and integration into traditional effective tactics in warfare was a surprising development and made frontier conflict more intense.[110] Warfare punctuated the news from the west from the beginnings of settlement, and events such as the Powhatan War, Metacomet's (or King Phillip's) War, and the Yamasee War were as prominent as, and the experience more immediate than, more formalized European conflicts such as the War of the Spanish Succession King William's War (1689–1697), Queen Anne's War (1702–1713), the War of the Austrian Succession (King George's War, 1740–1748), and the Seven Years' War (the French and Indian War, 1754/56–1763). The *Boston News-Letter* for August 19, 1706, reported from Piscataqua, "The Skulking Indian Enemy killed a man at Dover." A letter sent from the Niagara garrison in July 1763 reported a New Jersey soldier and two sailors based at Lake Erie attacked and scalped.[111] The genteel coffeehouses and the well-appointed drawing rooms and parlors of the Boylstons and John Copley must have seemed a different world from that of Carlisle, Pennsylvania, described in the *Boston Evening-Post* for August 20. 1764. The "melancholy intelligence" from Carlisle told of a pregnant woman assaulted near her home by a Native American raiding party, "murdered, scalped, and otherwise most horribly abused . . . , ripping her belly open & taking out the child, which they left lying beside her." There, too, Ensign Smith led seven men in a "scalping party" to root out the enemy, but found Crow's Town and Beaver Creek "abandoned and the houses burnt" or deserted in terror. Adding to the disembodied terror was the men's own inability, as "they found a few tracks, but did not see but one Indian during their long march, and him they could not come up with." The world must indeed have appeared a scene of incomprehensible, irrational violence and mayhem, what Linda Colley styles, "dimensionless fear."[112]

A surprising amount of "News from the East" filled British American newspapers and magazines.[113] Much of this information from the eastern frontier emanated from the Ottoman Empire, realm of the worst of the autocrats, the Great Sultan and Grand Turk, and the domain of that "Great Imposter,"

Mohammed. Frequently reported was news of wars, particularly between the Ottomans and Russia, and an interested reader could follow the course of international events as they unfolded beyond the Mediterranean Sea. The *Boston Gazette* for October 20, 1741, reported from Petersburg, Russia, that the "Turkish Ambassador has given the Court strong Assurance of the Porte's Resolution to preserve the Peace between the two Empires," but there the Russians and their allies kept several fleets of galleys armed and manned in the event of a breach.[114] "Advice" from the "Frontiers of Persia" told of an impending defense of the city of Cars, awaiting an assault of two hundred thousand men.[115] When the *Boston Chronicle* for September 14, 1769, described the first major battle of "the present war," the editor was not recalling the recent French and Indian War but rather the then-raging conflict between the Turks and Russians, a humiliating defeat for the Ottomans. "Advice . . . from the Frontiers of Persia," "the Latest from Constantinople," and "A Letter from Smyrna," often first page entries, greeted the newspaper reader throughout the colonial period.[116] Violence was a customary path to resolving international disputes, catching the eye especially of men such as the Boylstons, whose trade might one day bring their vessels into the Mediterranean. The king imposed summary judgment on the Reis (chief) who had taken the ship into Algiers, beheading him; another Reis who had taken an English ship suffered a lesser punishment, losing his teeth and beard.[117]

Revolts from within likewise fractured the stability of the Ottoman Empire. Beginning with their earliest newspapers, British Americans read of rebellions and revolts that painted the Ottoman East as bedlam. Reports of "a very sudden, unexpected and great Revolution" in Constantinople depicted a decadent domain, vulnerable to the visions of "a single Janissary, who pretended to be a Prophet." Western reports, especially those from British travelers, instilled an underlying Whig perspective in their descriptions, as in the article in the December 31, 1730, issue of the *Boston Weekly News-Letter* explaining that the danger to political stability lay in the tyranny of the Ottomans, in the "Indolence of the Sultan and the ill Conduct of the Vizier," whose defeats in their frequent wars lost them public support.[118] Adding to the instability was the challenge of governing a large empire of diverse religions and cultures. News of rebellion came frequently, of "laying waste" to villages and requiring a military response. Boylston could have read this in the *Boston Gazette* for November 7, 1768.

Ottoman rulers, whether in the Grand Porte or in the semiautonomous precincts of North Africa, imposed their own cruelties on their people.[119]

Much of Ottoman oppression took the form of tribute taxation. As Americans such as Boylston awaited Parliament's reaction to Boston's tea party, they were also reading about yet another war looming out of Constantinople. The news was old—from September of 1773—but rang familiar themes. The news was pertinent to their situation—new tax burdens to pay for foreign wars. The Sublime Porte proposed to lay "a fresh tax" upon Jews, Franks (Europeans), and Greek Christians and ordered the kingdom of Egypt to raise one and one-half sequins within two months and local officials "to be squeezed of large treasures, and the riches of the great Mosques . . . to be used on any particular emergency."[120] Although the English king's subjects on both sides of the Atlantic had for centuries embraced their relief from taxation without representation, British Americans complained about their burdens from local and colony demands, as Franklin's figure Father Abraham observed in *The Way to Wealth* (1757). With the imposition of the Sugar (1764), Stamp (1765), and Townsend (1767) Acts, newspapers paid even more attention to wrenching taxation elsewhere. In the winter of 1764, readers of the *New-York Mercury* learned that Morocco's bey had taken to the field to demand "exorbitant sums" from outlying provinces, and his subjects in the Rar (Rif) Mountains and Tetuan (Tétouan) were "in the greatest consternation."[121] Reports such as this reinforced the idea that violence was a customary path to resolving domestic, as well as foreign, disputes in other parts of the world. It was not uncommon, for instance, to read disturbing news such as an account from Constantinople: "For some days past many excesses have been committed in this capital. . . . The government, to remedy this evil, hath judged it proper to put to death some of the authors of these disorders."[122] Poverty was common throughout Europe, and American readers were accustomed to reports such as one from Scotland in which a gentleman observed that "the distresses of the poor in several parts of that country almost exceed belief, and the opulent inhabitants are hourly in expectation of an insurrection."

Acts of wanton cruelty, from the sultan down to the common people, were featured in the newspapers available to Boylston. The *Boston Chronicle*, in September 14, 1769, for instance, reported on "an odd sort of diversion" among the people of Smyrna who entertained themselves by placing hens' eggs in the nest of a female stork, whereupon other storks "to revenge the disgrace . . . destroy her by pecking her to death."[123] Yet, apparently, it was easier to excuse the cockfighting in which Virginians engaged, but which New Englanders found reprehensible, because such were the customs of countrymen and erstwhile business partners.[124]

Natural calamities likewise rocked the Ottoman world, augmenting the sense of a dangerous and disorderly region and agitating coffeehouse conversations with warnings against voyages to the Levant. Accounts of plague, earthquake, tsunami, and drought may have made it seem that the Protestant Jehovah was bent on punishing the region for its false religion. Plagues and epidemics struck Europe and America with regularity, of course, but the "fatal news" from the East frequently calculated the loss of life in the tens of thousands rather than the tens and hundreds who perished in the colonies' seaport towns.[125] Reports reminded readers in Boston, Charleston, and Williamsburg, who were accustomed to outbreaks of smallpox or yellow fever, that more virulent diseases stalked the Mediterranean world.[126] From Basra and Baghdad came "very alarming" news that a recurrence of plague had taken three hundred thousand souls. The news came with advice for a merchant who might be considering investing in this part of the world. English traders had become "accustomed to many vicissitudes in that part of the world" and "doubt not riding out the present storm."[127]

Nowhere in the colonial imagination was this triangulation between a decadent West and cruel and wanton East more evident than in the waters along the Barbary Coast. Whether in print or by word of mouth, early Americans learned of Barbary captivity largely through a European literature that described a range of sufferings. Men could be sent to mines to quarry stone for the breakers. Undernourished, beaten, worked in hot weather, captives died in droves, a fortunate few ransomed. Such was the fate of Miguel de Cervantes, who described the horrors of his five-year captivity in several works, including the influential *Don Quixote*.[128] The news from North Africa delivered a similar chronicle of instability and violence into British America's public sphere, and formed the consciousness of three generations of Boylstons. Coffeehouses collected news of captured ships and ransomed sailors throughout the entirety of the colonial period. They may well have served as collection sites for the ransom drives that Cotton Mather and others organized. One of these came in 1700, when Benjamin Alford of Boston and William Bowditch of Salem observed that "their friend Robert Carver of the latter port was taken nine years before, a captive into Sally [Salé]; that contributions had been made for his redemption; that the money was in the hands of a person here; that if they had the disposal of it, they could release Carver."[129] The imprisonment of Alford, Carver, Joshua Gee, and other Yankee tars held captive in Salé, drew early America's most articulate voices into a conversation that cast the East as a den of tyranny.

As early as 1722, under the banner of James Franklin's *New-England Courant*, the earliest permanent newspaper in the British American colonies, the Boylstons would have read that the bey of Morocco ordered the capture English ships in retaliation for an English boycott of trade with the Ottoman semisovereign kingdoms of Morocco, Algiers, Tripoli, and Tunis along the North African coast—the lands known as Barbary. Nor could they expect that the British ensign would cover their own ships, as they learned in journals such as the *Boston Weekly News-Letter* in the winter of 1737. Writing from Gibraltar, Dutch ambassador Henry Lynslager lamented that "some Christian Powers suffer daily Insults from the Infidels of Barbary, and not only so, but received them too with so little Resentment and so much Complaisance, when another sort of Conduct would effectually humble the Pride and Insolence of those Robbers."[130] British American merchant ships may have begun sailing to the Sublime Porte by 1767, when William Lee Perkins, a Boston merchant, established trade relations in Smyrna (Izmir) for opium and rugs, and Perkins and his crews would have regaled coffeehouses and taverns with their own Barbary tales.

The news from Barbary bolstered the idea of the Levant as perilous and uncontrolled, but the alarms that punctuated coffeehouse conversations did not stop at the water's edge. The Barbary kingdoms were known to be among the most violently unstable in the world. In 1727, the coffeehouses of New York, Philadelphia, Boston, and beyond would learn that "the Moors" of Morocco retire to the Spanish colony of Ceuta "to shelter themselves from the Tyranny of Muley Hamet, and the cruel Wars between the Sons of the late King of Morocco, for their Father's Throne." Such rivalries occurred among European dynasties, but news of prosperity and advancement mitigated such dire reports. The news from the East was almost unrelentingly dire, however. In April of 1728, a dispatch from Ceuta, the Portuguese colony off the west Coast of Africa, informed readers that the king of Mequinez (Meknes) had dethroned his brother the king of Morocco, and that although the former promised peace to all, "especially the Merchants," partisans "continued committing great Disorders in the Country."[131] Two years later, letters from Ceuta reported a "bloody Battle" in which the king of Morocco defeated an alliance of rebels, with the loss of seven thousand killed or captured.[132]

Dire reports formed the background for the next generation of Boylstons, as well, and again, increased during the world wars. Most weeks, one could expect to see an account out of London, Leghorn, or Genoa, such as the one printed in the *New-York Mercury* for March 1, 1756, that reported a

Genoese pink had repelled four Tunisian xebecs, each with crews of two hundred men; over the course of a five-hour "noble and brave action," the eighteen defenders killed more than two hundred attackers while losing only one man. That the report was incredulous likely added to the sense that this part of the world was washed in misted fantasy.[133] Thomas and Nicolas would have known of the news out of Cadiz that a Barbary corsair captured a Portuguese galliot in July 1765.[134] The dominant story from Morocco over the winter of 1763–1764 was the plight of the English brigantine *Charming Kitty*, taken off St. Mary's Isle.[135] The king of Morocco ordered her release, but not before "the pirates had cruelly used the captain, and plundered great part of the cargo."[136]

The news from East Asia was just as conflicting, with promising elements of opportunity shaded by vexed warnings of peril.[137] Merchant families, such as the Boylstons, could follow the fluctuations of the Asian price current: in 1733, the (French) "East-India Company's Merchandizes sell at a much higher Price this Year than the last."[138]

More philosophical matters also grabbed the attention of British American readers. Essays on Confucian belief and practice were frequently reprinted.[139] More likely to catch a reader's eye were the periodic reports of religious conflict that flared up between competing sects. British American newspapers took particular interest in the plight of Christians in the East. The struggle between Christians and Muslims was noted in the autumn of 1741, when several journals carried a report out of Madrid that

> by Letters from the Philippine Islands we are informed, that the Mahometans continue to persecute Christians and Missionaries of the Isles of Calaminnes and Mindoro; that the Barbarians there had oblig'd to Christians to retire to the Mountains; that they had plunder'd the Convents of the consecrated Plate, &c. That on the 23d of October, 1739 the Moors of the Island of Tidor, after having strip'd the chief Missionary there, bound and whipp'd him inhumanly, and afterwards cut off his Hands and his Head, which they carry'd in Triumph tho' the whole Island, after having cast his Body into the sea; and that on the 20th May, 1740 the Moor's also took a Missionary Preacher, and stripp'd [off] his Cloaths, then dragg'd him aboard a Vessel by a Rope which they had fasten'd about his Waist.[140]

Boylston would have learned of similar atrocities in European wars and conflicts on the American frontier, even those perpetrated by his own countrymen, but, somehow, cruelty seemed heinous when conducted by alien peoples.

Whether committed in the East or West, the cumulative message from British American journals was one of peril.

At the moment when he sat for Copley's painting, Boylston would not have contemplated initiating trade with East Asia; practical and political factors would have prevented the possibility of sending a voyage beyond the Caribbean Sea. If he could have done so, he would have heard warnings to advise against it. A chilling description penned by the chief mate of the *Plassy* (identified as J. G.) recalled the particulars of a trade gone bad. The mate had boarded a Chinese junk anchored off Malacca roadstead "in order to dispose of some opium which I did to good Account," unsuspecting a "horrid scheme" by "those savages" to murder him and keep the proceeds. C. G. fended off his attackers, and despite two lance wounds, escaped by launching himself over the railing and into the launch tied up alongside, then making his way back to the *Plassy*. The Chinese had failed to capture the ship, although they "treacherously murdered" the captain.[141] The report reminded the Boylstons that the lands and seas beyond Boston Harbor composed a dangerous world.

Despite direct contact through the Atlantic slave trade, Africa remained as mysterious to American readers as faraway China or India.[142] What was this place, this little known world that preindependence British Americans called "Afric" or "Africa"? The few standard maps reproduced stereotypes that offered little accurate information. Bowles's map, for instance, featured a cartouche that depicted images of dark-skinned, nearly naked people. Jonathan Swift lampooned the vagaries passed on by pretended experts: "Geographers, in Afric maps, / With savage pictures fill their gaps, / And o'er unhabitable downs / Place elephants for want of towns."[143]

What little authentic news that reached Boston from Africa would also have disturbed the Boylstons' ideas of order. Most of it was couched in a language of mundane business reports: "Just arrived in the James River, from Africa, the ship *Apollo*, Capt. *Elias Glover*, with about two hundred choice healthy *Windward* and *Gold Coast* slaves."[144] Merchants such as Thomas or Nicolas Boylston were aware that disorder and tragedy characterized this part of the world, but it was not the disorder that modern sympathies would necessarily recognize. It took the form of news that reached Newport on September 5, 1763, from "a Gentleman, who arrived here a few Days ago from the Coast of Africa" who passed along "very discouraging Accounts of the Trade upon the Coast, and that upwards of 200 Gallons of neat Rum had been given per Head for Slaves, and scarcely to be got at any Rate."[145] This was a case of too much demand, in rum, for too scant a supply (of human capital), but news such as this upset markets and troubled men of trade, who wondered how to retail their rum; farmers, who wondered how it would affect prices for their bushels of wheat; and laborers, who wondered how it would affect their wages.

The waters off the Gold Coast, the Slave Coast, or the island of Gorée, named for commodities that Westerners craved or for the sites of fortresses that served as collection points, were a theater of near-constant conflict plied by privateers, men-of-war, pirates, and other interlopers. Here, the sufferings of human cargoes carried no weight in a merchant's ledger. Of more interest to a Boylston during King George's War (Austrian Succession), the *New-York Evening Post* reported the capture of a French slave ship, "with 150 Negroes is taken on the Coast of Africa," by the London-based privateer *Black Prince*, a reminder that European wars had global repercussions.[146] Likewise, the *Pennsylvania Gazette* for March 2, 1758, carried multiple reports of British slave ships that had been captured by French privateers and robbed of their cargoes—hundreds of African slaves.[147]

The brutality and immorality of enslavement was eclipsed under warnings of a different kind of violence—the commercial loss when investors' property rose up against them. Uncomfortable as it may be for modern readers to contemplate, perceiving these incidents through the eyes of eighteenth-century merchants and tradesmen frames such incidents as attacks on these men's livelihoods and assaults on their concepts of order, property, and liberty. This is significant. In this way, the manner in which British Americans perceived the dangers of the world insulated them from caring about the brutality they inflicted. For the most part, they did not have time to consider the dangers to others because they were preoccupied with threats to their own well-being. Dangers to their interests absorbed their attention and left little over for empathy for the plight of others. Accounts of slave revolts poured in from the Atlantic, and some ships never sailed far from Africa. Slaves rose up on board a ship off Gorée in 1764,[148]

Slave reports formed much of the news from Africa. The report from a 1769 letter sent by the surgeon of the *Dwight* is illustrative: "Alarmed" in the night by "a most horrid noise of the Negroes," "the dreadful Shrieks from . . . the People upon Deck," and "an uncommon uproar," Mr. Boulton raced to the deck, where he witnessed a terrible scene. In Boulton's telling of "the Insurrection," the oppressors were victims: one was "Poor Mullroy; another was "promising young Man." They were "murdered under the Windlass," "caught and cut into pieces," "laid upon Deck crying for Mercy, having his Arms and

Legs cut off," and butchered on the Main Deck. The captives were "the Villains," "the Wretches," "these unmerciful Butchers," and "a resolute Dog."[149] Take, for instance, the constellation of events described in the *New-York Gazette, and the Weekly Mercury* for June 18, 1770.[150] Readers learned of a slave revolt in an account framed to invoke sympathy for the oppressors rather than the African captives in an arched language that described: "a horrid Noise of the Negroes"; "dreadful Shrieks from . . . the People on Deck"; and "several of the People, whom the Villains were butchering on the Main Deck." In fact, phrasings such as "the People on Deck" distinguish grades of humanity, or even steal humanity from the ranks of the enslaved. In the winter of 1768, the *Pennsylvania Chronicle* and other journals presented worrisome reports of violence in Gambia: the "trade there is greatly embarrassed and interrupted by the hostile behaviour of the natives, who make every attempt in their power to destroy the English" at St. James Fort. The disturbance arose when the English refused to pay their customary fees, "established from ancient custom," to the local ruler; nevertheless, the report described the Africans as "savages."[151]

The doorway of a colonial bookstore also opened into the wider world, and Nicolas Boylston's next steps might have taken him in search of leather-bound folios, quartos, octavos, and duodecimos that could provide a measure of clarity in this too often disordered world. As early as 1717, one could find a catalog of "Curious Valuable Books," the library of the Reverend Isaac Pemberton, up for auction at Boston's Crown Coffee House. Although Pemberton's collection focused on divinity and philosophy, the offerings included a scattering of histories and travelogues for the Orient, including *Memoirs of the Chinese People* (357), *History of the Turks* in two volumes (433), *The Conquest of Syria, Persia, and Egypt* (496), an abridgment of Sir Walter Raleigh's *History of the World* (498), the first and second volumes of *The Spectator* (539), three volumes of *The Tatler* (540), and *The Turkish Spy* in eight volumes (541).[152] In Boston, Boylston might venture to Samuel Shaw's or John Mein's London Book Store or perhaps to Henry Knox's London Book Store in the Cornhill section of the city, where the future Continental Army general purveyed "Books in all Languages, Arts, and Sciences," as well as stationary and blank journals.[153]

At Benjamin Franklin's shop "in the Post Office" in Philadelphia, beginning in 1738, a customer could peruse a plentitude of books that described the wider world: the *Arabian Nights Entertainment, Chinese Tales, Mogul Tales, Persian Tales,* the *History of Genghizcan* [Genghis Khan] *the Great, Tamerlane,*

The Turkish Spy, and more.[154] Elsewhere in Franklin's Philadelphia, a would-be citizen of the world could step into David Hall's shop to purchase *Smollett's Voyages, Mahamot, Kuli Khan, Anson's Voyage*, and *Arabian Nights Entertainments*. In 1743, a merchant could browse through William Bradford's Philadelphia bookshop and pull from the shelves, along with Shakespeare, Dryden, Swift, and Bolingbroke, fantasies such as *The Turkish Spy, Persian Letters*, and *Gulliver's Travels*; theologies such as *The Alcoran of Mahomet*; and biographies that included *The Life of Mahomet*.[155] Another window on the world opened at "Mr. James Emerson's, the Sugar Loaf, between the River and Front-street" in Philadelphia, where a middling man or woman could leaf through the volumes of Robert Bell, "Bookseller and Auctioneer." In 1773, Bell's extensive sale catalog included law books, poetry, classics, commercial and navigational guides, histories, oratory and rhetoric, travelogues, and much more. An important portion of his titles brought the reader into the world beyond Europe's shores; a sampling included the standard titles of the time, such as Anson's *Voyage Round the World*, with forty-two copperplates, for £2 5s. (a less expensive edition was available for 12s.), *Receuil de divers voyages faits en Afrique et en L'Amerique* for 15s., Bell's two volumes of *Travels from Petersburgh to Asia* for £1 10s., Beekman's *Voyage to Borneo in the East Indies* for 5s., Lady Mary Wortley Montague's *Travels* for 6s., Lockman's two volumes of *Travels of the Jesuits into Various Parts of the World* for £1 2s. 6d., *Ancient Accounts of India and China, by two Mahomedan Travelers* for 12s. 6d., Dampier's *A Voyage to New-Holland* for 3s. 9d., la Salle's *Account of North-America*, with Montauban's *Voyage to the Coast of Guinea* for 3s., Robson's *Voyage to, and Six Years Residence at Hudson's Bay, with an Account of the Fur Trade, and of the Whale-fishery* for 6s., *A Voyage Round the World with Banks and Solander, in the Years 1768, 1769, 1770 and 1771* for 5s., Smollett's *Present State of all Nations, containing Geographical, Natural, Commercial, and Political History of all the Countries in the Known World, with Maps of Kingdoms and Views of Capital Cities* in eight volumes for £5 12s., *The Chinese Spy, or Emissary from the Court of Pekin, commissioned to examine into the present State of Europe* for £1 16s., and Salmon's *Modern Gazetteer for the Whole World* for 7s. 6d.

British America's windows on the world were not limited to the Northeast. In Williamsburg in the 1760s, one could find at the post office a broadside "Catalogue of Books to be Sold at the Post Office" that included a wide array of titles, including the octavo volumes of *Present State of the British Empire, in Europe, America, Africa, and Asia, Callander's Voyages, History of Greenland, History of California, Ulloa's Voyages to South America*, and *Charlesveoix's*

Voyages to North America; and the duodecimo volumes of *Arabian Nights Entertainments, Boyle's Voyages; Life of Robinson Crusoe, The Adventures of a Guinea, Persian Tales, Tales of the Genii,* and *The Turkish Spy.*[156] Here, he might also collect mail posted from the Atlantic and Caribbean seaports where he had correspondents. As Joseph M. Adelman observes: "In the eighteenth century post offices weren't free-standing buildings. The 'post office' as such was often housed in another commercial establishment, most often a coffeehouse or printing office."[157] Here, when this catalog was published, two printers—Joseph Royle and then Alexander Purdie—held the commission to serve as postmaster. "The most likely answer," Adelman wrote, "is that the post office was the easiest identifier for this advertisement, and that it was for books sold either by Royle or Purdie."[158]

In seaports large and small, as well as in modest villages, one could find books. In 1756, in New York, where he purveyed globes, "bookseller and stationer" Garrat Noel advertised on the first page of the *New-York Mercury* "a choice parcel of the most esteemed modern books" that would acquaint a gentleman with the world, such as Abbe Lambert's *Curious Observations on the Several Nations of Asia, Africa, and America* in two volumes, Spelman's *Expedition of Cyprus* in two volumes, Moore's *Travels into Africa,* Raleigh's *Works* in two volumes, a "curious new edition" of Anson's *Voyage,* a *History of Thomas Kuli Khan,* and *The History of Barbary.* Or if he had traveled to a more modest seaport, such as John Edwards's Portsmouth, in 1767, he would have found at the stationer shop on Queen Street, an assortment of books and supplies "as neat as any in Boston," including *Travels through Turkey.*[159]

Boylston's day culminated as it began, with news of the world demanding his attention. A daily diet of perusing the newspapers or delving into travelogues and the like encouraged refined conversation for its many benefits. The coffeehouse and the tavern afforded spaces in which a man on the make could imbibe what useful knowledge the world could bring—what eighteenth-century observers knew about it—but where could one engage in philosophical conversation and the rich exchange of ideas that ornamented genteel living? As in the coffeehouse, convivial conversations among polite society were the goal for upper and middling sorts.[160] Clubs such as Franklin's Junto in Philadelphia or Dr. Alexander Hamilton's Tuesday Club in Annapolis prided themselves on elevated inquiry and discussion "to argue and debate upon various Subjects, and to discuss points of a knotty and abstruse nature."[161] In Newport, meeting notices were posted for the Fellowship Club.[162] Men on the rise, men of substance and consequence, as they considered themselves, found club quarters at taverns or in members' homes a comfortable space where they could master a language of serious things over bowls of port and madeira. Conversation, it was said, "tends to polish our Minds, and Refine our Manners" and to infuse an affable and easy Deportment which will powerfully recommend us in all Companies."[163] An Anglo-American citizen of the world was sensible of the qualities that made a gentleman of commerce: "Honesty and plain dealing are the best Foundation of a lasting Trade and Commerce," and one should "carefully Endeavor to prevent all Deceits and Frauds therein."[164] Whether opulent merchants, such as the Boylstons, or up-and-coming farmers or tradesman, these colonists crafted a culture that worshipped the "God of Order" and feared the deity of Anarchy.[165] Every opportunity implied danger, because it carried risk. In good company, enjoying the goods of the world, dressed in the finest raiment, they experienced a form of living that came to define civilization so rigidly that it virtually excluded peoples who did not live as they did.

The *American Magazine* provides a sense of the topics discussed at "a political club" in Boston under the Rev. Charles Chauncy in 1744: parliamentary speeches, a description of Greenland, discoveries using a microscope, a subterranean city, "superstitious fears and their causes," and similar subjects.[166] The *Boston Evening-Post* for August 13, 1744, noted the items, an account of Alexandria, "the declention and destruction of empires, states, and kingdoms," and a "species of milk-white Indians."[167] The conversation of club members, given their broad interests, did not strictly adhere to political issues, of course. Natural history, philosophy and religion, economics (then called political œconomy)—all fell under the purview of club discussions.

One issue in particular concerned the physicians, tradesmen, and, of course, merchants who filled the clubs of British America—the Atlantic economy, and, by extension, its global interconnections. The British Empire grew steadily, if fitfully, over the eighteenth century, and British Americans watched and shared in its successes and disappointments. As men of the world, they needed to articulate their thoughts on serious things. And important among those things were the challenges of overseas trade. Here, in 1701, they could discuss an agreement signed at Galhilly between the English and Dutch in India that forestalled conflict. They could have read it in the *New-York Gazette* for January 20, 1701, or in the *London Magazine, or Gentleman's Monthly Intelligencer* for 1760.[168] They may have discussed the debates in the latest session of Parliament, carried in the February issue of the *London Magazine, or*

Gentleman's Monthly Intelligencer, and traced a sophisticated understanding of the complexities of the global economy.

> By this act, after reciting in the preamble, that the grievance complained of is not only a manifest discouragement and prejudice to the woollen manufactures of Great-Britain, but is also a means for affording relief to the enemy, and thereby enabling them to carry on the war against these kingdoms; therefore, for the more effectually preventing such disruptive commerce for the future, it is enacted, that, after passing this act, no woollen goods of the manufacture of France, shall directly or indirectly be imported, or carried into any place in the Levant Seas, within the limits of the charter of the Turkey company.[169]

The lengthy piece (65–72) printed in the London journal (excerpts appeared in British American newsprint) raised the specter of a world that threatened the Empire's economy and could be felt in Boston or Philadelphia.[170]

During the 1760s, a debate over arbitrary power consumed clubs, one that was connected to Boston's Tea Party and Massacre indirectly. Britons and Americans debated the policies of "Asiatic plunder" fomented by the East India Company in Bengal.[171] Print culture offered many examples, but nowhere more frequently, or more strained, than when referencing "the Turk." New York merchants could contemplate the association through a proposition put forth in the *New York Journal* for January 28, 1733: "Men in a Torrent of Prosperity seldom think of a Day of Distress, or Great Men that their greatness will ever Cease"—"thus the great Turk often uses his Bashaws."[172] At the end of the year, the same newspaper quoted from *Cato's Letters* to caution against reverencing a ruler for his title rather than his deeds, advising: "This is the Height of humane slavery! By this *Turk* and the *Pope* Reign! They hold their horrid and saying Sanguinary authority buy false Reverence as much as by the Sword."[173]

It was a commonplace of the Georgian era that an understanding of politics required a grounding in history and geography. Consequently, in sites such as the Tuesday Evening Club, in Annapolis, the Scottish physician Alexander Hamilton and his colleagues discussed Chinese and African antiquity, "that monster among imposters Mahomet," and "the Indian natives of America, and the Æthiopians of Afric, tho not quite so civilized and learned a people as the ancient Irish, nor such great Saints, bid the fairest for being the most ancient and unmixed people now in the known world, and therefore have on that Score the Justest claim to honor & precedence." Tuesday Club members considered them civilized, unlike the ancient Arabians.[174] In New York clubs during the winter of 1735, amid discussions of the libel trial of John Peter Zenger, publisher of the *New-York Weekly Journal*, gentlemen might have taken up an extended essay on Confucian thought published in Zenger's newspaper.[175] Their conversations engaged one of the great arguments of the age: Did commerce bring civilization? As Malachy Postlethwayt phrased the answer in *Great-Britain's True System* (1757): commerce had "greatly civilized the human race" as the mechanical arts had done in China and other parts of Europe.[176]

Club members might debate the importance of overseas trade to a country's prosperity and power.[177] But men such as the Boylstons were attracted to less fraught issues. They were interested in what they called natural history. In 1738, the conversation could turn to accounts of ginseng in the Susquehanna Valley. As the Pennsylvania and New York press reported, "We have the Pleasure of acquainting the World, that the famous Chinese, or Tartarian Plant, called *GinSeng*, is now discovered in this Province, near Sasquehannah."[178] The finding was a reminder not only of the interconnections with the world but also of the kind of economic opportunity that fueled the "useful knowledge" appreciated in Georgian America. Recent letters from India, by way of London, informed the world that Chinese authorities had approved "the Ginseng growing in America" as of the same quality as the Asian root and "have hitherto sold at so great a price.[179]

As early as 1721, merchants in Portsmouth could see a camel, "just arrived from Africa . . . the first of its kind brought into America."[180] In the autumn of 1768, table talk might have taken in Busson's *Description of the Orang Outang*, the "surprising animal [that] nearly resembles the human species."[181]

Plays commonly offered moral lessons for the drawing rooms and bedrooms of the gentility, but could also reflect larger ideas of the world. That George Lillo's *The London Merchant* was first performed in 1731 but was popular throughout the Boylstons' time (although not formally performed in Puritan Massachusetts) is instructive.[182] In act III, scene I, commerce is not only an honorable profession but one that will bring harmony to the world and civilization to its scattered peoples:

THOROWGOOD: How it has promoted Humanity, as it has opened and yet keeps
up an Intercourse between Nations, far remote from one another in Situation,
Customs and Religion; promoting Arts, Industry, Peace and Plenty; by mutual
Benefits diffusing mutual Love from Pole to Pole.

TRUEMAN: Something of this I have consider'd, and hope, by your Assistance, to extend my Thoughts much farther.—I have observ'd those Countries, where Trade is promoted and encouraged, do not make Discoveries to destroy, but to improve Mankind,—by Love and Friendship, to tame the fierce, and polish the most savage,—to teach them the Advantages of honest Traffick,—by taking from them, with their own Consent, their useless Superfluities, and giving them, in Return, what, from their Ignorance in manual Arts, their Situation, or some other Accident they stand in need of.

THOROWGOOD: 'Tis justly observ'd:—The populous East, luxuriant, abounds with glittering Gems, bright Pearls, aromatick Spices, and Health-restoring Drugs: The late found Western World glows with unnumber'd Veins of Gold and Silver Ore.—On every Climate, and on every Country, Heaven has bestowed some good peculiar to it self.—It is the industrious Merchant's Business to collect the various Blessings of each Soil and Climate, and, with the Product of the whole, to enrich his native Country.

Club members debated the benefits of the "true religion"—their own brand of Protestantism—against others, condemning especially papism and Islam, which they thought in league under the Antichrist.[183] Mohammed was the Imposter, and they relished rumors that suggested even Muslims were reassessing the "Orthodoxy of the Law of Mahomet."[184]

They explored the art of living, appropriating ideas from across the globe. In 1735 in New York, they might have discussed an anonymous essay published in John Peter Zenger's *New-York Weekly Journal* that extolled the life and advice of Confucius and printed nine of his precepts.[185] They could, indeed, follow an extended essay on Confucius's teachings in the *Journal* for November 15, 1736, through February 13, 1737; in Franklin's *Pennsylvania Gazette* from March 7 through March 21, 1737; then in occasional pieces in the *New-York Weekly Journal* for February 20, 1743. Not all of this writing presented a positive view of the philosopher. The *Pennsylvania Gazette* for January 21, 1755, printed a dispatch from Paris reporting that in China, "the Persecution still rages against the Christians" and the Portuguese missionaries there, "who oppose the idolatrous Worship of Confucius."

At the end of the war, a piece of doggerel would have caught the eye, "A Sacred Ode," reprinted from the *Scots Magazine*, "occasioned by the late Successes attending the British Arms": "Beneath the scorching Afric sun, / BRITANNIA'S flag triumphant flies; / BRITANNIA'S sons have nobly done, / GOREE and SENEGAL, their prize."[186]

As much as the crow's nest or deck, the colonial pulpit was a site from which one could espy the world. Furthermore, one did not need to have been literate or male. Defoe and Voltaire certainly shaped the global impressions of Boylston and his neighbors in the coffeehouse and the club, but British Americans boasted a long, although rather vicarious, acquaintance with the world, an awareness that had lodged deeply in the colonial consciousness. Among the first generations of founders were ministers who had made themselves necessarily conversant with the canon of British fifteenth- and sixteenth-century exploration and promotional tracts that described the process of "planting" settlements, and this plantation literature had introduced them to an imagined East. The library of Boston's minister Richard Mather included such titles as *Purchas, His Pilgrims*, George Sandys's *Travels*, and Robert Knox's *Historical Relation of the Island of Ceylon*. Son Cotton Mather's library, half of which was inherited from his father, likely included these titles, as well as editions of Richard Hakluyt's *Voyages*, Joannes de Laet's *Persia*, Richard Knolles's *History of the Turks*, and the *De Africæ Descriptione* of Leo Africanus (Al-Hassan ibn Muhammed Alwazzan, Alfasi). Various letters and sermons show that Cotton had read Du Ryer's translation of the Qur'an, incorporated into Knolles's *History of the Turks*, and quoted from a number of Islam's scholars, theologians, and mystics.[187] As Puritan missionaries John Eliot, Thomas Shepard, and John Wilson traced an imagined peregrination of the lost tribe of Israel from Jerusalem to Salem, so Cotton Mather and others posited the Scythians as ancestors of America's "Indians."[188] Their own musings on the East informed second and third generation works such as Mather's *Magnalia* and the unpublished *Angel of Bethesda*. Edward Taylor and Samuel Sewell incorporated the construct of Turkish idolatry into their cosmologies, presaging the decline of Turkish rule as a forerunner to the new age of Christian revelation, and Sewell's diary entry for February 10, 1708, noted a private day of prayer seeking blessings concentrically from Sewell and his wife, to his children, servant, province, colonies, and hemisphere, and also, finally, offering a plea to "save Asia, Africa, Europe and America."[189] In this private writing, he echoed the public perception of the East presented in works such as Rev. Nicholas Noyes's May 1698 election sermon, *New-England's Duty*, in which the Salem teaching pastor encouraged his audience to pray for Christ to "come & rain down righteousness on Asia, Africa, Europe and America" and to have faith that "the Mahometan Imposture and Tyranny will not always last; and that the Remnants and Fragments of the Grecian and African Churches will be gathered up, and restored."[190] And this frame of reference was not limited to the elite. In the early days of Massachusetts Bay, when democratic forces contested the power of the magistrates, people commonly framed the debate against an imagined East of tyrannical sultans, asserting that if the people did not have a check on the magistrates' authority, "they were as good to live in turkie as live under such a government."[191]

In titles such as Cotton Mather's *Memorable Providences* (1689), popular colonial ministers followed their English counterparts in framing the Turk as the quintessential enemy of Protestants, even at times imagining an uneasy alliance with the Catholic pope under the guidance of Satan's throne.[192] At other times, ministers such as Increase Mather likened the Turk to a pestilence and beseeched their own "true God" to "let loose the great Turk" upon Rome.[193] For Increase's prolific son, Cotton Mather, both Satan and the Turk were cut from the same cloth: "We say, *The Devil*, as we say *The Turk*, or The Spaniard; it means *any* or *every* part of that infernal *Rendezvous*.[194] Certainly, the image of the Turk filled religious disquisitions of Higginson's other colleagues in New England's Puritan ministry. As early as 1664, in the fray over baptism, the Rev. John Davenport of New Haven appropriated the image of the Turk to explore the boundaries of Church membership in his "Another Essay for Investigation of the Truth, in Answer to Two Questions." To justify the removal of apostate church members, Davenport appropriated "a *Turk* who is an *English-man* by Birth," observing, "it would be gross . . . *To say that Turks are Members of the Church of Christ*." He not only wrote of New England but established the idea that even one who "turned Turk" moved outside the pale of civilized peoples.[195] In response, Richard Mather likewise used the Turk to explore the explosive question in the controversy that led to the framing of the Half-Way Covenant.[196] Thomas Shepard also situated the Turk beyond the pale of civilization and Christianity. In *Wine for Gospel Wantons*, he warned of Anabaptists "that they would not have any children to be baptized: and so they make the condition of the children of the Saints of God, (dear to God) in as miserable an estate, as the children of any Turk or pagan, and but as lawful to baptize them, as a cat or a dog."[197] Throughout the eighteenth century, the imagined Turk continued to fill British American pulpits as a challenge and a threat to the Protestant order. The ministry defended the walls of Christendom in sermons that were spoken from the pulpit and printed in the bookshops, and Boylston's consciousness formed around this essential crusade.[198]

On returning home, Nicholas Boylston's senses were further delighted by global goods, from the Canton porcelain on his rosewood tea table,[199] to the

India chintz curtains that protected his bed from New England's frosty winters, to the Turkey rugs that softened a pinewood floor. The scent of hyson tea imported from China mingled with Malabar cinnamon, and the infusion wafted through Mansion House. The flavors of candied ginger from China and raisins (called sultanas in the West and *kishmish* in the Ottoman world, from where they originated) would have been an added pleasure. The soothing touch of silk in an Indian banyan and Arab-style tam that he donned, similar to those in Copley's rich portraits, would have added additional exotic layers of comfort.

Yet, by the time Copley painted them, on the eve of the revolution, Nicholas and Thomas Boylston's own little world was falling apart. Despite the self-assurance depicted in their Copley portraits, the Boylstons were caught between their own conservative sympathies and increasing calls from their neighbors to embrace the Patriot's cause in defiance of Parliament's new regulations. It is telling that they would have understand the onset of rebellion and revolution through references to a wider, dangerous world of Muslim tyrants and Chinese emperors.

Early on, then, British Americans had begun to associate the political and moral problem of slavery with the East. For Dr. Hamilton's Tuesday Club, the danger of Islam lay principally in its propensity to subvert reason and undermine individual liberty. In a thousand years, did ever a sole Muslim thinker question: "the existence of his fools paradise, the pleasures of which, chiefly consist, in the gratification of the most beastly of the Sensual appetites, in filthy loss, and abominable pollutions; ordinary absurdities indeed, as they are not quite beyond the reach of Reason, may be curable by Reason, but extravagant, and monstrous absurdities, and miraculous nonsense, under a holy and Sanctified Garb, is safe and thriving, because quite out of Reason's Influence."[200]

Drawing upon their own experiences and the contested political literature of Restoration England that situated a country faction of "true Englishmen" against a reputedly corrupt court party that used its wealth to seduce compliance, a Real Whig school of thought took hold in the colonies and formed the foundations of the revolutionary resistance that emerged during the 1760s. The resonance was particularly sharp in the language of Real Whig opposition that filled James Franklin's *New-England Current*, John Peter Zenger's *New-York Weekly Journal*, Benjamin Franklin's *Pennsylvania Gazette*, and the *North-Carolina Gazette*. Here, the widely influential essays of John Trenchard and Thomas Gordon, James Harrington, and John Locke cast "Asiatic despotism" as a familiar reference point that anchored the poles of revolutionary thought between tyranny and liberty. In *Cato's Letters* (1720–1723), Trenchard and Gordon asserted the idea that a doctrine of nonresistance in the "Turk's religion" had caused the Turks'enslavement. John Wilkes compared the movement of British troops into Boston in October 1768 to the tyranny he identified in his imagined Orient with the comment, "Asiatic despotism does not present a picture more odious in the eye of humanity." By employing a trope so deeply entrenched in colonial political thought, the language of Eastern tyranny contributed significantly to pushing the revolutionary argument forward. American Whigs found that a revolutionary language that pitted liberty, property, and vigilant resistance against slavery, luxury, and corruption was a particularly useful weapon in their struggle against English "tyranny" because the vocabulary seemed to aptly reflect the conditions they located in the imperial rule of the Hanoverian kings. From Williamsburg in 1766, Richard Bland incorporated the trope in his attack on the Stamp Act, "An Inquiry into the Rights of the British Colonies," warning, "For if by a Vote of the British Senate the Colonists were to be delivered up to the Rule of a French or Turkish Tyranny, they may refuse Obedience to such a Vote, and may oppose the Execution of it by Force." In 1772, in the pages of both the *Boston Gazette* and the *Essex Gazette*, "Oliver Cromwell" referenced the association in his alarm at "the Crown's decision to pay judges," which he saw as "THE FINISHING STROKE" that would render Americans "as compleat slaves as the inhabitants of Turkey or Japan."[201] Two years later, a promising King's College student named Alexander Hamilton penned "A Full Vindication of the Measures of the Congress," in which he compared the authority of the House of Commons to take away "that security to our lives and properties, which the law of nature, the genius of the British constitution, and our charters affords us" to that of the Grand Mogul.[202] The "Oriental" metaphor extended across the Continent, reaching into South Carolina, where Isaiah Thomas's *Massachusetts Spy* reported that the young men of Charleston would be staging the play *Busirus, King of Egypt,* channeling the revenues to Boston to offset the town's losses from Parliament's closure in the Boston Port Bill. The play was particularly appropriate because its plot depicted "an injured Gallant people struggling against oppression, resigning their All to fortune, and wading through a dangerous bloody field in search of freedom."[203] The *Massachusetts Gazette and Boston News-Letter* followed this tradition in its issue for January 2, 1775, with a piece of doggerel that compared lamented Lord North's policies to Turkish Tyranny and encouraged, "Be firm, BOSTONIAN's, steadfast, true, Yea ne'er submit to Turk or Jew."[204]

By 1776, the association of British policies and "Oriental" tyranny had become complete. In a 1776 Election Day sermon, Samuel West railed against the "Intolerable Acts" of the prior two years by indicting "this wanton exertion of arbitrary power," which had "added a piece of barbarity unknown to Turks and Mohammedan infidels," and calling on his countrymen to exhibit a "noble indignation against such merciless tyrants." In July of that year, the *Connecticut Courant* reinforced the trope, printing a letter that insisted, "Indeed, it now appears that America has no other Alternative but to submit to more than Turkish Slavery, or declare itself independent of Great Britain."[205] And two years after this, William Whiting displayed the consciousness of the Massachusetts countryside in a "Statement of Berkshire County Representatives," which warned that "the most tyrannical and despotic governments" used their powers to reduce their people "to as abject a state of slavery as the most miserable in Turkey now are."[206] Even after the revolutionary settlement, the trope served as a political compass to guide leaders between the poles of "mobocracy" and despotism. So, Jeremiah Atwater's sermon on liberty in Middlebury, Vermont, in 1801, reminded his politically astute audience—the governor and legislature of that state—that their republicanism differed from "monarchies" such as China and Turkey, where government was "supported by force . . . adapted to the worst view of human nature . . . [founded on] an opposition of interests between rulers and ruled, and the tyrannical oppression and extortion which always follow." In his 1802 argument for incorporating freedom of religion in the Connecticut Constitution, John Leland compared the state's certificate law to Islam, claiming that "Mahomet called in the use of law and sword to convert people." Likewise, in that year, when writing an oration to commemorate Independence Day, Noah Webster sought an example of "a rigor of despotism which no free nation would now bear" and found it in the histories of Sparta, China, Turkey, and Russia. And when Fisher Ames needed an example of the dangers of arbitrary power in an 1805 dissection of Jefferson's "monarchy," he compared it to the "impossibility" of finding a true system of justice in Turkey.[207]

Yet the Patriot side did not have a monopoly on a term so deeply entrenched in the colonial consciousness. An idea that expressed the furthest deviation from British American aspirations, from what most colonists hoped they were and hoped that this was how Europeans saw them, was too useful to have been limited to one political persuasion. And, so, when Loyalists lamented their treatment at the hands of Patriots, they compared their opponents to the Turks, occupying both the far side of the world and the antipode of civilization. So

John Adams observed at the funeral of the eminent Boston tea merchant, Richard Clarke, implicated in the tea crisis of autumn 1773, when William Tyng overheard one sympathizer saying, "There was never any Thing in Turkey or in any Part of the World, so arbitrary and cruel as keeping old Mr. Clark[e], at the Castle all this winter, an old man, from his family."[208]

By establishing in the collective consciousness the idea of the East as uncivilized, one effect of this trope in British American writing was to integrate the provinces into an imagined collection of civilized states. At the moment when colonial writers such as Bland and the editors of the *Boston Gazette* and *Essex Gazette* portrayed the inhabitants of Turkey and Japan as "complete slaves," in London, William Bolts's *Considerations on India Affairs* was decrying the East India Company for exercising "such unbounded despotism . . . as would be thought intolerable even in Turkey or Barbary."[209]

The trope of "Asian despotism" became so deeply embedded in colonial political culture that it could be found in sermons, almanacs, newspapers, travelogues, music, and even a protest against the poor fare of dormitory meals by Harvard College undergraduates. Provincial readers of the *New American Magazine* (1758–1760) could commiserate with Andrew Drummond, whose "Description of the Island of Cyprus, in 1745" offered this "view of ARBITRARY. POWER": "It is impossible for any Englishman with common sense to live in Turkey, without congratulating himself upon . . . the privileges of a British subject; and perhaps it would be [best] for our happy Isle, if her representatives had the opportunity of seeing what misery and desolation are the consequences of arbitrary power." In 1768, when tutors at Harvard College attempted to infuse more rigor in student recitations, rebellious undergraduates likened the administration of President Edward Holyoke to a "Turkish tyranny."[210]

Reflections

So what do we learn from Mr. Boylston's day? He was caught in a web of seaport life, as Nash writes. It comfortably nestled him, providing reassuring truths about life, men, and the world. In reality, the web trapped him in a world of racial and cultural illusion. The sources of knowledge he relied on are now the archives that historians of race and indigeneity now challenge as honeycombed with erasures and absences. They are, as Lorgia García-Peña writes, "silences . . . filled with fantasies that reflect colonial desires and fears."[211]

What filled these absences in the early modern mindset was a set of assumptions, changeable to the occasion, but mostly privileging white Americans. The original writing contained, as Bronwen Douglas describes, "embodied encounters [that] helped shape the written and visual representations" of other cultures.[212]

Yet this imagined East was not confined to the political sphere, nor was it constructed only as a metaphor for arbitrary power or corruption. The Orient became so much a part of the consciousness of ordinary Americans that they commonly referenced it in the mundane run of everyday life. As the Atlantic economy developed the ability to deliver the "latest fashions in season," British American and republican readers benefited from the frequent replenishment of books and newspapers, demonstrating an avid taste for travel books, especially those describing explorations of exotic lands.

In time, British Americans would become Yankees and catapult themselves across the oceans. Slowly, as they accumulated firsthand knowledge, they would learn how much of their "knowledge" was fictional and learn through experience that the world was an even more dangerous place than they had imagined. Wherever they sailed, they were outsiders—*fan quai* or *ferengi*.[213] Yet amid the accretion of accounts, reports, tales, and rumors that described the world beyond the Atlantic, it was the sensationalist stories of pirates and typhoons, of massacres and murders that were most resilient. The construct was dangerous for Americans, as they engaged what were for them new worlds—a new world in which they were independent, a new world beyond the familiar Atlantic, and a new world of the Other. As the republican experiment challenged fundamental assumptions in Europe, Asia, India, and Africa, so, too, did these new worlds challenge fundamental constructs in the United States.

CHAPTER TWO

Unholy Lands

In August 1788, John Ledyard—world traveler, raconteur, Dartmouth College dropout—found himself stranded in Alexandria, Egypt. His voyage through the Mediterranean had been difficult, plagued by interruptions, expenses, and disappointments. In a prickly state of mind, he found that the city, "once the emporium of the world," did not impress him. Writing to Thomas Jefferson, Ledyard scathed, "Alexandria at large forms a scene wretched and interesting beyond any other that I have seen: poverty, rapine, murder, tumult, blind bigotry, cruel persecution, pestilence."[1]

To Ledyard, the fables of antique classicists and modern travelers that had drawn him to the Egyptian desert were a mirage, painting images of what later generations might call a Potemkin village. "Sweet are the songs of Egypt on paper," he lamented, but these were fools' tales. As for Cairo—or Grand Cairo, as early Americans knew it—the city was "a wretched hole, and a nest of vagabonds. Nothing merits more the whole force of Burlesque than both the poetic and prosaic legends of this country." Even nature disappointed the wayward Yankee. After a five-days' passage along the Nile, famous for biblical tales—"You have heard and read much of this River, and so had I," he lamented again to Jefferson: "It is a mere mud puddle compared with the accounts we have of it," hardly wider than London's Thames or even the Connecticut River. Famous stories of its flooding were likewise "a lye." The pyramids were unremarkable, the temperatures no hotter than one would find in Philadelphia. As for the countryside, "Who is not ravished with gums, balms, dates, figs, pomegranates, with the Circassia and sycamores, without knowing that amidst these, one's eyes, ears, mouth, nose is filled with dust, eternal hot fainting winds, lice, bugs, mosquitoes, spiders, flies—pox, itch, leprosy, fevers, and almost universal blindness." The cautionary lesson he drew was "Let me be careful how I read—and above all how I read Ancient history!" Ultimately, the cleansing filter of American reportage would put the lie to European fables, an angry Ledyard asserted. Burn Savery's *Letters on Egypt*, and "laugh at" Thucydides, Leo, Herodotus, Diode, and Siculus, who "never traveled themselves, and lived besides in epochs very unfriendly to history," and who instead wrote to deceive readers.[2]

Ledyard was no cosmopolitan. He was a man *in* the world, but not a man *of* the world, someone who traveled across the globe, but not the citizen of the world so admired in this age of reason. Rarely leaving the Frankish quarter of European residents, the bounds of his intolerance did not allow him to take in foreign customs or appreciate alien peoples. To Ledyard, the lands and people he encountered were steeped in falsehoods, deceivers and dupes both. Consequently, he needed to do violence to the culture, albeit a verbal violence.[3]

A person such as Ledyard, steeped in the shallow waters of prejudice, needed defenses, physical and psychological. His strategy was to transform his fears and frustrations into a testimony of resentment. Writing to Jefferson from Cairo, on November 15, 1788, Ledyard opined: "The humiliating situation of [a] Frank would be insupportable to me—but for my Voyage. It is a shame to the sons of Europe that they suffer this arrogance at the hands of a banditti of ignorant fanatics. I assure myself that even your Curiosity and love of Antiquity would never detain you in Egypt 3 months."[4]

The early republic abounded in similar reports from American travelers who had braved "dirty seas" to make their fortunes or spread the Word of their own "true God" among the "wretched Turks."[5] Ledyard's version had particular resonance on the quays and in the parlors of "Yankee land." Such tales were popular because they built on constructs that had been situated in British American and American consciousness even before the first colonies were established. They distilled centuries of conventional wisdom, accumulated in ships' logs, seamen's journals, travelers' diaries, and newspaper accounts.[6] Through a distinct genre of vernacular writing—an Indies' trade literature—as well as oral tradition and material culture, Americans came together in an imagined community that was distinguished by both its sense of commonality, if not always unity, *and* its heightened sense of difference from other peoples in the Atlantic and beyond. The writing, word of mouth, and goods from their "eastern frontier" were popular because they contributed to a worldview that capped Americans' entry onto the world stage—the imperatives to define and defend the national character and to establish the legitimacy of the "new people."[7]

Encounters

Mariners seldom detailed their reasons for sailing to the Mediterranean coast of North Africa—the region that Americans called Barbary and Muslim inhabitants knew as the Maghreb. James Durand, for one, left only a trace of his motivation: "Resolved to go to sea." After several previous adventures—mishaps, really—Durand decided, "I would no more venture to sea in small craft." Then, a "rendezvous being open," he enlisted aboard the US frigate *John Adams*, "destined for the Mediterranean, against the Turks." For Durand, it seems, the toil of a sailor aboard a warship was preferable to the labor of a farmhand, or perhaps he could find no work to his liking. For merchants, it was the lure of trade that drew their vessels across the Mediterranean. For missionaries, it was the prospect of claiming souls. "All kinds of grain" were produced in Egypt, as well as garden vegetables, such as lettuce, cucumbers, and maize; melons, figs, dates, and palm oil. Suez was a great market for Arabian goods, such as calico, leather, coffee, drugs, and spices. Constantinople was "one of the finest cities in the world by its situation and port . . . where the merchants have their shops excellently arranged." Algiers produced "excellent salt" and saltpeter, lead, and iron. Smyrna (Izmir), the "Paris of the Levant," was another profitable, as well as accessible, destination. Until the early eighteenth century, half of its exports were Iranian silk, replaced by cotton afterward, complementing its cornucopia of olives, pomegranates, figs, and "an exquisitely flavored and seedless grape." Other products drew Yankee merchants, however, as Timothy Roberts writes: "Americans first came apparently to purchase raisins, but by the early nineteenth century a small American colony developed in the city for a different commodity, which was opium."[8]

Others articulated their motives in depth, if not always in eloquence. Missionaries needed to explain the purpose of their journeys to seek funding, both initial and continued. In the years following the revolution, many Protestant leaders believed that their religion was under attack, at home and abroad. At home, leaders of the new nation had committed the republic to religious pluralism. Washington had famously promised tolerance to the Truro synagogue in Rhode Island and the Treaty of Tripoli, ratified in 1797, had asserted, "The government of the United States of America is not in any sense founded on the Christian Religion." More extremely, in Boston, Dr. Thomas

Young had published his deist work, *Sermon on Natural Religion by a Natural Man* (1771), and, in Vermont, Ethan Allen had published his support of atheism in *Reason the Only Oracle of Man* (1784). Overseas, the long-standing menace of Catholicism seemed as entrenched as ever. Protestant leaders' response was to engage the enemy, within their country and overseas.[9]

As Christine Leigh Heyrman explains, in 1810, a generation of aspiring ministers began the Andover Theological Seminary in Massachusetts as a bastion of rigid Calvinist thought to combat the heretics and apostasies. This New Divinity evangelical movement exerted a profound influence on Americans' understanding of the world. As early as 1810, the leaders of the Boston-based American Board of Commissioners for Foreign Missions (ABCFM) had hoped to set up missions in the Holy Land and India. Within a few years, opposition from the British East India Company and indications of Hindu indifference focused the initiative to send missionaries to "without delay take possession of the Holy Land." Meanwhile, a tight group of Andover students, including Pliny Fisk and Levi Parsons, had formed a reading group interested in missionary work. The region offered particular appeal. Not only did it offer opportunities for conversion under the stable, if violent, rule of the Ottomans, it held sites of Old Testament miracles and New Testament resurrection. Now, the young theologians believed, it was one of the world's decadent regions, "the light . . . almost totally extinguished," falling into decline under the Muslims, and ripe for the kind of revival movement they had experienced at home.[10]

In September 1818, the group proposed a commitment "That a mission be established forthwith in Palestine." Consequently, they prepared to undertake a journey as a merchant might have planned a trading voyage, reading travelogues and missionary tracts and corresponding with English contacts. Much of what they read favored "the expediency of establishing a mission in Jerusalem." As Alvan Bond wrote: "The church, since the commencement of the present century, having awaked to bolder efforts, has watched 'the signs of the times' as they respect the Jewish and Mahommedan nations—nations which, like the walled cities of the Anakims, have seemed to defy whatever exertion the church could make to gain possession." Under the auspices of the ABCFM, they had a ready market of congregants, dedicated presses, and a robust distribution network. In November 1819, the Board sent their first American missionaries to build a Near East mission for the conversion of Jews in Palestine.[11]

But this would be an anxious endeavor. There was much of God's work to be done and little time to prepare. The religious atmosphere that sowed the beginnings of a second revival movement in early nineteenth-century and carried Pliny Fisk and Alvan Bond to the Ottoman Empire maintained that "the movements of the Holy Spirit and Providence" were astir throughout the world. A nationalist chord added to the sense of imperative. The evangelists believed that Providence had called the new nation into being, and, anticipating John L. O'Sullivan's 1839 consecration of the country's manifest destiny, they embraced a dual purpose of disseminating both Christianity and American "civilization across a benighted world." All that was required was agency—the men and women who had the conviction and courage to carry the Word into "heathen" lands. "The Lord is shaking the nations," one wrote. As Emily Conroy-Krutz argues, their urge to sweep across the world made them "Christian imperialists."[12]

A number of Americans traveled to the Ottoman realm as adventurers and explorers, and their purposes were often multifaceted. Globetrotter, writer, and diplomat John Lloyd Stephens's (1805–1852) motives were decidedly more parochial. Wearied of his New York law practice and longing to refresh his education in classical literature, Stephens embarked on a journey through Europe in 1834, making an impromptu detour to Egypt and the Levant and returning home in 1836 to publish his popular *Incidents of Travel in Egypt, Arabia, Petraea, and the Holy Land* (1837). He hoped "to give a narrative of the every-day incidents that occur to a traveler in the East, and to present to his countrymen, in the midst of the hurry, and bustle, and life, and energy, and daily-developing strength and resources of the New, a picture of the widely-different scenes that are now passing in the faded and worn-out kingdoms of the Old World."[13]

For his part, Edward Robinson offered a decidedly Orientalist justification for the journey that resulted in his popular and highly regarded treatise *Biblical Researches in Palestine and the Adjacent Regions: A Journal of Travels in the Year 1838*. "This is all I have to say respecting the work, as here presented to the public," Robinson explained in the preface. "We wish it to be regarded merely as a beginning, a first attempt to lay open the treasures of Biblical Geography and History still remaining in the Holy Land; treasures which have lain for ages unexplored, and had become so covered with the dust and rubbish of many centuries, that their very existence was forgotten." For Robinson, the Yankee visitor was not simply an observer but rather a kind of savior, recovering an antique heritage that an indifferent people had allowed to fall into decay. Salvation of the Holy Land and, consequently, of souls would come through a "strong desire to visit in person the places so remarkable in the history of the human race" toward "the preparation of a work on Biblical Geography."[14]

That Robinson recorded his experiences—really, his perceptions of what happened, and more epistemology than ontology—was important. Of greater consequence, however, was the book's reach, as its multiple editions found thousands of readers across the world and over a century and a half. The "unexpected favor" of a Patron's Gold Medal from London's Royal Geographical Society in 1842 made the book "a standard work in relation to the Holy Land" and accorded Robinson particular legitimacy with his international audience.[15]

In planning his 1848 exploration of the Dead Sea and Palestine, William F. Lynch had to justify the appropriation of federal funds to a skeptical public. In testimony to Congress, editorials, and his 1849 *Narrative of the Expedition to the River Jordan and the Dead Sea*, he asserted a threefold purpose: to "promote the cause of Sciences, and advance the character of the Naval service"; to "strengthen the bulwarks of Christianity in the East"; and to extend the American presence across the world.[16]

In the early republic, one approached a sea voyage as a soldier or sailor might anticipate an impending battle. As late as the 1820s, overseas travel was precarious, even within Mediterranean confines, and the English traveler Thomas Robert Joliffe would dedicate his *Narrative of an Excursion from Corfu to Smyrna* (London, 1827) to "the surviving companions of his tour." The 1835 catalogue of the Library Company of Philadelphia framed a passage into the Mediterranean as a daunting prospect. A sampling of titles offers a glimpse of the tales that Americans read, heard, and passed on: A. Fothergill's *An Essay on the Preservation of Shipwrecked Mariners*, Archibald Duncan's *The Mariner's Chronicle; being a Collection of the most Interesting Narratives of Shipwrecks, Fires, Famines, and other Calamities Incident to a Life of Maritime Enterprise* (1804–1805); and Cyrus Redding's *Shipwrecks and Disasters at Sea* (1833). The Library's holdings created a forbidding impression of the Maghreb, the northwestern coast of Africa that was home to the infamous Barbary pirates, based on *An account of the shipwreck and captivity of M. de Brisson; containing a description of the deserts of Africa, from Senegal to Morocco* (1789); *A Journal of the Travels and Sufferings of Daniel Saunders, jun. A Mariner on board the Ship Commerce, of Boston, Samuel Johnson, Commander, which was cast away Cape Morebet, on the Coast of Arabia, July 10, 1792* (1794); *The Narrative of Robert Adams, a Sailor, Who Was Wrecked on the Western Coast of Africa, in the Year 1810, Was Detained Three Years in Slavery by the Arabs of the*

Great Desert, and Resided Several Months in the City of Tombuctoo (1816); Judah Paddock's *A Narrative of the Shipwreck of the Ship Oswego, on the Coast of South Barbary, and of the Sufferings of her Crew among the Arabs; Interspersed with Remarks on the Country and its Inhabitants* (1818); Archibald Robbins's *A Journal, Comprising an Account of the Loss of the Brig Commerce, James Riley, Master, upon the Western Coast of Africa; also of the Slavery and Sufferings of the Author, and the Rest of the Crew, upon the Desert of Zahara, in the Years 1815, 1816, 1817* (1817); and James Riley's *An Authentic Narrative of the Loss of the American Brig, Commerce, on the Western Coast of Africa, in 1815; with an Account of the Sufferings of her Surviving Officers and Crew: and Observations Historical and Geographical* (third edition, 1818). These stories of shipwreck, enslavement, and suffering were not limited to the shelves of Philadelphia's Library Company. They were available to a wide audience in the form of chapbooks, newspaper selections, compilations, and dramatizations and passed through hearsay, gossip, and retelling.[17]

The dangers that awaited a fragile vessel of wood and cloth in the open seas were described as so many and so ferocious that it was common for cautious merchants and mariners to tie up their affairs in preparation for the afterlife. When Isaac Hinckley began his voyage "Bound for Mocha in Arabia . . . where Christians are little belov'd," he added his prayer, "May God send the good ship to her desired ports in safety." The emotional weight of a maritime departure created fertile ground for premonitions of peril. In September 1840, embarking for Zanzibar, Sandwith Drinker lamented: "A few of us leaving the land of our birth, and friends most dear, possibly for the last time. (Yet, how few of us ever ask the question, Am I prepared not to return?), others, returning to their native clime, fondly anticipating a happy meeting, with those from whom they have been so long separated, yet little heeding the moistened eye of their comrade, who has perhaps for the last time, parted with Father, Mother, Brother, and Sister. How truly painful are such leave takings, and how frequently is the sailor obliged to endure them."[18]

In his "private journal," Drinker advised that anyone traveling to a distant land must "accommodate" themselves to unfamiliar sights. It seems, however, that he was not prepared to take his own advice. Unwilling to accept responsibility for himself or to blame the economic conditions that led him from home, his resentment lay ready to be projected onto the natural world and other peoples.[19] Drinker had been married on March 17, 1840, and departed for Arabia on August 8, voicing his regret to his newly wed spouse, writing, "I do trust and consider that this separation will be but for a short time; let us comfort ourselves with the knowledge, that we are in the hands of that good being who protects his own, on the ocean, as well as on dry land." Perhaps to "inoculate" himself against what would be new and strange, Drinker spent his free time "profitably," reading John James Blunt's *History of Christ* rather than perusing the plethora of histories and geographies that would introduce him to the Ottoman world.[20]

Yet, as technologies and navigational knowledge advanced, American travelogues increasingly reported that the passage to the Mediterranean was not particularly daunting, as a voyage to India or China would be. Aboard the warship *John Adams*, James R. Durand penned a common entry. Departing New York in April 1804, he recalled, "We had a very pleasant passage until we came to the Western Islands, where we were often becalmed."[21] A generation later, steamships made the passage faster and more pleasant. Biblical scholar Edward Robinson brought his family along on the cruise from New York to Liverpool, a "favorable voyage" of only eighteenth days.[22]

Despite their trepidations, and following the defeat of the Barbary powers by 1816, most accounts described the passage into the Mediterranean as uneventful and even pleasant. However, notorious accounts of shipwreck and capture along the coasts of North Africa and Arabia, where treacherous shoals and sunken rocks claimed many Yankee vessels, continued to fill the public sphere. A cautious navigator kept abreast of the latest pilot guides, followed the advice of experienced captains, and kept on his guard. After all, a stranded mariner could not expect the kind of fortuitous rescue that Alexander Selkirk experienced a century earlier. Selkirk had been abandoned on an isolated island in the South Atlantic but was recovered when the explorer and privateer Woodes Rogers happened upon his location. His story would become the inspiration for Daniel Defoe's *Robinson Crusoe*.[23] Nor could one expect the same treatment that Richard Cleveland described when his ship *Caroline* wrecked near Le Havre: "The peasantry had come down in great numbers, . . . and with such demonstrations of humanity and kindness . . . supported us to shore. . . . The inhabitants showed no disposition to take advantage of our distress." Instead, in the idle hours of watch-and-watch, notorious tales swept across decks, as crews recalled the loss of the *Commerce* in 1792 or the *Medusa* off the coast of Senegal in 1816.[24]

The shoals and rocks of Mediterranean harbors could be as dangerous as those of the al-Maghreb and West African coasts for an American pilot, ravaging even powerful warships. Lighthouses were rare, and even approaching a bustling port such as Alexandria, Egypt, John Stephens fretted "as we had been running several hours along the low coast of Barbary. . . . Night came on, however, without our seeing it."

The most notorious example for Americans was the loss of the USS *Philadelphia* in the autumn of 1803. Attempting to blockade the harbor of Tripoli during the Tripolitan War (1801–1805), on October 31, Captain William Bainbridge ran his ship aground on an uncharted reef. With the *Philadelphia* "wrecked on Rocks between 4 & 5 Miles to the Eastward of the Town of Tripoli" and the crew's "labour & enterprise . . . in vain," Bainbridge realized "our fate was direfully fixed" and surrendered the warship. Bainbridge and his 307-man crew were captured and held in a *bagnio*, or prison, for nearly two years. Americans learned that such was the case wherever a traveler passed. Those who romanticized the Nile River, for example, were disabused of their Orientalist fantasies by George Bethune English's 1822 *Narrative of an Expedition*, which described fearsome cataracts, dangerous rapids, jagged reefs, furious whirlpools, and treacherous currents.[25]

The short sail across the Mediterranean offered fewer nautical challenges when compared to the voyages to India, China, and the Palau Islands that were engaging other Americans, but it was an adventure for the American lawyer, Stephens. Approaching Alexandria, he described the English schooner that carried him in terms that a Yankee mariner might have used on entering a Fijian bay: "Slowly we worked our way up the difficult and dangerous channel, unaided by a pilot, for none appeared to take us in charge." By 1838, the voyage posed little inconvenience for Edward Robison, a professor of biblical literature at the Union Theological Seminary, who made the passage from New York to Liverpool in a "favorable" eighteen days with his family. His journey to Alexandria was gentle, "never retarded for an hour, nor scarcely for a moment rendered uncomfortable, by any unfavorable state of the weather." The challenge was not transportation, but information; he could not learn if "any steamer was running from Trieste to the Levant" despite "diligent inquiry."[26]

Nature did not pose extraordinary challenges for a cruise into the Mediterranean Sea or Arabian waters beyond what a mariner could expect in the Atlantic. Yet, another peril, particular to the Ottoman Empire, vexed Yankee voyages and reinforced an American view that the world was dangerously disordered and required Yankee intervention. The ill-fated cruise of *Essex*, a merchant ship out of Salem, Massachusetts, testified to the concerns that distressed mariners who ventured into this part of the world. In the summer of

1806, the *Essex*, under Captain Joseph Orne, voyaged to Mocha (al-Makha), the Arabian port famous for its distinctive blend of coffee. What happened next came in fevered reports that terrified American readers that autumn. Tricked into bypassing Mocha, with its European factories and Muslim safeguards, and sailing up the coast to a more vulnerable port, Orne accepted the company of Mahomet Ikle and incautiously allowed thirty of the rais's men aboard his ship. That evening, Ikle's pillagers massacred the crew of the *Essex* and took the ship. The loss of the *Essex* and its crew underscored the threat of state-sponsored terrorism that characterized the Ottoman East from the 1780s into the 1830s in penetrating terms that inflected the imaginations of generations of Americans. Most notorious were pirates who terrorized the Barbary, or North African coasts; almost as well-known were scavengers who pillaged shipwrecked vessels along the Arabian and Saharan coasts.[27]

Many historians have tackled the conflict known as the Barbary Wars, the assaults on American ships from corsairs of the North African states and the US Navy's retaliation. Tripoli, Tunis, and Algiers—quasi-independent regencies nominally belonging to the Ottoman Empire, along with the independent sultanate of Morocco—had waged an *al-jihad fi' l-bahr* (holy war at sea) against Christian shipping and coastal villages since the sixteenth century in search of slave labor to build cities and wharves, serve as concubines, and barter for ransom. Historians such as Robert Davis estimate that as many as 1.25 million captives were taken from European ships and coastal villages. They struck England's Cornish and Devon coasts in 1625 and 1645 and the "stolen village" of Baltimore, Ireland, in 1631, and carried hundreds of men, women, and children into slavery.[28]

In 1784, the "Barbary pirates" targeted vessels flying the stars and stripes. Within months of Congress's approval of the Treaty of Paris, American mariners learned that the price of independence would continue to tax their voyages. On October 11, "Sallee Rovers," pirates operating out of the Moroccan port of Salé, captured the *Betsy*, along with Captain James Erwin and the crew, in the international waters off Cape St. Vincent. Then, on July 25, 1785, an Algerian xebec surprised Captain Isaac Stephens and easily captured the schooner *Maria* out of Boston, three miles off the Spanish coast.[29] The same month, a third American vessel fell prey to what was becoming the Barbary menace, when the ship *Dauphin*, Philadelphia, commanded by Captain Richard O'Brien, was taken by an Algerian corsair.[30] The vessels were taken into Barbary home ports, where the crews were enslaved and held for ransom. Before the year was out, a full-fledged program of state-sponsored terrorism was in place.[31] As Martha Rojas observes, "Between 1785 and 1815, US ships were repeatedly captured in the Mediterranean: twenty-two by Algiers, six by Tripoli, five by Morocco, and two by Tunis. As a result, over seven hundred US sailors were held captive in North Africa."[32] The assaults from Barbary would not end until American marines had marched "to the shores of Tripoli."

For the nascent nation, rescue was out of the question. The War Department oversaw a "paper navy," selling the last ship of the Continental Navy, the *Alliance,* in June 1785. British minister Lord Sheffield neatly summarized the American dilemma: "The Americans cannot protect themselves. . . . They cannot pretend to a Navy." Consequently, American mariners followed Isaac Hinckley's strategy. In his 1809 voyage around East Africa, Captain Hinckley had the crew fashion quakers—wooden replicas of cannons made for show—and at the end of September, he logged, "Shipped the wooden guns; we now show 20 guns and look as rakish as a half wet swab."[33]

"Thank God that I was delivered from the hands of the Algerines," wrote an unnamed ship captain from Lisbon in October 1783. His letter to his ship's owners registered the anxieties that defined Ottoman rule for a generation of Yankee mariners. The "wretched Turks" had transformed the Mediterranean into a danger zone, reported the less fortunate Captain William Furnass of Berwick, Maine, whose *Olive-Branch* was captured five miles off Lisbon in 1793. Languishing in an "Algerine" prison, Furnass lamented, "In case something is not done soon the whole Western Ocean will be infested with their cruizers, as they . . . are fitting everything as vessels of War to cruize against the Americans."[34]

The horrific reports of the *Betsy, Maria,* ~~and~~ *Dauphin,* and over thirty other Yankee vessels assailed Americans at home and on the oceans. Out of this experience emerged what Hester Blum has called "the first coherent body of American sea literature known as the Barbary captivity narrative." In time, one could find this language of liberty, defining an American republic that again brought together Virginians and Pennsylvanians, Carolinians and Vermonters against a common tyranny. American bookstores stocked, stages performed, and poets wrote of Daniel Saunders's *Travels and Sufferings . . . on the Coast of Arabia* (1794), John Foss's *Captivity and Sufferings of . . . a Prisoner in Algiers* (1798), Jonathan Cowdery's *American Captives in Tripoli* (1806), William Ray's *Horrors of Slavery . . . in Tripoli* (three editions by 1808), Thomas Nicholson's *Captivity and Suffering* (1816), Judah Paddock's *Narrative of . . Sufferings . . . while in bondage among the Arabs* (1818), and Eliza Bradley's *Six Years a Slave in Algiers . . . Confined in a Dark and Dismal Dungeon, Loaded with Irons* (1820)—all in multiple editions—and other accounts from their countrymen captured off Gibraltar or "wrecked on the coast of barbary." Their accounts seeded a vision of an anarchic, lawless Ottoman Empire dramatized in Susanna Rowson's *Slaves in Algiers, or A Struggle for Freedom* (1794), Royall Tyler's *The Algerine Captive* (1797), and the anonymous1802 play *The Tripolitan Prize*. And, in his 1839 *The History of the Navy of the United States of America,* James Fenimore Cooper reminded naval buffs that the first action by an American naval vessel involved a Barbary rover. Even those narratives that were later discovered to be fictional influenced American ideas about the East. Readers could not have known that the *History of the Captivity and Sufferings of Mrs. Maria Martin* (1807) and *The Narrative of Robert Adams* (1816) were not authentic accounts, and they, too, filled the circulating libraries of seaports and rural hamlets. In the same way, thousands of ships' logs and private journals were carefully deposited in local marine societies or added to athenaeum reading rooms. As Lawrence Peskin shows, these accounts "played an important role in national self-definition during a crucial time in the new republic's young history."[35]

These accounts intended to depict American experiences abroad—to say something about the American and his values. But they relayed, equally, something about the world, and they did so in ways that complemented what merchants, missionaries, and travelers described. News reports, such as that of the 1806 *Essex* massacre, also identified the culprits as "the Arabs" and employed a language of visceral terror, incorporating terms such as "the slaughter," "headless corpse," "mutilated remains," "faithless Mahomet," and "notorious pirate," portraying the Ottoman world as perilous for Americans. In other accounts, the "Algerines" were "merciless *Barbarians*," "a parcel of ravenous wolves," and "barbarous masters" who imposed "unexampled cruelty" on Christian captives.[36]

Capture was traumatic. Taken from the *Polly*, out of Newburyport, Massachusetts, in 1793, John Foss described his immediate impression of "dreadful perturbations," punctuated with "terrible shouting, clapping of hands, huzzaing." The strangeness of the attackers' "dress and long beards" indicative of "Moors, or Algerines," so different from "the Christian habit" of Americans, unsettled him further.[37] Furnass observed of his 1793 capture, "We were stripped of everything when taken but in capacity [captivity] for [a] lifetime, loaded with chains."[38] The rais, or corsair captain, told Foss and the *Polly*'s crew that they "must immediately experience the most abject slavery, on our arrival at Algiers, which we soon found to be true."[39] Some villains were more feared than others. Trepidations increased if the captors were "Algerine," Foss reported, because "the Algerines used the most severity towards christian captives, of any state in all Barbary."[40] Regardless of nationality, the capture incorporated rituals of enslavement, similar to what West African victims experienced in the Atlantic slave trade, geared to foster "the horror of our situation . . . impossible to describe." Instilling a sense of uncertainty, about the present and the future, was another early step in capture, and remained a counterpoint to the brutal routines of labor that awaited prisoners. Our "minds were filled with horror, and dreadful apprehensions of the fate we might experience, and expecting additional severity on our arrival at Algiers," observed Foss. Rumors run rampant brought "disagreeable apprehensions of being separated, and sold into distant parts of the country, and at every call of all hands, painful sensations would disturb our breasts." James Leander Cathcart, of the *Maria*, captured in 1785, remained a slave for eleven years. Anxiety, for the present and the future, fostered a sense of despair, and men committed suicide or withered away. Furnass reported that his friends were "destitute of everything but horror, unless a peace should be made by our people, I expect to linger out my days in this cruel place."[41]

"I was purchased by the Arabian merchants, and taken off across the desert; I was suffering under the most excruciating bodily pains as well as the most cruel privations." James Riley's words from his 1815 *Narrative* touched a nerve in American identity. With the nearly 1 million African Americans enslaved in their home country in 1800, the experience of enslavement—of becoming the slave rather than the enslaver—was novel and deeply disturbing for the remaining 4.5 million. As Lawrence Peskin observes, the Barbary encounters forced Americans to think about their the new republic as a "captive nation" in ways that challenged the association between national identity and white supremacy and reoriented their place in the world.[42]

Captives such as Foss made clear their status as slaves, describing his account as "a short narrative of some of the most particular occurrences, which happened while I was in this abject slavery, and the common labor, and usage of the slaves." In retelling their experiences, they defined the Ottoman. The "Algerines" were "our keepers," "task-masters," and "drivers," and "our Masters."[43]

The "white slavery" endured by Barbary captives disturbed American society in ways that transcended ideology. The bagnios were work camps, not unlike the plantations of Georgia and the Carolinas where the enslaved grew their captors' tobacco, cotton, and rice, but here they broke and lugged rock for the wharves of Algiers, Tunis, and Tripoli. Here, the captive sailor William Ray experienced in 1803, "Turkish masters" divided captive mariners by "their several employments" as carpenters, blacksmiths, and coopers. Others were "denominated cooks," whose "employment was to bring water from a well, about a quarter of a mile distant, for the whole of us to drink." Regardless of the task, Furnass noted, all were sentenced to "hard labor from sunrise till dark."[44]

Others, less fortunate, "were distributed into different gangs, as we called them; some to the castle, to carry stone, dirt, lime, and mortar, where they were making repairs." Foss described "the hardest day's work, I ever underwent before.—The dreadful clanking of the chains, was the most terrible noise I ever heard. And never during my whole captivity did I feel such horrors of mind, as on this dreadful morning." Each morning, prisoners were marched out to quarries, where enormous blocks of rock were blasted out of hills, then "hauled by the slaves, two miles distance, which weigh 40 tons. They roll them to the bottom of the mountain, where is a convenient place to put them on a sled. Here . . . all the Christian slaves belonging to the Regency, are driven out to haul them to the Quay, which is about two miles from the place where they are loaded." Foss estimated that some seven hundred men pulled sledges to a quay, where the rocks formed a breakwater for the harbor. The pace under a scorching sun was relentless. To push the captives, Foss recalled, drivers were "continually beating the slaves with their sticks, & goading them with its end, in which is a small spear, not unlike an ox-goad, among our farmers."[45]

Conditions within the bagnios mirrored the trauma of enslavement and work. Barbary "slavery far exceeds death," Furnass wrote in 1793. Captives reported how malnourishment compromised their health and made the work more difficult. Ray recalled, "Towards evening, some coarse, white bread was brought, and we were all ordered out of the prison, and as we were counted in again, each one received a small white loaf, of about twelve ounces." Augmenting their misery, the Eastern diet did not agree with many mariners, whose standard fare was salt pork, hardtack biscuit, and rum. When the crew of the *Maria* arrived in Algiers, they were fed "camel's flesh, which prevented us from tasting it [which] enraged our Master." Deprived of their favored meat and liquor, they subsisted on a daily allotment of oil and two "black barley loaves, coarse, and full of straws and chaff." At other times they were fed "what the Turks call *coos-coos* which is barley ground very coarse, and neither sifted nor bolted; with which they occasionally fed us." Many would have perished from malnutrition had it not been for supplies from American and European diplomats and merchants. In his accounts, Furnass melded his personal horror with pleas to national honor, writing, "The labour is very hard, and they give us nothing but bread and water, and so little of that, that it is hardly sufficient to sustain life; and unless our humane Congress gives us some small allowance to alleviate our sufferings, we must continue in the most abject slavery."[46]

The dark, damp bagnios fostered illness. Cathcart recalled of his first night, "We stretched ourselves on the bare bricks where we remained all night, tormented with vermin and mosquitos, and at daylight, were driven down to the marine to unbend the sails and do other necessary work on the Cruisers that had captured us." Ray concurred, recalling, "We had nothing to keep us from the cold, damp earth, but a thin, tattered sail-cloth; the floor of the prison was very uneven, planted with hard pebbles, and as we had nothing but a shirt to soften our beds; and nothing but the ground for a pillow, and very much crowded in the bargain, the clouds of night shed no salutary repose." A year in the cramped, close bagnio brought smallpox for Furnass, who survived, but lost two companions. Peskin identifies plagues striking the bagnios in 1787, 1793, 1794, and 1796, putting the prisoners "on the verge of eternity," in the words of captive Richard O'Brien.[47]

The punishments inflicted on Barbary prisoners contributed to an American vision of a region that was barbaric and, lacking the gentle hand of "progress," astonishingly cruel. "We were counted in, one by one, and as we passed the grim jailor, were under the humiliating injunction of pulling off our hats. Those who refused this devoir were sure of a severe bastinadoing," noted Ray. When their captors turned away, some daring souls might drift into town, and find alcohol to wash away their suffering. On these occasions, their

> keepers perceived it, and proceeded to exhibit exemplary punishment, and sate, at once, their thirst of revenge. The instrument with which they prepare a man for torture, is called a bastone; It is generally about four or five feet long, and as thick in the middle as a man's leg, tapering to the ends. At equal distances from the center, it is perforated in two places, and a rope incurvated, the ends passed through the holes, and knotted. This forms a loop. The person is then thrown on his back, his feet put through the loop, and a man at each end of the stick, both at once, twist it round, screw his feet and ankles tight together, and raise the soles of his feet nearly horizontal. A Turk sits on his back, and two men, with each a bamboo, or branch of the date tree, as large as a walking-staff, and about three feet in length, hard, and very heavy, strip or

roll up their sleeves, and, with all their strength and fury, apply the bruising cudgel to the bottoms of the feet. In this manner they punished several of our men, writhing with extreme anguish, and cursing their tormentors. They were then hampered with a heavy chain at each foot, but the next day they were taken off.[48]

The accounts of captives John Foss, William Ray, and James Leander Cathcart deepened their countrymen's ideas of the Ottoman Empire as a backward domain where tyranny and enslavement thrived and deepened the revolutionary construct of a nation that was, as Paine noted in *Common Sense*, "an asylum for the persecuted lovers of civil and religious liberty," or an oasis amid a world of "merciless barbarians." A hallmark trait of tyranny, an element appropriated from English Whigs during the lead-up to the revolution, was its arbitrary nature.[49]

The account of Captain James Ervine, "now a prisoner at Mogador, South-Barbary," in June 1785, was one of many accretions that fostered the image of the East as the locus of arbitrary rule. After landing at Tangier, Ervine was "ordered to Morocco" and "carried before the Emperor," who informed his party that "he was at peace with our nation," only to then be "ordered to this palace, where we are to remain prisoners until Congress may think proper to send an ambassador." Situating a language of command against one of relocation, Ervine used his position as prisoner ironically, exploiting his own powerlessness to capture the traits of an idealized tyranny that Americans found most disturbing—its arbitrary willfulness.[50]

The plight of American captives and the overbearing demands of the pashas became tropes in the public sphere of the early republic. When Congress sent John Lamb to negotiate ransom payments for the hostages, newspapers followed his tortuous diplomatic efforts. In its issue for October 14, 1786, the *Salem Mercury* offered its readers a reflection on "Commerce," provided an account of Salem ships at the Cape of Good Hope, and from London, on July 30, the disappointing news that "Mr. Lamb was not received by the dey of Algiers, and was obliged to return without being admitted to a negotiation." Inland, farmers might follow the ongoing negotiations juxtaposed against reports of Indian raids along the frontier and feel that the nation was vulnerable on all sides. In its September 15, 1787, issue, the *Worcester Magazine* of rural Massachusetts reported on the negotiations between Lamb and the dey of Algiers for ransoming twenty-one American captives. Lamb offered $10,000 per prisoner, but the dey insisted, "You shall not have them for less than fifty thousand." The negotiations would continue, the magazine reported, "But we do not hear that the captives have been yet liberated." Through the publication of such passages, American editors were able to represent a national character, and to do so as a people committed to liberty, enterprise, and Christian values—traits that readers could imagine they shared with the captives. In 1802, in the *Balance and Columbian Repository*, Colonel David Humphreys represented Algerian rulers as "wicked and rash," depicted Americans as a force to "chastise that Haughty but contemptible power," and called for Yankee tars to protect their ships from "the hazard of falling into the possession of these pirates."[51]

Perhaps the most notorious example of the region's rule of men over law was that of the USS *George Washington* in 1800. As mariner Samuel Patterson recalled in an 1817 account of his "adventures and sufferings," the *George Washington* had carried tribute to the newly installed dey of Algiers, Bobba Mustafa. As the frigate prepared to depart, "the Dey made a most unexpected and extraordinary demand," commanding Commodore William Bainbridge to carry the dey and a retinue to Constantinople. Bainbridge complained, but had no recourse. The details printed in the country's news journals only heightened the sense of national outrage. "You pay me tribute, therefore you are my slaves. You will do as you are told," Mustafa is said to have told the commodore. Whereupon the "federal flag" was hauled down and replaced with the red pennant of Algiers. Things turned again when the frigate reached Constantinople, where the pasha flew into a "great rage, refused to see "the unfortunate Algerine ambassador," and welcomed the first US warship to visit Constantinople, where its complement was indoctrinated into the topsy-turvy disorder of the Ottoman East. Despite his relief for the *George Washington*, the sultan could not stop the predations on Yankee vessels. A symbol of the disorder of the Ottoman Empire, he held little sway over the deys and beys of the autonomous Maghreb states.[52]

Mediterranean and African waters had been profitable arenas for seagoing pirates at least since the seventeenth century, but even the shores, too, proved unsafe for the unfortunate captain and crew whose shipwreck was plunder for local scavengers. In the early republic, reading circles knew too well tales of shipwrecked mariners whose miseries were exploited by coastal scavengers. Coastal scavenging was a worldwide activity, of course, and even in Europe, regions such as the Cornish coast were notorious for their wrecking culture. Americans, however, associated acts of treachery, depredation, and cruelty with the Ottoman and Arab regions.[53]

Sailor Daniel Saunders penned an influential depiction of his "misfortunes" and "suffering" that described the loss of the Boston ship *Commerce*, "cast away near Cape Morebet, on the coast of Arabia, July 10, 1792," a report republished often and used as a model for later captivity tales. Saunders sailed under Samuel Johnson, a commander ill-suited for navigating the Indian Ocean, where "the winds for the most of the time being contrary, and the weather boisterous, our voyage proved very tedious." Johnson had set a course for Bombay on the Malabar (western) Coast of India, but nearly a week of "strong gales of wind from the southward and westward" pushed the *Commerce* far off course. At 3:00 a.m. on July 10, 1792, "to our great surprise, and greater misfortune," Saunders recalled, "the ship struck ground." Hundreds of leagues from their destination, on the coast of Arabia, the crew of the *Commerce* experienced the horror of shipwreck: "The consternation we were thrown into by this unexpected shock—the darkness of the night which surround us—the dashing of the waves against our stranded ship—and the prospect of immediate death before us—created a scene of horror past description." As they attempted to make their way ashore, Saunders and his fellow crewmembers were taken by "savages, on camels, armed with spears, cutlasses and knives" who "robbed us of everything we had, even stripping the shirts from off our backs."[54] When Saunders published his memoir, *A Journal of the Travels and Sufferings of Daniel Saunders, jun. A Mariner on board the Ship Commerce, of Boston, Samuel Johnson, Commander, which was cast away near Cape Morebet, on the Coast of Arabia, July 10, 1792,* he incorporated a language of captivity that Americans would come to associate broadly with the Ottoman world. And when Amasa Delano met Captain Johnson years later, he heard firsthand of "the calamitous consequences" of the captain's mistake and related, in a phrasing that resonated with readers of Saunders's book and his own *Narrative*: "The crew, getting ashore in boats, were attacked by the Arabs."

Thirteen years later, the shoals along the western coast of the Sahara Desert tricked the crew of another *Commerce*. On August 28, 1815, as Captain James Riley navigated the 220-ton brig off Cape Bojador, the sudden roar of breakers shocked the captain, who mistakenly assumed he was hearing the winds of a storm and lowered the ship's sails. As furious waves drove the ship onto rocks and battered the wreck, Riley managed to get his eleven-man crew ashore. Captured by Bedouin nomads, they made an 800-mile forced march across the Sahara until ransomed. Both Riley and crewman Archibald Robbins published accounts of their ordeal in 1817, the year Delano printed his *Narrative*, that made "the Western Coast of Africa" synonymous with "Loss," "Sufferings," and "Slavery."[55]

Captain George Nichols took "every requisite precaution"; he advised the owners of the *Active* as he anchored off Muscat in 1802: "Respecting the natives here, I always found them to be very friendly, but it is dangerous to irritate them and to permit many of them to be on board your vessel at a time. They always have their knives with them, and there have been instances of their taking vessels, and I imagine they are always willing to take advantage of a good opportunity to do a like act."

The accumulated warnings from worried mariners such as Nichols contributed to a general sense of the Muslim Mediterranean and Arabian waters as a place rife with various dangers in which a traveler passed at his own risk. Such was the sense with which Stephen Young, stranded in Europe in 1794, alluded in a vexed letter to his brother William, asserting, "I have recd. a letter for you from your Uncle in Blacklaw & another from Doctor Lyman [Newcomb] which I have sent with the bearer Charles White who is a member of Mr. Ellis congregation here. It is here reported that there is much danger of going to America in an American bottom for fear of the Algerines so that some are deterred on that acct. I wish you would give your mind respecting this. S.Y. April 28, [1794]." Warnings too often went unheeded, however, and this neglect resulted in tragedies such as the notorious massacre and loss of the *Essex* in 1806.[56]

Yet another peril awaited Yankee travelers who entered the Ottoman domain, and this for many was even more distressing than the threat of capture by corsairs or marauders. The possibility that Christian travelers might lose their faith and "turn Turk," through force or seduction, instilled further anxiety into a journey. A Yankee mariner could encounter Muslims even before touching at an Ottoman port of call, and the contamination of contact distressed those who did. Such was the challenge for the dyspeptic Philadelphia sea captain, Sandwith Drinker. Drinker's voyage from New York to Muscat and Zanzibar, 1840–1841, commanding the *Sultana* (*al-Sultanah*) for the sultan of Zanzibar, al Hajj Ahmad bin Na'aman bin Mushin bin Abdulla el Kaabi el Bahrani, under the direction of the first Zanzibar ambassador to the United States, (Ben Namen) Ahmad bin Na'aman, provides a record of the American response to Muslim encounters.[57]

What Drinker saw aboard the *Sultana* discomforted him. Studiously attendant to his own religious practices, he was particularly attuned to monitor those of others and found his experiences only confirmed the criticisms he had read previously. While he spent Sundays "profitably," reading Blunt's *History of Christ,* he groused that his lascar crew was unmindful of the Sabbath, as "religion with them appears a mere matter of form." Of bin Na'aman and his prayers:

> In performing them he appears only to be anxious that nothing may be neglected which the law requires. It is all outward, the heart is not interested. Like the Pharisees, they have every outward appearance of sanctity, whilst the inward parts are full of corruption. How unlike the precepts of the Koran was the religion taught by our blessed Saviour Bloodshed, and persecution were for its votaries, instead of those who refused to adopt it. A decisive proof of its purity, & divinity is the great change in habits, feelings, and dispositions, which all experience who are brought under its influence. The stubborn will which is inherent in man is subdued and brought in conformity with his, who established and died for it. . . . For centuries amidst revilings, and persecutions it has continued steadily and triumphantly, o advance 'till it has spread unto the utmost parts of the habitable Globe, whilst the religion of the prophet has as surely and steadily declined.' . . . The day will most assuredly come when all Nations will be brought to acknowledge the religion of the Cross.[58]

Drinker represented evangelical Americans who believed that contemporary Muslim practice was no less fake than when Mohammed introduced it 1,200 years earlier. He questioned the sincerity of holidays such as Ramazan (Ramadan), in November 1840, sneering: "The whole merit of keeping this fast, consists in abstaining from food. . . . Humility is out of the question, and so is prayer." His observation of his Arab crew was certainly distorted, ignoring the insincerity of his Christian countrymen, but unshakable. He put little stock in their complaints that it was difficult for them to work while fasting; instead, he complained, "The Arabs much resemble the Pharasees, selecting the most conspicuous place in the ship, to perform their devotions, putting on every outward appearance of sanctity, whilst the heart is wholly destitute of the vital spirit of religion. I shall really be glad when the month is past as my officers complain of being obliged to work when they cannot eat." The narrow field of Drinker's views was not his alone. The conceit that sincerity was a monopoly of travelers from Europe and the United States appears as an early Orientalist theme of Western observations of the Other.[59]

Believers in "Mahommedanism" felt none of the healthy "restraints" that molded religious discipline and were subject to "licentiousness, avarice, and deep duplicity," he pronounced. Furthermore, the newly married Drinker was appalled to learn that Muslims were "allowed as many wives, as they can support, a few only of the rich avail themselves of this privilege, most of them considering, that one woman is quite sufficient to manage."[60]

Yet Americans such as Drinker did not find all Muslims lacking in "moral character." He identified Hassen Bin Ibrahaim, a commander in the Ottoman navy, as "an exception altogether to the general Arab character." What made Ibrahaim different was his extended education in Calcutta, command of the English language, poise, grooming, openness to news of the world, and willingness to set a Western-style table, even allowing "silver knives and forks, tumblers, wineglasses, and an excellent glass of wine." He was, then, the kind of cosmopolitan citizen of the world that American travelers imagined they were.[61]

Ibrahaim was an exceptional other. This allowance did not enlarge Drinker's narrow prejudices, however. The captain's position was consistent with racist thinking, as historian Ibram X. Kendi shows, that singled out some African Americans as "extraordinary Negroes" who had not just risen above their station but also transcended the purported limitations of their race. They were the exceptional few, who could demonstrate promise but would never be fully accepted by whites. The remnant wallowed in a condition that Benjamin Franklin described and that Drinker applied to his lascar crew, as "dark, sullen, malicious, revengeful and cruel."[62]

For their part, Fisk and Parsons hoped that contacting British and American intermediaries who had traveled through the Ottoman region could help to prepare them for their mission; these contacts proved deeply disappointing, however. Moreover, the ensuing conversations portended a danger that threatened not just their mission but the very survival of Christianity. Even before leaving Gibraltar in 1819, they met the notorious apostate Bostonian George Bethune English. English had "turned Turk," taken the name Mohammed Vehbu Effendi, and served in the artillery of the Egyptian pasha, along with another American who had taken the name Khalil Aga. Another who "turned Turk" was John Perl, the sole survivor of the 1806 massacre aboard the Salem ship *Essex*. Then living in in Yemen with his Muslim wife and children when American missionaries met him, Perl had forgotten much of his English. Worse still, he had converted to Islam. In their sojourn, they would encounter more *Renegadoes*, such as English and Perl, than they would make converts to their "true God."[63]

Tales of apostacy concerned travelers and frightened their loved ones, who feared the seduction of other religions on weak minds. As his daughter Harriet prepared to embark for Canton in 1829, Seth Low wrote to her of his fears: "Thousands are willing to admit that there are a great many good things in the scriptures, but deny them as an entire system of moral government given to the world by God. They are willing also to believe that the Alcoran contains a great many excellent precepts, and, therefore, would have you believe it is as good as the bible. But . . . the Alcoran is not true as a system because it gives God a character inconsistent with the perfections ascribed to him in the scriptures." Apparently more concerned about her soul than her body, Low warned his twenty-year-old to remain "steadfast and immovable . . . to the end." Other twenty-year-olds about to embark into this imagined heart of darkness feared for their own souls. The danger of cultural contamination was infectious, according to James Durand. In Cairo, he observed, Christians "practice a holy cheat on Easter holidays, by pretending that the bodies of the dead on those days arise from their graves, to which they peaceably return."[64]

In a place often imagined as "exotic, ornate, and mysterious," it is no surprise that Americans found even the climate and weather of the Maghreb confounding. Jedidiah Morse noted a curious paradox in his *Geography Made Easy*, asserting, the air was "naturally delightful, serene and salubrious, yet the inhabitants are frequently visited with the plague." Travelers from the northern states of New England, especially, found the heat of the Mediterranean intimidating. Confined aboard the *Enterprise* in Alexandria harbor, Durand "gathered from the conversation of the learned; who had greater opportunity than myself" to go ashore that the summer months in Egypt were almost intolerable. "From March to Nov.," he recorded, "the heat is almost insupportable to Europeans. During the whole of the season the air is inflamed, the sky sparkling, the heat oppressive to all unaccustomed to it. The other months are more temperate."[65]

Whether inhabitant or visitor, one had reason to fear North Africa's climate. The winds that navy sailor Durand had learned of carried not just oppressive heat; he learned that Egyptians described the southern winds, in particular, "poisonous." He warned readers of his *Life and Adventures*, "Woe to the traveler whom this wind surprises remote from shelter: when it exceeds three days, the plague is an epidemic; it commences when the Nile begins to fall, and lessens when it begins to rise: Ophthalmalgia, dysentery, leprosy, dropsy, &c. are the diseases of Egypt which take place."[66] As in the lands of the Old

Testament, pestilence stalked the Ottoman world, bringing death to inhabitant and stranger alike, and, with each outbreak, stoking fears of the East.[67] A three-year plague came to Smyrna in 1739, taking 20 percent of the city and a greater number in the epidemic of the 1770s.[68] About the same time, plague decimated the Arabian port of Mocha, taking half of the port's population and the city into economic descent. Epidemics struck the region so regularly that, it was said, an inhabitant might state their age in reference to the year of a plague.[69]

The infamous yellow flag, warning of the danger of pestilence, and the lazaretto, where visitors were expected to quarantine themselves, were the first sites to greet visitors and informed them that they had now "entered the borders of the oriental world." This rite of passage into the Ottoman world was felt most harshly by the captives of Barbary corsairs, held for years in the bagnios of Morocco, Algiers, Tunis, and Tripoli. In 1787, Americans learned of the dire situation in an account from British ambassador Charles Logie, who had been "obliged to confine himself to his own house above a year, on account of the plague" in Algiers. Logie reported that three hundred victims were dying each day in the capital, but, fortunately, among the "unhappy American captives . . . only 3 out of 22 have been taken off by that distemper." The apostate mercenary George Bethune English, who fought for Egypt's Mehemmed Ali Pasha, could confirm Durand's warning, suffering a bout of the "distressing" eye disease ophthalmalgia along the Nile in 1820, inflicting "such acute anguish that I could get no sleep but by the effect of laudanum." Soon after, he contracted dysentery. Fifteen years later, John Stephens marked his entry into "the Land of Egypt" by noting "unfavorable accounts of the plague" and reciting Psalm 91:6: "The plague was in every one's mouth, and I was not sorry to have so early an opportunity of escaping from a city where, above all others, 'pestilence walketh in darkness, and destruction wasteth at noonday.'" When Edward Robinson entered Egypt from Greece, he learned to his good fortune that "all persons coming to Egypt from any part of the Turkish empire, were subjected to a quarantine of three weeks." Yet Christians were not immune to pestilence, and he had to be wary, observing of the plague's devastation at el-Kāhirah, "now universally called Musr," what Americans knew as Cairo, "In 1835 the plague made fearful ravages in Cairo, sweeping off not less than 80,000 of its inhabitants." Americans suffered from bouts of epidemic disease also, but in an effort distinguish their republic as exceptional, assigned the causes, or blame, for smallpox and yellow fever to others. Many newspaper accounts traced the origins of the yellow fever outbreak that struck

Philadelphia in 1793, for instance, to the flight of refugees from Saint Domingue (Haiti) that "vitalized a distrust of outsiders."[70]

Disease affected those under God's blessing. As soon as Fisk and Parsons landed in Smyrna in January 1820, incidents confirmed their imagined "Land of the Turk." In April, insurrections broke out in Greece against the oppression of Ottoman rule. By July, an outbreak of plague at Malta already imperiled the American mission. Parsons fell "an early victim to disorder, to which severe hardship and an unfavorable climate contributed."[71]

Yankee travelers' impressions of the Ottoman Empire depended on how they arrived—as merchants, missionaries, explorers, or captives. If one came as a free person, perhaps to trade for rugs and opium in Smyrna (Izmir), as did the Perkins family of Boston or the Chews of Philadelphia about 1803; to convert Orthodox Christians or even Muslims, as did Pliny Fisk and Levi Parsons in 1820; or as a tourist, as did New York lawyer John Stephens in 1835 or biblical scholar Edward Robinson in 1838; one found a land of paradoxes and contradictions that served to befuddle common sense and to elevate one's own country as a "civilized" nation. However, they came, American travelers felt a sense of strangeness—the novelty of the place and the sense of their own alienation as *Kafirs*, outsiders.

Visitors wrote of their arrival as an assault—as new sights, sounds, and smells overwhelmed their senses—that commenced even before landing at Alexandria, Smyrna, or Constantinople. When Charles Tyng spied a fleet of Turkish merchant ships at Leghorn in the 1830s, it was the sailors' "peculiar dress" that caught his eye, marked by "turbans of different colors, loose trousers drawn in round the ankle, and very short waisted jackets." About the same time, Edward Robinson foreshadowed his Ottoman adventures at Corfu, noting that "the first specimen we saw of a Greek population [was] also the worst. The streets were thronged with ragged, cut-throat looking fellows,—fierce, rugged, weather-worn visages, who might well have sat for Byron's pictures." At the landing at Alexandria, John Stephens described the kind of commotion and noise that others would find at Calcutta and Canton and that left him with a dizzying sense of culture shock. The people who flew about him, in particular, startled Stephens, and he observed, "Just as we had passed the last reef pilots came out to meet us, their swarthy faces, their turbans, their large dresses streaming in the wind, and their little boat with its huge lateen sail, giving a strange wildness to their appearance, the effect of which was not a little heightened by their noise and confusion in attempting to come alongside."[72]

Entering Constantinople or Alexandria after 1784, the "new people," as the Turks denoted them, would have encountered one of the world's great civilizations. For a mariner out of Hartford such as Captain James Riley, "the novel objects and scenes which I had an opportunity of witnessing in the country of the Moors" felt mysterious, puzzling, and enchanting. Walking the streets of Constantinople, a visitor would have experienced a truly global city and picked up the refrains of myriad languages; observed the variety of costumes worn in Bombay, Canton, Oman; and viewed an astonishing mix of architectural styles, featuring the Romanesque-style Galata Tower (1348 CE). The capital of the Ottoman Empire, of course, crowned a Muslim world, the center of "Dar al-Islam: the belt of Muslim societies from West Africa to the Pacific." Consequently, for Yankee visitors, the hundreds of minarets that dominated the landscape celebrated a "false God" and a prophet who appeared in their books as a lascivious whoremaster. Their "true religion" was, of course, Protestant Christianity, and although these monotheisms came from the same fonts, like siblings, they developed a scathing hatred for each other, scarred by centuries of war.[73]

Yet the world of the "Turk" was far more complicated than American writers conceived. As Christine Isom-Verhaaren writes, "Ethnic, religious, dynastic, and geographic terms all have their limitations when used as adjectives to describe the peoples who resided within the boundaries of the Ottoman polity. This is compounded when how those terms have been used in the recent past obscures rather than reveals their meaning during a previous period."[74] Even the peoples on the peripheries of the empire, ranged along the Maghreb or in Arabia, "were deemed outsiders by the administrative elite" in Constantinople.[75] Isaac Hinckley learned the fragmented, fractious nature of the Ottoman world on reaching the port of Aden in October 1809. Conflict between "Arabs and the Woaboes [Wahabis] had caused a scarcity of coffee," making it impossible to load a cargo there—the purpose of the voyage.[76]

American visitors did not fully understand what they were observing or comprehend the meanings of Ottoman customs and manners. Much of what they thought they were seeing frightened them. Yet, from their accounts, it appears that seldom did they ask questions, instead asserting racist assumptions as explanations for behaviors they described as "strange," "singular," and corrupt. These encounters gave them an outlet for surfacing pockets of deep racism. James Durand, a sailor who served aboard the warships *John Adams, Enterprise*, and *Constitution* in 1804, described his culture shock on arriving in Egypt, observing, "All Egypt is overrun with jugglers, fortune-tellers, mountebanks, slight-of-handmen, &c." All was unsettling, and even women, especially dark-skinned women, in exotic dress sent him in flight. In Algiers, "Being once on shore walking the streets, I chanced to meet a Turkish woman walking towards me dressed in black, with a white muffler on, nothing to be seen but her eyes. The novelty of her dress, together with the strange appearance of the streets (which were covered over-head) threw me into a strange surprise: and I must say, that I, in this time of life, although a stout hearted tar, ran at the approach of woman." Thirty years later, Edward Robinson wrote that he, too, had been assaulted by the strange garb of Muslim women, "muffled in shapeless black mantles, their faces wholly covered except peep-holes for the eyes." In 1848, Lieutenant William Lynch had opportunities to observe, if not converse with, women in Constantinople and reported that they "looked like ghouls risen from the graves."[77]

Among the many paradoxes that Yankee travelers found in the Ottoman realm was a surprising degree of mobility. One could arrive as a free person, even as one's countrymen and countrywomen languished in a putrid Algerian or Tripolitan bagnio. American travelers found a freedom in the Ottoman Empire that a visitor would not find in Canton or even India. One was free to go almost anywhere, provided that one took the necessary precautions to fend off bandits and marauders. Even a meek classical scholar enjoyed freedom of movement, as Edward Robinson observed: "At Cairo, . . . we took time, and made several excursions from the city to places in the neighborhood." However oppressive Pasha Muhammed Ali was to his own people, Robinson credited him with rendering "the countries under his sway secure" for Western travelers. A few years later, Navy Lieutenant William Lynch was able, "in part with the officers, in part alone, [to visit] some of the principal mosques, the seraglio, the arsenal, and the fleet."[78]

This mobility, however, left newly arrived visitors exposed to the perils of culture shock. One was never permitted to feel completely secure or independent. When they arrived in Smyrna, Timothy Roberts writes, "most foreigners, called 'Franks', were normally met by a guide and hustled by donkey ride along 'Frank Street' to the city's casino, which had rooms for billiards and card playing, a library complete with European newspapers, a ballroom, and a gambling hall." Nor was the prospect of threading his way through the numbers and variety of peoples the sole threat to Edward Robinson's sense of security. In his account, the path to the Western, or Frank, quarter, led him "through narrow, crooked, dirty streets and lanes, running between dead walls or ill built houses with flat roofs."[79]

The fears that Drinker and Robinson recorded were described by others when they arrived, experiencing diversity as disorder. In his 1824 *Memoir*, missionary Levi Parsons expressed his dismay: "I cannot describe Smyrna. . . . The people are of all ranks and complexions. . . . What would you think of a man approaching you, of gigantic stature, long beard, fierce eyes, a turban on his head . . . long flowing robes, a large belt, in which were four or five pistols and a sword?" Another Andover product, Robinson found even more deranged circumstances in Alexandria, where, "The moment we set foot on shore, we needed no further conviction, that we had left Europe and were now in the oriental world." Navigating their way through a heaving throng of "Egyptians, Turks, Arabs, Copts, Negros, Franks; complexions of white, black, olive, bronze, brown, and almost all other colours; long beards and no beards; all costumes and no costume; silks and rags; wide robes and no robes . . . endless confusion, and a clatter and medley of tongues, Arabic, Turkish, Greek, Italian, French, German, and English, as the case might be."[80]

After their country's independence, as Americans such as Fisk and Parsons penetrated deeper into the far reaches of the Empire, the meanings of "Turkish tyranny" became more varied and complicated. Before 1700, historians have traditionally maintained, the sum of knowledge that British Americans held about the Ottoman world would barely fill two quarto newspapers, suggesting that "due to their limited circulation their impact is difficult to determine."[81] Yet, by the mid-eighteenth century, Americans such as Nicholas and Thomas Boylston could read about Muslims through a sophisticated British print network of books, newspapers and literary treatments during the colonial period.

More recently, historians such as Nat Cutter have found a richer trove of print culture available from European presses, passing widely into the public sphere, and much of this made its way to the British American provinces.[82] The Ottoman world described in their geographies and encompassed in their maps (virtually all published in London) presented an amalgam of great luxury and withering poverty, of concentrated power and widespread enslavement. As historian Jürgen Osterhammel explains the origins and power of this Orientalist mythology: "The fabled East of flying *djinns* and flying carpets, but also of violence and debauchery, found its literary monument at the dawn of the eighteenth century in Antoine Galland's translation of the *Tales from the Thousand and One Nights* before being rediscovered . . . by William Beckford (1786)." It is difficult to know how many colonists read or heard Montesquieu or the *Persian Letters*. Still, there is ample evidence that some impressions of the "terrible Turk" made their way into popular consciousness. As with China, much of what crept into the colonies was fable. But inauthenticity did not discount its influence. Rather, the more sensationalist the account, the wider its distribution, and the more likely it was to take hold in the public consciousness.[83]

Although historians have tried to trace early American impressions of the world to their constructions of Native Americans, commonly describing the indigenous peoples of the Americas as "uncivilized" and "savage," it was the image of the "terrible Turk" that most forcefully influenced their ideas about the world and its peoples. Through the pens of merchants and missionaries, such as Pliny Fisk, and Barbary captives, such as John Foss and James Riley, the early republic abounded in such tales of American travelers who braved "dirty seas" and "wretched Turks" to make their fortunes or spread the Word of their own "true God." Through the telling and retelling of such tales, the idea of the Ottoman Mediterranean as a fount of imperious deys, pashas, "infidel Algerines," "wicked and rash" despots, and "wretched Turks" introduced another form of tyranny, one different from that of China's mandarins, to the American consciousness. In this version, tyranny was steeped in luxury and self-indulgence, whose pirate minions terrorized the seas and enslaved the innocent. This became concretized into a national trope. As we see in other themes, this was a construction inherited from centuries of European writing but reinterpreted to emphasize the superiority of Americans' own republican institutions. In this way, Americans contributed to the Western idea of the Middle East in a compelling mythology that imagined this part of the world as a site of unbridled tyranny and false religion.

After independence, as Americans began to sift into the Ottoman realm, willingly or otherwise, they encountered this "tyranny" in the form of a limitation on their movements. The sultan required foreigners to be accompanied by a dragoman or janissary, an Ottoman security officer, as James Durand noted, "whose authority generally protects them from insult of the natives." For Robinson, this dependence on a guide or servant insinuated a sense of dependence and vulnerability. The impoverished countryside of primitive roads and a dearth of inns and conveyances meant that he had to rely on a stranger, whose language, manners, customs, and, especially religion, were alien to him, and whose religion he held in existential antagonism. "Thrown back wholly upon his own resources, . . . he must hire a boat for himself, unless he can find a companion to share it with him; he must provide his own bed and cooking utensils, and also his provisions for the journey, except such as he can procure at the villages along the Nile." Consequently, a servant who could scope out provisions cook, purveyor, and interpret was essential. At home, one might imagine crossing a frontier with relative freedom. In Egypt, however, Yankee travelers lost this freedom. Edward Robinson was such a traveler, complaining of his dependence on a ragged, uncouth guide: "[A traveler] will soon find himself very much in the power of this important personage, who will usually be able neither to read nor write; and the discomforts and vexations of this relation of dependence will probably continue more and more to press upon him, until he has himself learned something of the Arabic language, or is fortunate enough (as I was) to fall in with a companion to whom the language is familiar. If the traveler has time, he will do well to purchase the chief necessaries at Alexandria."[84]

In November 1820, Fisk and Parsons toured the area of Egypt, Syria, and Damascus "for the purpose of visiting the places where once stood and flourished the seven churches of Asia. Their intent was not so much to learn as to proselytize, and the contents of their baggage revealed the mindset they had brought: "We carry a trunk, and two large sacks, filled with Testaments, Tracts, clothes, etc."[85]

They did record the sights, through a skewed lens, identifying the spiritual and physical impoverishment of a people who lived under the tyranny of Muslim rule. Time and again on their journey, they would encounter signs of the destitution they saw in Ottoman life. Describing their first stop for refreshment, Fisk introduced the trope of poverty:

> At half past twelve stopped for dinner, at a Turkish coffee house. It was built of
> mud and small stones; and was about ten feet square and ten high. The roof
> was of pine bushes. The ground served for a floor. The front was entirely open
> to the road. The furniture consisted of a sofa, pipes, and coffee cups. The Turkish
> landlord sat on the sofa, with a pipe in his hand, and a sword and pistols behind
> him. He invited us to sit down with him, and a young Arab slave brought us
> sweet meats and coffee. After eating of food which we carried with us, we
> obtained a watermelon of the Turk, and resumed our journey.[86]

Further on, readers could be reassured that their assumptions of Ottoman backwardness were correct: "Found difficulty in procuring a lodging; at length put up in a hut occupied by a Turk. It was about 10 feet square, the walls of earth, the roof of bushes and poles covered with soil and grass growing on it. There was neither chair, table, bed nor floor in the habitation. The Turk seemed to live principally by his pipe and his coffee." Readers would learn little about the people of the empire—their beliefs, their struggles, their dreams—but what these descriptions lacked in detail Fisk hope to make up for in repetition. Consequently, he iterated, at Haivali, where the name indicated "quince" but where there were few quinces to be found: "The streets are narrow and very dirty, and the houses mean. You see no elegance, and very little neatness." This existence was not much different from that of many Americans who eked out lives along the Western frontier, as British travelers such as Francis Trollope, Harriett Martineau, and Basil Hall enjoyed informing their English readers and outraging their American audiences, but that was not the point Fisk wanted to make. The thrust of his writing was not to foster empathy but to raise a storm flag. If the Turk somehow conquered America and imposed Islam upon a Christian nation, a frontier existence might be the future of the republic, a kind of reversed manifest destiny.[87]

In the republican vision of the new nation, ignorance was the handmaiden of poverty, and readers were reminded that following missionary accounts such as Fisk's were a way to protect Christianity at home. He brought home the point in describing a dilapidated khan, or caravansary, where they "found three or four Greeks about the khan; but all of them very stupid and unable to read, and either unable or unwilling to do much for our comfort." Later, while dining at a khan where they had deposited some religious tracts, the landlord expressed his astonishment at the republican idea of education: "It seemed to him a new and a wonderful thing, that men should go about, giving away books for nothing." How was this news received within the Baptist community? What did they make of Fisk's comment that he had left tracts for "such as wish for them, are able to read." It is not clear that literacy rates were any higher there than on the American frontier.[88]

As missionaries, whose purpose was conversion and success was measured in tracts delivered and converts made, where they went and what they did differed from the places and actions of other travelers. Fisk sought out schools and colleges, as well as religious leaders. He also followed an itinerary based on a contemporary reading of the Bible. His entries compose a kind of survey, documenting the churches and religious schools he encountered. Notable are the number of formerly famous Christian churches that had been taken over by Greeks or Muslims. This was a way of documenting the need for missionaries in the struggle against Satan's ignorance. This provides a lens for understanding what place meant to evangelical missionaries, and what this place meant to New Divinity missionaries such as Fisk.

And, so, Fisk found what he expected to see, at least in the landscape of the Holy Land. He had read that Ottoman rule had left holy sites in a decrepit condition, and, indeed, everywhere he saw signs that the pashas had allowed sacred places to fall into ruin. Fisk's itinerary read like a list of dead and wounded soldiers following a battle: "on our left hand, near the road, the ruins of a town, which, we concluded, must have been the ancient Myrina." Like John Ledyard, Fisk struggled to locate significant sites. Instead, he could only approximate where they might have been. Along the seashore, he reported, "Strabo speaks of Myrina as situated here, or not far distant; and some maps insert the name in this place." Closer inspection brought no further satisfaction, and Fisk lamented the decay, writing, "Many pillars of granite eight or ten feet long, and a foot and a half thick, and some fragments of marble, were scattered on the ground. Among them was a large statue of white marble. The arms and part of the head are gone. The body is about six feet long and three thick. Once, perhaps, it was an object of worship; now it lies entirely neglected, as we trust all relics of idolatry will be, at some future day. No walls remain, and there is no building on the spot."[89] The overall sense was that a "false God" left only false impressions to ridicule Christian pilgrims.

In the end, Fisk and Parsons made no converts and had scant influence on the Ottoman Empire. Parsons never recovered from the debilitating illness he acquired in Malta; he died at Alexandria in 1821. Fisk continued the mission but succumbed at Beirut in 1825. Their larger influence was upon readers at home, as missionary reports became the most important source of information about the world for many Americans. Through the renderings of disappointing experiences, Fisk and Parsons reaffirmed the impressions of the East left by Puritan sermons and Barbary captivity tales. The world, especially the Muslim part of it, was a perilous place for American travelers and their values.[90]

Other Americans followed, and they corroborated the idea of Ottoman decadence and danger. Increasingly, other Yankee travelers, neither merchants nor missionaries, determined to preserve the vestiges of the Holy Land, came to see, write, paint, and soldier. The Boston apostate George Bethune English was there at the same time as Fisk, and throughout the course of an expedition up the Nile River, he explored the ruins of Egyptian temples and Christian monasteries. Like Fisk, he lamented, "The peoples who now occupy the territories of nations extinct or exterminated have profited neither by their history nor their fate. What was once a land occupied by nations superstitious and sensual is now inhabited by robbers and slaves."[91]

Explorer and adventurer John L. Stephens, a New York lawyer, who on a whim abandoned his European tour to see the Ottoman world for himself, brought a different perspective to his travels, but his writing played the same chords of "Turkish tyranny." His 1836 travelogue, *Incidents of Travel in Egypt, Arabia, Petraea, and the Holy Land,* became a best seller and reprintings enabled him to leave the profession he loathed and explore the world further. *Incidents of Travel* would not bring his readers to fresh ways of seeing the world, and in Stephens's writing it would remain a dangerous land.[92]

Arriving in Alexandria in December 1835, after an anxious night coasting along the Barbary shore and finding no landmarks, Stephens scorned "the Land of Egypt" as a decrepit wasteland of ruins. "The ancient Pharos, the Lantern of Ptolemy, the eighth wonder of the world, no longer throws its light far over the bosom of the sea to guide the weary mariner," he wrote. Like Fisk and Parsons, Stephens was not interested in observing the empire as it was in his own times. Rather, his frame of reference was an earlier era, the lands of Pompey and Alexander. The sight of lateen sails on quaint dhows crowding Alexandria harbor, he recalled, carried him "back in imagination to the days of the Macedonian conqueror, of Cleopatra and the Ptolemies."[93]

But it was the work of man that troubled Stephens more, and he left readers with images of once great civilizations that had been allowed to fall into decay. His first stop, and his first "incident" of disappointment, was at the once great entrepôt of Alexandria. "I felt myself among the ruins of one of the greatest cities of the world," Stephens philosophized:

> All this intermediate space of sandy hills, alternating with hollows, was once covered with houses, palaces, and per-haps with monuments, equal in beauty to that at whose base I stood. Riding over that waste, the stranger sees broken columns, crumbling walls, and fragments of granite and marble, thrusting themselves above their sandy graves, as if struggling for resurrection; on one side he beholds a yawning chasm, in which forty or fifty naked Arabs are toiling to disentomb a column long buried in the sand; on another an excavated house, with all its walls and apart-ments almost as entire as when the ancient Egyptian left it. He is riding over a mighty sepulchre, the sepulchre of a ruined city, and at every step some telltale monument is staring at him from the grave.[94]

The Alexandria canal provided an entry point for Stephens to explore the Muslim failure to build upon the achievements of the classical world.

Drawing upon the trope of "Turkish tyranny," he mused, "In regard to the time in which it was made it certainly is an extraordinary work; and it could only have been done in that time; in such a country as Egypt, where the government is an absolute despotism, and the will of one man is the supreme law."

The consequences for Egyptian society were devastating. The canal was a great work of a modernizing society, and the pasha deserved credit for this, Stephens thought, but it came at a horrible price: a "wanton disregard of human life, and the melancholy fact that it proved the grave of more than thirty thousand of his subjects." The remainder of Egypt's population fared little better in his estimation. As he traveled, Stephens gazed "through long rows of Arab huts, where poverty, and misery, and famine, and nakedness stared me in the face, one glance at its majestic height told that this was indeed the work of other men and other times." For Stephens, it seemed as if humanity had devolved into a demi-human state, and his *Incidents of Travel* introduced Americans to a land he described as "between ambling donkeys, loaded camels, dirty, half-naked, sore-eyed Arabs, swarms of flies, yelping dogs, and apprehensions of the plague." Everywhere he looked, "wild, fly-way looking Arabs" or "a sore-eyed Arab boy" would meet his gaze.[95]

Stephens had used "the departed glory of Egypt" to warn his countrymen about the perils he found in the world. Furthermore, he implied, only the efforts of the West could reclaim the lost glories of the Holy Land, once "the mother of art." Now, it was Europeans who were "raising her from the ruin into which she had been plunged by years of misrule and anarchy." Should Islam conquer Christianity, through force or suasion, Europeans would become slaves to "Turkish tyranny," as the Egyptians and Syrians had. Poverty and ignorance would be their fate in this life, and damnation in the next. The Ottomans represented, then, the world as a dangerous place. The threat they signified was different from the forms Americans found in India, China, and the South Seas. But, being more proximate and of greater consequence, many Americans, and evangelicals, in particular, came to see it as the greatest threat they could face.[96]

Looking over Alexandria, "it was impossible to enumerate the variety of its riches and beauty," Stephens quoted a Saracen general. In its heyday, the city "contained four thousand palaces,. four thousand baths, four hundred theatres or public edifices, twelve thousand shops, and forty thousand tributary Jews." And, in Stephens's telling, the loss of classical civilization could be attributed to one source—Islam. The Ottomans had inherited and squandered the achievements of the classical world, letting its glorious architecture, art, music, science, and philosophy wither. Stephens eulogized the collapse by writing: "When it fell into the hands of the Saracens, . . . like everything else which falls into the hands of the Mussulman, it has been going to ruin, and the discovery of the passage to India by the Cape of Good Hope gave the death-blow to its commercial greatness. At present it stands a phenomenon in the history of a Turkish dominion."[97]

No one could be more interested in the ruins than biblical scholar Edward Robinson, who combined his interest in recovering sites of biblical passages with locating sites he associated with the classical world. He filled his *Biblical Researches* with discoveries that harkened back to Greek history, that were "enough to awaken all our classic feelings, and call up vividly before us Ulysses and the great 'Father of Song.'" Yet Robinson, like Fisk and Stephens, was often disappointed in his searches, even in Athens. Carried along in a fiacre, the traditional cart, he reflected,

> This drive was accompanied by sad feelings. The day was cloudy, cold, and cheerless. The plain and mountains around, the scenes of so many thrilling associations, were untilled and desolate; and on every side were seen the noblest monuments of antiquity in ruins, now serving to mark only the downfall of human greatness and of human pride. Nor did the entrance to the city tend to dissipate these feelings. Small wellings of stone, huddled together along narrow, crooked, unpaved, filthy lanes, are not the Athens which the scholar loves in imagination to contemplate. Yet they constitute, with a few exceptions, the whole of modern Athens. Even in its best parts, and in the vicinity of the court itself, there is often an air of haste and shabbiness, which, although not a matter of wonder under the circumstances in which the city has been built up, cannot fail to excite in the stranger a feeling of disappointment and sadness. This however does not last long. The force of historical associations is too powerful not to triumph over present degradation; and the traveller soon forgets the scenes before him, and dwells only on the remembrance of the past.[98]

Conditions did not improve as Robinson's party reached Alexandria, once "that renowned city," but when he arrived, "scarcely a vestige now remains." Once a bustling entrepôt of 160,000 souls, the city now barely supported 40,000. What lay before the scholar, and what he represented to his extensive group of readers, was reminiscent of Rome overrun by Vandals and Goths: "The hand of time and the hand of barbarism have both swept over it with merciless fury, and buried its ancient glory in the dust and in the sea. Her illustrious schools of theology, astronomy, and various other sciences; her noble library, unique in ancient history; her light house, one of the seven wonders of the world; all have utterly vanished away, and 'the places thereof know them no more.'" The loss was catastrophic, according to Robinson, presenting himself in the guise of the American citizen of the world. Almost exactly fifty years after his countrymen had created a new nation, this global citizen came to the Ottoman Empire to bemoan the loss of the classical world that had originated the "civilization" his country represented. He reported back to America and Europe that "her former structures have perished, has been dug over, and the foundations of her edifices turned up" to create "works of the Pasha." What were once "ornaments in the Greek style of architecture" now were now sites of "loneliness and desolation"; "the straggling and neglected tombs of a Muhammedan cemetery only serve to render the desolation more mournful."[99]

The hand of the pasha and the sultan, of the dey and the bey was felt everywhere in these once holy lands. The manner of population—the "indolence and procrastinating habits of the Egyptians and Arabs"—inverted American values and made the efforts of his entourage "a slow and wearisome matter." Yet manners reflected deeper, more troubling aspects of the culture. Under the hand of the Ottomans, the Holy Land had become not just ancient, but backward. Robinson's track took him through dust-infested villages where he found "only the squalid abode of filth and wretchedness; mud hovels, not high enough to stand up in, built on mounds accumulated in the course of centuries from the ruins of former dwellings."[100]

Worse still, like Pliny Fisk and Levi Parsons, Robinson was distressed with the sight of once glorious monuments now degenerated into scatterings of rubble, reminiscent of Coleridge's "antique land" of Ozymandias. It was "impossible to wander among these scenes, and behold these hoary yet magnificent ruins, without emotions of astonishment and deep solemnity," he lamented. "Everything around testifies of the vastness, and of utter desolation. Here lay once that mighty city, whose power and splendor were proverbial throughout the ancient world." The temple of Dendera now housed only "dilapidated tombs." The famous biblical city of Nilometer, which as early as 860 CE had displayed advanced architectural features such as pointed arches, lay "now half in ruins." For Robinson, the pyramids, more than other ancient sites, symbolized the evils that had laid waste to the country. These "earliest, as well as the loftiest and most vast of all existing works of man upon the face of the earth," erected at the cost of so many lives and so much treasure, had been "erected chiefly, if not solely, as the sepulchres of kings. Wain pride of human pomp and power." A "Turkish tyranny," then was the real legacy of the ancient world. In Egypt, it was "its famous ruler, Muhammed Aly," who personified the modern Ozymandias.[101]

"This extraordinary man, with native talents which in other circumstances might have made him the Napoleon of the age" had introduced manufacturing and engineering schools, built up the army and navy, and established a profitable cotton farm. Ali was not, however, a Washington nor even a Henry Clay or John Quincy Adams. His modernizing program was carried out "only for himself—not for the country." With a "barbarian eagerness," the requisite taxes had beggared the population "by draining them almost to exhaustion." Consequently, Egypt was "what she so long has been, 'the basest of kingdoms.'"[102]

American interest in the Ottoman world began to peak during the antebellum era for the reasons that inspired Robinson. Some went to seek the Holy Land, others to explore the classical world and its ruins and relics, others to advance what they saw as scientific frontiers. A decade following Edward Robinson's journey to Palestine, William Francis Lynch, a Virginian and a lieutenant in the US Navy, set out to survey the Jordan River and Dead Sea. What would be "the US Navy's first and only scientific expedition to the Ottoman Near East" produced yet another publication that carried Americans, if vicariously, to the world of the Ottomans, Lynch's popular 1848 tome, *Narrative of the Expedition to the River Jordan and the Dead Sea.*[103]

Lynch's exploration would be as dangerous a mission as that of Fisk and Parsons, and more so than those of Stephens and Robinson. Climate, logistics, and bandits had routed two earlier efforts, as expedition leaders died of malaria and dehydration. His own journey was daunting, although ultimately successful. Along the way, however, he recorded the same observations as had his Yankee predecessors. The landscape, although "truly Asiatic," was uninteresting, even disappointing. Landing at Smyrna, the port presented romantic associations, and Lynch crowed, "It was Ismir! Infidel Ismir! Christian Smyrna! The setting sun empurpled the neighbouring mountains, gilding here and shadowing there, in one soft yet glorious hue, lending a characteristic enchantment to our first view of an Oriental city." The port and its people, with its ethnic diversity and exotic ways, however, disgusted the lieutenant, presenting a sense of things to come. "We landed and passed into the streets, the narrow, winding ways of Smyrna," Lynch recalled. "How strange everything seems! After all one has fancied of an eastern city, how different is the reality! The streets are very narrow and dark, and filled with a motley and, in general, a dirty population—passing to and fro, or sitting in their stalls, for they deserve no better name. Greeks, Armenians, and Jews, seem to prevail." When offered an opportunity to partake of the famous baths, the fastidious Lynch protested that these were "far too public for our ideas of propriety." The revulsion was not only cultural, as he feared, "for it was not only necessary to avoid the camels and little donkeys, but also dirty, ragged, staggering, overladen porters, whose touch threatened not only to communicate the plague, but also whole detachments of the insect tribes of Egypt."[104]

Out of the city and en route to Constantinople to secure a firman—permission to travel to his destination—from the sultan, Lynch found the landscape as dull as other travelers had. Sites of classical and biblical importance betrayed their heritage. Everywhere he found indications of decline, such as "a once formidable castle" in Smyrna. Even the site of one of the world's famous battles was a disappointment, as Lynch recounted, "The plain of Troy, so familiar to every classic reader, now barren and unattractive, save in its associations."[105]

The Ottoman Empire itself was in decline, and, along with Stephens and Robinson, Lynch believed the degeneration was represented in the person of the sultan. The American described the ruler of the Ottoman Empire as a feeble and facetious creature, a "man, young in years, but evidently of impaired and delicate constitution, his wearied and spiritless air was unrelieved by any indication of intellectual energy." But it was in the sultan's people, from capable military and political officers to abject servants, that Lynch traced the decline and fall of this empire. They entered the sultan's presence "with heads bowed down and their left hands upon their breasts." Even the ruler's secretary exhibited "more awe than I had ever seen depicted in the human countenance," Lynch told his Yankee readers. For their part, the Americans, unacquainted with palace etiquette, made a noisy and awkward impression, their footsteps reverberating throughout the corridors "with untutored republican firmness." These were the signs, he observed, of a "general and spreading opinion, that the Ottoman rule upon the European side of Turkey is drawing to a close. This impression has become so prevalent, that hundreds, when they die, direct their remains to be interred on the Asiatic side of the Bosporus. It is sad to think that, from the destruction of the Janissaries by Mahmoud to the present time, the very advancement of the Turks in civilization should increase the weakness, and precipitate the dismemberment, if not the downfall, of the empire!"[106] Belying this sumptuous welcome, the ruler with the "feeble and almost tottering" gait governed a domain that was itself as feeble and almost tottering. He could not protect them from the multitude of ills that tore at the fabric of the empire. As he made his way from the palace, Lynch knew that the firman he held and the dragoman who escorted him provided scant security, and he recorded, "As to protection against the Arabs, it could afford none whatever; for Eastern travellers well know that, ten miles east of a line drawn from Jerusalem to Nabulus, the tribes roam uncontrolled, and rob and murder with impunity." To this he could have added the threat from plagues, earthquakes, bandits, rebellion, and primitive infrastructure. Americans had come to expect more from a government. From their revolution, they felt entitled to certain inalienable rights, and they increasingly expected that governments would safeguard their lives, liberties, and properties both at home and abroad.[107]

Reflections

During the summer of 1820, as Americans argued the meanings of freedom, enslavement, and statehood in Congress and over kitchen tables and as white "pioneers" pushed against the country's continental boundaries under the guise of manifest destiny, four thousand miles away, missionaries Pliny Fisk and Levi Parsons found a "lost boy" in the deserts of Yemen. Fisk and Parsons were on a mission to recover the Christian roots of the Holy Land as a means of extending "American civilization" beyond the shores of their republic. The encounter did not bode well for their success. The young man was none other than John Perl, sole survivor of the 1806 massacre aboard the Salem ship *Essex*. Even before this chance meeting, Perl's identity was uncertain, known variously as "a Dutch boy named John Hermann Poll," as an American named John Poll, and as John Porl. The accounts in American newspapers described his fate at the hands of "the faithless Mahomet" Mohammed Ickle, who "kept the lad whose life he had spared, as a slave until 1812, when Death kindly freed him from his cruel bondage." This was another fable from an unholy Land.

The John Perl whom Fisk and Parsons encountered was not the John Perl whose loss the country had mourned more than a decade earlier. Fisk and Parsons were horrified to learn that one of Salem's own was now Abdallah Mohammed. He had "taken the turban" and was living in Yemen with his Muslim wife and children. The encounter was a disturbing sign of the power of the "false God" they battled, who was more likely to draw Christians to Him than to surrender believers to their own efforts.[108] The impotence that the American missionaries felt in that moment underlay the country's evolving relationship with the Ottoman East. Today, Americans boast of their exceptionalism and their ability to project their economic influence and military might "to the shores of Tripoli." The posturing has its origins not in conquest, however, but in a sense of weakness: an abiding fear of the influence of the Muslim world and its ability to project its own power across the seas remains an element of American identity.

Captivity Narratives

At the moment when Virginians, New Yorkers, and Carolinians began to call themselves Americans, direct encounters with the Ottoman East began in the form of "clear and present dangers."[109] Robert Allison, Lawrence Peskin, Hester Blum, and Pauline Strong have documented the importance of these Barbary captivity narratives in contributing to "some of the exceptionalist genealogies of American literature."[110] As Malini Johar Schueller, along with Allison and Peskin, has shown, Americans' fear of Islam has deep roots, extending well before the modern paranoia over "Islamoterrorism."[111] Grafted onto the entrenched tropes conveyed in two centuries of European Barbary captivity tales and a century and a half of sermons, newspaper reports, and their own chilling Native American captivity narratives, accounts of Americans imprisoned in North African bagnios carried particular resonance for a country unsure of its place in the world and, indeed, its own legitimacy.[112] Although their own ideas of the boundaries between concepts such as Ottoman, Turk, and Muslim were murky, most Americans held a potent revulsion for the peoples of the Mediterranean even before direct contacts. As the most sensationalist writing from the Ottoman Empire, American versions of Barbary-captivity tales fostered the strongest impressions upon the national consciousness.[113]

Central to the Barbary-captivity accounts was an anticonquest narrative. In this trope, Yankee ships went to the East in a virtual state of commercial grace, seeking only innocent trade. By extension, missionaries traveled to the East in an peaceful effort to teach Arabs about Christ. This interpretation masked the reality that the missionaries who arrived in 1819 came to the Ottoman Empire on an errand of conquest, not to acquire territories, but to claim souls. Renegadoes such as John Herman Perl and George English Bethune complicated the story, signifying the doctrinal strength of Islam that threatened the American mission and its manifest destiny of spreading Christianity.

Orientalism

One cannot interpret early American encounters in the Ottoman Empire without referencing the seminal work of Edward Said and his reinterpretation of the concept of Orientalism introduced in his eponymous 1978 text. Although some scholars have taken exception to nuances of his argument, Said demonstrated convincingly that a steady drumbeat of texts fascinated American readers, who learned that that the Ottoman East was both a web of tyranny and purveyor of a legacy of false prophets, led by the chief deceiver, "Mahomet."[114] Like Allison, Peskin, and others, I would push the beginnings of this American obsession with a dangerous East to the beginnings of national identity. As early as 1788, Yankee newspapers were insisting, "Everyone who has been the least versant in history, will know, that Arabia, Persia, Egypt, and the different provinces of the East, have, for more than a thousand years, been under the power of the Mussulmans, or followers of Mahomet, and governed by despotic princes, who, bearing the titles of Caliphs, Sultans, or Sophis, have pretended to be successors of that prophet, for executing his pretended commission from heaven."[115] Consequently, although their own ideas of the boundaries between concepts such as Ottoman, Turk, and Muslim were murky, most Americans held a potent revulsion for the peoples of the Mediterranean.

In Lisa Lowe's study of eighteenth-century Orientalism, Europeans imagined "the oriental world as an exotic, uncivilized counterpart of Europe," balanced against "representations of the European world as knowing, stable, and powerful."[116] Early American travelers to Dar-es-Salam continued the trope of innocents abroad "encountering strange and disorienting customs and practices." Historians such as Alison Games, Linda Colley, Gerald MacLean, and others have described the overseas experiences of British travelers in ways that complicate Edward Said's *Orientalism* (1978). They have connected these travels to the construction of national identity.[117] Along with Nabil Matar, Ros Ballaster, Katie Sisneros, Nat Cutter, and other scholars, Lowe asserts that these constructions "addressed national anxieties about maintaining hegemony in an age of rapidly changing boundaries and territories."[118]

I contend that the element of fear plays a role. The ruins that captivated and disappointed the missionaries Fisk and Parsons and explorers such as Stephens, Robinson, and Lynch represented an obstacle to republican ideals such as progress, individualism, and the advancement of science. Shelley expressed the dangers of decadence and decay powerfully in his 1818 poem *Ozymandias*, and others followed, anticipating the American experience in the

East.[119] As the evangelicals believed that Americans had a duty to send missions abroad to Christianize a benighted world—Christian imperialism, as Conroy-Krutz puts it—so secular authorities called for Americans to carry the light of their republican revolution into the world. In some explorers, the secular and sacred missions were fused. Decadent lands were an obstacle to this republican responsibility. Ruins symbolized a threat in this body of writing, specifically a threat to the perception of an American mission. Although O'Sullivan did not present the term "manifest destiny" until 1846, the idea was seeded with the American victory in its War of Independence. Valedictorian essays made the connection between American liberal progress and Eastern decadence, using the traverse of the sun as their exemplary symbol. It was America's providential duty to bring progress to the world (the torch had been passed, as a later American president put it) generationally and geographically (as American social observers waxed in poetry and prose)—to bring light into the darkness of tyranny, ignorance, and poverty. The tension between luxury and poverty, power and submission, beauty and cruelty challenged the order that Americans sought to bring or impose and threatened to thwart the spread of the manifest destinations of the Ottoman Empire.

CHAPTER THREE

"Unfeeling Mandarins" in Canton and Macao

In the late summer of 1772, it was commonly observed, the world was on the move. Even "the quality," such as Nicholas and Thomas Boylston, were not immune to upheavals that were turning the world upside down. The Boylston family broke apart during the opening fracas that became the American Revolution. Nicholas died in August 1771, after a lengthy illness, leaving a £1,500 bequest to Harvard College. Brother Thomas, accused of being a "stingy merchant" who horded coffee and sugar during the revolutionary crisis, sailed for Britain in 1777 and the tenuous comfort of exile. He never returned to Boston. Fractious loyalties divided the town, and luxury goods such as Chinese teas, Indian calicoes, Japanese coromandel screens, and even silk shoes became signifiers of partisan loyalties. One former friend and neighbor whom Thomas left behind was Harbottle Dorr, fellow merchant, supporter of the Patriot cause, and avid reader. As tensions built up during the 1770s, Dorr collected newspapers and pamphlets and annotated the accounts and advertisements he found that helped him to understand the complicated world around him. From his shop "almost opposite the Cornfield in Union Street," he could not help but situate Boston's "disturbances" into a global perspective.[1]

As Dorr picked up his copy of the *Boston-Gazette, and Country Journal* for September 14, 1772, his eye fell upon an "Extract from Political Essays Concerning the Present State of the British Empire, a new Work just published, said to be written by one of the first Characters in the literary world." The "first Character" was Arthur Young (1741–1820), English reformer, travel writer, and agricultural expert. With considerable prescience, Young imagined a world "the *total* converse of the present case;—America to be the seat of government, and Britain the dependent," a world indeed turned upside down in which, he prophesied, "America" would launch an empire that would become unparalleled in world history. He compared this imagined America to the "Persian empire under Darius," the Roman empire in its utmost extent," China, the "Great Mogul's," and the Russian empire—sites of which a cosmopolitan colonist such as Dorr would have been quite knowledgeable. "None of the ancient empires therefore, nor the present one of China, which fell prey to a handful of Tartars, can be compared to this of North America, which will as surely exist, as the land is now in being that will once be trod by the first people the world ever knew," the essayist predicted.[2]

Americans such as Harbottle Dorr would have embraced the global vision that Young imagined, even if in 1772 they could have little confidence in its imminent manifestation. An empire like the one Young described would have been a magnet for the teas, spices, and silks they craved. Yet, to participate in this global economy, independent Americans had to sail to the far side of the world, navigating through the world's most daunting typhoons, pirates, and shoals. The farther a ship sailed from its home wharf, the greater the danger it was in; the farther a ship sailed from shore, the more dangers it encountered. Even when a Yankee traveler reached China's sole trading port of Canton, further challenges threatened the enterprise. To participate in the trade meant that mariners ran the risk of losing themselves in it.

An expansive, globe-girdling empire, even one that abjured colonial conquest, brought dangers. Some of these were common to both the Ottoman world and the China trade: the specter of political "tyranny" and natural calamity. Other forms of encounter seemed more particular to the China trade: extended voyages, navigational perils, tropical diseases, the vagaries of the monsoon seasons, more serious threat of domain piracy, and, especially, the specter of commercial corruption. Or so it appeared in the logs, journals, and publications that mariners produced. From their first direct contacts in August 1784 up through the First Opium War that erupted in 1839, Yankee traders, missionaries, and sojourners described China in these terms, often eliding similar experiences in other parts of the globe and in their own Atlantic backyard.

Encounters

American encounters in China began, famously then and now, in 1784, with the cruise of the *Empress of China* to Canton.[3] Independence from Britain's trade regulations and rising trade opportunities across the Indian Ocean opened the world to Yankee mariners in search of the spices, textiles, and porcelains of China.[4] Yet there was no one China that American travelers encountered, and newspaper readers found no fixed or distilled description of China in the pages of the many "voyages to . . . China" printed in the years following American independence. Each traveler's account was authentic, if subjective, and each described a China that was true to one's experience, but travelers experiences varied according to the writer's personality, the journey's purpose, and the vagaries of a voyage. They shared, however, an emotional experience common to the long-distance traveler: the sense of foreboding that prevailed aboard a ship that sailed into unfamiliar waters and that at times erupted into substantive fear and even panic. Of course, perils threatened any cruise, whether aboard a ferry crossing Philadelphia's harbor or a circumnavigation "round the world," and the essential elements of peril were as dire as they were dangerous, whether in Boston harbor, the Baltic Sea, or the Bay of Bengal.[5] Distance—nearly fourteen thousand miles, spanning four to six months from Alexandria or Philadelphia to Canton (Guangzhou)—made the loss of ship, cargo, and lives more likely and magnified a traveler's anxiety. The duration of an overseas voyage—including the repetitive days and nights of empty ocean, unpalatable food, and vile water—weakened a traveler's defenses and made him more vulnerable to the dangers of shipwreck and capture and less tolerant of the "singular" people he would encounter. After months at sea, on reaching a foreign port, travelers complained of the bustle and hurry, the overwhelming noise and confusing languages, the strange smells and tastes that left the "griffin," or green visitor, feeling disoriented.[6]

Within the pages of the merchant's daybook or the sailor's journal, all of this added up to risk. Voyages were investments—of capital or time, materials or lives. For a merchant, these investments required heavy capitalization, more than one alone could manage. A bad cruise could wipe one out. Merchants solicited investors in local newspapers, such as Boston's *Independent Chronicle*, which advertised for June 23, 1785: "Proposals for building and outfitting a ship for the East India trade. . . . Any citizen who wishes to become interested may have an opportunity. A single share is only $300." Consequently, merchants and supercargoes, in particular, were under great stress to acquire cargoes that would gain a profit in markets that were half a world away and six months in the future, and in the post-Revolution maritime world, investors were under great pressure to find men who could navigate the intricacies of global trade. Central to the task was the imperative to keep an ear to the ground and gain knowledge about complicated global forces. It was all a gamble, as investors wagered capital, sailors risked their labor and lives, and families chanced the time away of husbands and fathers and uncles against the possibility of profits that could catapult one into wealth or, at least, provide enough for a plot of land or a stake in a shop. The increased risks of sailing to China heightened the stakes, the price that would be paid if the voyage failed, and enhanced the sense of danger and a crew's sensitivity to anything that posed a threat.[7]

The expense could eat into profits and torment a travelers' thoughts, whether merchant or ordinary seaman. Merchants came to the East to earn a competency—a *lac*, as Canton merchant Nathaniel Kinsman later phrased it—that would enable a man to retire from the perils of the sea, purchase land, perhaps a farm, provide for his family, and leave something to his children.[8] Allowed a small amount of space on the *Cordelia*, seaman Charles Tyng invested in umbrellas and hoped to augment his roughly $15-per-month wages when he could find a buyer in port.[9] Even a well-to-do merchant had to economize. Sent out to Canton to handle the family's business affairs there, Sullivan Dorr summarized for his father that "to live respectably it will cost 10,000 dollars independent of factory expenses, after the ships depart; I shall have to pay 300Z) for [a] chop to get to Macao, and the same up." Dorr noted that his yearly expenses could be "lightened by 3 or 4 clubbing together, and if Consul Snow remains, [I] shall club with him and a Philadelphia Supercargo." Little had changed by 1838, when Robert Bennet Forbes reported to his wife, Rose, in Boston that he could live quite well in Canton if he "don't give parties & receive comp[any]."[10]

Forbes's genteel lifestyle was out of the reach of working-class people, but a cruise presented opportunities for them, also. To participate in the game of chance that the China trade epitomized, a working man could serve before the mast, investing his labor and time as those of an ordinary sailor, hoping to exchange in Canton a few hats or umbrellas for a bolt of nankeen that would fetch a fair price in the markets of Boston or New York. The precarity of an East Indies cruise increased the risk. The farther a ship sailed from its home wharf, the greater the danger it was in; the farther a ship sailed from shore, the more dangers it encountered. The longer a man sailed, the more the journey deprived him of his family and friends—the lament of many such as Richard Cleveland who complained, "Three years had now elapsed since I had had any accounts from home."[11]

Necessity drove people to sea. Samuel Shaw had been a Boston bookseller and officer in the "late War," but in 1784 his prospects were so poor that a voyage to China appeared the only way to salvage his career and provide for his family. Indeed, it seemed as if his family of a mother, brothers and sisters, and cousins and nephews tilted on a precipice of poverty. Two of his brothers went to sea for the same reasons and after they died there, the need for Shaw to return to sea became more pressing until he died off Cape Town. Richard Cleveland described the China-trade mariners as people "whom business shall lead to Batavia, for there can be no other inducement."[12]

Many described the experience in China as less an adventure than a sacrifice, made often in desperation, to gain a competency and entrance into the commercial community at home. As Robert Bennet Forbes described to his wife back in Boston in April 1839, "I sometimes think the ship I have taken was not justified by any state of affairs, that it was a cruel sacrifice. Then a pain comes to me & the reflection that I could only have remained home in a state of dependence, that I must have incurred obligations which could never cancel. By coming here I have done all I could to retrieve my fortunes & procure an independence."[13] The same demands fell on what would become some of the country's most eminent families. Robert Bennet Forbes made two sojourns to Canton, both necessitated by economic pressures, and complained vehemently in letters to wife Rose about his sacrifice.

There were too many ways to lose money on a voyage. Storms, hidden shoals and reefs, buccaneers and privateers, scurvy and tropical fever, and Native attacks all posed threats to the cruise.[14] All of these were beyond the view of the merchants and investors, who, like Shakespeare's Antonio in *The Merchant of Venice*, could only wait in anxiety to learn the fate of their ships, cargos, and crews. Despite every effort to protect a delicate cargo of silks and teas, moisture, rain, and salt water inevitably damaged at least a portion of the cargo.[15] The challenge for a captain was to get as much of it to port in a salable condition as possible—one which prompted many to inscribe their journals with a phrase such as, "So God send the good ship to her Desired Port in Safety. Amen." Such were the calculations of Amasa Delano, freighting skins from the Falkland Islands to Canton in 1806, writing, "But they procured between twelve and thirteen thousand skins, with which they arrived safe at Canton, though some of the skins were damaged by being wet, in consequence of the schooner being upset while entering the China seas."[16]

Predicting customer tastes was as precarious. Failure to anticipate changing tastes and fashions from one season to another could leave a merchant's cargo or sailor's adventure without a market even across the Atlantic. Advertisements were replete with phrases such as "for the season," even before independence. Initially, merchants did not expect that "primitive" and "savage" people could also disfavor goods that no longer fascinated the eye. Joseph Ingraham learned this lesson in July 1792, recording "the things which they esteemed highly when I was here before were now of little value. To my great surprise tablespoons were eagerly enquired for-articles they would scarcely accept as a gift when I was here before. For collars one skin was offered, and clothes were scarcely noticed." Consequently, on the return passage from Macao, he adapted: "All my passage from Macao I had my smith at work making daggers in every form I had seen among these people . . . had executed them vastly well indeed." Yet, even then, Ingraham "was again disappointed, for they scarcely looked at them. In short everything seemed changed, and those articles which were most valuable when I was here before were now of little or no consequence."[17]

Adding to the stress and impatience, a merchant and mariner needed to plan carefully for the season. "The proper season to leave the Malabar coast for Canton is from the first of April to the middle of May, by which means you will have sufficient time to stop in the straits of Malabar, to purchase tea, Pepper, butter, amica fruit, red canned, sea swallow (called béche de mer by the Portuguese, and Trepong by the Malays), birds nests, all of which, if well laid in, will net a handsome profit at Canton," observed William Elting in 1802. But one could not anticipate every variable or even the timing of a ship's arrival. Coming to Canton late in the fur or tea season, after other ships had flooded the market for imports or depleted the market for quality exports, could ruin a voyage's prospects, as Ingraham found in December 1791, when he "found, anyway, from minute enquiry of well informed and disinterested people that the price that sea otter skins usually fetched was no longer to be obtained." With the *Grace*, the *Gustavus*, and Dorr's *Hancock* anchored at Larks Bay and collecting pelts from the indigenous Nootka, Ingraham estimated eleven thousand furs languishing in Canton's closed market, "which may readily account for the decrease of the former price." Ultimately, the cruise of Ingraham's *Hope* lost money, and he found it difficult to secure another posting. A similar problem—overcompetition—stalked Edmund Fanning's winter sealing voyage a decade later near South Georgia Island in the South Atlantic: "As there was every reason to believe, that soon after the winter should break up, and the summer season set in, many vessels in the same pursuit would arrive. . . . When the summer season set in, seventeen sail of sealing vessels, mostly ships, with their shallops, arrived at this island." Explaining the failure of his first cruise, Delano reported, "Those who know all the circumstances said that if we had arrived at Calcutta six months sooner, or six months later than we did, we should have made a fortune"—a rationale many commanders drew on to account for a failed China voyage.[18]

American travelers tended to accept delays caused by storms or market forces as God's will, forces with which few were inclined to argue. "But hazards of this kind always exist, and we went beyond our depth, and suffered the unhappy consequences," Delano philosophized. Setbacks produced by human hindrances—assaults, stiff bargains, impractical demands, refusal to hunt—spawned blame, especially when the Other was assigned responsibility. Rarely does it seem that white Americans applied the same filter to other white people. Merchants struggled to find ways to protect against losses. From his counting house in Salem, Elias Hasket Derby, for instance, used several strategies: contracting sales of imports to a wide array of customers, working with Hamilton to create a bonded warehouse system that allowed the merchant to keep goods for months before paying taxes, and re-exporting goods to other markets. Adding to the anxiety, a merchant in Baltimore or Philadelphia might not have known how well a voyage turned out for a year or more, as it could take that long to dispose of a cargo. Even if a ship had made a profitable cruise in the China markets, shipwreck in another part of the world could spell disaster. This was the plight of merchant-captain Edmund Fanning of New York in March 1802. His *Aspasia* produced a tidy profit, wiped out by the wreck of his *Regulator*: "With her valuable cargo being all uninsured, was of course a total loss; thus creating a gap which the *Aspasia*'s voyage was not able to fill up." Fanning lamented, "Had this misfortune not occurred, the adventure would have been very profitable, and perfectly satisfactory to all concerned."[19]

Tearful adieus set the stage for the arduous cruise that would take harrowing months to complete. The Canton expatriate William C. Hunter reminds us that travel to the East was a rare occurrence still in 1820s because it was so dangerous. All knew that departure meant that friendships and relations would likely be sundered. In the early years of Western voyages to the East, the records of East India companies presaged what would become a tradition for American travelers. The August 1685 minutes of the British East India Company's Committee of Shipping noted, "It is ordered that Anna Peddy Jane Davis and Darcey Johnson have liberty to goe to their Husbands paying their Passages. And that Thomas Lewes Acquaint them that Children dye fast in those long Voyages." Documenting his departure for Canton on April 26, 1838, Sandwith Drinker offered a lament, writing, "This morning at 10 A.M., I took leave of my friends, and uncomfortable, and alone, . . . and with a heavy heart, went on board."[20]

Parting left travelers and well-wishers both in an emotional maelstrom as grisly tales flooded imaginations with thoughts of pirates, typhoons, and cannibals. Before her departure to Canton in May 1829, Harriet Low shared her fears with her "dear father," lamenting: "We have not heard of anything but shipwrecks and piracies lately. . . . I dread nothing so much as those merciless demons, and that is too good a title for them. . . . I believe I have suffered as much in anticipation as I shall in reality, for it has been the subject of my day and night dreams." For their part, Low's parents had other, no less anxious, concerns. They feared that the seduction of exotic religions could beguile her young mind and condemn her weak soul to damnation. "Multiplied and intense apprehensions" filled their imaginations with thoughts that sojourning "among a heathenish or idolatrous people, especially if intelligent, you may be led to suspect that the rigid principle of the Christian religion may be justly stigmatized as bigoted," and she be lured into darkness. Recounted in so many journals and letters, the emotional toll shaped the ways in which visitors to Canton constructed their experiences. Departure on a long-distance voyage instilled, further, a well of resentment for anyone who could be made a suitable scapegoat.[21]

Upon his return home, a traveler could expect to learn of the demise of those he had left behind, or they would hear that he would not be returning. Returning to New York on April 18, 1799, Edmund Fanning framed the cruise in terms of pathos:

> After an absence of two years from home, on a voyage around the world, or
> elsewhere, the feelings on obtaining sight of one's native land again, from
> which they have not heard during such time, are not to be expressed; thoughts
> upon a hundred different subjects fly also through the mind—a multitude
> of questions also arise, tending to give pain by the incapacity there exists
> satisfactorily to answer them—while with the utmost anxiety, the mind flies
> from one subject to another; these giving birth to others, are rapidly followed
> by those long dormant, but not forgotten remembrances of the condition in
> which all were left, hopes, doubts, fears and expectations rapidly succeeded
> each other. How will be found our near and dear relatives and friends? Who
> still remain among the living? How many, and which of them have gone on the
> long voyage of eternity? Who have been consigned to the tomb? and what shall
> we find the situation of our beloved country to be? All these questions and others,
> crowd through the mind at once, and remain unappeased until we once more
> gain the family circle, where they can be answered.[22]

Belying a romanticized literature of adventure, the most common theme revealed in China-trade letters, mariner's diaries, logs, and journals was the enervating monotony, the debilitating sameness of an extended passage. On his 1799 voyage to China, Sullivan Dorr found little to pique his interest. Writing to his father, Ebenezer, in Boston, he groused, "I kept no journal, the sea so barren of incident, and possessing so sterile an imagination shall not trouble you with the trite occurrences of the cruise."[23] Others kept journals to fill idle hours and hold boredom at bay, and these provide us with a clearer sense of the passenger's experience of a journey to China. Thirty years after Dorr's passage, Harriett Low made the same voyage aboard the ship *Sumatra*, and experienced the same ennui. Her remarkably comprehensive journal noted for Tuesday, August 11, 1829, the psychological toll the cruise took on her: "Tuesday 11 Fine wind, pleasant weather. Making our way swiftly toward Java head. I cannot realize that I am so many thousand miles from home. For almost 3 months now we have been floating on—from wave to wave we are driven—without change of scenery except of weather—my prospects of happiness all lying in the future—which is hidden."[24]

Idle hours and an unchanging horizon wore on a crew and especially passengers, who found little else to while away the time except to log their complaints into letters and diaries that would be consumed by a home audience. Dullness fostered a sense of privation, which they expressed in petulant correspondence. Amos Porter no doubt was missing the Green Mountains of his home state of Vermont in March 1803, aboard the *Penman*, bound from Canton for home, with strong winds from the north and "frequent showers of rain and unpleasant weather," which rendered him seasick. His summary of ocean travel was despondent: "Notwithstanding the many pleasant hours . . . in one of these voyages . . . there is a sufficient number of trials in the bad ones to make one sick of the sea, as well, and seasick and almost sick of life."[25] To recover a sense of orientation, travelers calculated the distance traveled, but this strategy did not always ease the feelings of loss. On his cruise to China, Nathaniel Appleton seems to have become obsessed with measuring the time away, yet gaining little comfort. In November 1797, he recorded, "We have been out but 34560 minutes & it appears to me as many ages since I left Salem."[26] Amid the tedium, home and family took on particular salience for overseas travelers whose voyages deprived them of the familiarity of hearth and neighborhood for years at a time. The loss and loneliness they experienced were a source of common commentary in their journals. "After so long a separation," Samuel Shaw reflected in 1789, "the sensations of friends so near to each other, on such a long-wished and unexpected meeting, may be better imagined than described."[27]

As the technology of shipbuilding and navigation advanced, making a cruise faster, shorter, and safer, a few passengers recorded the occurrences of the voyage "trite" or a "frolic." For Nathaniel Bowditch, who asserted, "I found the terrors of it far less than what I had an idea of," the initial experience of sailing did not match the forebodings. Beneath the monotony lay an atmosphere of tension, however. For one thing, mariners could seldom be certain where they were. Although John Harrison and other instrument makers were honing the chronometer from the 1760s on, merchants were not prone to investing in a costly, delicate, and mercurial device, even if it offered an improved method of determining longitude. Even a sextant might be an extravagance for a tight-fisted merchant. Despite Sullivan Dorr's insistence that "I would recommend putting one in every Vessel you may be concerned in, the expense being amply paid by enabling one to take advantage of a knowledge of the exactitude of his situation," the investors—his father and brothers—balked at the extravagance. Investors were indeed reluctant to invest in seaworthy vessels, and mariners urged them to demonstrate less parsimony.

Dorr's correspondence home was filled with pointed warnings against skimping on instruments, materials, and even unreliable vessels. As soon as he settled into Canton in the autumn of 1799, Sullivan Dorr wrote home with a gentle reminder: "The *Hancock* two months before they reached the coast began to leak, requiring 4 hands to the pump most of the time and Crocker cut up 6 foot of the kilson to find the leak, without so doing; its a chance if she don't break in two, he intends putting her on shore, and the *Dispatch* will accompany her; don't buy such ugly ships, if you mean to be successful in the Northwest business." So fragile were the ships that Dorr was reluctant to send home one, the *Hancock*, which he found "so wormy that perhaps she will go home, not being trust worthy."[28]

Up through the South China Sea, bearing under the Southeast or Southwest monsoon, the crew and passengers could find other hints of their approach to China. Even the vessels they observed from a distance took on a startlingly strange appearance, with their junk-shaped hulls, rattan sails, and eyes painted on the bow. Charles Tyng described his view from the deck of the *Cordelia* in 1815:

I think we were about a month on the way [from Hawai'i], and when we
approached the shores of China, we saw many of the Chinese vessels, or
"junks," as they are called, most strange looking craft, nothing like our vessels,

either in hull or rigging. The hull looks like a bunch of boards put together in a most clumsy manner, apparently open at the bow and the stern, not painted, excepting two large eyes, one on each side of the bows. The rudder is a large square thing, entirely different shape from ours. Their anchors are of wood with a big stone lashed on the crown. The stern is much higher than the forward part, it rises from the centre, something like a pair of steps, altogether a strange looking thing, at first sight, but one soon gets use to them after a while. They have one large mast a little forward of the entire centre of the vessel with a large lateen sail, curiously made of bamboo, and rushes. It seems a big unwieldy affair to a sailor. They also have another small mast on the stern, with a small sail, of similar shape as the large one, no bowsprit and no other sails than these two. All their vessels large and small, as well as their boats, have eyes painted in the bows. I asked a Chinaman why they painted eyes on their vessels. He replied, "How can see no got eye?"

Tyng's gaze described a strange place of "singular people" whose ways deviated unnervingly from the standards of civilization that he expected.[29]

China traders, from opulent merchant to ordinary Jack Tar, had more to concern themselves with than tedium. Mariners could expect to encounter "squally, dirty, disagreeable weather" anywhere, and the seaworthiness of their vessels also provoked worry.[30] A passage to China was not an ordinary voyage, however. The distances, uncertainties, and wear and tear on hull and body exacerbated the terrors of the deep. Fickle typhoons, or "typhongs," in the South China Sea, "well-fitted to inspire alarm," toyed with mariners' expectations, as Tyng observed as the *Cordelia* bore into the South China Sea. He recalled, "As it was about the change of the monsoons, which is every six months, from S.E. to S.W., it had been blowing from the east to the southeast, and now the S.W. were commencing which would be fair to Canton, and during these changes the weather is very various—calms, gales, and sometimes severe typhoons. Now it was light winds and calms, and we had a long passage to Canton River."[31] Relying on past experience or uninformed opinion could have devastating consequences. Joseph Ingraham saw it this way: "Shipwreck is often the fate of mariners, but more especially those who pass through unknown seas, which must often be the case with those who circumnavigate the globe. However they may endeavor for their safety to tread the steps of others who have preceded them, yet by various unforeseen causes they will at times fall in with dangerous shoals or lands seldom frequented and not well known. Except guided by the all seeing Eye of

Omnipotence it is impossible for the best of men to guard against every such danger which may occur."[32]

Another Bostonian, Charles Bernard, would have concurred, and described the terror that he experienced in the South China Sea: "The violence of the gale was now dangerous and terrifying. The roaring, mountainous billows appearing enraged that we had as yet escaped their power, rolled furiously towards us; their foaming tops seemed to dash their spray to the clouds, and to have united with the dense atmosphere to hide the dangers and horrors around us from the pitying eye of heaven. Our ship was lying with her lower yards in the water, and we looked every moment for the hurricane to sweep us forever from the society of the living." In such terrifying conditions, frightened sailors—"except those whose fears had paralyzed their energies"—struggled to clear a deck heaving with shattered, piercing spars, tangled rope, torn sail, and burst bulwarks, "using all possible means for the preservation of the ship, and the lives of those on board."[33]

The crew of the *Massachusetts* was reminded of the value of a seaworthy ship as they approached Macao from the South China Sea in September 1790, the beginning of the winter monsoon season. "[We] experienced a severe typhoon, split the main sail, foretop sail, and foretopmast staysail. But owing to our ship's being an excellent sea boat, we weathered the gale, and suffered only trifling damage compared with some other ships," recalled second mate Amasa Delano. The *Massachusetts* was both well-built and fortunate. "One Dutch ship was totally lost amongst the islands in Canton Bay, together with all the crew," Delano added. Not all Yankee vessels were as soundly constructed as the *Massachusetts*, however. Nine years later, Nathaniel Appleton was making a longer, less direct passage to China in the *Concord*, a lurching ship he described as "so crank that it is with difficulty you can walk the deck." Consequently, "I shall be an amphibious animal before I get home, for I live as much under water as over it, the ship is so wet." New technologies advanced the state of shipbuilding, but fifty years later Joseph Sewall recalled the terror that pervaded the USS *Saratoga* when "a delinquent spar" gave way, all hands agreeing that, "If we had had that stick aloft in the typhoon we encountered a fortnight later, very likely we should have lost our masts and gone to the bottom."[34]

Brutal storms—what Charles Barnard styled a "war of elements"—imperiled the lives of passengers and crews; from the merchant's perspective, they endangered his investment in vessels, cargoes, and equipment.[35] This was the point of view presented by merchant Sullivan Dorr to his father in 1799, when he observed, "Mr. Gray's ship of Salem met with a sad disaster in the straits of Gasper, . . . a squall took the Ship and carried away her topmasts." The timing could not have been worse. Unfamiliar with the hidden reefs and shoals of the Straits, the captain had ordered "two boats a sounding . . . and they were enabled only to take one boats crew on board leaving the mate and seamen in the other." Fortuitously, there was another ship in the vicinity, and the crew in the lost boat "were fortunately picked up in the Straits of Sunda by the *New Jersey*, and have arrived here [safely]." It was "a critical situation" for the men and the ship, but Dorr was especially disturbed that the ship had limped into Canton late in the tea season and "from their account it is impossible for the Ship to catch (as the Chinamen say) Canton this season."[36] William Elting expressed a similar conclusion about the loss of the *Ontario* in 1799, noting that the crew was taken off the ship, but "the cargo totally lost."[37]

This was Dorr's opinion when reporting to his father that the family's ship, the *Hancock*, tackling the treacherous waters off Cape Horn, had developed a leak. The crew pumped their way across the Pacific Ocean, "once in four or six hours," and anchored at Whampoa in November 1799. He relayed no information about the crew, only "this much is in case you may effect any Insurance; shall have the leak inspected, and every prudent measure taken for the preservation of her cargo home." Others were not as fortunate. In the same season, the *Nancy* was "a great loss."[38]

A ship might survive, but the effects would be traumatic and scarred even old hands, such as Joseph Ingraham. In November 1790, the Boston sea captain described a storm of "frightful thunder and lightning," clouds "in great perturbation," and "darting flashes of sharp lightning all around." It was a frightening spectacle, he recalled, "one of the most awful pictures I ever remember to have been witness to." Another tempest, striking Ingraham's *Hope* on a sealing voyage in the Falklands in 1791, "left us all in a tremor, myself in particular." Thankful that the gale had struck in a well-traveled path where rescue was possible, Ingraham apprehensively contemplated the next leg of the journey that would carry the *Hope* beyond the Land of Fire (Tierra del Fuego) and into the greater expanse of the Pacific: "Such an accident at some period of a voyage round the globe would unavoidably end in the destruction of the vessel and crew ere they could reach a port where the damage might be repaired," he fretted. Friends and loved ones shared in the loss and their memories contributed to the sense that the world posed awful dangers to travelers. A decade after his brother Thomas was swept into the Pearl River in a typhoon, Robert Bennet Forbes passed the spot and confessed to his wife Rose in Boston, "I can not help feeling a little dull though the long years have elapsed since that fatal gale. Ten years ago to day or yesterday perhaps, the remains of that Brother were deposited in their present home. That when he died we were just beginning to feel like Brothers, has always been a source of great uneasiness to me." One did not have to have weathered a typhoon or lost a loved one in a storm to feel shaken, as Forbes knew. When he returned to Macao in 1838, he learned that just a week earlier "there happened a hard ty-fong in which an English ship foundered with all her crew and one large junk besides several minor damages." He confided philosophically to his wife, Rose, "its uncertain my dear whether we are going too slow or too fast in this world." These were the tales that would inspire later writers such as Joseph Conrad to chronicle "adventures in the South Pacific."[39]

Old hands adapted, learning the gales and currents driven by the seasonal monsoons of the South China Sea, following ancient routes pioneered by Chinese, Indian, and even Arab traders to Malacca and beyond. Chinese traders, likewise, used these winds to send their trading junks to Taiwan and to the Philippines, where, Nathaniel Bowditch reported, one could find the "great numbers" of Chinese junks dominating the indigo trade at Manila the beginning of the year.[40] In March, dry monsoon winds blew out of the northeast, and in the 1780s Yankee captains began to take advantage of these to venture out of Canton into the Indian Ocean. By midsummer, the winds of the southwest monsoon rose up out of the Indian Ocean, bringing drenching rains—as much as thirty inches of precipitation over two months—and propelling the sails that would carry ships back to China. Ambitious traders such as William Elting frequently weathered these late autumn winds, taking his chances to squeeze out more profit: "In the trade on the Malay coast requires you to stay as long as possible." Elting had mastered the tactic of sheltering under the lee side of Sunting Island if the seas grew too rough. Others learned to simply comply with the monsoon winds, as the *Cordelia* did in the straits east of Java, "which made our passage longer, which was a little over one hundred days," sailor Charles Tyng conceded. Many would not take the risk. As one captain's clerk observed in 1852, it was an "unlucky cruise" that was "timed with the autumnal change of monsoon." In its voyage to Japan in 1853, the flagship *Mississippi* under Commodore Matthew Perry followed a circuitous course to keep the ship away from hurricanes that swept the Indian Ocean in the early part of year.[41]

As a vessel flying the "flowery flag" of the United States, what Chinese observers could discern from a distance as the American pennant, neared the

Ladrone Islands and Chinese shores, ironically, further dangers threatened its passage. The timing was especially problematic. During the period of 1780–1810, the fledgling United States was struggling to establish its economic footing, and leading American merchants turned their eyes to the Indies and China trades.[42] As David Armitage, Eliga H. Gould, and others describe, the consciousness of the emerging nation was expansive and open to the world, careful to demonstrate "a decent respect to the opinions of mankind" and anxious "to assume [its station] among the powers of the earth."[43] But the new people lacked a navy or even the finances to build one, enhancing their sense of national impotence. During these years, as the threat posed by Barbary corsairs increased and privateers, licensed by protagonists in the French Revolution, roamed the Indian Ocean, complicating the recovery and insulting national honor, organized piracy was in resurgence along the coasts of the South China Sea and Malay Archipelago, and out of Taiwan and Japan, even invading the Pearl River.[44] To all, seagoing buccaneers were "the scourge of the Eastern seas" and "the enemies of all mankind."[45]

During most of the period between 1790 and 1810, the southern and southeastern coasts of China were under the grip of powerful pirates who controlled the flow of traffic to the sea. The South China Sea and East Indies were congenial places for pirates. As late as the 1850s, John S. Sewell proclaimed, "If any part of the world might seem to have been originally designed for a pirates' paradise, the southern coast of China is the place."[46] Indeed, the organized piracy of the East surpassed even the state-sponsored buccaneering of the Mediterranean. Bribing officials, conniving with local rulers, and building fleets that intimidated even the imperial navy, Chinese corsairs often operated in the "space between" peaceful activities such as trade or fishing and synchronized assaults on merchant shipping.[47] Many of these *wokou* were Chinese traders who had turned to piracy in response to the Ming and Qing prohibitions against their own subjects' participation in overseas commerce.[48] Chinese pirates colluded with Tâyson rebels in Vietnam and later Bugis buccaneers to pour pillaging fleets out on villages and ships, and even "Japanese" pirates were known to attack unsuspecting ships in these waters, although many were actually Chinese crafts in disguise. In the Guangdong (Kwangtung) province, by 1805, a confederation of seventy thousand men ravaged the seas in two thousand vessels. A lull followed the defeat of the pirate fleets in 1810, but from the 1830s through the 1850s, sporadic attacks on Western vessels resumed. The summer and winter monsoons determined when these fleets sailed, as they did for indigenous raiders from Sumatra,

Java, Borneo, Malacca, and the Celebes. This latter arena centered on the slave marts of Jolo in the Sulu Sea and the islands of Riau and Lingga above the Sunda Straits.[49]

Piracy did not remain contained around the Ladrone Islands. Rather, it invaded the Pearl River and kept American mariners in a state of near constant anxiety. As Dian Murray notes, "Repeated pirate occupations of the Pearl River severed communication between Guangzhou (Canton) and Macao and disrupted the trade." In 1802, when Amos Porter visited Canton to sell a shipment of ginseng, the city was under martial law. Guangzhou's governor, known to China traders as John Tuck, imposed a curfew, and police searched everyone entering the city's gates. Tuck attempted to torture his captives, who would only reveal that their leaders hid within the walls of Canton itself. Ordering the imperial navy to sail out to fight the pirates, he soon found his fleet "surrounded by 30 or 40 thousand insurgents" and had to call for reinforcements. Consequently, even these severe measures did not bring the stable conditions that *fang quai* merchants needed.[50]

Americans blamed the imperial government for the eruption of lawlessness that threatened American lives and trade. Harsh measures, misguided policies, and ineffectual results seemed reminiscent of the conditions they found frustrating under King George III, and they hoped for more from the Chinese emperors. By early 1810, the *Salem Gazette* and other American papers were posting warnings from Canton:

> The Ladrones are disaffected to the Chinese government, and are daily increasing in power, are very daring, making frequent excursions up the rivers, burning and plundering the villages, and massacring all that attempt to resist them. Their force at sea, is estimated from 900 to 1000 junks, of from 3 to 28 guns and powerfully manned—their connections and abetters on shore, are much more numerous and widely disseminated through the maritime provinces, who amply supply the rebels with provisions and ammunition. The efforts to suppress them by the Vice-Roy of Canton, is feeble, and of no effect, he having no confidence in those he sends against them, as they are as often inclined to act with the Ladrones, as against them—so wide is the disaffection spread, that the lower order of the Mandarins are not to be trusted with executing the orders of Government.[51]

By 1805, as the Jefferson administration was intent on reducing its own navy to a coastal fleet of gunboats, an armada lurked around the Ladrone Islands, perched at the very entrance to the Pei-ho River. Some seventy thousand men in four hundred ships made up the "red fleet" of the Ladrone freebooters, or Ladrones, as Europeans called them. What made this navy so frightening to Yankee seamen was its leader and its purpose: a pirate fleet under the female leader Shi Yang upset the American desire for free trade and female subordination. In August 1809, her pirates posted notices around threatening to attack the city itself. In response, American shipmasters and merchants joined their European counterparts in paying protection money to ensure safe passage.[52]

Still, capture was possible. The travails of John Turner, first mate aboard an English country ship in 1807, were common knowledge on the China Coast, and reached American bookshops in 1814 as *A Narrative of the Captivity and Sufferings, of John Turner, First Officer of the ship John Jay, of Bombay, among the Ladrones of Pirates.* Turner recounted some rather gruesome practices, "peculiar horrors" and "shocking treatment," that captives endured, and, no doubt, American readers shared his reflection that "their cruelty . . . has made an indelible impression on my mind." Disturbing, also, were the reasons why the pirates found it easy to recruit volunteers. As Turner wrote: "Some of these were, doubtless, vagabonds, induced by poverty and idleness to embrace this criminal mode of life, but many were men of decent appearance, and some of whom brought money with them. The only reason I heard them assign for their conduct, was that the Mandarins of their district, were unjust and they came there to avoid their oppression."[53]

American vessels were just as vulnerable to the Ladrone pirates, as a young Boston captain learned two years later. William Sturgis likely felt secure as his vessel, *Atahualpa*, lay anchored in Macao roadstead in 1809.[54] A British East India Company fleet of twelve Indiamen and several Royal Navy warships, including a sixty-four-gun man of war, *St. Albans*, were anchored at Chumpee.[55] Another cruised off the Straits of Sunda. Yet, on August 18, twenty Ladrone junks attacked the *Atahualpa*, while observers watched from shore. Captain Sturgis was able to ward off the pirates and maneuver the ship to safety. Although the New York papers tried to reassure readers that "there is not the least danger" for Yankee ships that sailed in consort, a sense of danger lurked beneath the headlines. The imperial government, "so arbitrary and oppressive to its subjects," appeared "supine" before the pirate threat.[56]

The traditions of buccaneering in Southeast Asia, reaching back for centuries, were certain to offend America's republican sensibilities. Appropriating traditions of tribal war, Eastern sultans and "datus" employed pirates to enhance their authority, measuring their power in numbers of slaves rather than miles of territory and asserting the legitimacy of treachery, deceit, trickery, and pillaging as political tactics. In response, journals such as the *Gazette of the United States* celebrated Yankees' defense of their ships and opposed these Eastern traits to American courage and determination. In May 1789, the *Gazette* chronicled one such attack and cheered, "Capt. Metcalfe, in the brig Eleanor, belonging to New York, lying in the river Tigris, was boarded we understand by a number of Chinese banditti; but by the spirited conduct of the crew, who brought a gun, loaded with grape, to bear on them, they were repulsed with the loss of some of their gang."[57]

Toward the end of this century and into the next, popular historians such as Charles E. Trow, Ralph D. Paine, and James Duncan Phillips would extol these incidents as adventures constituting "a record of American achievement." Many readers were taken in by this romanticized version of things. But others, and particularly those who read about them, drew a lesson in terror and danger that defined this part of the world then and later.[58]

Nature's perils did not subside even when a vessel dropped anchor at Whampoa Reach, some sixty miles up the Pearl River and just a dozen miles below Canton. Instead, threats took on different, more confounding forms. China suffered from pestilence, even as its 350,000,000 people saw historic prosperity by the eighteenth century, as did much of the world throughout the years from 1300 through 1800. In the late eighteenth century, a form of bubonic plague, quite different from the pathogens that have historically bred in farming environments and to which the population had built up immunities, struck China.[59]

Some Yankee visitors found the climate debilitating; others found it killing. At a time when the Little Ice Age lowered temperatures around the globe and people were inured to cooler climate regimens, the letters that Asiatic travelers sent home groused about the heat of "this unhospitable climate."[60] That most Yankee mariners hailed from the northeastern states, where cold temperatures penetrated even into the summer months, gave their accounts a particular salience.[61] William C. Hunter, a Russell & Co. partner who spent three decades in Canton, filled his notebooks with observations on Canton's heat, with entries noting "the thermometer at 96 [degrees] in the cool" and "the thermometer then stood daily at from 90 to 96 in the shade." When Sullivan Dorr arrived in Canton in September 1799, one of his first impressions was the effects of the climate on Western residents. "The thermometer half the Year is up from 84 to 100, sufficient in time to warp the strongest constitution." In May 1819, just three years after New England's 'year without a summer," John

White of Salem recorded at Mintow, off Sumatra, "The thermometer at noon stood at 80°, and in the afternoon we had a squall from the south-west with heavy rain." Even East India Company residents who had adapted to the climate "look like so many bread and water fed Gentry." Company physician C. T. Downing would have concurred. Based along the Pearl River in the 1820s and 1830s, he observed, "As all the parts of China to which Europeans have access are within the Tropic of Cancer, the heat during a part of the year is excessive. At the time when the south-west monsoon prevails, from April to October, when the wind comes directly from the hottest quarter, the thermometer rises frequently as high as 96° or 100° in the shade, and every means must be used to protect the body from the burning rays of the sun."[62] The effects, he concluded, were dangerous: "The constitution of Europeans is not fit to bear up against the oppressive heat of the summer season, and they, therefore, feel weak and languid, especially if they have in addition been residing on the coasts of India before their arrival in China." For his part, Dorr hoped that "with care one may be able to weather the climate."

One strategy for staying healthy was moderation in everything. One had to exercise vigilance, as ordinary pleasures could weaken an immune system and make one susceptible to tropical diseases. En route to Canton, Charles Tyng described his dining strategy at a party in Batavia: "Mr. Paine sat at the head of the table. Behind him stood a servant with a large fan, the handle resting on the floor, made of peacock feathers, which he kept twisting one way and the other, so that by both operations there was quite a cool breeze passing through the room. Wine passed freely of several kinds, and they all drank glass after glass. I was on my guard, for the little brandy and water I took when I first arrived was enough to warn me to take no more."[63]

East Asia's climate was not just uncomfortable; the stifling heat and humidity, and the rapid transitions between cold and arid air, produced tropical fevers that filled the graveyards of the "outside barbarians." Physicians such as Downing maintained that Western visitors died in droves because their "unsuitable apparel" was inappropriate for the climate. Disease was not as prevalent in the expatriate communities of East Asia as in the Ottoman Empire, but tropical fever felled many visitors who displayed an inability to adapt to Canton's climate. Too many letters homeward read like one sent by Rebecca Kinsman in 1846, reporting the death of John Roger of Salem: "He died at Woosung the port of Shanghai of fever, and my husband has the melancholy duty to perform the giving the information of this sad event to his friends at home. Death performs his work faithfully everywhere, with you & with us, one is taken here another there, may we also be ready."[64]

China—indeed all of Southeast Asia—was a great killing field for the *fan quai,* or "outside barbarians" who filled the expatriate neighborhoods of Canton and Macao. In Singapore, a British missionary advised prospective Americans, "You are aware that no American constitution could [survive] working in the field" in Southeast Asia, a sentiment that justified African American enslavement in Georgia, South Carolina, and Mississippi. No one, rich or poor, was immune. On his second voyage to China in 1786 in the optimistically named *Hope,* Samuel Shaw's business partner Isaac Sears barely survived past Batavia and died almost immediately upon reaching Macao. Shaw's last visit was curtailed when he contracted tropical fever in India and died at the Cape of Good Hope in 1794. Two years later, Captain John Tucker, Master of the *Light Horse,* out of Salem, succumbed. He had been "retired from service for some years. He was induced by Mr. Derby's persuasion and probably the strong argument of the sum of $3000, being a large amount for that day, influenced him to undertake the voyage but it cost his life. He was attacked by the climate fever at the Isle of France from which he did not recover but lingered on the return voyage and died at home in March, 1788."[65]

Tropical fever took the lives of Salem merchants William Henry Low in 1834 and Nathaniel Kinsman in 1847. Thomas Handasyd Cabot, cousin of the privileged Forbes family, sailed to Canton with John Murray Forbes at age nineteen and died of smallpox at age twenty-one. Like so many others, his remains added to the Protestant cemetery in Macao. More susceptible were the ordinary sailors whose diet and labor routines made them targets for the pathogens of the South China Sea. Dr. Downing observed,

> The common sailors in the ships lying at Whampoa are the most subject to the disease, and many circumstances tend to debilitate them, and thus render them liable to be attacked by the endemic maladies of the place. . . . After toiling in the noonday unloading the vessel, they suddenly, when the cargo is all delivered, are reduced from a state of great activity to one of almost absolute quietude. For, when the ship is painted and the hold put to rights, there is nothing left for them to do which requires active exertion. The want of exercise is shown to be one of the principal causes of the attack of ague, from the fact, that during the whole time after delivering the cargo, intermittent fevers are very prevalent, but, as soon as the teas come down and the stowing commences, there is scarcely a case to be found on board that ship.[66]

Interspersed within entries of ships logs that recorded latitude and longitude, winds and currents, and other commonalties of an ocean passage, one could find rhythmic notations of fever, scurvy, and death. They filled the diary of mariner John Richards Child, who noted, for instance, the deaths of a boatswain and captain William Dorr at Whampoa in 1813. And they filled the *Narrative* of Captain Amasa Delano, who recorded the loss of Daniel Malcomb: "died and was thrown overboard in the Straits of Sundra, 1791." In his popular 1817 account of three voyages from Boston "round the world," Delano famously produced a three-page chart that detailed the fate of the officers and crew who had sailed aboard the *Massachusetts*, bound for Canton, in 1790. Of the sixty-one men, forty-eight (78 percent) were no longer living, many having died from disease and accidents at sea. The East, especially, had been a dangerous place for American mariners. They had "died at Macao" and "died at Canton," were "lost overboard off Japan" or "murdered by the Chinese near Macao." Their remains were scattered across the East, "buried ... outside of Batavia roads," "buried under the walls of Macao," and "thrown overboard in the Straits of Sunda." The fatalities of ships' officers were somewhat lower, but still daunting. In September 1802, at the start of Canton's tea season, two Yankee captains succumbed to tropical fever. With thirteen vessels in port, this represented 15 percent of the total. Officer, crewman, or passenger, all likely received the Episcopal rites that were standard aboard Yankee vessels.[67]

At sea, scurvy and smallpox decimated crews with remarkable efficiency. Yet conditions in port were as bad. The Doctor explained,

> The country, as has been mentioned, is for miles on either side of the Canton
> river low and swampy, and very properly laid out in paddy-fields, as the rice
> requires for its proper cultivation, a great deal of moisture and a very considerable degree of heat. But that which is so necessary for the health, and in fact
> for the existence of the vegetable, is highly injurious to the animal. While we
> see the grain flourishing, and rearing its head with strength and vigor above
> the surface, we find man depressed and too often sinking beneath it. This
> applies of course only to the foreigners; the Chinese are, like the paddy,
> indigenous to the country and therefore habituated to the climate; but the
> stranger seems faint and depressed, and out of his proper element.[68]

One could not help but fret about one's health and the dangers posed to it in a tropical climate. As Charles Tyng ruminated on his own bout with cholera, he concluded that this was a miserable way to die: "How very lonesome it is to be sick at a hotel in a foreign country. How long were the days and nights, I might say nights, for it was so dark during the so-called day, that the gas had to be kept burning to see across the room."[69]

The semitropical ecosystem spawned other kinds of problems, and these could be equally dangerous. William C. Hunter, an old China hand, described the infestation of cobras throughout Canton, Macao, and Hong Kong. Pak-Hak-Shay, as his Chinese servants named the "very venomous snake, with black and white or yellow transverse bands," were especially prolific after monsoon rains. As Hunter recalled, they were "washed into the river by heavy rains, [and] carried by the water to the Square. In the rainy season this would be frequently overflowed to a depth of twelve or more inches, up to the gates of and inside the factories, where the snakes thus found their way." Breaching the factory walls, they could move from room to room. Once bitten, a victim could expect to survive only a few hours.[70]

The first stop for merchant vessels would be Macao. A peninsula on the edge of the Celestial Kingdom, Macao had become an outpost for the foreign community, but by September, most foreign merchants would have returned to Canton or were in preparation for leaving, part of the ebb and flow that made life in China seem unstable. American crews could make out the three-hundred-year-old fortress, government buildings, and churches—ruined remnants from a time when Portuguese galleons ruled the oceans and, in 1557, defeated a vast pirate fleet in the South China Sea. Portugal's reward from a grateful Chinese emperor, and a singular concession to "outside barbarians," was the freedom to occupy Macao. The Portuguese had chosen well. Protruding from the end of the peninsula into the South China Sea, the sole European jurisdiction within the Celestial Empire offered a "Mediterranean, even Moorish aspect to the maritime gate to China," still described as a place of "extraordinary beauty." As historian Jacques M. Downs tells us, "To weary sailors, the lush green vegetation, the Praya Grande arching eastward toward the bay, and the swarm of small boats racing to be first at shipside" provided relief from months of boredom and work.[71]

Americans were immediately drawn into a befuddling system of rules and requirements. Upon anchoring in Macao Roads, a flotilla of sampans and boats swarmed toward the ship, filled with men who "clamored" to be selected as comprador, an on-site ship's steward. As William Elting recalled, "When you make the land & are near the Ladrones, a Chinese pilot will come on board to carry you into Macao Roads, bringing the ship to anchor. The pilot will then go on shore, to report to the head mandarin at Macao of what nation you are: should there be any women on board, application must be made to the Bishop & Synod of Macao, for leave to put them on shore, and they will not be permitted to go up to Whampoa in the ship."[72]

After a voyage of six months or more, the captain, officers, supercargo, crew, and passengers were anxious to get ashore. Supercargoes such as Elting had business to get to— indeed, getting down to business was the whole point of the journey—and were especially impatient to get to Canton. His sense of urgency would not be met with a complementary efficiency from the hoppomen, or customs officers, however, and he complained, "As soon as the mandarins at Macao are satisfied in all their enquiries, he orders of a river pilot, who never comes on board until you have laid 24 hours in the road, and brings a chop (a license) to pass the Bocca Tigris the mouth of the Canton river, [illegible] the ship to Whampoa."[73]

In Captain Edmund Fanning's 1833 travelogue, *Voyages Round the World*, American readers vicariously experienced the frustrations that an American merchant could expect to encounter in the labyrinth of Chinese regulations. In his August 1798 landing at Macao, as Fanning told his audience, "for a commencement I was met by an unexpected difficulty, and one that at first was like to have caused a vast deal of trouble before it was removed." Fanning was astonished to learn that, having earlier rescued survivors of an English wreck off Tinian Island, he would not be allowed to carry them upriver to Canton because several of his charges were women. Despite repeated efforts, he lamented, "Nothing was sufficient to induce these officers to vary or make any allowance for a case (as this) not contemplated by their laws. Afraid of having his head taken off, the mandarin always replied, 'It no have China custom; how can, do.'" Throughout the anecdote is the implication that Fanning has entered a commercial Wonderland in which his republican vision would be "Not much enlightened, or greatly pleased with this sublime reasoning, [and] rather heavy hearted at so dark a beginning." Even after the impasse was negotiated, Fanning discovered that further obstacles would hamper his progress, and that only "after a series of tedious and vexatious examinations at five chop houses on the way up, I arrived in three hours time." Fanning returned in September 1801 to find that the Western impetus for progress and change had had little effect on Eastern traditions: "Everything was moving forward as usual; the same routine, the same regulations, not an alteration or improvement to be observed: the Chinese are a peculiar people in this respect, and tenaciously adhere to old customs and forms." C. Toogood Downing advised his readers that the illiberal restrictions had not loosened by 1838, although "Attempts have lately been made . . . to traffic with the natives in various inlets along the coast, but without success. Prejudice has assisted the action of the laws, in preventing all intercourse with strangers, but that allowed by the despotic government of the Celestial Empire." China not only failed Western expectations of "progress"; the empire was "stagnant" when compared to empires such as that of the Ottomans, "important changes [have] already taken place in the oriental character and feelings; and new causes are daily springing into operation, which will necessarily render these changes not only permanent, but progressive." What was the source of this "inefficiency" and lack of "enterprise"? Americans traced it back to the corruption of the mandarins, averse to making waves that would imperil their revenues.[74]

After months at sea, on reaching a foreign port, weary, anxious travelers, their nerves stretched, found themselves overwhelmed by the rituals of arrival. Under such conditions, travelers did not hold a particularly charitable disposition toward the greeters and gawkers, the compradors and mandarins who inhabited the wharves of Macao. Yankee voyagers frequently recalled that their first impression of China was one of bewilderment. The commotion of activity, a babble of languages, a confusion of rules, an onslaught of strange sights ricocheted into an exaggeration of what they had experienced in other ports. They complained of the bustle and hurry, the overwhelming noise and confusing languages, the strange smells and tastes that left the "griffin," or green visitor, feeling disoriented. Adding to the confusion as the ship moved upriver, more men seeking a position would be encountered at the central anchorage at Whampoa Reach and at Canton. Arriving at Macao on Tuesday, September 29, 1829, after a tiresome voyage of four months, "an immense quantity of Boats in which whole families live indeed 2 or 3 [illegible]" astonished Harriet Low. She reported back to her family sights that were unimaginable in the streets of Brooklyn, scenes that inverted fundamental ideas of family and gender: "The women steer the boats and frequently have an infant slung to her back. The common mode of carrying children among the poor class and the poor little thing only has a shaking if it cries. They sometimes use their children very cruelly." For Low, this China was strange, and in ways that prompted the disgust of a refined, antebellum middle-class woman.[75]

Travelers needed news, and, armed with letters of introduction or instruction, they sought out contacts in the Western business community. They found quarters, caught up on rumors of war, revolution, or typhoon, and, of greatest consequence, gleaned what news they could about business conditions here and at home. Here, they could reunite with old friends, who provided credible news and advice. As Joseph Ingraham of Boston described his 1791 arrival at Macao, "For convenience in transacting my business I was under the necessity of taking part of a house in Macao, which I did with my friend Captain Coolidge." Here, too, foreign captains were required to report their arrival at the custom house, which they learned was called a chophouse, to receive a "chop," or permit, to continue upriver to Canton, sixty miles upriver. They likely had their first introductions to one or more mandarins, the Manchu imperial officials infamous for their haughty bearing and fastidious preoccupation with propriety. The captain or supercargo contracted with local Chinese merchants to provide services and furnish supplies. Here, too, the captain arranged for a pilot to guide the vessel up to the mouth of the Pearl River.[76]

Ostensibly, these local guides were experts in maneuvering through the shoal waters that led into the Boca Tigris. In fact, the consensus among American crews who had just sailed half the globe was that these "outside pilots" were useless. Yet an imperial edict dictated compliance. For a tightfisted Yankee such as Captain Benjamin Shreve, who paid $60 for a pilot to take the *Governor Endicott* upriver in 1819, these earliest impressions of China, then, invoked a strange, fantastical, and somewhat corrupt land. The Celestial Empire was, he believed, a place in which one was required to hire incompetents. For a green hand such as Charles Tyng, first impressions likewise created a sense of the fantastic:

> We sailed up the Yellow Sea, on which Canton is situated, or I should say in which the river empties on which Canton is situated, and finally saw the land, which was not very high, and as we drew near, a pilot boat came alongside and put a pilot aboard, to me quite a curiosity, with his shaved head, excepting his long queue hanging down behind, and his curious dress. It was quite a funny sight to me. His shows and cap took my fancy. He was as great a sight to me as I was to the Sandwich Island Indians.[77]

From Macao, the vessel sailed fifty miles up the Pearl River to its destination at Whampoa Reach. And with each mile the Pearl seemed to fill with ever more boats, bustle, and commotion. The profusion and variety of watercraft awed English physician C. Toogood Downing, who recalled, "Nothing strikes the stranger with more astonishment on his first visit to China, than the almost endless variety of craft which is seen upon the river."[78]

They next passed Ling Ting, or Lintin Island, recognized by its singular promontory, known as the Solitary Nail. By the 1820s, Lintin was the anchorage for opium store ships, floating warehouses. Opium clippers such as the *Frolic* and the *Red Rover*, whose whimsical names belied a nefarious operation, their holds filled with chests of Mawha opium, sailed from India, directly for the isolated site. Ahead loomed the imperial fortresses on either side of the river, built to project the empire's power against any who would dare to intrude. The Portuguese had dubbed the site the Bogue, or Bocca Tigris, the Tiger's Mouth, but what Americans saw were the decaying shambles. Charles Tyng was one who found the sight undaunting, and years later he recalled, "We entered the mouth of the river, between two fortifications, one on each side, singularly formed, being built on the side of the hills, which sloped gradually to the edge of the river. They were in shape of a half circle, the circle part being up the hill, and the straight part along the river, where the cannon were placed, all surrounded by a white wall, so that the whole interior of the forts could be seen as we sailed by. Any kind of an armed vessel could destroy such fortifications in short order by shot and shells."[79]

At the Bogue, ship's officers prepared to meet more customs officials, either taking a boat to one of the forts that dominated the passage or ordering the mates to reef sails to await the mandarins' visit aboard the ship. They were now at the gates of China proper, in an interior administrative district, and the genteel world of Manchu officialdom. Introductions were followed by a ritual repast, perhaps tea, sweetmeats, and liquor. Shrewd Yankees saw all as a façade for further dunning, however. The Hoppo's agents demanded payment for another chop, one that would allow the ship along the next leg of its passage. In 1816, Charles Barnard described the tidewaiters as "Pharisee-like, [who] compel all to pay their 'tythe of mint, anise, and cinnamon.'" Adding to these complications, arrangements for pilots who had the expertise to guide a ship upriver were necessary. Licensed, professional, and skilled, this cadre was not only of a different set from the estuary guides but, fortunately, also of a different caliber. American navigators frequently complimented their expertise. Under their careful watch, the vessel then sailed upriver to Whampoa anchorage, some thirteen miles below Canton.[80]

Such was the way things were done in China. Americans learned to master the intricacies of customs, expectations, assumptions, rules, and regulations that characterized the China trade, but not without reporting their own abiding frustration. The "new people" prided themselves on their pragmatism and informality, and, so, Chinese adherence to arcane forms and precedents often befuddled American travelers. Patience could be rewarded with measured regard. William Elting learned this lesson about 1803, explaining, "The captains and supercargoes are allowed as a great favor, to wear a flag in their boats, which serves as a pass to there, without being obliged to stop at the different Hoppo houses, but all other boats must stop to be searched and have their chops examined." Such indulgences were an exception to the capricious rules of the mandarins, however, and Americans often chafed at what they saw as a frustratingly slow tempo. Elting expressed his dismay that in the thirteen miles from Canton to Whampoa, one encountered "five Hoppos, or chop houses, which to call and stop at, are very troublesome particularly if in haste to reach town." He was not alone in thinking the attention to form as an interference with more important values such as efficiency. Arriving at Macao in August 1838, and anxious to get a head start on the tea season, Sandwith Drinker paid a cumshaw, or bribe, to make the passage upriver without securing authorization from the customs officials. His journal recorded a narrow escape from the Hoppo's dragon boats:

> A little after sunset we entered the Bocca Tigris, passing the numerous Forts, erected there, and during which our cautious Chinese Captain, stowed us away under hatches covering the same with mats, ropes, etc. lest we should be discovered by the celestial cruisers. (No Chinese boat is allowed to take a foreign passenger without a special permit from a Mandarin.) But with all our precautions we were suspected: We were now well nigh to the last Fort, and just as we arrived abreast of it, we descried a Mandarin Boat, in full chase of us, pulling bout 30 oars. The first glimpse of them fired the hearts of our crew, consisting of about twelve in number, who being well aware of the penalty for having foreigners on board, were plying their oars with superhuman strength. But with all their efforts, we could perceive they overhauled us rapidly. A few more minutes during which nothing was to be heard but the hard breathing of our crew, as they toiled at their oars. Suddenly they set up a hardy and triumphant cheer of victory. We jumped up and to our great satisfaction, found that they had given o'er the chase.[81]

What an American saw on approaching the island of Huangpo, or, in the garbled pidgin of Western visitors, Whampoa, varied according to season and era. An exquisite eight-story pagoda topped the island and Western vessels anchored in the bay, ranging in size from hulking 1,200-ton Indiamen to modest Yankee schooners. By the 1840s, in high trading season, the masts of a hundred Indiamen might loom over the island.[82]

At Whampoa, Americans were initiated into a new community, with different figures and personages, different rules. The eagle did not always mix well with the dragon, and the new people often found strange or tiresome the need to follow the entrenched traditions of "olo custom." As a vessel dropped anchor, her captain waited for the creaking machine of imperial bureaucracy to move into operation. In the early days of the China trade, this might have required an audience aboard ship with the Hoppo. Customs checks had become conventional practice throughout the ports of the early modern world. In China, however, there were uncertainties and surprises. Historian Robert Peabody describes the ritual this way: "Soon after a vessel arrived at Whampoa, and before she could open her hatches and discharge any cargo, the famous ceremony of 'Cumsha and measurement' had to be performed by the Hoppo himself. At such times, the Hoppo, or 'harpoo,' came down to Whampoa from Canton in his barge, accompanied by his attendants, together with the Hong merchant acting as security for the ship." Charles Tyng, ever a careful observer, described the action from the ordinary seaman's perspective:

> We finally arrived at Whampoa, and came to an anchor. Very soon a large "harpoo" boat came alongside and made fast to the side of the after part of the ship, also a comprador's boat. . . . The harpoo boat is more of a custom house affair, it is curiously built, has in the middle a room covered with a circular bamboo top. This is for the mandarin, or custom house officer. He has a little table in the center, with his writing materials, as he signs all the papers connected with the discharge or loading of cargoes. These papers are called "chops." This part of the boat is entirely devoted to him. The after part of the boat is one story higher, also covered with a bamboo cover. There are two or three China men, or women, who have charge, and live quite comfortably. I very soon formed an acquaintance with them, and they were always very kind to me. They would make a nice omelet, which I liked, and I learned to count in the Chinese language, which I have not forgotten to this day.[83]

On their first voyages, Americans could hope to learn the intricacies of the customs rules from European residents; within a decade, more trusted countrymen could provide guidance. This was a fortunate situation for captains such as Nathaniel West, who commanded Elias Hasket Derby's *Grand Turk* from Salem in 1786. The *Hope*, out of New York, had arrived just ahead of the Turk, and aboard was Major Samuel Shaw, who had served as supercargo—a vessel's commercial agent—with the *Empress of China* when she had made the first American landfall in Canton in 1784 and who was back in China as the recently appointed first US consul. Shaw explained the peculiarities of doing business in Canton. Under the Eight Regulations issued by the emperor, West would first have to find a Hong merchant to act as agent for the vessel, certainly an arrangement preferable to the risks in the less established markets that Charles Endicott found in Sumatra or Nathaniel Bowditch in Manila. Shaw recommended Pinqua, with whom he had dealt, and he made the necessary introductions. He also found a comprador to provision the *Grand Turk* while the ship anchored at Whampoa. With the arrival of the Hoppo, they learned that the intricacies of trade included an elaborate fee structure: 100 percent cumshaw; 50 percent "Hoppo's opening barrier fee"; 10 percent to superintendent of the treasury; 10 percent for "transport of duty to Peking and weighing in Government scales"; 7 percent to cover difference in weights between Canton and Peking; and one-fifth of 1 percent "for work of converting." Only after Pinqua signed a bond guaranteeing payment did the Hoppo then issue the required "permit to open hatches."[84]

The payment of port fees was galling to Americans. Benjamin Shreve laid out $4,000 for measurement and cumshaw for the *Governor Endicott* in May 1820. Salem merchant Elias Hasket Derby found Canton's port fees exorbitant, and by 1790 he concentrated his trading voyages in the Indian Ocean. To Shreve and Derby, the Hoppo personified both the confusion and corruption of the East and a counter to the republican values their new nation represented. William Elting, trying to earn his competency in the China trade between 1797 and 1803, believed that the term *Hoppo* was applied to the official who sought to constrain Western traders and to use his position to extort cumshaw from them. The Hoppo also assigned the customs boats that conveyed his officials and guarded the Indiamen to prevent smuggling. Unlike anywhere else in the world, Hoppo boats were stationed at the bow and stern of a ship anchored at Whampoa. Hovering over all and getting into everything, were the Hoppo's officials, who weighed each piece of cargo before it could be offloaded into the boats bound for Canton, then weighed again. The weights rarely agreed, Elting complained, because the watermen engaged in "chicanery" and were "so very dexterous at the trade of embankment." Consequently, he advised installing "three men of the ship's company in each boat, to prevent plundering because "despite of your [illegible] care, they will steal a great deal." In his 1809 visit, Thomas Ward of Salem complained, "there is no villainy that they will not be guilty of if possible." Seven years later, Captain Charles Bernard could verify Ward's complaint, describing an aborted evening burglary even as the ship *Trumbull* was departing Whampoa.[85]

The comprador was an essential cog in what Americans described as an engine of corruption. Always a male, he was the local intermediary who procured provisions and services for a ship and crew anchored at Whampoa and for the Western residents who lodged upriver at Canton. Tyng remembered: "the comprador is a very important personage, every vessel has to have one, who are hired to attend to the ship during their stay. They attend to everything." In the trading hongs at Canton, the stewards "also occupied the position of housekeeper [and] hired the clerks and house-boys, and generally supervised the running of the establishment." His role was similar to that of the dubash or banyan in India, or a travel guide within the Ottoman Empire, whose services rendered the Yankee griffin in Canton dependent. "[V]ery much in the power of this important personage" and finding it difficult to trust someone whose language and reasoning were often incomprehensible, expatriates frequently lamented a sense of vulnerability. Preoccupied with both his own exposure to strangers and the drive to make as much profit in as brief a time as possible, the fan quai rarely appreciated how the comprador contributed to Chinese society, providing jobs for dozens of his kinsmen. The comprador's fee in 1780 was about $250 per ship, "but the fee was merely nominal, as his real income came from the commissions and perquisites which he obtained on everything he bought, according to a system long established and recognized as 'olo custom.'"[86] Relations with the comprador varied. Edmund Fanning laid out his requirements of the office as he sought "a trusty servant, who speaks the stranger's language, and attends to your person in your walks, to act as interpreter." He approved of a system in which "the usages and customs of trade at Canton, make it easy for supercargoes to attend to their business there with dispatch; in fact, more so than at any port of the world I have visited." Not every captain appreciated the comprador's services nor trusted his honesty. Many complained that the system left them dependent on someone and vulnerable to exploitation, and, experiencing "imposition to perfection," were outraged at instances of rampant corruption throughout Chinese society that filled their journals and letters home.[87] Aboard the Boston vessel *Columbia* in 1791, John Boit implicated "the *Rasscles* of the Chinese" when a dozen hogs, meant as provisions for the homeward voyage, were poisoned." He noted that the carrion were taken up by the "half starv'd wretches" of the river, adding, sardonically, "they was very nice in their Cookery," feasting on entrails and dead rats, combining two powerful tropes that left refined readers in genteel Boston and Philadelphia disdainful of the Chinese character.[88] Similarly, in his log of *Minerva* from Salem to Canton in 1809, Thomas Ward left a scathing indictment in his journal:

> You will now or before perhaps have some applications for the birth of ship Comprador, and they are all without exception a set of cheats, & this they will vouch for, if you should doubt their rascality. . . . They will expect a Cumshaw of 260 or 280 dollars for the Liberty of cheating you out of twice that sum, & that too with your consent as it were, as you are knowing to the fact, without having the power to prevent it. . . . The price of every article must be named in the agreement & he bound as fast as you can bind him.[89]

Chinese regulations stipulated that a fan quai vessel hire a translator, or "linguist, "in order to ensure smooth relations and few misunderstandings.[90] Here, too, however, Americans became acquainted with a government in which form was more important than function. Although the linguist served as "a sort of customs inspector and official interpreter combined," his title and commission belied ability. William C. Hunter's wry humor expressed his countrymen's cynical sense of the linguist's role: "Next to the Hong merchants, other Chinese were closely allied to the foreign community as 'Linguists'—so called, as it used to be remarked, because they knew nothing of any language but their own. They were appointed by the Hoppo to act as interpreters, and were duly licensed."[91] Like the comprador, Tyng found, "They speak a broken English mixed up with Portuguese, some Dutch, and French, the same as most of the Chinamen who come about the ship. It is rather difficult to understand them at first, but one soon gets used to hearing them." Yet "getting used to" working through mandarins, compradors, and linguists meant, Americans recorded, becoming enmeshed in corrupt Chinese ways. Sullivan Dorr expressed his suspicions in regular letters to his merchant father and brothers in Rhode Island, confiding in October 1799, "from circumstances am apt to think our tea topers will have enough in America, and cheap too. Between 14 and 15,000 thousand chests went to America last year, and the quantity this you shall have if the linguist don't deceive me." A few weeks later, he added, "The *Mary* of New York is said to be at Macao, together with ships here and expected, will make eighteen sail, the linguist has just left me promising to give me a memo, of the Cargo of the respective ships, but the Chinamen will lye."[92]

The narrative of early American encounters in China described a panoply of dangers, from the planning of the voyage to the vessel's return to home port. One threat stood out, in particular, the specter of corruption that could undo the whole purpose of the enterprise, and it was at Whampoa that Yankee travelers were drawn into another level of what they described as China's web of corruption. Thomas Ward articulated the general grievance in 1809. In addition to grousing over the "rascality" of compradors and the "impositions" of hoppomen and mandarins, he railed against another favorite target of his venom, Canton's shopkeepers, advising "there is no villainy that they will not be guilty of if possible." Old Synchong, for instance, was a "close fisted old miser, gets drunk every day, but performs his contracts & whatever you can bind him to."[93]

Some historians concur. Paul Van Dyke, Stephen Platt, and other scholars detail a long tradition of rampant corruption at all levels and in a plethora of forms. One could find it at the highest levels of government, in which imperial ministers squeezed funds from revenues that should have gone to flood control, famine, and epidemics. From this core, corruption spread like a cancer through the middle ranks of government, where "the system of civil appointments became fertile ground for bribery schemes" that included down payments to acquire a position followed by annual payments. American merchants heard rumors of this extortion, but, on Canton's peripheries, were not in a position to observe it directly. However, corruption infected them at "the lowest levels," and "where the vast imperial governing apparatus reached the level of the common people, this pyramid of graft resulted in widespread petty oppression." Platt describes an entrenched system of "petty oppression and outright cruelty by minor officials towards the populations they governed—especially the peasants and those on the margins of society, who were most vulnerable to their extortions. Such victims had little or no effective legal recourse if they were harassed or beaten or had their meager property taken by greedy officials. All they could really do, if they were desperate enough, was to revolt."[94]

Van Dyke locates this system of corruption residing particularly in smuggling operations in which Chinese and fan quai colluded. The roots of the system were deep, going back to the beginnings of Portuguese residence at Macao in 1557. Three contraband networks, originally centered around Macao, then shifting to Whampoa, and finally centered at Lintin Island in the early 1820s, circumvented the empire's customs houses.[95] The focus on Lintin coincided with the shift that the British East India Company and Americans made from paying for Chinese goods in silver to bartering in smuggled opium. The corruption that American traders described in their accounts, and for which they wholly blamed the Chinese, was a system in which they, in fact, were deeply complicit.[96]

With the vessel berthed, measured, and assigned its Chinese comprador, linguist, and Hong merchant at Whampoa, the fan quai captain, supercargo, and passengers donned formal waistcoats and hats from their sea trunks and prepared themselves for a short pull upriver and the rites of meeting business agents, partners, or supervisors. They boarded another sampan or fast boat, described by Captain Sandwith Drinker as a "small lateen sail boat, with a wretched cramped cabin, but possessing excellent qualifications for sailing" the Pearl River.[97] They now sailed (or rowed) the thirteen miles upriver to the trading center at Canton (Guang Fuchew or Guangzhou) proper.[98] C. Toogood Downing made the trip many times, recalling, "The usual way of going to the city is by the ships' boats; but there is another mode of conveyance which is very tedious, on account of the stoppages to which the boats are subject by the local authorities. This is by the dollar-boat; a rough, creaking vessel, with a house and chairs for the accommodation of the passengers."[99]

Travelers were plunged into Canton's color, noise, and churning commotion. As they approached, "a low, rumbling sound commenced and soon increased to a loud-heavy, humming noise, which never here ceases, during day and night. This buzzing sort of serenade is caused by the beating of gongs, firecrackers, etc., etc., mostly among the river craft constantly on the move up and down the river."[100] The assault on their senses increased as they neared the city. Charles Tyng recalled his 1815 visit:

> For two or three miles from the landing the river was covered with boats, in which families lived, all the time, scarcely ever going ashore. How they existed is the greatest wonder. A passage through this floating town was always kept open as a public road, by a sort of police guard, who did not mind using their bamboo clubs to keep order. It was only a little wider than required for the boats to row through, so that we were close to, on both sides of this high way through this floating town, and could look into their houses, as it were, and see all that was going on. They would good naturedly greet us with the word *pangui, pangui,* which I understood to mean stranger, which I learned afterwards was "foreign friend." The banks of the river were quite low. There is very little tide in the river, not more than a foot difference between high and low water, which is generally the case in the tropics. It is the same in Havana, which is in the same latitude as Canton.[101]

The fast boat brought foreign visitors to Jackass Point, gateway to the foreign enclave. Tyng described the site as the only "place for foreigners to land, which is a large space, fenced in on two sides, with the factories, or hongs, on the other sides, fronting the river." The term *factory* was an import from India, and connoted the office of a business agent, the intermediary or "factor." Yet the factories nestled outside of Canton's walls were unlike the commercial sites that Americans found in Calcutta or Madras, and not at all like the global cities similar to the Dutch posts of Fort Orange (later New York) or Cape Town (est. 1652). Experience had prepared most for living in "exotic" foreign neighborhoods such as the Frankish quarters of Smyrna or Alexandria, where they could come and go as they pleased, but Canton's confined space challenged their idea of an expatriate community. The port's origins were shrouded in mystery, according to William C. Hunter, who resided in Canton from 1829 to 1844. Before them stood whitewashed façades, the factories of the Western merchants. These were not the mills or manufactories that would emerge in New England after 1790. Rather, they were the business offices, living quarters, and warehouses. These twelve acres were a site of confinement, intended to isolate the cultural contagion that the imperial authorities believed fan quai visitors carried. Samuel Shaw knew the place well and observed,

> The limits of the Europeans are extremely confined; there being, besides the quay, only a few streets in the suburbs, occupied by trading people, which they are allowed to frequent. Europeans, after a dozen years' residence, have not seen more than what the first month presented to view. They are sometimes invited to dine with the Chinese merchants, who have houses and gardens on the opposite side of the river; but even then no new information is obtained. Everything of a domestic nature is strictly concealed, and, though their wives, mistresses, and daughters are commonly there, none of them are ever visible.[102]

Canton was one of the world's great cities, its perhaps one million residents producing arts, sciences, crafts, and trade in a rhythmic—they described it as regimented—order. It was, as well, the site where American merchants would find one of the world's most bureaucratic and regulated trading cultures. Americans saw in international commerce an opportunity to extend their republican vision to the world and to "humanize men by refining their manners and morals." Yet this conceit—along with the privileged concepts of reason, progress, and other artifacts of Western Enlightenment thought—would be sorely tested by the corruption that characterized Canton's business practices in American accounts. Representations of heroic commerce did not have a place within the Confucian value system that structured Chinese thought, however, and even in the bustling port of Canton such mercantile activity merited not approbation but condemnation. As merchants, purveyors of use-less goods, Chinese officials considered "them allied with the lowest and vilest orders of the people, to break through the best institutions of the country, and to deprave the morals, and thus to alienate the affections of those whom they consider their children."[103] China's mandarins, many trained in the values of a Confucian hierarchy, made every attempt to regulate and restrain the excesses of what they saw as unseemly conduct. The tensions that arose from conflict-ing value systems were inevitable. Racism played a part, as well. Americans were likely to levy similar complaints against other peoples, including Euro-peans, but attributed the cause to customs or government rather than the character of the people.[104] They could not see that the imagined culture of cor-ruption was a net in which imperial officials and merchants were also caught.

Most odious were the infamous Eight Regulations established by the im-perial government to protect the Chinese from the taint of the fan quai and reissued or increased by the imperial government until the Treaty of Nanking in 1842. They precluded a variety of practices common to the West and used by merchants in virtually every other port in the world. Americans learned, for instance, that they were prohibited from year-round residence in Canton, riding in sedan chairs, owning firearms, employing Chinese servants, or loan-ing money to Chinese merchants. They were to be closely supervised by a merchant of the co-hong, who would serve as an intermediary for all commu-nication between the fan quai and imperial government. Perhaps most griev-ously, foreigners were not allowed to bring women to Canton. Under the im-perial regime, even one's movements, so necessary to the regular flow of business activity, were constrained, Shaw complained, by the requirement that "every Chinese, excepting the co-hoang and persons in office, is obliged to have a chop for visiting the factories, which is renewed every month, and for which servants, and even coolies, hired at three dollars a month, must pay half a dollar."[105]

Once a "griffin" clerk or supercargo had settled into the routines of factory life, another layer of dependence regimented his life. The tyranny of the work-load compromised the health and broke the spirit of generations of expatri-ates. Where sailors looked at ports as an exotic, exciting, change of pace from the monotony of shipboard life, residents felt oppressed by that very world from the smallness of it. Even before the establishment of American merchant "houses" in Canton in the 1810s, an agent such as Sullivan Dorr was observ-ing that his many incumbent duties left him scant time for pleasantries. "Ac-cept my thanks, for the papers and pamphlet, have not read them yet. They can't but afford considerable local amusement," he wrote to his brothers. The drudgery of an incessant workload was complemented by pangs of homesickness that further weakened an expatriate's defenses. Dorr was one who learned how much family meant to him, writing home in 1799, "[I] shall send something on a future occasion to my nieces and Eben's boy. the rouges don't know I love 'em, nor even myself until I was deprived of them by absence, which will tend to instruct me to appreciate the society of my friends, and become more humanized myself."[106]

Expatriates lamented that they felt this invasion of their rights most severely in the enforced isolation of the factories. Suspicious of its own people, and especially of foreigners, the Qing regime regulated everyone's movements and constrained the travel and correspondence that the fan quai insisted were vital to the regular flow of business activity. Amos Porter echoed this appraisal in 1803, commenting on the flow of authority from emperor to mandarins to the people, noting, "This is a country that's everything from oppression."[107] Consequently, Western visitors who resided in Canton's factory site described their lives as lived, in Jacques Downs's poignant phrasing, in a "golden ghetto." Where the mandarins who enforced the imperial policy of isolation and confinement aimed to prevent outsiders from contaminating the virtues of the Celestial Empire, Americans—the "flowery flag devils"—depicted the illiberal restrictions of a decadent civilization. The site of resident life came to symbolize their enforced separation and isolation.

The monotony sapped a traveler's fortitude even in port, where manifest threats to life and limb had fallen away. Harriet Low gave voice to her disorientation in an entry from Saturday, October 10, 1829, in which she sighed: "I saw a ship passing up to Canton from our door this morning. I watched it for a long time, hoping that I should see the stars and stripes, but could not make anything of it but an English signal." Reaching out to his wife in Boston, Robert Forbes lamented his time in China: "[I wish] to stay only long enough to get my Competency—whether that can be done in one or two years after 1 January 1840 remains to be seen & the period is too distant for poor humanity to look forward to—of one thing you may rest assured[:] I shall not stay an hour after I can see my way clear to have enough to live upon in a very moderate way at home."[108]

The isolation of the factories intensified the disdain many Americans felt for the "singular" Chinese people. In his second tour of duty in Canton's trading regimen, Robert Bennet Forbes expressed the resentment he felt in leaving Boston again, taking careful note of the many petty indignities he suffered, and commenting on one, in particular: that "you may judge from this little incident how sensitive a man becomes when away from all he holds dear."[109] He held the officials who carried out the imperial policy of enforced isolation and separation and who sought to prevent outsiders from contaminating the virtues of the Celestial Empire—the mandarins—even more culpable than at the emperor himself. The mandarin symbolized all that was wrong with China—its corruption, its crude and cruel forms of justice, its gaps between wealth and poverty, all ramifications of a despotic system of governance that Americans called tyranny. Where Yankee fan quai knew and used the names of Hong merchants, compradors, and even servants, mandarins remained anonymous in their correspondence.

The regulations limited trade opportunities further by determining that fan quai merchants could transact business with only a dozen Chinese merchants, and they constituted a strange, mysterious body. "The day after your arrival at Canton, the Cohong or directors of the Chinese hong merchants will wait upon you," observed William Elting. Even the names of this brotherhood exemplified the curious mysteries of doing business in China. "There are 10, whose names are as follows: Pankequa, Manequa, Yanqua, Houqua, Lunqua, Hunqua, Consequa, Manhop, & Suequa," and it took time to understand how a fan quai should greet a "qua," or "Sir."[110]

Some Americans held the Hong in high estimation. Samuel Shaw, the first American supercargo to encounter the Hong merchants, was in this camp. They "are a set of as respectable men as are commonly found in other ports of the world. They are intelligent, exact accountants, punctual to their engagements, and, though not worse for being well looked after, value themselves much upon maintaining a fair character." Shaw may have experienced good relationships because he was the first American and he was shepherded through by doting Europeans. Others certainly fostered close partnerships, both personal and professional—Robert and John Forbes with Houqua, for instance. Many, however, fretted about the fairness of cargoes and prices, anxious about their complete dependence on their Chinese counterparts.

Yankee traders preferred to work within the comfortable familiarity of kin networks. Pioneering the Canton trade in 1799, a jaded Sullivan Dorr had been burned by unreliable American captains and supercargoes and was not about to extend trust to a people so distant and different, who he regarded as duplicitous. Writing home to his family, he described the Hong merchants as extravagant in their promises. They were "very ready to [give] credit," and the cautious Dorr decided to "put them to the test, but should not be disappointed if they should refuse, they are capable of such duplicity." Furthermore, "none of them get a hide from me, without a previous receipt of goods, on board ship." For every Houqua, there was a conniving Consequa. The East India Company, he learned, had returned some $60,000 worth of mixed teas from the Hong merchant. Despite the careful attention of the fan quai merchant, one might still find himself "egregiously cheated, for over the packing place, some of them have trap doors through which they drop old good for nothing teas, in the dust of packing." Despite his efforts, Dorr, too, fell into a trap, lamenting, to his brothers in 1799, "You will notice in [my letter] to my father the difficulty [I] am in about ginseng, entertain hopes of being cheated out of only 250! to 600D. confounded knaves I hate them." Chunoquai, "an arch rouge," was no better, sending "forty five chests of Hyson tea, 20 of which are good, the remainder not so good." Dorr determined he "will not give him a sous, a greater scoundrel never lived, and am happy I have got thus much." Matters were made worse when collusion between his security merchant and a servant threatened his reputation as well as his profits, but he could not identify the culprits with certainty. All Dorr could do was to bemoan his plight, writing, "the dissimilarity of language and of manners lays one under a vast disadvantage, for they will sell you before your face and you not know it, but it is certain I used every caution, it is prohibited. I would not have my feelings sported with in such a manner again."[111]

The empire's mandate that fan quai traders work only through the Hong merchants added to the sense of dependence that Americans experienced in Canton. Dudley Pickman provided a thorough guide to trade in Canton knowledge in his instructions to Captain Benjamin Shreve, piloting the *New Hazard* out of Salem in 1815, writing, "The most important thing in your voyage is in securing your ship. You had better not employ a Man of doubtful character at any rate. Engage with a security merchant of the first Character even at rather higher prices for your goods and you will be sure to have a good cargo and without being delayed beyond the time stipulated for. There are generally about 12 security merchants, with one of whom you must engage of those who were in the Hong in 1805, when I was at Canton, 5 or 6 did much American Business." Recognizing that the success of the cruise depended on choosing a trustworhty Hong merchant, Shreve knew he was in a vulnerable position.[112]

Having "immersed the Ship in roguery" at Whampoa in 1811, Captain Ward's distaste was exemplified in the petty officialdom of compradors and Hong merchants through which he had to work and whose greed, he believed, ate into the profits of the voyage. Middlemen such as Consequa for instance, epitomized the vices of the East, and Ward described him as "Rich—roguish—insinuating— polite—sends some excellent cargoes—some bad Cargoes—not attentive enough to business and a man with whom you cannot talk with safety, as he will promise everything & perform what he pleases—not to be seen always." The advice that merchant Dudley Pickman sent to Captain Benjamin Shreve, about to cast off in the *New Hazard* in 1815, was likewise cautious: "Hooqua does business for [the] Perkins house, [and is] considered very rich, close, to be depended on. . . . I should prefer him to any of those now in the Hong who were there when I was at Canton. Ponqua [is] too poor to deal with. Chunqua Mr Ingersoll [thinks is] 'a big Rogue' [and] I should have nothing to do with him. Conseequa [is] a very uncertain man; I should not have perfect confidence in him, [though] some of the Philadelphians are very fond of him."[113]

Elting admired the Hong merchants, but found them to be sharp negotiators. His advice: "If you come to market early and expect other ships to arrive soon afterwards with the same kind of articles, your cargo is composed of, I would advise you to take the hong merchants' first offer, provided it is clearly the Price you expected, yes probably buy your refusal, they will have you, and perhaps not return . . . well knowing that you cannot dispose of your cargo to any other and that from Canton you have no market left to claim or go to."[114]

American charges of corruption within the factories were longstanding. Cheating, in the form of adulterating the product, was especially rife in the tea trade. To package the tea tightly in wooden chests, seminaked coolies, or barefooted lower-class laborers stomped for several hours on the pilings, "not very Cleanly." Amos Porter observed that coolies packed inferior bohea teas into chests, as their "sweat ** spittle, and many fulsome substances are inter mixt with this tea, which renders it almost unfit for use." To decrease their costs at this stage, the packers surreptitiously mixed lesser grades of tea into the chests, and then introduced new names for the result. Porter complained that a fan quai trader, "at this day rarely get a single Chest what is genuine," and by 1802 paid several times the cost of a chest in the mid-1790s. Consequently, experienced residents keep their suspicions alert. "A sample of Ginseng I do not send, can't get it, have been several times, to one who promised; they are all infernal liars," Sullivan Dorr lamented to brothers Joseph and

John Dorr, in Canton, on November 6, 1799. Dorr had been in Canton for perhaps a year when he wrote, "[I] shall take care and place my confidence in none as Joseph says, repaying their proffers with compliments, knowing my own business shall not subject myself to the Duplicity of any one, keeping the staff in my own hand."[115]

While the heat, disease, typhoons, and Ladrones pirates of the South China Sea threatened the well-being of Americans who ventured beyond Good Hope, still other calamities could ruin a voyage. On the wharves of Macao, Whampoa, and Canton, pilferage and corruption could eat away the profits and render the cruise a failure. For a supercargo such as Samuel Shaw or an ordinary sailor such as Charles Tyng, the mysteries of the China trade—a *cumshaw* to the mandarin, a *singsong* for the Hoppo—represented the "roguery" that both violated fundamental republican sensibilities and eroded any chance one had to gain a "competency." At the center of this cesspool of corruption were the empire's mandarins, the Qing officials whose spies watched and reported on every aspect of fan quai life. In the accounts of Thomas Ward, Harriet Low, and other Yankee visitors, mandarins were groomed to be greedy and never missed an opportunity to profit from their position as gatekeepers of the imperial domain. Americans may certainly have ambivalence about their Hong partners, but their disgust for the "unfeeling mandarins" was unrelieved. As Edward Robinson learned in Egypt, "The people in general do not ascribe their oppression so much to the Pasha, as to his subordinate agents," so in China it was the mandarins who took the blame for onerous regulations. The empire's bureaucrats were the bane of their efforts to do business in Canton, Americans reported, and the butt of much derision in the correspondence that informed American beliefs about the world.[116]

In American accounts, finding novel ways to profit from the office seemed the raison d'être for the privilege of wearing the mandarin's button, overriding any responsibilities a mandarin had to his post. In August 1798, during a visit to the Bocca Tigris, Edward Fanning observed how deep this corruption lay. Fanning wanted to inspect the integrity of the forts that guarded the strategic Pearl River and found that, overriding any considerations of imperial security, "the mandarin in command at the fort, . . . in consideration of the small sum, or *cum shaw* of a Spanish dollar, not only gave permission to take our walk, but also directed [an] officer to show us to the fort."[117] Amos Porter's 1803 sojourn in Canton confirmed Fanning's observations, and further implicated the mandarins in a system of extortion that he found both pervasive and debilitating, compromising the virtues Americans claimed on behalf of their own republic. "Supported from the earnings of the lower order of subjects" and finding "no bounds set to their demands," Porter asserted, "by their avaricious disposition the poor or lower order of people are squeezed . . . of their last cash." The bureaucrats' tight regulation of foreign trade infiltrated every aspect of expatriate life, public and private, and approached the level of that scourge of republican virtues—tyranny.[118]

Those who had traveled into the Holy Land or been captured by Barbary corsairs or who trafficked opium from Smyrna to Canton would have found the situation familiar. The Qing emperor was reminiscent of the Grand Turk, his pashas and beys and deys imposing power in ways as cruel and arbitrary as Canton's mandarins.[119] The decapitations, the *bashido,* or foot beatings that were common in Ottoman punishment, and the capricious, onerous duties and fees that Yankee mariners found in the Ottoman domains corresponded with the summary executions, the cangue (a "broad wooden collar that locked around the neck" and left the victim to perish by hunger or thirst), death by a thousand cuts, and the Hoppoman fees they lambasted in China. Yet, in the lands of the Turks, there was often greater freedom of movement, even for Christian missionaries. As Yankee traders William C. Hunter and Robert Bennet Forbes huddled inside their Hong compound in 1838, biblical scholar William Robinson was passing freely through Ottoman Egypt and crediting its tyrannical pasha: "In one respect, the energy of Muhammed 'Aly deserves all praise; although the severity by which it is attended may not always be the most justifiable. He has rendered the countries under his sway secure; so that travellers, whether Orientals or Franks, may pass in their own dress throughout Egypt and Syria, and also among the Bedawin of the adjacent deserts, with the same degree of safety as in many parts of civilized Europe."[120]

The cultural and linguistic barriers that divided the Celestials and the barbarians made the mandarins seem incapable of that most revered of Enlightenment traits, the capacity for reason. Imagining themselves as paladins of a vernacular Enlightenment, Americans could not fathom the principles underlying the Eight Regulations, the embedded corruption, the passivity of the Chinese people, the rejection of "progress" that they believed their own republic represented. Fanning reported that the mandarins might appear civil enough, but this was merely a feint of etiquette. As he described one encounter, "On entering, his mandarinship, with his hands closely clenched together in front, and thus moving them quickly up and down, with the body slightly inclined forward, actions on the whole somewhat resembling the shaking of a person afflicted with the paralysis, welcomed us with a *chin ching* (How d' ye do?) making the while a great many bows, in rapid succession, and as many professions of friendship."[121] But, in expatriate correspondence, the mandarins were represented as incapable of the kind of reasonable engagement that marked truly "civilized" decorum. Furthermore, the tyrannical hold the officials maintained over them hindered the populace from cooperating with the fan quai. Consequently, when twenty-one-year-old Thomas Handasyd Cabot died of smallpox in 1835, his family in Massachusetts arranged for his remains to be shipped home to Brookline but received no help from the officials; in the words of Robert Bennet Forbes, the "superstitious ideas of the Chinese prevented them from aiding."[122] Their fear of reprisals from mandarin officials created barriers between the peoples, constituting a cultural "great wall" that precluded empathy and understanding.

Through the years of the Old China trade, American travelers echoed the complaints of Fanning, Forbes, and others against what they described as the tyranny of mandarins. Missionary Henrietta Shuck, for instance, encountered an example of this bureaucratic oppression as soon as she landed in Macao. A Chinese boatman, she recorded, refused to land Shuck and her infant child, fearing the officials would learn of this violation of the Eight Regulations, as the mandarins charged additional fees for landing fan quai women. Instead, he rowed her to a Western ship, where she asked for passage to shore.[123] Nor was there recourse in a system that controlled every communication and whose purpose was to keep the emperor in the dark regarding developments in Canton. Thomas Randall saw little recourse in trying to reach the emperor, noting in 1791, "The idea of a representation, concerning the frauds and impositions of the Chinese to the Emperor, would deserve attention were there not the danger of making things worse."[124]

In the writing of their encounters in China during this time, American travelers described a system that was overseen by "stubborn and unfeeling mandarins" whose rule matched corruption and inefficiency with degrees of brutality and cruelty that offended the refined republicans from the new nation.[125] Yankee merchants and supercargoes who prided themselves on their fastidious gentility were presented with unrelieved scenes of horror on a daily basis. Within the confinement of the factories, they could not avoid the sight of chained bodies writhing in the cangue collar that left the victim to perish by hunger or thirst. Screams pierced the quiet of the factory floors as notorious malefactors suffered various punishments. Barely a mile from the factories lay the execution grounds; the sight of decapitated bodies "in various stages of decay" formed part of the landscape.[126] Of particular insult, Canton's mandarins staged these public displays to incite terror among the Chinese population and the fan quai, and Americans recalled their horror for years afterward. When Chinese authorities captured the pirate leader Apootsae in 1809, the mandarins ordered him executed by the "thousand cuts," or *lingchi*, and he was slowly hacked to death.[127] Boston Brahmin Robert Bennet Forbes complained of one such episode. Returning from a yachting party on the Pearl River in February 1839, he was "confounded to learn that a Chinese implicated in some way with the opium trade had been executed in the public square in front of our factories."[128]

Canton's mandarins deepened the impression that China's legal system was arbitrary as well as cruel when they denied fan quai pleas to even see the Empire's legal code. As historian Li Chen observes, provincial governors refused to make Qing legal codes available and, in a curious twist of logic, asserted that the "public nature" of the laws "could not with propriety be granted to the inspection of Foreigners without the express permission of the Emperor." When a purloined copy did make its way through the expatriate community in 1817, fan quai fears were aggravated when they read how completely they were subject to the "tyranny" of "that remote and apparently benighted nation." They would learn the unpleasant truth, to their dismay, the Chinese penal code provided: "In general, all foreigners who come to submit themselves to the government of the Empire, shall, when guilty of offenses, be tried and sentenced according to the established laws."[129]

Samuel Shaw encountered instances of mandarin injustice during his first visit in 1784 and was especially affected by what became known as the *Lady Hughes* affair. On November 24, aboard the British warship, an unfortunate sailor manning a cannon obeyed an order to light off the traditional salute for a departing ship. When the cannon misfired, several Chinese subjects, including a mandarin's servant, were killed. Guangdong's provincial governor, Shuchang, demanded that the gunner surrender to imperial authorities for trial. When the culprit failed to appear before the mandarins, they seized the ship's supercargo, triggering a "general alarm" among the foreign community. That the events occurred during the height of the trading season sealed the fate of the unfortunate gunner. Outmaneuvered, British officials turned him over to the imperial police. When Shaw returned from his second voyage to Canton in 1786, he reported, "It must occasion pain to every humane mind to reflect that this poor fellow was executed by the Chinese, on the 8th of January following."[130]

Such was the trade-off that Americans would come to accept, the sine qua non for the privilege of trade with the Celestial Empire, but it was a devil's bargain that they were not prepared to acknowledge easily. As Teemu Ruskola observes, "Indeed, in an 1815 communication to the British representative in Canton, the American consul expressly acknowledged China's jurisdiction over Americans in the city, stating 'that the citizens of the United States have for many years visited the city of Canton in the pursuit of honest commerce, [and] that their conduct during the whole period of intercourse has been regulated by a strict regard and respect for the laws and usages of this Empire, as well as the general law of nations.'" American travelers could vent their outrage in their correspondence homeward, but they were not prepared to challenge the mandarins' authority and, hence, abandon a profitable trade. A sailor's life, they would learn to admit, was not worth the risk.[131]

For American travelers and their readers, the most disturbing incident came in 1821 off Whampoa Reach, amid the opening of the tea season. The incident began innocently enough. Preoccupied with the bustle of removing from their summer residences in Macao upriver to the factories in Canton, Yankee merchants prepared for the arrival of vessels such as the American ship *Emily*. The 284 ton Indianman sailed under Captain Cowpland out of Baltimore, and arrived at Whampoa even before the season commenced on May 15, 1821. By September 23, the ship's lading completed, the officers and crew prepared for departure. Customarily, mariners bought souvenirs before departure—knickknacks such as fans, incense, and firecrackers. Customarily, also, disagreements ensued, as differing languages and customs triggered misunderstandings that fueled angry words and led to assaults. This time, the records agree, Francisco Terranova, identified as a sailor from Sicily serving aboard the *Emily*, quarreled with one of the thousands of Chinese boat women who offered services and goods. Apparently—here the story is muddied by various versions—Terranova dropped an olive jar onto Ko-leang-she, who then struck her head on the gunnel, fell into the river, and drowned.[132]

Perhaps the tragedy could have been resolved as easily as Fanning had done earlier, reconciling Ko-leang-she's family with recompense, as the British believed the case should have been.[133] Instead, it erupted into one of the most notorious examples of mandarin "tyranny" and another cause célèbre that demonstrated the dangers the world presented to Americans who ventured beyond their native shores. Following form, the authorities demanded Terranova's surrender for trial. Captain Cowpland stoutly refused, but agreed to a shipboard trial witnessed by representatives of the East India companies.

His compromise did not satisfy the mandarins, however, who ordered a blockade around the *Emily*, and American trade suspended. This decided Terranova's fate. The sailor's surrender to the mandarins was followed by a hurried trial and immediate execution. Once Terranova's body was returned to the *Emily*, the new viceroy, Ruan Yuan, issued an edict, asserting that as the Americans had

> behaved submissively, it is proper to open their trade in order to manifest our compassion. The Celestial Empire's kindness and favor to the weak is rich in an infinite degree; but the nation's dignity sternly commands respect, and cannot, because people are foreigners, extend clemency. . . . Now it is written in the law when persons outside the pale of Chinese civilization shall commit crimes they too shall be punished according to law. I, therefore, ordered them to take the said foreigner and, according to law, strangle him, to display luminously the laws of the Empire. In every similar case foreigners ought to give up murderers, and thus they will act becoming the tenderness and gracious kindness with which the Celestial Empire treats them.

The viceroy's language was telling: The Chinese showed "compassion," "kindness," "tenderness and gracious kindness," and "favor to the weak." But China's "dignity" and national honor were at stake and, so, China could not offer mercy. In order to "display luminously" the laws of the empire, Terranova had to die. For their part, the Americans "behaved submissively." This was a discourse directed to please the emperor, but, for Western audiences, and especially within the United States, the viceroy's words would fester and erode any sympathy they felt for China.[134]

American reports lambasted Canton's mandarin officialdom and excoriated both the Chinese and US governments.[135] The State Department evidently took the position that Americans in China violated the empire's laws at their own risk, for it made no protest in the matter. British critics, meanwhile, took notice of American "weakness" in submitting to Chinese jurisdiction.[136] As for the complicity of the American community at Canton, missionary S. Wells Williams observed, "The American merchants were really helpless to carry the trial of Terranova to a just conclusion against the Chinese law, which peremptorily required life for life wherever foreigners were concerned, and gave him up on the assurance that his life was in no danger."[137] The American press held its own trial in the public sphere, accusing the Chinese of further injustices. The *Chinese Repository*, published in Canton by missionary Elijah Bridgeman, described it as a misunderstanding or comedy of errors: "Here ends the account of the 'mock trial.' It needs no comments from us. The fate of the unhappy sailor is well known. How the Puanyu (or Pon-ue) knew in his heart the man was guilty, it is not easy to understand. When it is said, 'God would punish him,' we suppose the linguist used the word *jos* as a translation of the Pwanyu's words for the gods of his nation."[138] In the refined parlors and coffeehouses of Boston and Philadelphia, the *North America Review* also took up the expatriates' defense—too late for Terranova himself—by implicating the mandarin's management of the case. The trial, asserted the *Review*'s editor, violated a republican sense of justice: without taking the time necessary to investigate the context, "it appears that a charge of murder was immediately brought against Terranova." Nor was the accused permitted to bring in his own witnesses—"the most respectable American merchants at Canton"—or even an interpreter to cross-examine the Chinese witnesses. The verdict was foreshadowed, the *Review* insisted, when "Pac-qua, the security merchant of the *Emily*, and Cou-qua, the linguist, being called, fell on their hands and knees, to hear the demands of the Pon-ue, of which the Americans could get no interpretation." Even their dependable ally, Houqua, wilted before the authority of the mandarins, as the *Review* groused: "Hou-qua and the linguist, although repeatedly urged by those assisting the prisoner, evidently did not translate the half of what was urged in his defense. Whenever either of them attempted an explanation, he was silenced by the Pon-ue." Under such circumstances, this could not be considered "a fair and impartial trial."[139] Given the inquisitional nature of the trial, what hope could any American have if he was unfortunate enough to be caught in the mandarins' web?

The lesson that Americans drew from the Terranova incident was that Yankee travelers needed to be on their guard in this part of the world, as the dangers from a corrupt commercial system and a tyrannical bureaucracy threatened their profits and even their lives. A few significant figures led an exodus from the mandarin tyranny. Stephen Girard, John Jacob Astor, and John Perkins Cushing took the opportunity to leave the China trade.[140] Yet others admitted the weakness of their position, lodging a feeble protest to the Chinese authorities ("We consider the case prejudiced"), but ultimately recognizing: "We are bound to submit to your laws while we are in your waters, be they ever so unjust. We will not resist." Even the Americans who most resented Chinese jurisdiction observed reluctantly that, "as a question of the law of nations and casuistry, it would bear an argument whether the United States could rightfully go to war against the Chinese for administering their own laws on persons voluntarily coming within their jurisdiction."[141]

Reflections

26 April 1845,

My dear Husband

I happened yesterday to go out to see the cow and found she appeared to be very hungry, and not a spear of grass to be seen and [our Malayan servant] John told me that there had none been brought since thee went away, *four days*. I told the Comprador I should cut his account half a dollar, and if he did not get some very soon—*a dollar*. This was about twelve o'clock, but he did not get any till between four and five. Mr. Wetmore has been scolding him about it this morning, but I do not suppose it wiil do any good—the Rascal; how I dislike him.

When Nathaniel Kinsman read his wife's complaint, embedded in four years of correspondence between Canton and Macao, he heard the frustrations of a mother who felt exhausted, alone, and vulnerable. Rebecca Kinsman had dutifully followed her husband around the world, from Salem to China, to raise their children in Macao as he labored in the firm of Wetmore & Co. in Canton's factories. Most of us can identify with Rebecca Kinsman's plight. In this letter, as in so many she sent to Nathaniel and home to her extended family in Salem and Philadelphia, Kinsman represented herself as a victim of China's decadence, corruption, and tyranny.

Yet there is so much that is missing here, so much below the surface of the text that might challenge this rendering of Kinsman's correspondence. Like her readers, we hear Kinsman's voice, but we do not hear from the cowman. We do not hear about the scarcity of fresh grass on Kinsman's small plot of land, the cost of animal feed, the difficulty of exercising the cow. We hear later from Rebecca that Chinese cows were uncommon and remarkably thin, but we do not hear her connect these facts. We are left asking, What was the cowman's experience? Who were his fan quai? What was his China trade? How did the literary strategies that American travelers such as Rebecca Kinsman employed justify their criticisms of the Chinese through a language of silencing, ridicule, and victimization?

Distortions

A close reading of this side of the archive reveals an arched vocabulary that demeaned cowmen, compradors, mandarins, and shopkeepers. Yankee travelers resorted to strategies, in practice and in the retelling, that erased the Chinese from the China trade or rendered them as incompetent, duplicitous, or vicious. Yankee travelers' interpretations framed the Celestial Empire as another zone of danger in which their residence in a foreign city was tolerated, even as their own tolerance, much less acceptance or embrace, was extended to the Chinese.

That we know little of what the people of Canton thought of American traders illustrates the problem of colonial archives described by scholars such as Marisa Fuentes.[142] The selective nature of collecting papers, privileging one point of view, prevents us from gaining a balanced and authentic sense of early American encounters in the East. And we see in the accounts of Shaw, Ward, Fanning, and Elting a rather intentional decision to silence Chinese voices.

This project of absenting the Chinese from an emergent narrative begins with names, or, rather, with the exception of the Hong merchants, the decision to leave Chinese people nameless. Rebecca Solnit, Marisa Fuentes, Lisa Lowe, Michel-Rolph Trouillot, and others have probed the use of language in the colonial archive, but they have been especially penetrating in explaining the role of absences and silences.[143] Solnit writes, for instance: "In the deep past, people knew names had power. Some still do. Calling things by their true names cuts through the lies that excuse, buffer, muddle, disguise, avoid, or encourage inaction, indifference, obliviousness."[144] We see an example in Rebecca Kinsman's letters, as she refers to her servants as "My Amhah"; "the Comprador"; "My tailor"; "the Cow-Man"; "the House-Coolie"; "these Chinese women"; "the young Cooly whom we disliked so much"; and the like.[145] We see something similar, as Damien Shaw points out, in 'Kinsman's earliest letter from Macao on 4 November 1843': describing the city as a collection of "Jews, Parsees, . . . Malays, Bengalees, Lascars, then there are Coffers . . . to say nothing of Europeans." This certainly suggests that some expatriates were developing a cosmopolitan consciousness. But, as Shaw observes, "it is striking, however, that no Chinese are included in this tableau as they constituted, after all, the majority of Macao's residents." We read this erasure of the Canton Chinese again and again in the archive of Yankee China traders.

Many of the texts in the China trade canon also served to devalue and delegitimize the people of Canton and Macao. The language of this trade was a language of debasement and distortion. Rebecca Kinsman found great faults in her Chinese servants, who made a "fuss" when serving tea because "[n]either the Comprador nor the boy knew in the least how to bring in tea." A "young Cooly" was fired for the "unpardonable" crime of "smoking a cigar upstairs."[146] Others were simply annoying. Kinsman's expectations that the Chinese should become familiar with the middle-class mores of her native Salem, rather than that she should learn their ways or even their names, reveals an essential truth about the American experience there—one that rendered the world dangerous in Americans' writing. Another of Macao's American expatriates, Harriet Low, was typical in ridiculing Chinese pronunciation, in passages such as, "putty off a little, that have mandarin fashion." During the four years Low spent there, she immersed herself in Unitarian doctrine but never reached out to the disadvantaged around her, never tried to teach, and never took pains to learn anything about the Asian practices that she found so repellent. In China, she studied Spanish and French but did not bother to learn Chinese. Underlying this language of ridicule was a privileged concept of free trade. Salem traders expected the Chinese to open freedom to trade where and what the Americans' wanted, with no responsibilities on their part. Low was not an exception. A patter of mimicry embedded the pages of American accounts as a pattern of interaction and discourse that Natalia Molina calls a racial script, "the ways in which the lives of racialized groups are linked across time and space and thereby affect one another. . . . Once attitudes, practices, customs, policies, and laws are directed at one group, they are more readily available for and hence easily applied to other groups."[147] Indeed, reading chronologically, from Samuel Shaw's accounts in the 1780s to Sullivan Dorr's in the 1790s to Nathaniel Kinsman's, Harriet Low's, and Amasa Delano's during the antebellum era, we can see how a racist construction of the Chinese emerged from the layers of accounts that accumulated in the American public sphere.

Dependencies

We might construe the discourse of Kinsman, Low, and others in terms of anger, hostility, belligerence. But something else leaks through their diatribes. Significantly, in demeaning the shopkeeper Tom Birdman, who was " without doubt as great a villain as ever went unhung," Thomas Ward confessed, "we were frequently obliged to deal with [him] some way or other." The necessity of working with Chinese agents at every level of activity fostered an uncomfortable sense of dependence that rendered the fan quai vulnerable and brought further anxiety about the security of the voyage. Ward's language was petulant; he represents himself as victim. Certainly, in a ship's log, he would seek to defend himself against charges of overspending. He claimed he was set upon, virtually assaulted, "without having the power to prevent it." In this construction, the Chinese—all of them—were to blame for his vulnerability. Here, we find a paradox of imperial discourse: Americans represented themselves as victims, eliding the expansion of their nation across the globe and casting "the projection of American power as inevitable and benign and as fundamentally different from European imperialism (conceived as a metropolitan center harshly dominating a group of alien colonies)."[148]

This analysis is not an attempt to make a case that the frustrations and fears of a voyage to China and residence in Macao and Canton excuses the hostility that American expatriates showed toward the Chinese or that it necessarily fostered a posture of aggression. Rather, I want to document how Yankee travelers could justify their belligerence by representing themselves as victims, and how this imagined victimhood influenced readers at home. This phenomenon was most fertile where encounters with indigenous peoples blended into the threatening natural environment. Global voyages made perfect laboratories for this dynamic.

Many historians refer to the relationship between early America and Canton by that overworked term, *cosmopolitan.* But scholars such as Henk Driessen and Isaac Land question whether this perceived cosmopolitanism was truly a shared experience. Driessen observes that "maritime towns have functioned as hinges between empires, continents, trading blocs and nation states," but that the exchange of ideas did not necessarily accompany a commerce in goods.[149] It is a mistake, then, to assume that the appearance of Chinese export goods in America's entrepôts and museums indicated a greater level of cosmopolitanism. What was lacking was a greater measure of understanding and tolerance. Instead, Isaac Land labels the relationship one of "antagonistic tolerance," and includes it as one of several "port town paradoxes." As Land writes, "while tolerance in some form clearly correlates with traditional port town activity, regimes of coexistence always contain the potential for tipping in one direction or another."[150] Land recognizes that incidents of tolerance depicted in the China trade canon were selective, used when useful to the interests of Yankee merchants and missionaries, dropped when intolerance served an underlying purpose. More often than not, then, China traders found it useful to depict China as one more part of a dangerous world.

CHAPTER FOUR

Hindoos and Fakirs in India

During the night of September 16, 1861, Charles Storrow was in trouble. His ship, the *Boston*, fifteen thousand miles from home, coasting the Bay of Bengal, was bound in "heavy rain and fog, and we were watching in great anxiety for land till nearly dark." As passengers and crew strained their eyes for hidden shoals or sudden shoreline, their repeated hails brought no pilot, only eerie silence. Storrow's journal tells the story:

> Today is marked by quite an unusual adventure. By eight o'clock had got no pilot and could see no signs of any, and it was proposed that a visit should be made to the 'Mary Ann' if that stranded vessel should indeed be her. [After a pull and sail of six miles,] we arrived at the craft, which indeed bore the white figure of a female on her bow and '*Mary Ann*, Boston' painted on her stern. Strange thing and one that I little expected when I bade goodbye to the *Mary Ann* on Commercial Wharf last November that when I should see her next it would be to plunder her wreck at the entrance of Basseiw River.[1]

Charles Storrow's India was a dangerous part of the world. Belying the common term for the globe's Eastern quarters, the region was anything but *oriented*, and the transposed wreck of the *Mary Ann* was a harbinger of the disordering that Storrow and other Americans would document in the Indian Ocean.[2] Disturbing moments such as the one that Storrow recounted appeared all too frequently in the accounts Americans left and contributed to a marked sense that danger and disorder stalked this land.[3] The disorientation that Americans described in encountering the subcontinent bore some similarities to what they found in China and the Ottoman Empire. But it was in India that they depended particularly on the kindness of strangers, of European expatriates and Indian intermediaries. The subcontinent was fragmented into dozens of realms in which American traders had to negoti-ate a myriad of ecosystems, polities, regulations, languages, and currencies. Consequently, India represented great opportunities, but this was a place in which Yankee traders felt particularly vulnerable and a culture in which they felt their values especially threatened.[4]

Encounters

Americans sailed to India for the same reasons they sailed to China and the Ottoman Empire. India was a place of dreams. It offered the promise of adven-ture and the hope of a "competency," a nest egg that would purchase land or shops for young men starting out. India promised hope for old men, too, who had been financially "shipwrecked" and lost fortunes and gambled on a chance to regain their footing. Debt could catch up eventually with a mariner, as the downwardly mobile Delano and Pickman families learned. Samuel Shaw learned this humbling lesson after the War for Independence, left nearly in-solvent from Congress's inability to pay veterans and responsibility for family finances after the deaths of his father and brother. Thomas Smith was another who sailed to India to recover his finances, holding a letter from his mother Hannah that read, "Your father's estate was rendered insolvent, but I do not feel anxious, but that I can provide for myself, and my rents are paid punctu-ally." Still, she cautioned, Smith would need to manage his own future.[5]

The first Yankee voyage to the subcontinent foreshadowed the uncertain-ties that challenged the anxieties accompanying later cruises. When the ship *United States* cleared Philadelphia on March 24, 1784, just a month after the departure of the *Empress of China* from New York, the four-hundred-ton ves-sel was "bound for China," carrying Virginia ginseng, naval stores, copper, miscellaneous hardware and a "considerable sum in dollars." The ship never completed the voyage to its destination. Instead, the captain changed course to Sumatra, then India, and reached Pondicherry (Puducherry), the French-held port on Coromandel (southeastern) Coast at 6 p.m., December 26, 1784. Here the crew was welcomed warmly by the French governor and veteran of battles against his English competitors, the Marquis de Bussy. But, when the *Chesapeake* arrived at Calcutta in autumn 1787, Captain John O'Donnel had concerns about the reception they would receive from the East India Company (EIC), whose recently appointed governor-general was none other than Lord Cornwallis, who had suffered defeat at the hands of a combined French–American army at Yorktown six years earlier. The Irish-American mariner was worried "to know in what manner the Americans were to be received."

EIC officials were wary of American entry into the Indian Ocean and steadily plotting the removal of French, Dutch, and Portuguese competition. But the Americans brought silver, and their agile ships could manage navigation into the modest ports their own bulky Indiamen could not reach. Even two years later, the *Salem Gazette* and other newspapers reported on the arrival of the *Chesapeake* in Calcutta with the observation: "The *Chesapeake* was the first American vessel allowed to hoist the colours of the U. States in the river Ganges, and to trade there. When Lord Cornwallis, the Gov. General, then at a great distance up the country, was applied to by letter from Calcutta, to know in what manner the Americans were to be received, his answer was, 'On the same footing with other nations.'"[6]

Over time, Yankee merchants mastered the details for an Indian Ocean voyage, building on a thousand years of experience from Native navigators. Arab and Bengali mariners who had navigated "this fierce unbounded sea" of the Buddhist *Jakatas* for centuries had learned the winds and currents of the Indian Ocean well and accumulated lifetimes of expertise upon which Westerners grafted their maps. Later generations followed texts such as Ahmad Ibn Majid al-Najdi's ca. 1490 guide, *Kitab al-Fawa'id*, and its wisdom was appropriated by the Portuguese in the sixteenth century, the French in the next, and the British in the next after that. By the late eighteenth century, Western navigators were learning for themselves to chart the waters that the *United States,* the *Chesapeake*, and hundreds of Yankee ships after them would ply. This knowledge was incorporated into a map that would become essential, J. Bayly's ca. 1782 *A New Map of the East Indies*, followed by the 1879 *Bay of Bengal Pilot*. As Americans entered the India trade, European geographers were codifying the accumulated knowledge from hundreds of years of navigating the shores, and sailors could read in tomes such as Milburn's *Oriental Commerce* (1813) that south of Bombay lay the port of Paniani, and "Near this place there is a remarkable gap in the mountains, called the Ghauts, through which the N. E. monsoon blows in general stronger than on any other part of the coast." At Surat, "the navigation up the river . . . is very difficult, in consequence of the sands frequently shifting." Countless Europeans had paid a high price for this kind of knowledge, as had countless Indians, Africans, and Arabs before them.[7]

Even so, inaccurate charts could lead even a cautious a navigator into peril, as Isaac Hinckley learned in October 1809, noting in the log of the *Reaper*, "My charts are not good." The maps he had brought, he learned, "are old, and I suppose incorrect"; consequently, he would have to "take my chance with my own judgment." For some, uncertainties created opportunities, and a mariner such as Nathaniel Bowditch, young and inexperienced at sea—but who had mastered the art of "working lunars" (celestial navigation) and was fluent in French and acquainted with Spanish—could land a position as shipmaster bound for the Indian Ocean.[8]

In planning a ship's destination, merchants scanned a befuddling abundance of markets—French Pondicherry, Portuguese Goa, Dutch Tranquebar (Tharangambadi), British Madras (Chennai), and Calcutta (Kolkata), among many smaller ports. Historian Glenn Gordinier has documented an example in the voyage of the Boston brig *Reaper* in 1809. This would be a complicated enterprise, entailing many unknowns. To diversify the risks, a temporary consortium of fifteen merchants planned the one-time project, employing a modest, two-masted vessel of two hundred tons and selecting Isaac Hinckley as the brig's captain. The *Reaper* freighted New England lumber, but, as had China, India had little demand for American goods, and so the merchants had to augment the cargo with three chests of silver, likely Spanish milled dollars obtained from their West Indies endeavors. It was up to Captain Hinckley to convert the specie into local currency in India. In a similar ca.1793 voyage, Amasa Delano elected to sail to the Malabar (western) Coast. He learned that the name denoted "mountaineer," referring to the mountains of Hindustan, from which it was said the coastal people came. But it was pepper, "a very important article of trade in this country," along with the areca nut, wild cinnamon, and cotton goods that drew him. When William Elting made his voyage to China, a Mr. Hunter provided him with a "testimony" of the markets along the way. He explained, "The articles of trade, from the bay and the Malabar coast are chiefly, pepper, sandalwood, put chick, shark fins, ola Halmer, elephant teeth, rhinoceroses horns." In addition, "the articles of trade from the Isle of France are cotton and chiefly ebony wood, which is always at a high price, . . . if its disposition, Quality, and dearity."[9]

Whatever the itinerary, mariners knew that the disposition of ship, crew, and cargo was not in their hands to determine, as Captain Benjamin Carpenter intuited when he began his record in a tenuous spirit: "Journal of my Intended Voyage (by God's Permission) from Boston to the East-Indies in the good Ship HERCULES. Departed Boston May 14, 1792."[10]

A voyage beyond the Cape of Good Hope entailed extraordinary risks, as Delano learned. He bet on the Indian markets along the Coromandel (southeastern) coast, and lost everything, lamenting: "Those who know all the circumstances said that if we had arrived at Calcutta six months sooner, or six months later than we did, we should have made a fortune. . . . But hazards of this kind always exist, and we went beyond our depth, and suffered the unhappy consequences."[11] Indian Ocean markets required complicated calculations—guesswork, really. India had little use for New England rum, fish, spermaceti candles, pork, and beer; consequently, merchants such as Charles Storrow and Samuel Shaw needed to trade fish, lumber, and Caribbean sugar for Spanish milled dollars, the standard international coin of exchange of that time.

A voyage to India was long, tedious, and wearing, mitigated only by virtue of being shorter than a journey to Canton. Ships' logs and mariners' journals recorded duration and distance as a measure of accomplishment in their modest vessels. Leaving sight of familiar places brought pangs of regret, as in the entry of William Augustus Rogers, supercargo aboard the *Tartar*, bound for Bombay (Mumbai) in 1817: "[At Thatchers light off Cape Ann] Here I cast one *'longing lingering look'* to the shores of my native land. And how fortunate was I in the consolatory thought that I left behind me many an anxious friend, who would rejoice at my prosperity or feel an anxiety for one who had left them in pursuit of an honorable independency."

To hold on to his connections with his native Salem, Rogers drew an image of a ship on the title page of his journal, and inscribed, "Baker's Isld., Light."

> Like a star on eternity's ocean.
> Oh what can sanctify the joys of home,
> Like Hopes of gay glances from oceans troubled foam?

Likewise, Salem supercargo Benjamin Carpenter sketched an image of Boston Light as his vessel passed on its passage to India in the *Hercules* in 1792. Landmarks such as lighthouses "were deeply felt markers of departure and arrival," historian Susan Bean notes.[12]

Voyagers sought to keep monotony and homesickness at bay by reading books and keeping journals, as Amasa Delano observed, "to employ and amuse my mind in this work, and to spend, in a rational and profitable manner, a number of months which might otherwise have been left a prey to melancholy and painful meditations."[13] Many travelers measured their passage in days and distance. Reaching India in 1800 in the *Belisarius*, Dudley Pickman remarked, "Arrived at Madras after Passage of 111 days from Salem. Distance run per log, this passage, 14,240 miles."[14] Spanning five months and two oceans, in January 1818, William Augustus Rogers recorded, "At 6 a.m. R.S.R. discovered land from the fore yard. The high lands of Ceylon, . . . this is the first land I have seen for 135 days! . . . It seems like my native land. But that land, the loss of the dearest of all friends a son can boast, has deprived me of almost all pleasure when I think of it."[15] Approaching his destination of Bombay, he recorded his sense of relief. "After being at sea 160 days and experiencing every vexation from wind and weather, added to the privations ever attendant on so long a passage, we arrived on the 16th at Bombay," Rogers noted.[16] The duration of a voyage was a reminder that travelers were now on the far side of the world and reinforced their status as outsiders—*farangi*, used across South Asia, equivalent to *fan quai* in China and *kafir* in parts of the Ottoman world.

Like the cargo, the crew's disposition posed further uncertainties on a long-distance passage. Purveyors of maritime fiction such as Melville, Michener, Stevenson, and Conrad spun tales of hearty men pitted against the sea, a primordial struggle of man against nature. In fact, as Marcus Rediker and Peter Linbaugh observe, the elemental struggle was often one of men against men and of social class against social class. Complicating conditions further, the vessel flying the Stars and Stripes rarely carried a Yankee complement; instead, a "motley crew" of divergent races, religions, and ethncities posed as much a danger to the good order of a ship as did nature.[17] Officers and crews were too often divided, as bad food, incompetent navigation, harsh discipline, and disappointing results triggered reprisal. For officers and passengers, a "motley crew" stoked fears of mutiny that added to the underlying tensions aboard ship.[18] Edmund Fanning took his vessels out of New York to his native Middleton, Connecticut, to find the New England crews he trusted. Sullivan Dorr similarly wrote to his brothers from Canton: "I cannot but repeat my solicitations that you will obtain good no[r]thern sailors, not valuing two or three Dollars per month extra wages, it will be made up by peace and order on board Ship, without which your vessels will not succeed on the Northwest Coast." Such selectivity was rarely possible. Bowditch described one muster out of Boston as "a curious set" that included "Negroes, Mullatoes, Spaniards, &c." The "&c." could include French, Portuguese, and Italians, Protestant and Catholic, enslaved, indentured, or free. On the *Frolic*'s last voyage, to San Francisco from Hong Kong by way of Bombay, the ship carried two American officers and a crew of seventeen Lascars and Malays, with a Serang (Native) boatswain.[19] The large presence made sense, according to Jeffrey Bolster's calculations, showing one quarter of American sailors were African American, often consigned to menial roles as cooks and stewards.[20]

Between the Cape of Good Hope and Cape Horn, as opportunities to abandon a ship increased, a captain's "pickings" might well include Indian lascars, Malayans, Chinese, Japanese, and the occasional Queequeg from Hawai'i. Such was the challenge for Sandwith Drinker, commanding the *Sultanah* to Zanzibar in 1840.[21] His observations on *Sultanah*'s sailors and dignitaries were commonplace, however. They were lascars, Indian maritime workers, from Bombay and the "very gleanings of the rough-scum of India." All work was God's work in Drinker's estimation; consequently, the lassitude he believed he perceived in the crew was a sin. As a group, he found them "about as worthless, idle set of wretches as I ever met with, [without] any pretensions to discipline." Unable to provide a cure for the first mate's lingering illness, Drinker attributed it to lassitude, recording: "Abdallah, my first officer, has scarcely been out of his bed since the Pilot left us. He has fallen away almost to a skeleton. I believe, however, it is as much laziness as sickness, that induces him to keep his bed. It is evident I shall receive little assistance from him this passage."[22]

Drinker recorded his deep sense of isolation; it seemed as if the safety of the ship and the success of the voyage were on his shoulders entirely. He described Juma, his African servant, "altho part African exceedingly intelligent," yet struggling to learn the principles of navigation."[23] Part of the problem lay in the fact that "their ideas of geography are so very different from the correct, it will be a long time before he understands the theory of it," a problem he shared with Captain James Cook's officers, who were at pains to comprehend the geography of their Tahitian navigator, Tupaia.[24] As for the diplomat, Ben Namen, Drinker took him to task as "so little of a sailor, I cannot trust him on deck alone, (If I could get him there.)"[25]

Nineteenth-century Americans appear to have taken stock in another quasi-Christian adage, the aphorism that cleanliness leads to godliness, and disparaged what they perceived was a lack of hygiene among foreign peoples. The Bible-clutching Drinker recorded his disgust with his lascar crew, writing: "I never met with a more filthy set of beings in any country. . . . All are exceedingly filthy, in their persons and dress; every Saturday evening they rub themselves with coconut oil, which gives their persons intolerable stench. They consider it a preventive to Rheumatism and cold."[26]

Encountering India meant navigating through its monsoons, those seasonal winds that so thoroughly and pervasively affected every aspect of life across the Indian Ocean. William Marsden, the EIC agent in Sumatra, understood this. Of the monsoon seasons, he wrote, "a different order takes place" in the tropics, "and the year is distinguished into two divisions, usually called the rainy and dry monsoons or seasons."[27] From September to June, the winter monsoon blew in from the arid deserts of northeast Asia, bringing drier, more pleasant air. In a place such as "Moombaee" (Bombay), one might see one rain shower in four months.[28] From June to September, the summer monsoon swept up from the southwest seas, brining torrential rains to western India.[29] This was the best time to sail from London, observed English visitor George W. Johnson, and the earlier in the season the better, "because the ship then arrives in India about the commencement of the cold season, beginning at the end of October, and the new comer is thus more gradually initiated in the inconveniences of the climate."[30]

The climate and weather of the Indian Ocean that they encountered usually confirmed a mariner's apprehensions. When Dudley Pickman described Calcutta from the *Derby* in 1803, he noted, "The rainy season commences in May and continues till September, sometimes raining for several days almost without intermission, and scarcely a day passing without some showers."[31] On leave from the US Navy in 1819, Lieutenant John White of Salem was impressed by the regularity that the climate imposed on human affairs, commenting, "The maritime commerce of Cochin China, like that of many other parts of Asia, is regulated by the monsoons."[32] Ten years later, Harriett Low, a passenger aboard the *Sumatra* was so taken that she wrote from the Cape of Good Hope, "In the several parts of India these monsoons are governed by various particular laws."[33]

Encountering the Indian Ocean's monsoons, one could expect a pleasant voyage when managed correctly. In December 1798, Edmund Fanning reported a rather routine crossing, "unattended by anything more than the usual occurrences of similar voyages; watching the wind, trimming sails, making and mending, constituting our daily business."[34] Such was the experience of William Augustus Rogers, aboard the *Tartar*, from Boston to Bombay, who observed, "Saturday Jany 31 1818. Brisk breezes & fine weather."[35] Yet the weather conditions of the Indian Ocean were fickle, and assuming the weather would be constant was one of the most grievous errors a mariner could make, as Rogers learned later in June, recording in the log of the *Tartar*:

June 3, 1818

Heavy distant thunder & lightning—9 AM the weather changed & in one hour was not a cloud to be seen—This has been a most unpleasant night & the ship in the greatest danger during the 2 squalls, I know of no situation more terrible, nor of one in which man feels his impotence & littleness, when compared with that Deity who wields the Thunder & directs the lightening, than in such as storm.[36]

The cyclones and the typhoons of the Indian Ocean could match those of the South China Sea, and the scenes of destruction filled the horizon. Rogers recalled "a dismasted E.I. ship from China to Bombay—about 900 or 1000 tons—had experienced a blow off the Nicobar Islands and lost his main topmast and mizzen mast."[37] A seasoned mariner would have fought through Atlantic gales, but in an unknown and distant region the stakes were higher and one felt more vulnerable, especially along an uncharted coast. Such was Charles Storrow's experience as his ship coursed the Bay of Bengal, as he jotted, "At daylight passed Prefraris Island, then came on heavy rain and fog, and we were watching in great anxiety for land till nearly dark, when the clouds lifted, discovering Diamond Island about 8 miles distant. . . . While we were on the lookout for land, through the fog, I experienced very strongly that feeling that I've read of, but hardly realized, namely the wish that we were out at sea where there is safety, instead of being near the treacherous land."[38]

Ignoring the experience of European guides brought trouble, as Bryant Parrott Tilden learned in 1815 as his ship *Canton* made slow progress through the Malay and China seas at the change from southwest to northeast monsoons.[39] Trouble could swiftly become tragedy for the careless mariner, as Amasa Delano learned. He wrote, "It is not advisable to work against the monsoon much at any time. Not regarding this, we were twice very near to a loss of our vessels on this coast."[40] At the cluster of islands known as Bombay, or Moombaee, Rogers advised, "In the south west monsoon however, in thick weather, vessels are often obliged to lay off and on several days before they can get in. Great care should be taken not to mistake a bay formed by Malabar Point and Bombay Island called Back Bay for the entrance to the harbor. It is full of rocks and shoals. You can ride with 1000 ships at your anchor in the N E monsoon but in the S. W. a very heavy sea sets in."[41]

Knowledge of the seasons was essential information for the merchant who sought the highest quality in cinnamon or opium, as well as the captain who sought to navigate precarious waters. American travelers knew of the fate of the Royal Navy's three-decked warship, the *Superb*, lost off Tellicherry, the principal English settlement on the Malabar coast (latitude 11°45′ North). Milburn's *Oriental Commerce* had described a secure harbor, advising, "In fine weather, ships anchor in the roads in five fathoms, the flagstaff bearing N. E. by N. off the town 14 to 2 miles; but when there is a chance of unsettled weather, they should anchor well out in 7 or 8 fathoms." But, in 1782, during the southwest monsoon, the fleet had "anchored in 5 and 54 fathoms, a heavy sea began to roll in, which made [the *Superb*] strike on the anchor of another ship," and sink.[42] The journal of William A. Rogers, aboard the *Tartar* along the Indian coast from 1817 to 1818, brought cautionary advice to the captains of the Salem East India Society. Rogers's jottings warned, "In passing along the W. Coast of Ceylon, care should be taken to distinguish the Hooy Mount from Adam's Peak, which although very lofty still may be mistaken for one or other."[43] From discussions with Rogers and his colleagues, Salem mariners might learn as much about sailing the Malabar or Coromandel coasts as schooning outside Salem harbor.

Complicating navigation was the unnerving sense that conditions were always variable, and a safe harbor in one season could be treacherous in the next. At Karical and other ports along India's Coromandel Coast, a Yankee skipper learned: "The marks for anchoring vary according to the monsoon: in the southerly one bring the flag-staff to bear W. S. W. in five or six fathoms; and in the northern monsoon it is to be brought to bear west. By this means the passage becomes easier to boats passing to and from the shore."[44] "It is not considered very safe in the southwest monsoon, though the ground is good," observed John White in June 1819, anchoring in the Tonkin Gulf of Cochin, China (Indochina), "but in the opposite season it is an excellent harbor."[45] Nor were the monsoon winds constant over the entirely of the Indian Ocean. Where mariners reported a rainy southwest ranged from June to September in India, William Marsden reported that on Sumatra's west coast, a dry southeast monsoon began about May, followed by "the NW. monsoon [that] begins about November, and the hard rains cease about March." One needed to take care during the transitional months of "April and May, October and November, generally affording weather and winds variable and uncertain."[46]

As in China, the climate of the Indian Ocean impaired the health of indigenous residents as well as foreign visitors. Visitors such as Amasa Delano found the elements particularly unhealthy in the northeastern province of Bengal, site of the bustling port of Calcutta. Likewise, an English visitor in the 1840s described the entrance to the Hugli River:

The first land, the features of which are dissectable, is Saugor Island, one continuous low and even waste, covered with genuine jungle. . . .

A noontide, like "the burning fiery furnace," chilling night fogs, and the miasma arising from putrefaction unparalleled in intensity, gather (at Saugor) the European quickly to his grave, whilst the rapid and extreme vicissitudes from moisture to dryness, break and crumble down his dwelling, with a rapidity unapprehended by a tarry-at-home in the temperate zone.[47]

The enervating heat of India's dry season, contrasting with the chilling winds of the wet season, brought discomfort and death. At sea, mariners' journals recorded deaths as regularly as they marked latitude, longitude, currents, and weather. In port, distressing news greeted a crew even before they lighted ashore. Pilot boats brought the first news a traveler had seen in months; some of this information was welcomed, much was fraught. William Scollay learned:

From a *Register* of the year belonging to the pilot, first learn the sad news of my poor cousin Peter Innes's death. My friend Mr. Cherry who chanced to have the first perusal of the book perceived in part for Thomas, requesting him to communicate the melancholy circumstance to me, which he did somewhat abruptly on returning to the cabin when I had just [illegible]. He died at Panang on his way to Amboyna, where he was going as assistant to the resident of the island on Dec 27 1810, the day of the ship's arrival. The letters which his mother & sisters received from him as he was about embarking were dated Nov. 27, one month before, written in a high [illegible] of spirits & apparently animated at his brilliant prospects.[48]

Death stalked India, and no one was safe, at sea or in harbor. Benjamin Carpenter lamented, on August 17, 1793, "Died on shore Capt. Jacob Oliver, of the American ship *Dispatch* of Boston—his Death was deeply and sincerely lamented by all who knew him."[49] When the *United States* anchored off Pondicherry in 1784, for instance, surgeon Thomas Redman wrote that by midday the heat kept all whites indoors except for those in palanquins, "which are carried by the black boys on their Shoulders."[50] With the *Ruby* anchored at Madras six years later, Captain Benjamin Carpenter calculated the cost of his visit with a note about the weather: "The sun is so powerful and the heat so excessive that you cannot live without a palanquin. This will cost you two rupees."[51] Departing Ceylon on September 10, 1861, William Storrow complained, "Nothing to do, and no energy to do it, so completely does this intense heat overpower me. The breeze is dying away, and but for the protection of our awning we should dive too."[52] When Captain Dudley Pickman anchored the *Belisarius* at Madras, 1799–1800, he recorded, "The weather during our stay was pleasant, except when the land wind blew, which was extremely hot. The thermometer stood at about seventy-five to eighty in the shade. No rain fell during our four weeks stay. Sometimes there is no rain for several months, till the rainy season sets in, when they are almost deluged. We saw a few camels here, employed in carrying burthens. Scarcely any birds, except crows, which are very plenty, coming into the house and almost taking things from table. They keep [up] a hideous croaking."[53]

The rhythm of a rainy season, June through October, followed by drought, filled the European cemeteries, the Indian funeral pyres, and the subcontinent's sacred rivers. In 1807, as an omen of what lay ahead, Captain David Pulsifer counted corpses floating by as his ship sailed toward Calcutta, recording, "It is not uncommon to see Dead Bodys Go past Every Day, More or Less."[54] Merchants such as Samuel Shaw succumbed to the lingering, painful liver ailments of tropical fever. The graves of many would be marked by navigational notation, if at all, such as that of thirty-three-year-old John Adams, who perished aboard the Salem Indiaman *George* after a lengthy illness, on March 18, 1821, in latitude 1°53′ North, longitude 31°36′ West. This John Adams would be remembered in popular histories, as his "body was committed to the deep, with the usual impressive services, which affect all so deeply and are so lasting on shipboard."[55] In Madras, Delano reported, "The climate is excessively hot, but is relieved by sea breezes."[56] During his stay at Madras, Benjamin Carpenter advised, "The sun is so powerful and the heat so excessive that you cannot live without a palanquin"—well worth the two rupees expense. By late December, conditions improved, and Captain John Crowninshield could observe, "very pleasant as it all ways is this time of the year. . . . Now is the best time of the year in the south West monsoon. It runs very strong indeed."[57]

The favorite leg of a voyage was the homeward cruise, as Marcus Rediker writes, and this was certainly true for an Indian Ocean passage. A crew did look forward to one stopover, in particular, and this was at the British-held island, and for a while the domicile of Napoleon Buonaparte, St. Helena. The South Atlantic winds and currents that directed a ship homeward made the island, over a thousand miles off Africa, more convenient than the Azores for refreshing supplies. St. Helena's fertile volcanic soil produced a bounty of fruits and vegetables, palatable wines, salutatory herbs, and decent food that could cure some of the many ailments a traveler could acquire in India.[58]

Climate diseases ran rampant throughout India, impeding business and imperiling lives. In the northeastern state of Assam, Englishman George Johnson warned in 1843, the climate was "direful" and "malarious," to the degree that "no European can exist there during June, July, August, and September." He ticked off a list of merchants and officials who had "perished within the preceding twelve months, [including] Mr. Duffield, Dr. Lamqua, Mr. Murray, Mr. Matlay, and Mr. Paton, have fallen before its death-blast." At times, EIC officials "had not an individual able to superintend, or to move about among the people, who were equally sickly." Diseases such as cholera struck high and low alike. The effort to transport "a gang of Dhangah coolies" to tea fields failed, "for cholera appearing among them, midway between Hazareebaugh and Assam, they took fright [and] the whole gang disappeared in one night, and no trace of them could be found!" It seemed as if all of nature on the sub-continent conspired against human agency. In the struggle to "civilize" parts of India, the EIC was losing, as "the jungle has been allowed to increase to a fearful extent, and when nature is thus neglected, she is a deadly opponent in her warfare against man." The dangerous climate meant that the political apparatus moved in spits and spurts. During the 1840s, Bengal's supreme court could not maintain a necessary cohort of chief justices, as one survived only the first six months, another the first three months, and another the first month of their arrival in India.[59] Not only did the losses complicate the efforts of Yankee skippers to complete their trade expeditiously; but also the extended anchorage imperiled the lives of officers and crew.

As in China, the extravagant lifestyles of the expatriate communities in India may have compromised a *farangi*'s immune system. Dudley Pickman observed this in his 1803 voyage to Calcutta aboard the *Derby*. Within the factories, he noted, the European traders "live in great style," enjoying "good tables and very expensive wines, and engaging in "very little exercise."[60]

High living among Western visitors, many believed, inflamed a pernicious liver ailment. As Delano described: "The liver becomes inflamed, an abscess is formed, and an incision is made in the side of the patient for relief. Sometimes he dies, but more frequently recovers."[61] Recovery did not come for many, however, as notable traders such as Samuel Shaw and William Henry Low filled graveyards across the Indian Ocean.

As a vessel plunged past the Coromandel Coast and toward Calcutta, another particular peril lay ahead. Many ships were lost and lives perished in the "notoriously turbulent Bay of Bengal, terror of mariners past, still and flat in the winter monsoons, raging when the summer monsoons riled the waters with silt and storm."[62] Ann Hasseltine Judson, a missionary aboard the brig *Caravan* in 1812, fretted: "We are now at anchor in the Bay of Bengal, and dare not go any farther tonight, as we have not yet got a pilot. Everything before us is uncertain. Whether we shall ever again be on land, or where we shall live, is known only to our heavenly Father."[63]

In the northeast province of Bengal, as a vessel approached the British factory at Calcutta, the Hugli River, a branch of the Ganges, awaited as a notorious gauntlet. The Hugli was a "difficult and dangerous" river cautioned Amasa Delano, aboard the *Eliza*, in 1803–1804.[64] Guidebooks and experienced sailors both advised slow, steady, watchful navigation up the eighty-one-mile passage to Calcutta, with an experienced pilot to navigate through sunken wrecks, lurking sandbars, and submerged logs. More dangerous still, the Hugli was "a treacherous river," generating eight-foot tidal bores that could easily capsize the small American ships, advised Captain Dudley Pickman, aboard the *Derby*, in 1803–1804.[65] In the writing of the day, the attempt to try the river's "bore of the tide" was so daunting that writers such as Delano framed their narratives as navigational guides. He cautioned, "A pilot must be obtained soon after you pass Point Palmyras. At the junction of the Hugli and the Ganges there are dangerous banks, and ships are lost upon them."[66] As a passenger, Ann Hasseltine Judson felt even more vulnerable, praying "We have been very anxious to get a pilot." As she told the readers of her *Memoir*, she spent the night in terror:

> Last night was the most dangerous, and to me, by far the most unpleasant we have had. The navigation here being dangerous, on account of the sand-shoals, the pilot came to anchor before dark. The sea was high, and kept the vessel in continual motion. About ten, the mate came down, and told us the cable had parted, and the anchor gone. I thought all hope of our safety was entirely gone, and immediately began to inquire into my preparedness for an entrance into another world. The thought of being shipwrecked was exceedingly distressing: and I could not but think the providence of God would preserve us on account of this infant mission.[67]

Nearly fifty years later, English passenger George Johnson shared the fears of Delano and Judson. Over the course of a stressful night, as repeated hails for a river pilot went unavailing and passengers "became better acquainted with the shallow soundings in which we were navigating, and the eternally shifting sands we were approaching . . . the anxiety displayed by our captain" spread to all.[68] The bore could easily capsize vessels the size of Isaac Hinckley's brig, *Reaper*.[69] In 1810, it took a pilot five days of plodding navigation to bring the *Reaper* upriver to Calcutta. The downriver trip was as daunting, as the pilot managed to pull the ship through powerful currents and tides by daylight, six hours each day, each night anchoring until a change of tides or dawn brought favorable conditions.[70] In 1821, it took the *George* eight days to sail from the Bay of Bengal and six to return.[71]

The Hugli was not the subcontinent's only navigational hazard. India's coastline was so long and so varied that a cautious navigator sometimes had to take extraordinary precautions. At times, no pilot appeared, as Charles Storrow learned to his disappointment in 1861 and William Augustus Rogers found at Bombay in February 1818; when Rogers "hoisted colors for a pilot, but none coming off," he piloted the ship *Tartar* into the harbor on his own. At harborless Madras (Chennai) along the Coromandel or southeastern coast, the surf was so treacherous that scenes of *masula* boats ferrying European goods and passengers through the waves became a favorite subject of colonial artists.[72] Approaching Madras in 1800, Dudley Pickman observed with caution, "The surf is always rough—sometimes very high, and throws the boat onto the beach with great force and rapidity. When the boat strikes, some of the boatmen jump into the water with a rope which they carry on shore, and with which the boats are hauled as far up, out of the surf, as possible."[73]

At the entrance to the Bay of Bengal, a Yankee ship faced its first encounter with the subcontinent's native sons. Local pilots, or *serangs*, and a lascar crew created a memorable, if not always favorable impression. Edwin Blood, arriving in Calcutta in May 1854 was struck by the costume of the lascars aboard a pilot boat: "The boat . . . was manned by 8 Lascars or native sailors. They of a dark copper color with straight black hair & beautiful. They were not overburdened with clothing, bare headed, with a loosely fitting jacket and pants rolled lightly up to the body exposing their bare legs the whole length.[74] George Johnson derisively described his arrival in a Calcutta pilot boat in February 1839 by noting that "the motions of her native crew was a sight of most amusing interest to us griffins, and ludicrous were the surmisings as to the duties and offices of sundry turbaned fellows among them."[75]

A dark element lurked beneath the feigned humor. Immediately, upon seeing the pilot crew, the condescending amusement that Western visitors displayed betrayed their own sense of dependence upon people who looked and acted so different. George Johnson expressed the sense of vulnerability, recalling, "The importance of the pilot establishment maintained there was intimated to everyone on board, by the anxiety displayed by our captain to get one of the fraternity to take us in charge that night; and, when we became better acquainted with the shallow soundings in which we were navigating, and the eternally shifting sands we were approaching, we fully participated in the skipper's anxiety. This anxiety was not to be allayed that night, for although we hoisted the usual signal, and burnt blue lights at intervals during the darkness, no pilot came to our invitation." Yet Westerners rarely trusted the people upon whom they needed to survive.[76] As in Canton, a Yankee felt both dependent and cheated, as Captain John Crowninshield implied as he boarded a pilot for the Hugli River passage up to Calcutta on December 14, 1797, complaining, "In the stream gave the pilot my Note for 121 Rupees for piloting the ship up—she drew 10 1/2 but we must pay for 11 if she draw above 10 &c."[77] The lasting impression left in their travelogues was that the land and waters of India were dangerous. Equally threatening, to one's life and profits, were the people.

For those destined upriver for Bengal province, pushing through the Hugli's vicious tidal bore was just one challenge met, as William Scollay, writing to relations in Boston, reported in 1811. "Multitudes of tigers" freely roamed the shores and feasted on travelers who were foolish enough to take to land without a guard. Anchored off Sagar Island at the mouth of the Hugli River, Scollay reported, "People often carried off here and it is very dangerous going ashore. Shortly after our arrival a sailor belonging to an Indiaman who was taken from between two others and borne off. All attempts to save him [in] vain. His piercing cries heard to the last. A son of Sir Hector Morris was carried off by one of the furious animals many years since. He extricated himself from the tiger and expired on board the ship."[78] When Storrow visited Ceylon, much of the island remained "unexplored, native jungle," where Westerners hunted elephants and tigers and were "constantly meeting with venomous snakes, such as the cobra di capello" and boa constrictors.[79] Little had improved by 1854, when Captain Edwin Blood observed, "Terrible hot; Temp 91°. Sharks, water snakes, & pleanty of land insects bout us all day."[80]

In journals and logs, festooned with motifs of national eagles and Stars and Stripes that anchored a traveler's memories to hearth and home, the first sight of India's indigenous people appeared as unnerving as its creatures. Sailing up the Hugli River, missionary Howard Malcolm described an eerie and primitive shoreline, a "dead level and unbroken jungle [that] gives the whole an aspect excessively dreary, well suiting to one's first emotions on beholding a land of idolatry."[81] The scenery was unpleasing, and beneath "a savage underbrush" along the river banks, Scollay observed, were villagers who appeared "even more savage then the rude wilds in which they dwell."[82] Moreover, the shoreline was unrelieved of any of the familiar markers of "civilization" to greet the traveler, unlike, the Bostonian referenced with some irony, "the shipwrecked mariner on desert coast"—Defoe's Robinson Crusoe—for whom the sight of a "murderers gibbet" indicated he had returned to a civilized country. In India, Scollay complained, with no hint of irony, that "for long intervals scarce another mark of humanity can be discerned," with little "to distinguish the shores of the Hoogly from the savage haunts and solitary wilds of our American wilderness."[83]

After, in Scollay's words, "what for me had been for six tedious months a scene of annoyance, disgust, mortification & uneasiness," a traveler was hardly prepared for the sense of disorder that marked a griffin's landfall in an Indian port.[84] Unfamiliar sights, sounds, and smells stunned missionary Miron Winslow, who recalled, "On a first arrival here, one finds himself so completely in a new world, that he is bewildered. . . . If the moon should fall from heaven, he would not be surprised, but think it the way with the Bengal moons."[85] On reaching Bombay in 1818, the extraordinary noise and commotion left William Augustus Rogers equally disoriented, "after being at sea 160 days and experiencing every vexation from wind and weather, added to the privations ever attendant on so long a passage."[86] The sight of land and the odd displacement of a familiar name shook a traveler's nerves, as when Rogers observed Ceylon on January 23, 1818, recording: "This is the first land I have seen for 135 days! With what pleasure was the distant crags of Adams Peak."[87]

From the moment of arrival, the griffin felt exposed on every front and, consequently, less at ease, less tolerant, and less forgiving. Newcomers described themselves reeling from every sight, sound, smell, taste, and texture as strange and disorienting.[88] In Calcutta's harbor, Ann Judson was "almost stunned with the noise of the natives."[89] Rogers reported the dizzying assault on his senses in Bombay, where "in passing from the bundar I was, as may be easily imagined, forcibly struck by the appearance of everything around me. A stranger, the first moment he sees an Indian city is probably more astonished, his curiosity more awakened, perhaps delighted, than it can be in visiting the first European cities."[90] European cities could not "excite half the emotion that you feel on first seeing" a South Asian enclave. Here were buildings "of a style totally different from any we have ever seen," streets teeming with the range of humanity dressed in every attire from genteel European to the "turban's Turk," the loose pants of the coolie, and seemingly of every nationality, ethnicity, and religion.[91]

So shocking was the appearance of the serangs, lascars, guides, purveyors, and, in countless numbers, beggars that some American visitors questioned the humanity of the indigenous peoples who assaulted their senses. Culture shock marked William Storrow's first contact in Calcutta in September 1861. Here he found men who were "copper-colored, very intricately tattooed with red and blue, so that almost made us think they wore figured blue trousers, while in reality they are utterly devoid of such appendages."[92] Strange, inverted gender customs likewise amazed their field of vision, as a disbelieving Storrow fretted.

> We found here a custom of labor altogether new to us, viz: for our work, women and girls were the laboring class; all our ballast was discharged, and all our rice loaded by girls and women from six to sixty years of age; they are divided into gangs under female supervision, all obedient to one make head or chief, called the coolie gong. They are admirable workers, and I believe we never had cause to complain of them. In loading ships with rice in bags the men do all the labor; carrying the bags on their shoulders, while the women take their loads in baskets, proportioned in size to the strength of the owner.[93]

Yet this India would be a place in which Americans' confidence in their own civilized behavior could be questioned. To the dismay of Captain Benjamin Carpenter, his own appearance complicated efforts to make business connections at Madras in 1790. Advising the *Ruby*'s owners in Salem, Carpenter warned, "An attention to your person as well as uniformity of conduct is necessary to make you appear in any favorable light to the haughty Indians who have a very miserable opinion of the Americans, and their ignorance and shameful behavior hitherto has justly merited their censure."[94] A journey to this part of the world, as in Constantinople or Canton, shook a Yankee traveler's certitude, and left one feeling elemental doubts. There was always the opportunity to use the experience to foster feelings of humility and humanity. Carpenter may have done so when he reflected: "Let me be in what port I may, not to neglect this attention. . . . From the Governor to the meanest citizen I have made it my study to please. Let a man's occupation be what it will, you may have occasion for his aid." Yet few did. Most accounts refracted their own newfound vulnerabilities into arrogance toward the inhabitants they encountered.[95]

Language was another thing to disturb a griffin's composure. As in China and the Muslim world, words carried meanings not easily understood; new words had to be acquired and remembered if the voyage was to be profitable.

And there were so many. Upon anchoring in any port eastward of the Cape of Good Hope, an American could expect to be surrounded by dozens or even hundreds of pinnaces or canoes offering provisions for barter. In Canton, these vessels were called sampans and *hawpoo* or dragon or crab boats; in India, they were dinghies, *dinghy-wallahs*, *pawuchwags*, pattamars, *kedgers*, and country boats.[96] In Canton, one needed to deal with mandarins and compradors and hongs. In India, it was *sicars*, serangs, lascars, *khansamahs*, *khitmutgahs*, banyans, and dubashes.[97] Harriet Low and Robert Bennet Forbes complained that Canton's noisy Joss days, filled with the crash of firecrackers, disturbed their routines. In Calcutta, likewise, Benjamin Carpenter and William Rogers confided to their diaries their frustrations when "This day being the Gentave [Hindu] Holiday, we had no Caulkers." Later that summer, he would record, "August 13 . . . Came onboard Francis, a Bengal Portuguese," whose Catholicism added to the babble.[98] The noise and commotion engendered a sense of dependence not only on others but also on persons they found annoying and, that capital of Yankee sins, frivolous.

It was all just so much noise to a Yankee or English griffin, such as George Johnson, who complained of "the noise, the unintelligible vociferations of the rowers or dinghy-wallahs, of the numerous craft of that description who come upon deck to solicit employment, is totally bewildering to the uninitiated."[99] Depending on the disposition of the griffin, a lascar crew's appearance might be reported as industrious, even entrepreneurial. In the early years of American encounters in India, a traveler such as William Rogers of Salem used his journal to perform the roles of Yankee gentleman, cosmopolitan citizen of the world, and sympathetic observer of the human condition. Off Ceylon, he recorded that the "many canoes of a singular construction filled with natives nearly naked [that] came off to trade away their fruit" constituted no particular threat, and their Native crews "were honest, intelligent, & good natured. . . . The natives appeared very poor indeed, but very honest."[100] More frequently, however, a newcomer could not get past cultural differences that were so at odds and frightened the dainty gentility of the Atlantic's mercantile world. William Scollay, for instance, described indigenous Indians in deplorable terms, as:

> much nearer in affinity to baboons than human beings. On seeing them one is
> almost inclined to consider the opinion maintained by Lord Mimbroddo relative
> to our general [illegible] from these animals to be founded on something like
> probability. Though one may be apt to dispute his position that the inhabitants

of the Nicobar & Andaman Islands in the Bay of Bengal have not yet entirely worn away the whole of the tail which was once the common appendage, but still retain a visible stamp. Yet from the striking resemblance in physiognomy & in the posture of sitting one is led to his lordship's opinion with no small degree of complacency. Their only clothing a piece of cloth around the waist, smoking the hubble bubbles, a kind of hookah formed from a cocoa nut seemed to be their principal relaxation from labor. Their paddles resemble spoons more than oars. They are made out of bamboo. Their anchor a stone secured in two pieces of wood crossed.[101]

Scollay may have been disaffected by the erratic behavior of his drunken pilot, a "loquacious, swaggering, consequential fellow."[102] Scollay's racism allayed his anxieties in other ways. Discounting the mass of humanity which filled India, more than one hundred million, simplified the need to comprehend the complexities of another culture, relieved him of the need to treat Indians as people, and enabled him to focus on the economic purposes of the voyage.

As in the Ottoman world or in China, even the strange clothing, or rather the lack thereof, assaulted the senses. And, as in China and the Ottoman world, the pervasive poverty that enveloped travelers stunned Western observers, but in India it was even worse. Dependence made newcomers' first encounters with the indigenous people even more galling. They needed help from the very people they found ridiculous and revolting, especially on arrival, when the "comfort and benefit derivable from the services of a native attendant, are never more apparent to the stranger than upon his first arrival."[103]

Calcutta had been opened as a British factory-fortress in 1690, yet, fifty years later, transport was still tenuous. "Thomas intends going to Kedger, higher up to obtain a budguou for our conveyance," Scollay reported in 1811, "but gives up his intention on learning from the *sicars* or black agents who had come on board that none can be procured at this place."

The complication of geography and culture meant that making one's way in Madras was different form Pondicherry, and was different still from Calcutta. Upstream at Kedgeree, the sense of strangeness met the eyes in all forms. Like Canton's curious vessels—crab, hawpoo, flower, and dragon boats—Calcutta's coastal fleet defied expectation. "Meet many of the *donies* in country vessels as we sail up the river. Their construction & appearance very singular, square rigged with one mast & curious bows. They usually go down to the Coromandel coast & return with the monsoon, performing in this manner one voyage in the year. Breadth of the River Hooghly at Kedgence."[104]

Upon arriving in any foreign port, a vessel's officers first had to contact the local authorities and customs officials. With its hundreds of indigenous principalities and kingdoms, overlaid with Portuguese, Dutch, Danish, French, and British colonial administrations, India lacked the centralized governance that regularized trade in Ottoman ports and Canton. As in Canton, Americans were a "new people," and their first contacts with European colonial officials were awkward. Official visits were required everywhere, but a captain needed to learn who commanded authority and what the protocols were. In 1790, Benjamin Carpenter sailed the *Ruby* to Point de Galle, Ceylon (Sri Lanka), where he met with the governor, then to the French factory at Madras, where he waited upon the intendant. In 1810, Captain Hinckley of the *Reaper* first reported to the Police Office to deliver his ship's register, then to the Custom House to drop off the vessel's cargo manifest.[105] These meetings could be whirlwind affairs, leaving an American visitor stupefied. Or so Rogers reported of his arrival at the Custom House in Bombay, where, under the watchful care of two dubashes, or guides, "Here I was, the moment I landed thrust into a palanquin and carried off to our merchants' house whose names were Nowrajee and Jahangheer Nasserwanjee."[106]

Where in Canton the various East India Companies made accommodations available in the foreign factories, an extended stay in Madras or Bombay or Calcutta required that one search for lodgings. Taverns were available but inferior. Dudley Pickman from the *Belisarius*, 1799–1800, found: "There are several taverns here, but their charges are enormously high, and, it is less reputable to live at them, than to keep house. The Americans whose business brings them to this place, take a house and furnish it, and hire a sufficient number of servants."[107] Besides the expense that cut into profits, there were other considerations, as Captain John Crowinshield recorded in Calcutta in December 1797: "I got an early dinner & went on shore to engage a house & after seeing several I concluded to take the largest & the others I saw where not only small but have no go down or stores, & are a long way from the custom house & all goods must go there before you can export them & the cooly hire would be more & this house which I have taken (it is larger than I wanted) has sufficient room & large go downs but the price is high. 125 Rupees per month."[108]

Two years later, R. Cleveland complained, "The multitude of servants, which custom required for the establishment of those even, who were desirous of living in the most frugal manner, was alarming. Mine, including palanquin-bearers, cooks, stewards, and waiters, amounted to eight, exclusive of my

black man, George; a number that seems enough to ruin a man of small fortune, till it is considered how very small is their pay, and how little their food
costs compared with ours."[109]

In Calcutta, Hinckley rented a small house for $7.06 per day for his lodg-
ings and business office.[110] The cost was almost the monthly wages of the
Reaper's sailors, and so seemed an extravagance that, along with the many
port charges, added further to the costs of the voyage. To economize, John
Crowninshield moved his own furniture into "the house I have took to reside
in." At Madras in 1790, Benjamin Carpenter advised, "It is better to take a
small house and preferable to living at the tavern and vastly more convenient.
Your house expenses will be about a pagoda [madras currency worth 8 shil-
lings, or 3½ rupees], whereas at the Tavern two pagodas a day."[111]

A frugal and well-connected world traveler could share the burdens of
housekeeping with his countrymen and acquaintances. Richard Cleveland of
Salem benefited from connections in Calcutta in November 1799, recalling:
"Here I met again my worthy friend Captain Lay, of whom I bought the cutter, and of whose kind hospitality Captain Hassell and myself availed ourselves till we could procure and prepare a house. For a hotel, or a public
boarding-house, was a thing unknown in this country." In Bombay in February 1818, after berthing the *Tartar*, William Rogers jotted in his journal, "Capt.
R & myself, with Mid. E Orne went on shore— found here the Malabar, took
lodgings in a fine house in Military Square occupied by Capt. Orne & son."

As at Canton, finding other Americans, even fellow townsmen, in an Indian
port provided a measure of relief from the monotony and homesickness of an
extended journey and eased the "pain of unbelonging."[112] The accommodations that American sea captains settled on in Indian ports worked toward
exclusion, however. In a faraway port, travelers sometimes found scant company to refresh their souls. Captain Dudley Pickman of the *Belisarius*, was disappointed to find in 1799:

> At Madras, I met very few Americans, and, except in business, formed no
> acquaintances with the English residents. Of the former, was Captain Cheever,
> born at Danvers where his relations now live, has been twelve or fifteen years
> in India, master of a country vessel, has acquired but little property and will
> probably never return to America. . . . Mr. Stephen Minot of Boston, lived for
> several years in Salem with Captain N. West, now trades between Isle of
> France, and Tranquebar and Madras, probably covering French property,
> principally prize vessels which he brings back from Mauritius for sale.[113]

With fewer opportunities to listen to and learn from Indian men and women, their understanding of the country and its peoples remained necessarily shallow. It became difficult to develop empathy or concern for a people with whom they had few interactions, and these concentrated on matters of trade and profits. And, as Henk Driessan, Michael Pearson, and Isaac Land have pointed out, it is difficult to characterize these Americans as cosmopolitan.[114] In his 1811 sojourn in Calcutta, William Scollay evidenced his sense of privilege in describing his first experience in a palanquin: "The first entrance into a palanquin is attended with no small degree of awkwardness on the first attempt & beside the jolting & unpleasant motion the idea of pain to the sweating & grunting bearers on whose shoulders your hearse-like machine is borne is far from making this mode of conveyance agreeable to a beginner, tho' custom in a few days wonderfully [illegible] us to all similar ideas, & we soon enter into the vehicle & hear the grunts of the bearers with as much influence as the most luxurious Indian."[115]

In settling into the Indian conveyance, Scollay took pains to situate himself between the "luxurious Indian" and the "grunting bearers." In this way, he was able to employ two conventional tropes that allowed him to represent himself as both the "exceptional" American and the sympathetic victim. Except as props, perhaps, neither the lives of Bengal's thirty million people nor the wrenching poverty that ground many of them down nor their desperate search for work appeared in the pages of Scollay's travel journal or interrupted the opulent lifestyle of *ferengi* visitors. So Scollay and other American expatriates could imagine them simply as an undifferentiated degraded mass.[116]

Wherever in the world a merchant traveled, the success of the voyage necessarily invoked relationships of trust with strangers. A Yankee supercargo knew, and feared, that the success of his voyage was in the hands of people whose language he could not understand, whose motives he could not predict, whose beliefs he could not fathom, and whose values he could only dimly penetrate. In their hands lay his reputation, his competency, and his future. The sense of dependence undermined the trader's self-esteem and left him resentful of the people who controlled his fate.

Independence was not an option in the Indian marketplace, however. The journals of captains and supercargoes describe a patchwork of myriad markets more confounding than what they found in Constantinople or Canton, the mysteries of each of which had to be unlocked if a voyage was to make a profit. In any voyage, the plight of the supercargo was to fear for the success of a voyage that could leave him wealthy or bankrupt, his reputation intact or in tatters; as more layers of complexity were added, opportunities for success diminished. Such had been the fate of Robert Morris, who financed the *Empress of China*, and later of Amasa Delano, who returned to the Massachusetts shipyard where he had spent his youth as a broken man, and many others. His 1817 *Narrative* was testimony to the dangers that India posed for even an enterprising Yankee. Consequently, successful merchants such as Morris's partner, Thomas Willing, and Stephen Girard preferred to finance partial cargoes rather than entire ships, and New York merchants commissioned only half a dozen Indian voyages before 1800.[117]

Americans had ventured eastward of Good Hope in 1784 to find markets and goods that would allow them to bypass the familiar emporia of the Atlantic and Caribbean. After the Revolution, Europe's empires raised duties and increased regulations to limit participation by the merchants of the new nation, who needed to look farther afield for opportunities. New lands created new opportunities but added more risk. Language was another thing to disturb one's composure. As in China and the Muslim world, words carried meanings not easily understood; new words had to be acquired and remembered if the voyage was to be profitable. In India, Americans found a cornucopia of goods that taxed their knowledge and increased the risks that the cargoes they fetched would fail in the home markets. In Calcutta, one had to master a cotton-goods market that was "particularly challenging as there were hundreds of different kinds of cotton cloths, each with unique qualities, and each with fluctuating financial worth," designated first by village or region of origin, then by kind (mirzapore chintz, and the like). One had to further gauge the quality of gruff goods such as sugar, India's second largest export commodity, and know how bags of sugar should be stowed in the ship's cargo hold. Gordinier explains, "The real key to successful trading in Calcutta was familiarity with the local market. Daily visits to the bazaar were required, otherwise the unwary westerner could pay as much as 25 percent too much for his purchases."[118] The variety of goods, as well as the quality, value, and currency or barter exchange, could be daunting. In Benjamin Carpenter's sojourn in Madras in 1790, he purchased cotton and silk textiles, sugar, indigo, ginger, saltpeter, leather, jute, linseed, and cowbear—"a small hard substance from the gall of bullocks and is used as a medicine in India—it is in great demand at 120 pagodas per maud."[119] Elias Derby Jr.'s journey to India, in 1803–1804, fetched a cargo of cotton textiles, raw cotton, sugar, ginger, and copal (resin used in varnishes), which he sold at Boston.[120] Hinckley in the *Reaper* needed to learn about rattans, sago, cassia, pepper, ebony, sugar, and other gruff goods.[121] In Bombay, Amasa Delano learned the properties of *kayar*, "made from the busk of the cocoa-nut," for ships' cables, and, in Calcutta, "a kind of hemp called *jute,* eight or ten feet long after it is dressed. It is excellent in all respects, but will not bear tar, and therefore is not suitable for the use of ships."[122] In 1790, in Calcutta, Captain Benjamin Carpenter complained that "the markets are so fluctuating with dry goods that I think it dangerous to meddle with them." And, everywhere, the supercargoes needed to master a hodgepodge of currencies—pagodas in Madras, rupees in Calcutta, lakhs elsewhere.

In their early days of contact, the India that Americans encountered was as much a European as it was an Indian place.[123] Rarely did an American mariner stray from the port where he supervised the sales of cargo and maintenance on his ship, and few took the time to meet a pasha, nawab, or a *ryott* (inland farmer).[124] The War of 1812 left William Lee of Boston stranded in Calcutta, for instance, but his letters home rarely said a word about the Indian peoples or cultures.[125] By the time the *United States* dropped anchor in Pondicherry in December 1784, much of the Malabar and Coromandel coasts were pocked with French, Dutch, Danish, Portuguese, and, of course, British factories (fortresslike trading posts). Or, rather, they were the domains of East Indies companies of merchants from these countries. The English were in ascendance, consolidating the gains they had made over three decades. EIC armies and administrators were in Madras along the Coromandel Coast, Bombay along the Malabar, and Bengal in the northeast, although only in the latter was their control secure.[126]

In many of the world's ports, cultivating a faithful mercantile relationship could be relatively straightforward, in others complex and fraught with difficulties. Benjamin Carpenter found Calcutta's populace "more sociable and friendly" and "ready to assist you in everything" than those of Madras or Ceylon.[127] Yet, as Glenn Gordinier writes, "Unlike the Canton market, which was relatively straightforward, the Calcutta textile market was very complex," requiring eight functionaries to move cloth from country weavers to Western merchants: *pycars, gomastahs,* peons, *hiscarars,* sircars, and, driving the process, the banyan, or *banian.* Wherever a ship anchored, however, various officials met the captain with a dizzying array of invoices. In loading even a simple commodity, such as sugar in Calcutta, he would face "ten separate charges that were paid in order to cover the cost of packing, weighing, storing, protecting, and clearing the bags of sugar."[128] "The role of the banyan," Gordinier observes," "was indispensable."[129] In southern Indian ports such as

Madras, the banyan's counterpart was the dubash and a clerk, known as a conicopoly. The process of selecting a reliable banyan or dubash could be as chaotic for an American captain or supercargo as finding a comprador in Canton. Benjamin Carpenter described the essential roles, writing from the great cabin of the *Ruby*:

> When you first land at Madras you will have a number of the natives about you who will [be] very solicitous to serve you as a dubash or broker. . . . Pauls Vincaty is the best dubash in Madras. He has served me in two voyages and I have no reason to be dissatisfied with him. . . . You will also want conicopoly who will be of service to you in many little matters, such as supplying you with coolies, receiving your money, etc. The dubash is useful when you are at a loss for a market and will frequently dispose of your articles, when you have made every effort without success.

Carpenter added a caveat that incorporated part business advice, part cultural reductionism: "It is necessary to have one of their people, but not to be too precipitate in your choice. They are in general a [set?] of artful men and require well looking after."[130] In his view, the qualifications for choosing a banyan or dubash were a mix of business sense and personal qualities, especially dependability. So he recommended Ramdulolday, who was "very shrewd and capable, extremely avaricious, and possesses great talents for business"; Ram Chunder Banorjea, "a very smooth tongued man"; and Collisunker, "a shrewd man and industrious when pressed by business." As another indication of their effectiveness, Carpenter had inquired into their assets, learning that Ramdulolday "is considered to be worth three to five million rupees," Ram Chunder "is said to be worth five to ten lacs rupees," and Collisunker was "about as rich as Ram Chunder." Overall, Carpenter "was satisfied with the manner in which they managed the business I entrusted to them."[131]

Whether a banyan in Calcutta or a dubash in Madras, American traders were dependent on their knowledge, skills, and honesty. "Every mercantile house in Madras employs a head dubash, or broker, who is a native and does most of the active business of the house," Dudley Pickman reported. "It is absolutely necessary to employ a dubash, whose clerks (or conicopolies) attend to receiving, weighing, and shipping goods, etc., which on the part of the merchant is also attended to by natives. The more the whole of them can be overseen, and the less depended on, the better."[132] In Calcutta, in December 1797, Captain John Crowninshield described the competence that "my banian" proved across a wide range of areas: "trying to find a place to heave my ship down at & to see what kind of an agreement I can make with the man &c."; "has bought for me today several sorts of white cloths at different price & I believe they are lower than they have been this sometime past owing to the scarcity of specie"; "had [bales of cotton] all brought up to my house & put in the Go-downs before night"; and, in a catchall phrase, "I let my Banian have the above 48 Lumps of gold to try what he can obtain for them."[133] In Madras, in 1790, Benjamin Carpenter offered his thoughts on the vital responsibilities that the dubash had carried out. The conicopoly "will be of service to you in many little matters, such as supplying you with coolies, receiving your money, etc. The dubash is useful when you are at a loss for a market and will frequently dispose of your articles, when you have made every effort without success."[134]

Dependence bred suspicion and mistrust, however. Susan Bean describes the many ways in which a ferengi merchant depended on the insider, observing "The banian was essential. . . . He spoke English; he knew the market; he knew where to procure commodities and sell imports; and sometimes he supplied capital as well." "These webs of dependence," she continues, "nurtured trust when the transactions were successful and suspicion when they failed. The success often led to relationships that transcended pure commerce."[135] John Crowninshield expressed his frustration with the situation in 1797, writing, "A man you must have and a man that will make money out of you."[136] This vulnerable state was acute among American traders who, through instinct, experience, and training, grasped at control and bridled at weakness. In Delano's *Narrative,* Cleveland's *Voyages,* and a host of other accounts, American readers could also learn much about everyday life in India, and these descriptions, too, offered a "useful knowledge" that enabled them to anticipate the various dangers to life and enterprise in the ports of the Indian Ocean. Reports of corruption on the docks of Bombay and Calcutta, augmenting reports of Chinese "knavery" at the wharves of Canton and Whampoa, inflected American travelers' descriptions of the East and instilled lasting impressions of a corrupt and dangerous people.[137] In 1788, for instance, when the Indiaman *General Washington,* out of Providence, Rhode Island, anchored in Madras harbor, the supercargo reported back to the Brown family, "the whole life and study of the Indians is to cheat you." Yet the *General Washington* brought home a cargo worth nearly $100,000, and its owners continued trade with India.[138] Be wary in forming a household in Madras, Dudley Pickman advised, as "Some excellent servants are found here, but all much inclined to 'cheat master.'"[139] William Rogers concurred in his sweeping assessment that "the Hindoos [are] a low, cheating, brutal race, but a short remove from the brute creatures."[140] As for the indispensable dubash, his loyalties were to the Anglo-Indian mercantile house that employed him and not to the American client who would be gone within a month or two. Pickman warned his employers about employing Indian intermediaries, writing, "Some of them are very rich and faithful to their employers, even joining in any fraud or oppression they may practice on the countrymen of the dubash."[141]

Putting a premium on trust, Yankee merchants touted the "exceptional" Indian as abolitionists and others back in the United States touted the exceptional African at home.[142] Benjamin Carpenter employed this condescending language from his berth aboard the *Ruby* in 1790, advising the owners, "After your sales are finished and accounts settled, if your dubash has behaved himself well and has been faithful to you, you will pay him about 30 pagodas; and the conicopoly 20."[143] Dudley Pickman engaged in a similar kind of rationalization from his berth aboard the *Belisarius* in Tranquebar (1799–1800), writing, "The dubash, Tilly, returned with Mr. Reid to Tranquebar, who spoke highly of his attention, ability and faithfulness." For his part, Pickman was more circumspect, carping in his journal: "The Americans who trade here find it necessary also to employ a dubash. There are two only who devote themselves to this business, Vincaty and Villapoy. Neither of them deserves high commendation. . . . They require much looking after, and are not to be depended on, having the interest of the merchant from whom they expect future favors at least as much at heart, as that of their immediate employers."[144]

Having settled into a rented bungalow, perhaps smoking their cheroots after a sumptuous European-style dinner, waited on by fawning Native servants, American expatriates often turned the conversation to condescending chatter about the people among whom they lived and from whom they felt alienated. Yankee accounts often described Indians as so different from anything to which they could relate, so varied as to defy the effort to establish a pattern, and their behaviors so "inscrutable"—a favored term applied to Asians by the end of the century—as to defy reason; they were to be met with a harsh impatience.[145] This was especially so because Indians were seen as obstacles to the entire purpose of a voyage—to earn as much profit as possible. They frustrated American merchants and missionaries from the first moment of contact. When no pilot arrived to escort a vessel through a harbor, as Ann Hasseltine Judson found in 1812, William Augustus Rogers in 1818, and Charles Storrow in 1861, the motive was assumed as lassitude or impertinence.

A common topic was the need to be on guard against charlatans, who seemed ubiquitous and ever ready to part ferengis from their money. The Englishman George Johnson cautioned against buying furniture and clothes from "the itinerant vendors, or *box wallahs*, who call at your house almost daily. They invariably ask four times as much as they will take: if you know the value of the article in England, offer that, and it will always be taken."[146] Even the sepoys of the British army could not be trusted to safeguard foreigners— so Amos Porter heard in Canton in 1802.[147] When the governor of Bombay granted a sepoy guard for the Persian ambassador, a dispute broke out, and the sepoys killed several Persian attendants as well as the ambassador.

Much of the Americans' complaint against Indian "corruption" likely proceeded from projection.[148] Yankees were notorious among their own countrymen for their own sharp business practices. Beyond the Cape of Good Hope and out of the eyesight of other Americans, deception and cheating was a two-way street, as Benjamin Carpenter observed in 1790: "It is customary for the India captains to add twenty percent on the prime cost and then sell at twenty-five percent on the foot of the invoice so that instead of twenty-five they gain forty-five percent on the whole amount. The natives are unacquainted with the cost of goods in Europe and are easily deceived this way." In their correspondence, many employed secret codes to mislead competitors.[149]

Another link in the India trade was the merchant business office, known as a house. This could be British, Anglo-Indian, or Indian. American traders were known to use all three, as long as the local merchants could assign a banyan or dubash and conicopoly, handle currency exchange, and, perhaps most important, provide current market information. In 1790, Benjamin Carpenter listed the qualifications he sought in a Madras merchant, advising that an American trader seek out "men of property [who] carry on an extensive trade . . . very liberal in his dealing and is very attentive to strangers . . . well informed and will give you every information respecting your proceedings while in India." Carpenter, Pickering, and Rogers understood how great were the risks and how dependent they were on strangers with whom they had virtually nothing in common. Carpenter summarized: "To gain the friendship of such a man is by no means a small acquisition, especially in India, when you are liable to so many impositions. Before you make any contracts or do any business of any kind it is best to consult him. He will inform you of the state of the market and the customs of the place necessary to be complied with."[150]

Yankees employed a studied wariness even of the British mercantile houses in the ports of the subcontinent. Because Eastern markets showed scant demand for American goods, a captain or supercargo needed to convert specie into local currency. This complicated set of actions required the intermediation of a local commercial house.[151] Captain John Crowninshield felt his voyage compromised in January 1798, caught in the machinations of a Calcutta firm, fretting: "Messrs. Fairlie Gilmore & Co. have not sent me the 10,000 rupees I sent my Banian after the 29 ulto. I don't know what to think of it. It is not the way we do business in America. His seccar had the confidence to offer to mine 2,000 rupees." Curiously, when William Augustus Rogers anchored at Bombay, he did business with a Parsee house, yet was especially skeptical of them, chiding: "Most strangers are pleased with their characters, but I found too much dishonesty in the reputed intelligence in business, too much self interest in their good nature and too much licentiousness in their private characters, to entitle them to indiscriminate confidence. The poor are thievish to an extreme."[152]

"We shall have a fine time & a good opportunity to give it all a good & thorough over hall as we intend so to do it," recorded Captain John Crowninshield in December 1797. Crowninshield recognized that his ship, the *Belisarius*, "has been standing 37 months," and in that time proper maintenance on the vessel had been necessarily deferred. Fortunately, his port of call was Calcutta, where a traveler could find some of the best maritime facilities and nautical expertise in the world. Yet here, too, Crowninshield found himself dependent on others, and being ashore did not lessen his anxiety or enlighten his perceptions of the Indian peoples. He found it necessary to move ashore to manage the trade, leaving his second mate to oversee the vessel and cargo. The responsibilities were varied and great. The mate had to manage shipboard routines and oversee the discharge of the ballast of New England stones, careening and repainting the hull, sewing tattered sails, replacing masts. In addition, he was responsible for the careful off-loading of the *Belisarius*'s cargo and the loading of cotton goods, coffee, spices, and anything else the captain thought would fetch a good price in New England or European markets. Crowninshield was satisfied when he could record in his journal, "The mates have stript the ship all except the lower rigging-yards & top-mast are down."[153] The captain had confidence in his mate, but felt less certain about the Indian workers who carried out much of the labor.

The rhythms of the seaport included the ebb and flow of "the People," or ship's crew, who sought shore leave and frequently did not return.[154] In the spring of 1793, as Benjamin Carpenter's *Hercules* lay in Calcutta harbor, Carpenter noted, "Upon reaching Fort William, unloaded cargo and discharged several hands, at least one absconded." They would attempt to find a better berth aboard another ship, but their absence required the captain to make other arrangements, and Carpenter recorded for June 7, "A Sernag & 20 Lascars came onboard to do Ship's duty." He knew from his visit three years earlier that he must exercise vigilance, closely watching the coolies who helped load the *Ruby* for the return voyage, adding a memo for the ship's owners, "You must be careful to send one of your people in each boat, for the natives are so much given to thieving that unless you use this precaution, you must expect to lose many things." Even with confidence in a merchant house, the careful supercargo monitored market conditions daily, while keeping a close eye on ship maintenance and the loading of cargo.[155]

As a captain tallied up the port charges; the costs of food, lodging, and servants, banian or dubash; and the commercial house and godown disbursements; and weighed these against the uncertain markets in Europe or the United States, he feared the totals might well wipe out any profits earned. As in Canton, the atmosphere of corruption tainted everything, and the threat of corruption risked the success of the entire voyage. Reeling under "impositions," besieged by a host of ever-changing conditions, overwhelmed by the myriad annoyances of daily life in a foreign port, many Yankees turned to ridicule as a defense. The antidote for being beleaguered by the Other was, it seems, to lash out at those who least resembled themselves.

If a Pickman or Crowninshield felt his pocket picked by banyans, lascars and coolies, he responded by declaring them ridiculous and irrational. So, Dudley Pickman found emotional release in a sweeping dismissal of a Madras festival: "No celebrations take place without music and dancing—and in the night fire works are added. The music is without harmony. The dancing, if so it may be called, performed by girls whose business it is, consists of strange contortions of the face and body, accompanied by the clanking of large rings round their ankles, and horrid shrieking. Their movements are very horrid and clumsy. The fireworks are miserable. Yet all these being to the taste of those, for whose amusement they are exhibited, are very highly enjoyed by them."[156]

Hindu festivals were inconvenient for an enterprising Yankee. William Rogers offered some insight when he described the festival of Holi in Bombay in 1817, recording, "It begins by the suspension of all business and every occupation; everything gives way to debauchery and drunkenness," practices that were antithetical to the Yankees' Protestantism. Missionary Samuel Nott went further in 1816, indicting Hinduism for its assertion that "the means of attaining the spiritual state are, an entire separation from business." Dancing, singing, and the "little stumpy goggle eyed, no armed Juggernaut" featured at Hindu ceremonies not only delayed departure, but also they violated civic values such as hard work and enterprise and religious ideas of solemn order.[157] Consequently, where the intricacies of the India trade compromised the success of a voyage, and typhoons and tropical fever imperiled life and limb, another kind of pitfall endangered one's soul. This was the abomination of cultural contamination.[158] Even the most cosmopolitan visitors, such as Rogers, reviled Hindu practices, sneering: "Their religion is the most disgusting and at the same time the most degrading to the human mind that can be imagined. It unites everything frivolous and horrible, childish and cruel, with the most disgusting lewdness and superstitious bigotry."[159]

Like William Storrow's 1861 report of the wreck of the *Mary Ann*, many merchant accounts warned of the spiritual dangers of contact with India's many sects. As Protestants, these American voyagers perceived the nature of Indian religions—their variety, their forms, their doctrines—as assaults on their construction of the "true God." The tenets by which American visitors, whether merchant, missionary, or other, lived were unyielding. Based in the Ten Commandments, they held that there was only one true God, their Jehovah, and all other forms of belief were necessarily false. Their First Commandment dictated that there could be but "one true God," and they laid claim to Him. Yet, as Dudley Pickman recorded in 1804, "all religions are tolerated here."[160] Merchants described this menagerie of beliefs as a Babylon of heresy, and missionaries, whose whole purpose was directly threatened by this diversity, depicted India as "a Land of Darkness."[161]

Rather than explore differences in doctrine, merchant accounts tended to expose the Hindu practice as spectacles of deviance. In the journals of Pickman, Rogers, Joseph Webb, and others, idol worship, festivals, and the "various torments" of self-mutilation became abominations that affronted their God and transgressed the human condition. Depictions of self-abuse, such as swinging and hook vows, in particular, were detailed and graphic and would have astounded and repulsed readers of their journals. When Webb donated a set of hooks to the Salem East India Marine Society in 1833, his accompanying note described the apparatus as "two hooks, used by the Hindus for the purpose of transfixing and suspending the natives before the public to recover their cast when lost by some misdemeanor or for penance. In 1832, these identical hooks were inserted in the flesh, below the ribs, and the individual hoisted to the public gaze in Kolkata."[162]

Three years later, Charles Currier described the kind of infraction that could lead one to the hooks. If a servant performed work for a ferengi outside of his caste, "they lose their caste, to gain which they would be obliged to hook themselves in the back and swing on poles in the air and indoor some other paid for performance such as their priest might prescribe."[163]

The context, both religious and social, was important. Dudley Pickman, for instance, associated Hindu ceremonies with "some of the lower classes . . . generally wrought up by opium" or performed by "boys of fourteen or fifteen years of age." He invoked terms that invoked the sin of pride. Performers exhibited "pride" and "self-satisfaction," accompanied by festive music. They would "exhibit themselves," and "dress gaily." This was all false worship and the term "fakir," or "faker," religious mendicant, expressed his revulsion.[164]

William Rogers concurred. He castigated the Huli festival at Bombay in 1817 as loathsome and repellent exhibitionism: "It is near the temples dedicated to Maha Deva or Maha Deo that you will behold objects and witness scenes which degrades below the most abject of creation, that lofty supremacy of mind, which entitles man to that rank his God assigned him and makes us shudder with the idea that man endowed with reason and blessed with the prospect of immortality should so sport with his hopes and make a ship wreck of every quality of goodness and religion."[165] The temple seemed a manifestation of Hades itself. Under its extended verandah appeared "three images of most horribly grotesque appearance." These demons, "the images of two dogs in stone which they worship, expressing great terror," were besmirched with red paint and oils. To complete the hellish scene, the sounds were not the familiar hymns of a New England service. Rather, "Numerous bells are constantly ringing, tom-toms (a kind of drum) beating, which together with the scenery, their fires, howling and singing, almost tempted me to believe myself at the portals of the infernal regions."[166]

Perhaps more than the purported venality that Rogers reviled in these displays, he sought to peel back Hinduism's falsities. No one expressed these illusions more aptly than the fakirs, or religious medicants, who filled the streets and performed their offensive rites at religious festivals. Appalled at the behaviors that he witnessed, Rogers described "such tricks before high heaven as would make angels weep: "They build large fires in the streets (and some I saw in the Fort of Bombay) of their towns into which they throw some offering either sandal wood or coconuts and the oil and flowers. They howl and dance round them repeating the most obscene expressions accompanied with the lewdest gestures. Their fires are very large and have sometimes destroyed whole villages."[167]

More appalling were the forms of worship that Rogers documented:

I saw one measuring his distance from the temple by prostrations, lay flat and reaching out with his hands. Then rising and prostrating again. So doing for a half mile. One was a good natured crazy fellow who set upon a stone in a particular posture many years. Another was sitting before a very hot fire, under a burning sun, throwing ashes on himself. A third had held his left arm up perpendicularly so many years that it had withered and was immoveable. His hand was clenched and the fingers were like horn. His nails 2 inches in length and grew into the hand. One at a temple at Malabar point had held his hands clasped together till the nails had perforated the hand.[168]

Even more than Yankee merchants, missionaries contributed to their countrymen's construction of the subcontinent as another of the world's dangerous regions.[169] Their letters from "lands where the prince of darkness has long been adored" were published in periodicals such as the *American Baptist Magazine*, the *Missionary Herald*, and the *Panoplist* and republished after their deaths as devotional writings, making them both celebrities and martyrs in America.[170] As Emily Conroy-Krutz contends, these religious periodicals enabled Americans to see the globe from their parlors.[171]

Missionary sojourns began in 1812, drawing on funds from the same American Board of Commissioners for Foreign Missions, founded in 1810, that would send Pliny Fisk to tour the Ottoman Empire in 1819. In February, filled with hope and trepidation, half a dozen acolytes and wives departed Pickering Wharf in Salem. The timing was not propitious initially. In June, Congress declared war on Great Britain, and British EIC officials, never cordial even to British missionaries, ordered the Americans to leave.[172] They scattered to Bombay and Ceylon, but, soon after their arrival, the Judsons joined some British Baptist missionaries in Madras. Conditions improved the next year when Parliament's Charter Act of 1813 allowed missionaries to travel about the subcontinent.[173]

Although these missionaries' message was similar to that of merchants—Americans should understand that the world they inhabited and traveled through was dangerous and disordered—their writing reached a wider audience, an audience that counted success in a different currency. Where merchants counted bales of cotton and piculs of spices, missionaries counted souls saved and lost. And, like merchants and other travelers, they sought ways of bringing order to the world. Conroy-Krutz reads into the Indian mission a dual purpose: to civilize as well as to Christianize. The broadly cultural goal made this a reform movement as well as a conversion program.[174]

Indeed, Michael Verney notes that the correspondence of American missionaries was distinguished from that of merchants by its visceral rejection of Hinduism. Missionaries tended to be more critical and acerbic and revealed not just differences of practices and belief but also a fundamental divergence from humanity. Indeed, both Yankee merchants and the British EIC feared the disruptive potential of missionaries. Salem merchant Benjamin Crowninshield vehemently opposed their presence among the Indian populace, who were "perfectly satisfied with their own religion, [and] wanted no change."[175]

Against their depictions of depravity, Conroy-Krutz writes, "This larger project aimed to convert the whole world to an Anglo-American model of Protestant Christianity, defined not only by its theology, but also by its culture. Civilization was one of the benefits of the religion they preached, according to American and British missionaries in this period, and they sought to reform the gender relations, agricultural style, property ownership, dress, and recreation of the cultures they encountered." When Judson, Nowell, and others described Indians as lost, and as others described Chinese or Hawaiʻians similarly, this is what they meant.[176]

The writings of Ann Hasseltine Judson and Harriet Newell, members of the first American mission to India in 1812, were representative of the missionary imperative. Judson believed deeply in her own superiority as a Caucasian and a Christian, a citizen of "the country favored by heaven above most others."[177] Newell inserted her nationalism in letters home to Haverhill, Massachusetts, boasting, "In this land of darkness . . . where the enemy of souls reigns triumphant, I see the blessedness, the superior excellency of the Christian religion."[178] Judson believed, also, that anyone who lacked these virtues was bereft and needed to be saved. Her first real contact came with the arrival of a pilot boat in the Bay of Bengal and its occupants. Her observation—"one of them a Hindu"—expressed the astonishment of a young American that there were, indeed, such creatures in the world. As she described: "He exactly answers the description we have had of these poor benighted creatures. He looks as simple and feminine as you can imagine. What an alteration would a belief in Christianity make in such a degraded creature. If we have a favorable wind, we hope to get to Calcutta tomorrow. O, how soon will our labors in the mission begin! Yet we are happy, the time is so near when we may begin to labor for Christ in a pagan land!"[179]

For Judson, Newell, and their colleagues, the world's dangers lay in knowing the fate of those who would not be saved, who were, instead, damned to eternal torment. They believed it was their duty to help. Indeed, they did not have the luxury to stand around and watch in, what Newell scorned as, "criminal slothfulness." They believed it a Christian's duty to intervene and aid. On a "romantic" glide up the Hugli River to Calcutta, Judson considered her responsibilities in this dangerous world, reflecting, "Notwithstanding the scene is so pleasant, on account of the works of nature, yet it is truly melancholy when we reflect, that these creatures, so numerous, so harmless, have immortal souls, and, like us, are destined to the eternal world—and yet have none to tell them of Christ. I suppose the natives that live on these shores, for many miles, have never seen a missionary. I should so happy to come and live among them, in one of their little houses, if it was as large a field for usefulness as some others."[180] The terms she chose reveal her attitudes: from her perch aboard the *Caravan*, the people of Calcutta looked "sitting indolent," "so numerous, so harmless," yet relegated to "perishing for the want of the knowledge of a Savior" on "heathen shores of darkness and wretchedness."[181]

As merchants had recorded in their own accounts, missionaries paid particular attention to the spectacles of Hinduism. Festivals, with their disorder, noise, wanton exhibitionism, and, especially, "senseless, stupid idolatries," came in for harsh condemnation.[182] The sentiments of a Pickman or a Rogers were shared by Ann Hasseltine Judson, who watched a Juggernaut festival and employed a similar language of condescension: the idol was "only a lump of wood"; worshippers were "these poor deluded creatures"; and the "inhabitants of America know nothing of poverty, slavery, and wretchedness, compared with the natives of India."[183] Idolatry offended Mrs. Newell, William Ramsey, and Allen Graves, who expended much time in trying to wean potential converts from the "shameful character" of these representations.[184]

Other Hindu rituals and ceremonies were seen as affronts to the Protestant religious order. Missionaries deplored the ritual of hook vows, complaining that these were barbaric acts of submission that debased the worshipper and offered no honest deference to a divinity. In the rite, two rattan or iron hooks were pierced through the body and the penitent was swung from the hooks. Even before departure from Salem, they targeted this rite for banning. Seeing it on their own, they employed a language that associated it with barbarism. To this end, the ceremonial site was "a barbarous and frantic scene," and the penitent was a "deluded, perishing fellow creature."[185] The related rite of swinging came in for similar condemnation, as did the sati, the practice in which a woman would sacrifice herself on the funeral pyre of a deceased husband.[186]

Reflections

Touring Boston's Museum of Fine Arts, as we move from the Americana Gallery, with its Georgian furnishings and Copley portraits of Revolutionary figures, and meander into the African gallery, we enter other worlds of sight and sensibility. Here, exquisite Benin bronzes depict Portuguese soldiers who brought guns, powder, and new forms of enslavement to Africa in the fifteenth century. Entering the South Asian Gallery, we are again introduced to a world that Americans found strange, different, and dangerous. As we gaze upon the stupas and Buddhas, we encounter symbols that convey religious or political meanings that meant little to early Americans. Consequently, while a few people were curious and wanted to learn more, it may be that many were indifferent and dismissed these objects. Still others saw them as offensive to their own "true religion." As we gaze, we might recall the writing of Carpenter, Pickman, and Rogers and experience awakenings that are more scholarly than spiritual. We realize how little of India they penetrated, and how little of India penetrated them. We see how shallow were their experiences. They met few Native people, and the range of castes with which they interacted were few. Even for the missionaries who did interact with Brahmins, untouchables, and others, their relationships covered so little of the range of humanity. As did merchants, missionaries came for a single purpose, and this motive channeled the possibilities of their understanding, limited the range of their sensibilities, and confined the ambits of their knowledge. If they made sense of this world, it was only a dim awareness, confined within a conventional vision, a chimerical yet potent fusion of Christian theology and democratic mythology.

The Anticonquest American

"How to write about India?" queried British novelist Elizabeth Elton Bruce Smith on her travels through the subcontinent in the 1830s. As Kate Teltsher observes in her essay "India/Calcutta: City of Palaces and Dreadful Night," this was a resolvable challenge for Smith, who could draw upon the accounts of two centuries of European soldiers, sailors, traders, administrators, and missionaries to India. Americans, likewise, knew how to write about India, drawing on long-established conventions of writing about that country.[187] The challenge for Yankee voyagers was not how to write about India but how to distinguish their writing, and, to this end, their observations at times presented undercurrents of ambivalence about the European occupation and recent British conquest.

William Rogers offers a representative example. On his 1817–1818 sojourn to Ceylon and Bombay, he wrote admiringly of British palaces, forts, and administrative centers, but laced his account with observations that noted "the progress of that insatiable thirst of territorial expansion, which has marked the conduct of the English since the first settlements in India. . . . In satisfying their thirst for conquest, they have in India passed the barriers of justice and humanity; have created wars, and dictated peace; deposed their rightful sovereigns." Rogers was particularly disappointed on his voyage to Ceylon to learn the fate of "the king of Candy or Kandi, who has finally been conquered, dethroned, and enslaved by the British."[188]

The themes that run through the journals and correspondence of Rogers and other Yankee voyagers are expressions of what Mary Louise Pratt has called narratives of "anti-conquest." This is a style of travel writing that invokes "strategies of representation whereby European bourgeois subjects seek to secure their innocence in the same moment as they assert European hegemony, . . . in travel and exploration writings these strategies of innocence are constituted in relation to older imperial rhetorics of conquest associated with the absolutist era."[189] It was a style that Americans easily appropriated.

American travelers were ambivalent about British rule. They needed the accommodation of the EIC to trade in the subcontinent.[190] They sought legitimacy for themselves as gentlemen and for their country as a "civilized" nation, as did Samuel Shaw on his first voyages to Canton. British acceptance came where the Americans might prove useful. But not until after 1817 would Britain accept a formal US consul, and Yankee traders relied on a series of powerful unofficial consuls, given that, as John Quincy Adams explained, "it could scarcely be expected that a foreign commercial agent should be received there against their will."[191] And because British acceptance was tentative, and could be withdrawn at any time, the relationship was a delicate dance of acquiescence.

American anticonquest personas suggest an innocence or neutrality, as if the writer were simply moving through the world, empty of an agenda or intentions or assumptions. This style downplays the exploitation of resources and peoples by other coutnries. It had obvious advantages. It was calculated to create sympathy for authors and to coax the reader into empathy for them and antipathy toward their opponents and the obstacles they encountered.

The style also allowed Americans to assume the role of victims. We see this in anecdotes from Richard Jeffry Cleveland's 1842 travelogue, *Narrative of Voyages and Commercial Enterprises*, in which the vagaries of Britain's colonial administration and Royal Navy aggressions challenged Cleveland along his journeys. One Indian encounter in particular stood out. In December 1799, Cleveland had stopped over at Calcutta. Anticipating a stay of several months, he rented a house, and sent his loyal African American servant (or possibly slave), George, out for errands on Christmas Eve. George did not return; instead, a police messenger "informed me that a black man, who said he was in my service, had been taken up as a sailor"—that is, impressed into the Royal Navy. When Cleveland investigated, he learned that George had fallen to a press gang and was imprisoned "on board an Indiaman lying in the river below." The captian could not locate a magistrate until Christmas Day, "on the point of going to church." Cleveland's initial strategy was obsequious, employing "wth the humility of a person who is going to ask a very great favor of a man so very great." When the judge refused "in a tone which indicated a sense of the advantage he had over me," the American's sense of justice was piqued. The thirty-six-year-old Cleveland brashly challenged the older man, to try to impress him, and then "replied in a tone of which he had set the example . . . 'I am an American citizen, Sir, and one who is not unacquainted with what is due to that character.'" Eventually, George appeared at the lodgings, "accompanied by an orderly sergeant, who had been sent to conduct him to me."[192] Posturing an idealized republican innocence against British arrogance was one strategy in their anticonquest critique that relieved Americans from complicity.

Purity and Danger

William Augustus Rogers's visit to the Temple of Maha Deo in Bombay in 1817 introduces another trope that filled early American observations of India. Here he found that a large tank, or reservoir, was filled with "water [that] was dirty [and] stagnant, indeed had a most offensive stench." Not only did Rogers find the pool repellent, but also, he griped, "yet they wash in it, from religious notions of its efficacy. Round its banks are thousands constantly praying."[193] As a practical concern, the foul waters of India's rivers and tanks concerned Rogers and other observers as examples of poor hygiene and vessels for disease.[194] The Maha Deo tank served as a metaphor for deeper concerns of cultural contamination and religious pollution that repulsed Western visitors.

Scholars such as Jean Delumeau, Mary Douglas, and Peter Carmichael describe how contact with alien smells, touch, tastes, sounds, and sights can trigger sensations of danger expressed as disgust. Carmichael labels this kind of response to foreign cultures—the experience of revulsion—as "degraded, morbid, defiled, depraved" and describes it as "a species of ugliness even repugnant the imagination."[195] In early Americans' Indian encounters, concerns about polluted sites added more layers to what Delumeau calls the "permanent dialogue with fear" that underscored early modern life and, as we have seen, accentuated fears that acommpanied travel during these times.[196]

Americans were not unique in their depictions of revulsion. As Amina Marzouk Chouchene observes, a number of recent histories explore British anxieties across the emerging empire to contest "the rosy vision of Britain's imperial past" depicted by historians such as Niall Ferguson and Jeremy Black. These include Robert Peckham's *Empires of Panic: Epidemics and Colonial Anxieties* (2015), Marc Condos's *The Insecurity State: Punjab and the Making of Colonial Power in British India* (2018), Kim Wagner's *Amritsar 1919: An Empire of Fear and the Making of a Massacre* (2019), and *Anxieties, Fear, and Panic in Colonial Settings*, a collection edited by Harald Fischer-Tiné.[197] Perhaps the most famous moment in the literature of travel and exploration is Captain James Cook's encounter with Polynesian cannibalism. On his second voyage to the South Seas (1772–1775), Cook witnessed an act of cannibalism that "struck him with horror, and filled his mind with indignation against these cannibals" and had "such an effect on some of the sailors as to make them sick."[198] For Cook and his crew, eating human flesh transgressed essential boundaries that rendered the participants' humanity questionable, a reaction that Americans describe in their accounts of Hindu religious practices. These were the kind of anxieties to which colonizers, long-term residents who sought to impose a colonial order yet were dependent on Indian servants and allies, were especially susceptible.[199] Even short-term sojourners such as Yankee merchants and missionaries experienced their encounters as violations of their core beliefs.

For Americans, it was one thing to view "exotic" hooks and hookahs in the East India Hall in Salem, nestled within the shelter of conventional landmarks and among familiar faces; the experience was unsettling and dangerous when in Calcutta, immersed in a carnival of foreign languages, costumes, and manners. Americans of the early republic described their encounters in India in similar ways, and terms such as "disgust," "loathsome," and "offensive" fill their writing. India's exoticism was not only experienced as merely baffling but also perceived as an abomination and an offense against their God and country.[200]

Jeffrey Strout's work suggests that the boundaries between what Americans considered "civilized" and what Indians thought appropriate were impenetrable. What passed for work or worship in India, coming in layers of lassitude and irresponsibility or pride and exhibitionism contested the rhythms of shipboard labor and the measured psalms and solemn order of a Protestant meeting house. He locates the feelings of revulsion in the contrast with Americans' own experiences and conceptual realities: "The offense one takes depends upon the concepts one brings to the scene."[201] Rogers, Pickman, and others could not fathom the behaviors that disgusted them and apparently did not even inquire into the meanings and motivations underlying these rites because, as Strout theorizes, they were "too irrational or too depraved to profit from reasoned argument."[202] In the eyes of Yankee merchants and, especially, missionaries, the danger was not so much a threat to life and limb but a spiritual peril. In their minds, they had to contend with the very forces of darkness in India. A Hindu practice such as hook vows or the sati constituted "an anomalous or ambiguous act . . . more likely to seem abominable where it seems to pose a threat to the established cosmology or social structure."[203] India presented a very dangerous landscape to the missionaries that journeyed there, but that danger was as much from their own prejudices as it was from piracy and theft.

CHAPTER FIVE

Cannibal Isles

Deep in the Pocumtuc Valley in rural Massachusetts lies Historic Deerfield, a living history museum that commemorates the winter 1704 raid on the frontier village by a force of French soldiers and their indigenous allies. Within the museum's Flynt Center, with its sweeping array of early American material culture, one can find a remarkable collection of powder horns that mark the violence and instability of the colonial wars as imperial powers across the Atlantic wrestled for control of the continent's furs, fish, tobacco, and timber. One of these tools, inscribed "John Parker His Horn 1775," reveals a peculiar testament to how early Americans perceived the world as contest between civilized and savage peoples. Etched into the horn is an image of a canoe carrying eight Native Americans. One stands in the bow, holding a telescope; the others paddle a vessel festooned with severed heads, war clubs, and decorative art, symbols drawn from Native Americana but also from Polynesian cultures! Intriguing, too—the engraving seems to be based on an etching of a South Seas war canoe that had appeared in the *Gentleman's Magazine* for September 1773. Objects carry stories, and some artifacts tell several at once. John Parker's powder horn reveals how white Americans imagined the world then and how this vision would influence Americans' encounters in the wider world once they were free to roam it. Throughout, the trope of cannibalism marks their view of the peoples who lived "eastward of Good Hope."[1]

Indeed, relics and artifacts such as Parker's horn fill museums in the nation's metropolitan centers and along rustic byways. In the Woodman Museum in Dover, New Hampshire, the American experience in the East Indies is seen in pieces of Hawai'ian kappa bark cloth and a fearsome pointed war club. At Harvard University, a nineteenth-century poster advertising showings of a repulsive "Feegee Mermaid" and a serrated club represent the South

Seas encounters. In Boston's Museum of Fine Arts, bypassing the latest block-buster exhibit of a European master or the marvelous, tucked-away period rooms, visitors can wander into a South Seas exhibit that features Tongan war clubs and other ceremonial weapons. A ten-minute walk from the museum brings visitors to the venerable Massachusetts Historical Society, which houses a trove of South Seas ships logs and journals and a Hawai'ian fishhook fashioned from human bone.[2]

Americans knew the vast expanse that swept the earth's surface from Africa's Cape of Good Hope to America's Northwest coast by various names: India, Asia, the Asiatick Islands.[3] Its oceans were likewise dubbed the Great South Sea, the Southern Ocean, the Indian Ocean, the Pacific. The arc of planet that made up the Great South Sea that the Boylstons' imagined was the largest and perhaps the most unknown portion of the globe that adorned their parlor. Penetrating their imaginations were only the foggy accounts of Raleigh and Dampier; at the time that Copley was limning their portraits, Captain James Cook was planning the expeditions that would fill in the empty spaces. So gaping were the recesses that the Boylstons knew the place by various names—the South Seas, the Great South Sea, the Pacific, the Western Ocean—and the expanse of spread out territory, islands, and archipelagoes went by the name "India." As Françoise Douaire-Marsaudon expresses it, the South Seas were "invented" before they could be "discovered."[4] When in 1784 the Philadelphia merchant ship *United States* made its aborted voyage to Canton, it seemed to land at Sumatra, describing it as part of India.[5] Americans had much to learn about the Great South Sea and its interconnections with the Indian Ocean, South China Sea, and East Indies. Filling in for fact were rumor and mythology—unnerving tales of cannibals, pirates, typhoons, and sea serpents. This was a more visceral kind of danger than the tyrants and cheats and bureaucrats who threatened early America's global enterprise in Canton, Calcutta, and Constantinople. A voyage to the South Seas added fresh layers of dread to augment the threat of financial loss.[6]

A cornucopia of images represented the South Seas in early American consciousness, and carvings of palm trees and sandy beaches, coconuts and pineapples, great sea turtles and ravenous sharks festooned the paintings, mantles, doors, and wallpaper of the well-to-do. But one image, in particular, held the attention of young and old, prosperous or down-and-out. This was the cannibal of the South Seas, clutching an enormous, menacing war club. By the early nineteenth century, institutions such as the Salem East India Marine

Society and Nathan Dunn's Chinese Museum in Philadelphia drew crowds to exhibits of exotic goods that included war clubs, shell jewelry, hookahs, palanquins, and clay figures.[7] But it was the most sensationalist displays that captured the American imagination, especially impressions of Oceanic men engaged in combat. Amasa Delano, for instance, recalled that a Hawai'ian boy whom he had carried to Boston later performed on the stage there, "in the tragedy of Capt. Cook," a display that reinforced the image of savage and cannibal.[8]

Captain Benjamin Morrell paraded Polynesian "cannibals" and their battle equipage in peep shows, on the Broadway stage, and in a traveling show. Within days of their arrival in August 1831, Dako and Monday were performing in a show called "Two Cannibals of the Islands of the South Pacific." As Morrell's "protégés" drew large audiences at Tammany Hall and Reuben Peale's museum, the captain organized a traveling show to Albany, Philadelphia, Baltimore, and Washington in the winter of 1831–1832. Fijians and other Oceanic peoples played an unintended role in fostering this association. Mary Wallis, wife of a bêche-de-mer trader, recorded in 1851, "His Majesty presented me with a valuable and curious war club to show the Americans."[9]

Word of mouth carried stories, and stories sensationalized and prepared the mind for the worst. On Palliser Island, the Marquesas, in April 1811, for example, Boston supercargo John Richards Child observed, "The natives are said to be cannibals, very wild and savage. It is said there was a brig cast away upon those reefs not many years since and a greater part of the crew roasted and ate by the natives. The captain and two or three of the [crew] made their escape to Otaheite in the long boat."[10] When in 1819, some thirteen years after Mahomet Ikle carried away Orne's ship, that other *Essex* had been "stove by a whale" and sunk, leaving Captain Pollard and Mate Owen Chase to decide how to get their crew to safety. Although the Marquesas Islands lay one thousand miles to the west, the crew elected to sail their three whaleboats two thousand miles eastward to the coast of Chile. They had heard that the Marquesans were cannibals.[11] By the 1820s, when James Oliver sailed the South Seas, New Zealand "had ever been associated in our minds with all that is barbarous and inhuman in savage life."[12]

Early American readers learned their world geography in this way, associating places around the world with explorers such as Cook, La Perouse, Tasman, Magellan, Mendana, and Mendoza, who had made important discoveries "at the cost of great suffering and loss of life." After 1784, Americans could glance at similar maps to locate the graves of friends, neighbors, and loved ones.[13]

They memorialized Nootka Sound, where Native Americans massacred the crew of the *Boston* in 1803; the Straits of Singapore, where the *Putnam* had been taken and six crew members killed in 1805; Hawai'i, where Charles Derby succumbed to tropical fever; and the hundreds of beachheads and watery graves where the anonymous many lay forgotten.[14]

John Brown Williams of Salem had fallen under the spell of cannibal talk before he voyaged to New Zealand in 1842. He began his journal with a description of the island's "cannibal population, . . . as described to me" previously. From "certain but very complete accounts," he had learned "of their cruelties and barbarous ways." Few ships came to New Zealand before 1808, he had heard, "on account of their savage hostilities, treachery and barbarous treatment" of outsiders, whom they called *pakeahs*.[15] Holding to the popular notion that civilization followed commerce, Williams explained that the trade in "gun powder and muskets," ironically, "was the first step to civilization amongst them." But warfare had been incessant on the island, and, consequently, "with their weapons of war they were debasing, blood thirsty and their atrocities indescribable. [Captive children were] sometimes put to death and eaten; but the adults, and old natives were compelled to make the fire on which they were to be roasted, after being quartered and their head taken off and posted on the pole, imagine the feelings of such an individual. After the body is cooked the greater the animosity to those taken the more avaricious the appetite to devour them."[16] In an age of improvement, however, the use of modern weapons had reduced the frequency of wars and the barbarity practiced in them. Williams's experiences in New Zealand corroborated what he had absorbed in reading and hearsay, and he then perpetuated the trope in his own writing.[17]

Print, whether fictional or authentic, read alone or in groups, embedded these impressions of the Great South Sea deeply into American thought.[18] So novel was the extent of this expanse that most geographies included in it the East Indies, Oceania, and the American Northwest coast.[19] By 1835, the Library Company of Philadelphia's catalogue of holdings included "Round the World—South Seas—N.W. passage—Polynesia—Australia—N. W. Coast of America" as well as topics on "Voyages and Travels"; "Travels in Persia, China the East Indies, &c."; Oceanic geography, and shipwrecks.[20] Authors incorporated the idea of Pacific Islands cannibalism into all. Mary Wallis used her book's title, *Life in Feejee: Or, Five Years Among the Cannibals* (1851), to imbed the cannibal trope further into American consciousness. In the words of an admirer, "No account has been given to the public, which details so fully the past and present abominations of cannibal Feejee."[21] Others introduced their readers to the concept in tables of contents. Samuel Patterson described "My dreadful Sufferings at Feegee" (1817). Amasa Delano's *Narrative* listed topics such as "Savage Town"; "Battle with the Natives, Dr. Nicholson killed"; "Hostility of the Natives of New Guinea"; and "Treachery of the Malays" in the same year. Edmund Fanning added to the trope in his *Voyages to the South Seas* (1838) by reveling in topics such as "Cannibal war yells"; "Their cannibalism"; "A terrific savage"; "A white boy to roast"; and more. James Oliver's 1848 *Wreck of the Glide* included the headings "War dance"; "Barbarous customs"; "Attacked by the natives"; and "Massacre of two men." And the contents of Mary Wallis's *Life in Feegee* included "Massacre at Vewa"; "The Faithlessness of a Feejeean"; "Treachery of a Chief"; "Murder of Four White Men at Navu"; and "Cannibalism." "Cannibalism," "treachery," "faithlessness," "hostility," "barbarous," "massacre," "surprise attack"—this was the language of the East Indies and Oceania, or, rather, how Americans imagined the South Sea.

Encounters

Tucked away in a little corner of Oahu, obscured by vibrant greenery, lies a solitary gravestone, like so many others throughout the South Seas. Here lie the remains of a famous Salem name, that of Charles Derby, son of Elias Hasket. The stone reads, "In memory of CHARLES DERBY Esq., *late Commander* of the Ship Caroline, of Boston N–America. he died on this Island September 26th 1802. Ætat 32. his friends in testimony of his Virtue and their esteem have erected this Monument." When the news arrived in his hometown, the *New England Palladium* for March 29, 1803, added a few more details (although apparently misstating the date of his death): "At Whahoo, (one of the Sandwich Islands) 22d Sept. last, on his passage from the N.W. Coast of America to Canton, of a pulmonary complaint, *Charles Derby*, Esq. of Salem, late commander of the ship Caroline, of Boston, a young gentleman whose virtues insured esteem, and his death the regret of all who had a knowledge of his worth."[22]

Many American travelers, whether privileged or poor, perished in the Great South Sea, and many have no stone to mark their graves; for others, "decaying tombstones, half buried beneath earth and weeds, still tell the tale."[23] One would not find a grave marker for William Augustus Rogers. His final voyage ended not in Salem but at Bangkok, on an 1820 voyage to Batavia in the *Trexel*, when Rogers was washed from the deck of a houseboat while he slept during a gale.[24] The body of Daniel Malcomb, "noble, brave, and generous," was thrown overboard in Straits of Sunda in 1791, as were the remains of Nathaniel Shaw, somewhere between Canton (Guangzhou) and Bombay (Mumbai); Samuel Tripe, lost overboard in the Indian Ocean; and Jeremiah Parker.[25] In fact, a regular ritual of entry into an East Indies port was to hear the "small news" of relatives or acquaintances lost at sea, Nathaniel Bowditch learned at Manila in 1796.[26] Seven thousand miles across the Pacific Ocean, and nearly fifteen thousand miles from Salem, in another remote village, Kuala Batee, we might stumble across another solitary *koeboe*, or grave site, in the jungles of Sumatra. The inscription reads:

> This marble points to the grave of SHEWBUNTAR, who died at Quallabatto 13 April 1824: Æ 42. As he was ambitious of distinction, active, persevering, & energetic, success followed his efforts, and his dominion and reputation were widely extended. Personally brave, he was cautious & calculating. In more cultivated society, his fame would have been, probably that of a great conqueror in history would have recorded it. He had imperfections, as well as virtues. He was generous and open towards his friends, severe and implacable toward his enemies. The traditions of his countrymen Will preserve the memory of his abilities & his conquests. Strangers will recollect the kindness of his temper and the friendliness of his conduct.[27]

As for Batavia, C. Doogood Downing knew it as "the graveyard of Europeans."[28] The entry that Harriet Low noted in her journal for Batavia, on Wednesday, August 26, 1829—"what a graveyard it has been, and still is, for foreigners"—could be described for those who sailed the expanse from Good Hope to the Columbia River and down to Massafuega.[29] Nathaniel Bowditch, another Salemite, made similar warnings about Batavia, where it was "very sickly," and Manila, where he found March "very sickly, while the autumn months were not much better: "Shiver and fever are then very rife." Tropical fever respected no man's rank, he learned, "Seven masters having died."[30] The world of Low and Bowditch, as that of Daniel Malcomb, Nathaniel Shaw, and Samuel Tripe was a dangerous place, and the remains of hundreds of Yankee men and women molder unmarked in graves around the globe or at the bottom of a foreign sea.

As with voyages to Canton, Constantinople, or Calcutta, Americans sailed "eastward of Good Hope" for a multitude of reasons.[31] Some sailed for adventure; some to forget sorrows; some to save souls. Most ventured into the Great South Sea for the economic opportunities they found wanting at home, or, as Amasa Delano of Duxbury, Massachusetts, put it, "honestly and honorably, to obtain a competency sufficient to support myself and family, through an old age, should I live to see it."[32] Fables of lost cities of gold continued to lure some travelers, as they did Hernán Cortés and Francisco Pizarro centuries earlier. Sumatra, it was said, "produces so much gold that it is thought to be the Ophir mention[ed] in the Scriptures." And, within ten years, a Salem vessel would discover there a product worth more than gold—pepper.[33] Delano wrote of these impulses often. Reaching New Guinea in 1791, he reflected, "The island abounds with gold dust, or grains of gold as large as shot; with pearls; and, with the long nutmeg."[34] His sources had informed geographer Jedidiah Morse that Dutch Ceylon (Sri Lanka) was thought to be "the richest and finest Island in the world."[35] Imagined worlds of bounty and beauty, even a "terrestrial paradise" filled Morse's geographies, predicated on the conceit that his God intended men to cultivate empty places—to sow seeds and His Word. Whatever the reasons, each voyage contributed to a constellation of ideas, impressions, and images of the South Sea that was forming in the national consciousness.

Of the books, journals, and logs that made up an early American literature of voyaging "eastward of Good Hope," many were memoirs that recalled the "adventures and sufferings" of American mariners. Some of these "globe beaters" reached out to do more than gain a competency.[36] Amasa Delano, Edmund Fanning, and others imagined themselves as latter-day Captain Cooks and formatted their treatises as navigational guides that tracked winds, currents, shoals, and reefs that stood as obstacles to enterprise. As men who had survived the dangers that nature posed—sometimes barely—they hoped their writing would save ships, cargoes, and lives.[37] Delano, again, presented their motives in exalted terms, recalling his "ambition to excel others in achievements . . . to satisfy my own curiosity in a knowledge of the world, and particularly to know how far myself and others were imposed upon with exaggerated accounts of the world, and false statements of things a great way from home . . . to do a benevolent act now and then, and to leave an unblemished character behind me."[38]

Organizing a voyage was a complex affair in early America, as it is today, whether along the coast or across the Atlantic Ocean, but the extended distances of a South Seas voyage complicated every aspect of the trip, from collecting maps and accounts of experienced travelers to purveying the exotic goods that filled the cargo hold of an Indiaman just returned to port.[39] Preparations for a voyage into "barely charted seas full of dangers" often began months or even years before a captain knew his destination, a crew came on board, or a cargo collected.[40] Planning began with gathering information—frequently scarce, late, and false. Like Melville's Ishmael, they "swam through libraries and sailed through oceans." Yankee merchants haunted coffeehouses, taverns, and wharves to pick up any scraps of news that might yield useful knowledge of distant markets. They scoured libraries, their own or their friends'; ravaged marine societies and athenaeums; and poured over newspapers, maps, gazetteers, and travelogues. As the nineteenth century dawned, more books conveying more detail "corrected," or sometimes augmented, the many erroneous charts and hearsay. English-language books and foreign translations, original and in multiple editions and reprints, offered some guidance.[41]

Even a well-established market such as Manila confounded Yankee planners who could only guess at trends in taste and fashion when it opened to American trade about 1796. Nathaniel Bowditch bet on Portuguese and Madeira wines and brandy for the Spanish colony, and misjudged badly.[42] They prioritized reading, collecting histories, geographies, medical treatises, and, especially, travelogues. It is likely that they collected the plethora of pilot guides available from the 1790s. They could find the "Great South Sea" laid out, in whole or in part, on Bowles's *New Pocket Map*, as well as on Herman Moll's *Map of the East-Indies* (c. 1720), Emanuel Bowen's *An Accurate Map of the East Indies Exhibiting the Course of the European Trade both on the Continent and Islands* (1744), and James Thompson's *New Map of America* (1799). William Barker's rendering of Cook's map of the world, situating the Pacific Ocean at its center, with the Americas and Europe on its peripheries, could be purchased in Philadelphia in 1796 for nine dollars, about one month's wages for a sailor, but within the means of a merchant or successful sea captain.[43]

Pilot guides, increasingly reprinted in the United States, offered purportedly precise and "corrected" navigational directions for India and beyond. In 1791, Herbert and Dunn's *New Directory for the East Indies* was available in London.[44] In Philadelphia in 1801, James Humphreys printed Joseph Huddart's guide, *The oriental navigator, or, New directions for sailing to and from the East Indies: also for the use of ships trading in the Indian and China seas to New Holland, &c. &c., collected from the manuscripts, journals, memoirs and observations of . . . officers in the Hon. East India Company's service, and from the last edition of the French Neptune oriental, by Mons. D'Apres de Mannevillette*. This was a commercial as well as navigational guide and contained "a particular account of several new tracks and discoveries; to which is added The India officers and traders guide in purchasing the drugs and spices of Asia and the East Indies, with practical directions for the choice of diamonds and the use of Chinese touch needles in judging of the value of gold; likewise accurate tables of the weights, measures, coins, money, &c. &c. &c. of different settlements in India, from the latest and best authorities; the whole arranged and now first published in one volume." In 1802, there was H. M. Elmore's *The British mariner's directory and guide to the trade and navigation of the Indian and China seas. Containing instructions for navigating from Europe to India and China, and from port to port in those regions, and parts adjacent: with an account of the trade, mercantile habits, manners, and customs of the natives.*[45] In 1805, Scottish hydrographer James Horsburgh published his *Memoirs: Comprising the Navigation to and from China, by the China Sea, and through the various Straits and Channels in the Indian Archipelago; also, the Navigation of Bombay Harbour.*[46] From 1817, one could find multiple editions of Horsburgh's *India Directory, or, Directions for Sailing to and from the East Indies, China, New Holland, Cape of Good Hope, Brazil, and the Interjacent Ports / comp. chiefly from original journals at the East India House, and from observations and remarks, made during twenty-one years experience navigating in those seas.*

Of wide influence would have been the Reverend John Malham's two-volume *The Naval Gazetteer: or, seaman's complete guide, containing a full and accurate account, alphabetically arranged, of the several coasts of all the countries and islands in the known world.* Available in the Unites States in 1797, Malham's *Gazetteer* served as a conduit for mariners, dictionary compilers, and geographers. The text covered the world, yet he specifically located cannibalism in Africa. Along the Barabalemo River, "though ships' boats sometimes go into the rivers hereabouts for trade, it is very hazardous as well as difficult, on account of the cannibal negroes."[47] By 1813, Americans could also access William Milburn's magisterial *Oriental Commerce, containing a Geographical Description of the Principal Places in the East Indies, China, and Japan* (London: Black, Parry, 1813). Milburn complemented his careful descriptions of passages, shoals, reefs, and port facilities, gleaned from his own seven voyages to the East, with a history of "the rise and progress of the trade . . . with the Eastern world."[48] He provided, in addition to a geographical description, important commercial details, such as currency exchange rates and lists of goods available in each port.

When preparations for the first American voyage to Canton, that of the *Empress of China*, were underway in 1784, merchants Robert Morris of Philadelphia, Daniel Parker of New York, and other investors collected $120,000 of ginseng, cordage, wine, lead, iron, and Spanish dollars for a cargo.[49] The challenge of collecting a cargo required finding the best mix of goods for an unfamiliar market, thousands of miles abroad, at a future season. Such guess-work tested the skills and vision of the most successful merchants. And, too often, the American economy provided few items that would have been in demand by other peoples. Many enterprises required stopovers to collect an appealing cargo. When Joseph Ingraham sailed the brigantine *Hope* to the East in 1790–1792, he had to set a course first for the American Northwest coast with a hold of knickknacks to exchange for the otter pelts that he hoped would sell in China.[50] Ingraham's voyage was a failure, as the market for furs had collapsed by the time of his arrival. Similar problems were encountered by the most experienced of merchants and officers, and were the lot of the *Cordelia*, which left Boston in May 1815. This was a first voyage for sailor Charles Tyng, who secured a berth aboard the ship of his uncles, the eminent Boston merchants Thomas and James Perkins, sailing under Captain John King and First Mate Charles Magee. The *Cordelia* was loaded in Boston with $400,000 Spanish dollars in one hundred iron kegs, yet failed in efforts to load copper at Coquimbo or sandalwood at Hawai'i.[51] Amasa Delano provided his advice on how to outfit a vessel for a commercial voyage to the Pacific. A ship "ought to be new, good, and strong," its hull should be coppered "with fresh metal," and it should be armed with six to ten cannons (some long, for a China Sea voyage) and have strong rigging and a surplus of ropes, canvas, and the like. Provision should be abundant and of the highest quality, the casks airtight. And, importantly, one should "take plenty of livestock, and a great abundance of water."[52]

There were two approaches, one around Africa's Cape of Good Hope, the other doubling America's Cape Horn, or Tierra del Fuego (Land of Fire).[53] It is not accurate to assert, as some popular historians have done, that Boston ships favored the South American approach and Salem vessels the African course. Conditions and markets determined the route. Regardless of the vessel's course, a navigator needed to be well prepared. Delano advised: "Every commander should furnish himself with a good brass sextant, and so should every chief officer of any ship bound round Cape Horn, or the Cape of Good Hope . . . An instrument, books, and constant practice during a twelve month voyage, with a little instruction, would enable an officer to ascertain his longitude within ten or fifteen miles, provided he could get an object east and west of the moon." Practicing the necessary calculations was essential on an Asian voyage, allaying the anxieties of both officers and crew. As Delano observed: "This important point should not be neglected. It makes a sailor very happy, after being at sea for a hundred days or more, to know that he can take his books and instrument, and ascertain his situation on the globe within ten or a dozen miles."[54] A chronometer was advisable, as well, but the instruments were notoriously unreliable over an extended voyage and many merchants were unwilling to carry the expense.[55] To underscore the stakes, Delano shared his own anxieties with his readers, writing: "It is not delay only that is occasioned by not knowing the longitude, but the loss of hundreds of ships and lives. This should be understood, and regarded by all European traders from this country, as well as all ships on foreign voyage."[56]

The conventional wisdom, especially in the early decades of South Seas travel, that these were dangerous routes could be quantified in insurance calculations. As Elias Hasket Derby prepared his *Grand Turk* for what was then its longest voyage, taking insurance to reduce the risk, his London agents, Lane & Frazier, sought to warn him off the venture with the caution: "We could not effect the Insurance you order'd on the ship Grand Turk & cargo Ebenr West Master from Salem to the Isle of France & back. Our Underwriters are not fond of the risque, it being a new Trade to the Americans. Most of the ships in this kind of business are very particularly described, and the masters and Seamen well acquainted with navigation."[57] Ultimately, Derby supercargo Nathaniel Bowditch recommended that Americans—the "new men" of global trade—load their ships with Spanish silver only to the uncertain new markets that they encountered.[58]

The emotional cost of a cruise "to the South Sea [or] Pacific Ocean" could not be tallied, either. Delano lamented his 1803 voyage even before the ship left Boston:

> On my leaving America on this voyage, I was placed in a situation that caused me more anxiety than I had ever experienced at the beginning or any enterprise. I had with me my two brothers, who were all I had, and a nephew of seven years old, who was an invalid. I had entered into a contract, which was * * * * * *, that had more powerful effect on my feelings than all the other causes put together; and moreover I found myself less active in body and mind than I was at the age of twenty five years.[59]

Popular historians of the nineteenth and twentieth centuries elided the apprehensions that haunted the men and women who prepared to sail "eastward of Good Hope." As Delano continued, "All these important causes came under consideration, together with the extraordinary uncertainty of the issue of the voyage, as we had nothing but our bands to depend upon to obtain a cargo, which was only to be done through storms, dangers, and breakers, and taken from barren rocks in distant regions. All the foregoing considerations were sufficient to rouse the sensibility and put the mind of any man on a stretch."[60]

The voyage to the East was wrought with anxieties even before the first cable was cast aside. Gabriel Franchère described the emotional turmoil he felt in 1810 aboard the *Tonquin,* bound for the Northwest coast, still in New York harbor and already lamenting his voyage:

> One must have experienced it oneself, to be able to conceive the melancholy which takes possession of the soul of a man of sensibility at the instant that he leaves his country in the civilized world to go to have with strangers in wild and unknown lands. I should in vain endeavor to give my readers an idea, even faintly correct, of the painful sinking of heart that I suddenly felt, and that's the sad clients which I involuntarily cast toward a future so much the more frightful to me as it offered nothing but what was perfectly confused and uncertain.[61]

Sandwith Drinker expressed his regret embarking on an Indian Ocean journey with more brevity, writing, "This morning at 10 A.M., I took leave of my friends, and uncomfortable, and alone, . . . and with a heavy heart, went on board."[62]

Like the Indian Ocean or the South China Sea, the Pacific could swallow up a ship, its crew, and its cargo and leave no trace. Its waters make up one-third of the world's surface—sixty-eight million miles in area and sixteen thousand kilometers across—more than twice the breadth of the Atlantic. All the earth's continents could fill the Pacific, with room left over. As historian Ernest S. Dodge observes: "The size of the greatest geographical feature of the world is awesome to contemplate. . . . [The Pacific Ocean] is more homogenous, more diverse; the water bluer, the swells longer, the trade winds steadier, the typhoons more monstrous. It is the most unstable third of the world's surface."[63] But the Pacific is not empty. Congeries of islands, atolls, and archipelagoes fill its waters. Twenty thousand of its islands are the most isolated in the world, some more than six thousand kilometers from the nearest continent. Yet they are "bound together by ocean," connected by currents and the strongest winds in the world.[64] Early historians described the islands and atolls, and their inhabitants, as isolated from each other. Understanding little of these lands and their people, early Americans were not as impressed as historians are today, who describe "a people who achieved the greatest feats of maritime navigation in all human history" and "cultures that were not only pragmatic systems of survival, but were also rich in imaginative power and beauty, representing achievements of the human mind, tongue and hand as inspiring as any others in the world."[65]

The origins of the peoples of the East Indies and Oceania remain somewhat shrouded in mystery.[66] The East Indies, it appears, were settled by populations from Southeast Asia and, by the time the Portuguese encountered them, were divided into various domains of chiefdoms and city-states. From there, historians posit, two streams of migration "filtered" through the Melanesian islands.[67] There is no evidence of a simple route; rather, complex patterns of migration seem to have crisscrossed. New research reveals that Polynesian people had contact with South America by 1200 AD.[68] However people arrived in the Pacific, by 400 AD the habitable islands of the Great South Sea had been occupied across a sweep of ten million miles known as the Polynesian Triangle, marked by Hawai'i, New Zealand, and the Easter Islands.[69] By the time Americans entered the Great South Sea in 1787, parts of this vast area were in transformation. The eighteenth century saw a departure from the largely stable, steady growth that had characterized the Pacific cultures. Tonga had centralized into a unitary state, and Fiji, Tahiti, and Hawai'i were moving along this trajectory. In Polynesia, Fiji represented one form of cultural convulsion, beginning in the early eighteenth century, as "the traditional skirmishing and symbolic wars between petty communities gave way to wars which aimed at exterminating or absorbing and supplanting the enemy, and enlarging the territory and status of the victor."[70] Europeans could only dimly grasp these changes.[71] Abel Tasman had visited Tonga in 1643 and described it as a place of longstanding stability, but by 1799 a civil war among the islanders was tearing Tonga apart and would continue until 1852.

A perusal of the maps that were becoming available offered a sense of what awaited a voyage. Men who returned from a South Seas voyage bestowed a fearsome nomenclature on the site. Amasa Delano's *Narrative of Voyages and Travels* took early American readers through the Revenge Straits and Endeavor Straits off Timor and New Guinea in 1791, through the Storm Bay passage off Tasmania about 1793, and around Inaccessible Island in the South Seas in 1804, past Thwart-the-way and Cut-throat Creek.[72] To impose some sense of order and control, Yankee voyagers tamed these sites with titles that suggested an Edenic bounty. Over the course of a voyage through the Pacific, Edmund Fanning observed, "We got sight of Eooa, or Middleburgh Island"; the "Island of Tongataboo, or New Amsterdam"; and "the King's main island of Toconrobaj (subsequently named Sandal Wood Bay)."[73] Sometimes he knew the indigenous names—"(Turtle Island,) called by the natives Fatoa"—and sometimes he did not—"On the 26th, at 8, A. M., saw a small island, which I called, and very appropriately, Direction Island, (not having learned the native name of it)."[74] It did not matter to these Yankee voyagers. He felt comfortable enough with imposing Western names on occupied coasts that he dubbed the Palmyra archipelago Fanning's Islands. The confidence with which Yankee mariners appropriated indigenous lands and resources would contribute to their own economy, undermine those of the people they exploited, and frequently lead to misunderstanding and conflict. In their writing, they represented themselves as innocents, seeking only "fair trade," situating themselves as victims who did nothing to instigate or provoke an attack. Consequently, for American readers, even the place names would conjure up impressions of vulnerable ships in great danger.

It is likely that from a very early moment in Western exploration of the Pacific, some version of the adage "Below the Forties there is no law, and below the Fifties there is no God" came into maritime expression.[75] A day began with observing the weather and location, the ship's log recording the date, then "commenced with light breezes" or "commenced with gale." A captain or mate then noted latitude and longitude, the latter difficult until the chronometer became widespread, and so more a matter of instinct and hunch than precision. Mariners could expect to encounter periods of "squally, dirty, disagreeable weather" anywhere in the world, as Robert Child complained.[76] Nathaniel Appleton concurred, inking into the log for the ship *Concord*, bound from Boston to Canton, the lines,

> Remarks Thursday Jany 9th 1800 78th
> [Today] Ends small breezes, & hazy weather, & a plaguy, nasty, heavy, crooked, ugly, good-for-nothing, sea going.

Sandwith Drinker did not appreciate ocean travel any more than his fellow voyagers, noting in 1838, "How I do detest the Ocean, a ship and every [thing] connected with them. The more I see of them the less I like them."[77] In the works of Patterson, Delano, Fanning, and others, the Great South Sea took form as a series of harrowing challenges, a voyage through it more daunting even than a journey to Canton, the Ottoman Empire, or India. With so little knowledge at hand, so much distance to travel, and so much uncharted water, every passage constituted "a voyage of commerce and discovery."[78]

The Pacific Ocean was formidable also because of the typhoons and pirates that roiled its surface, and also from what lay hidden beneath. Disaster could strike a vessel even before the watch discerned any disturbance or discoloration in the waters ahead. It was a lesson that Edmund Fanning learned on a voyage in June 1798, and that became an important moment in his popular 1833 book *Voyage Round the World*. Describing a cruise through the western Pacific under a "quite pleasant" trade wind and "remarkably fine" weather, he lulled himself into thinking that "our voyage, it seemed more like a sailing excursion, or party of pleasure." He wrote that never "has there been any necessity, while sailing over or across the western part of this extensive Pacific ocean, to lay the ship by a single night, through fear of running her upon any hidden danger, the weather having been remarkably fine all the time, with moderate trade winds, ever keeping a good look out, and believing ourselves perfectly secure from this precaution." Suddenly, in the early morning hours of June 15, Fanning spotted lines of foaming breakers, "mast high, directly ahead, and towards which our ship was fast sailing." What they encountered was a Pacific motu, or low island, virtually invisible to a distant vessel.[79] The captain described this obstacle as "a coral reef or shoal, in the form of a crescent, about six leagues in extent from north to south; under its lee, and within the compass of the crescent, there appeared to be white and shoal water. We did not discover a foot of ground, rock, or sand, above water, where a boat might have been hauled up; of course had our ship run on it in the night, there can be no question but we should all have perished." As astonishing as the "appalling danger" they narrowly escaped was Fanning's own mysterious behavior during the previous evening. Claiming that he had never been prone to sleepwalking, he had repeatedly awakened and lumbered up on deck to advise the watch to keep a careful lookout. The crew's suspicion that the captain had lost his mind transformed to a conviction that only a loving Providence had saved them.[80]

Given the amount of time that Fanning spent in the South Seas, it is not surprising that his books frequently mention the trope "We narrowly escaped shipwreck." In another instance, a thousand miles southwest of Hawai'i, his ship avoided "one continued sheet of white foam along the horizon, breaking high, with a tremendous noise, on the coral reef that bound the coast, and about one mile distant from the ship" when at 3 a.m. on June 11, 1798, a vigilant lookout cried out, "Land ho! . . . direct ahead, and close aboard." Needless to say, "an hour passed in great anxiety."[81] The sudden appearance of catastrophic breakers was experienced by Wallis at Tahiti in 1767 and many others.[82] Often, realization came as a tragic postscript. When Fanning learned that his ship, the *Union*, had been lost and its crew massacred, he recalled the tragedy "of that celebrated and much lamented voyager, La Perouse, in his two large frigates, must, in all probability, have been similar to that of ours, and no doubt was the cause of his loss."[83] Fanning and La Perouse were not exceptional in this regard. Fanning's close calls led him to take a leading role in urging Congress to sponsor exploring expeditions to chart the Pacific, correct error-prone maps, imprint safer routes for whaling ships, and identify new locations for bêche-de-mer, sandalwood, and other goods for the Canton market.[84]

Some sites became notorious. The Palau Islands were known for their "treacherous reefs" where the *Antelope Packet* had wrecked in 1783.[85] The 150-mile strait that separates Australia from Tasmania, named for George Bass in 1783, was regarded for its precarious currents. Passing the Endeavor Straits that separated New Guinea from Australia, Delano was "apprehensive that we should not be able to go to the west of the gulf of Carpentaria, a gulf much dreaded by seamen because the wind makes so strong a draught inward, and it is so difficult to get out."[86] North of Tasmania were islands so daunting, "It must never be attempted to run through between these islands by any vessel." Here lay the aptly named Bay of Shoals, "a most dangerous bay," shallow enough "to take up a boat." Nearby, "the north, south, east, and west sides of Cape Barren are surrounded with rocks, shoals, and dangers, for some miles from the island; and must not be approached but in the daytime, and then with the greatest caution."[87]

Anchoring in the treacherous currents of Bass's Straits (now Bass Strait) on February 20, 1804, Delano remained until October, as the *Perseverance* settled in at Kent's Bay while the *Pilgrim* made two excursions among the fifty-plus islands of the straits in search of seals. In November, the ships made the Snares, off the southwest coast of New Zealand. He continued to think of himself as an explorer, culling the journals of earlier European expeditions for inspiration and quotable material. George Bass and Matthew Flinders had discovered the straits just six years earlier. The Fiji Islands were known to be a "dangerous archipelago" where "numerous sunken rocks" lay along the route from Coro to Tacanova, and so, in September 1829, James Oliver aboard the *Glide* noted that "the greatest precautions were taken to avoid danger."[88] The emotional toll was high, Oliver recalled: "The occasion was one of the most intense anxiety. Every man was at his post, and the stillness on board was broken only by the loud and hurried orders of the officers to the helmsman. The crisis was at hand. Within a few feet from the surface of the sea, and directly ahead, was discovered a large oral rock. . . . The next instant, the *Glide* struck with a tremendous crash."[89] Nature did not relent on the return, where the weary mariner 'shuddered' at "the boisterous waves, dashing with astonishing force against its rocky sides, and covering the greater part with a sheet of foam" on St. Helena Island and St. Paul's rock.[90]

In the Pacific Northwest, the mouth of the Columbia River barred passage to fur traders and explorers. Mapped by Robert Grey in 1792, the combination of bars, shoals, winds, and furious currents have made this the "graveyard of the Pacific," claiming more than two thousand vessels, rivaling the entrance of the Hugli River approaching Calcutta.[91] Aboard the *Columbia* ca. 1790, John Hoskins described the passage through Barrell's Sound as "dangerous, having many sunken rocks in its channel; the tide also here runs with considerable force." In March 1811, Lieutenant Jonathan Thorn attempted to bring the *Tonquin* across the Columbia's bar. He lost five men when a reconnaissance boat capsized in the surf; then two days later, three men more.[92] Washington Irving made the *Tonquin*'s crossing notorious in his history of the Astoria enterprise, concluding that the river was "rendered extremely intricate and dangerous by shoals reaching nearly from shore to shore, on which, at times, the winds and currents produce foaming and tumultuous breakers."[93]

Trader Gabriel Franchère was a "scribbing clerk" aboard the *Tonquin* when Captain Thorn ordered the hapless attempts on the river.[94] His 1820 book *A Voyage to the Northwest Coast of America*, translated into English in 1854, described an eerie sense that they were entering a new and forbidding land. Departing Karakakoua, Hawai'i on February 28, 1811, he wrote, "We . . . lost sight of the smiling and tempered countries, to enter very soon a colder region and less worthy of being inhabited." Even before they reached the mouth of the Columbia, he reported, the wind blew so violently that the captain gave the order to strike the top-gallant mast and top sails. Franchère reflected, "The rolling of the vessel was greater than all the gales we had experienced previously."[95] What awaited was even more daunting. The "entrance of the river . . . appeared but a confused and agitated sea; the waves, impelled by a wind from the offing, broke up on the bar and left no perceptible passage."[96] Franchère described "the horror of our situation" as "tremendous breakers" crashed over the ship; "the inquietude" of waiting to learn the fate of the exploration's missing crew members; and the survivors' realization that eight men would not return, perceived as "a bad augury [that] was sensibly felt" by the survivors.[97] Franchère recalled the loss poignantly: "In the course of so long passage the habit of seeing each other every day, the participation of the same cares and dangers, and confinement to the same narrow limits had formed between all the passengers a connection that could not be broken, above all in a manner so sad and so unlooked for, without making us feel a void like that which is experienced in a well-regulated and loving family, when it is suddenly deprived by death of the presence of its cherished members."[98]

A crew that had threaded perilous shoals and reefs faced further jeopardy in attempting to land a boat ashore. One could sail around Christmas Island and discover no dangers, yet "landing upon it appeared to be difficult."[99] Similarly, at King Island in the Bass Straits off Tasmania, water and wood were precious, but in 1804, Delano "did not consider it safe to anchor with the prevailing wind, which was from the southward; and as this was the only possible place on the east side in which water could be procured, I was obliged to leave it without wood or water."[100] No amount of planning might prepare a crew for lurking dangers. Fanning believed this caused the "lamentable fate" of the *Union* in 1803, the first vessel he sent to the Pacific in search of sandalwood. He reflected, "All on board either perished by drowning, or as they gained a foothold upon the rocks of the coral reef, were massacred by the natives."[101]

A mariner who survived the physical and psychological challenges of navigation might gain a reputation when he could correct errors found in the records of earlier explorers. Exploring the New Guinea coastline in 1791, Delano recorded, "Although this was not the place, where we were ordered to seek a strait through New Guinea, yet we hoped to find one. The bay was filled with shoals, and we could not advance without sending boats to sound the channels."[102] Similarly, in 1805, Delano failed to penetrate the shoals approaching Calleo, writing, "We went in this way in consequence of the information that we obtained from the *Naval Gazette*, and came very near to losing our ship."[103]

Worse dangers awaited. In 1829, off the Fijian island of Tacanova, with the *Glide* shattered against a rocky shoreline, water spilling into the ship as the crew feverishly worked the pumps, James Oliver fretted, "In this situation, with our destined port in view, almost hemmed in by rocks, liable, from the disabled condition of the ship, to be successfully attacked by the savages, and in continual fear lest the water should increase upon us, the sun set, and the darkness of a starless night gathered about us."[104]

The many "Oriental" directories, guides, and coastal pilots that promised to aid navigation to the East Indies were so popular because they were so necessary. The winds, currents, and constellations that moved a ship to its destination could also beleaguer or even sink a vessel, if not properly understood.

In planning voyages to the South China Sea and the Indian Ocean, Americans had to decipher the monsoons that drove seasonal winds, storms, and even currents. Yet the monsoons of the South China Sea varied across the watery expanse, moving differently from those that struck the Malabar Coast and the Bay of Bengal, creating microclimates that could change from year to year.[105]

Extending into the Pacific, seasonal winds challenged Yankee explorers to change course, trim sails, or brace for stormy weather. Amasa Delano's voyages were an exercise in vigilance, especially as his ship neared a coastline: "Of the Pelew Islands, the most southwest is Onour, whose western extremity lies in latitude 6°64′ north, and longitude 134°30′ east. This island, when a ship is seeking a harbor among the group, must be made in the south-west monsoon."[106] Returning through the East Indies, a mariner had to adapt again. Approaching New Guinea in a northwest monsoon late in December, his ship yielded before unexpected winds, diverting its return course to one less direct but safer. The mariner recorded, "We steered off the coast south and west; as the winds prevail so much from the north and west at that season of the year, we should never be able to make the passage in the north west monsoon, which would last as long on this coast as the north east monsoon blows in the China Sea, till the last of May."[107]

The monsoons likewise confounded John White in 1819 as he sailed the *Franklin* through the South China Sea to what he called Cochin China—today's Vietnam. In early June, he observed, "We had expected ere we had proceeded thus far to the north of the equator, to have fallen in with the south west monsoon, which generally commences in this part of the China sea early in May, but we attained the latitude of nearly 5° south, before we had any indications of this semiannual wind, and it was then so faint as scarcely to enable us to stem the current which had now again changed its direction, and ran very strong to the east-north-east; and it was only on the 4th of June, that we descried the Redang islands." Pushed along by mild westerly breezes, "co-operating with the prevailing monsoon, and inclining far southerly," temperatures hovered in the mid-80s and the voyage was comfortable. Yet the shift to the summer monsoon was not predictable, White learned. "The monsoon, which we had anticipated would at this season be regularly set in throughout the China Sea, became faint of the 26th." Reaching Manila towards the end of June, he used the alternating monsoon patterns to guide his course: "In the north-east monsoon, from October to April, which is the fine weather season, ships lie at anchor a short distance outside the bar, but in the Vendavales, or rainy monsoon, when the south-west winds prevail, they take shelter at Cavitè." Reaching the shores of Cochin China, he found the winter monsoon had set in two months earlier, and the

> heavy rains which had prevailed since our arrival, began now to abate, and frequent breezes from the northern quarter, indicated the change of the monsoon. Frequently after a day of calm weather, accompanied with great heat which would raise the mercury in the shade to 85° of Fahrenheit, a sudden northerly wind would spring up in the night, accompanied sometimes by rain, which would depress the mercury in a few minutes from ten to twenty degrees. As the season advanced, these breezes were of more frequent occurrence, and longer continuance, till the middle of December, when the periodical northeast wind was prevalent, and before the expiration of the month, fairly established.[108]

As unpredictable as the monsoons might be, currents posed a similar problem. Some were charted, but many had to be studied as they were encountered, adding to the anxiety of a voyage. And, as a ship entered the Great South Sea, the unknowns and the dangers increased. Consequently, American mariners made it their responsibility to add to the storehouse of human knowledge, contributing their mite to what William H. Goetzmann called "a second great age of discovery."[109] Part of its history incorporated a great age of mapmaking, as the need for precision became more apparent.[110] In his 1838 travelogue, Captain Edmund Fanning pondered a representative dilemma:

> What is the cause of those never-ceasing, or frequent, rapid, unaccountable, and variable currents, in all parts, or places near the equator on our globe, as they appear to be the same in the Pacific, in the Indian Ocean, and in the South Atlantic, between the continents of America and Africa? Are they caused by the force of the heavy gales in the variable latitudes on the surface of Neptune's element? Or by the daily rotation of our globe, as some will have it, and the trade winds? It cannot, I think, be the last; for if so, they would be regular, and always setting the same way, and not suddenly variable. It seems, therefore, all we can say relative to the explanation of the fact, is, that it is one of those mysteries known only to that Almighty Being, who created our globe, and placed it in its orbit.[111]

As John White navigated the *Franklin* from Banka into the China Sea, he likewise pondered, "The current, which had been setting strong to the eastward, since our leaving the Seven islands, now began to take a new direction, and run northerly; this easterly current and the light westerly winds which had attended us since our entrance into the China sea, had considerably retarded our passage, and rendered the time tedious and irksome."[112]

The uncertainties of a South Sea passage challenged mariners' courage. In his compendious *History of Sumatra* (1770), the English merchant William Marsden asserted that even the term "surf" was new to Westerners, and bracing waves of surf required particular mettle in both men and boats, as "countries where the surfs prevail, require boats of a particular construction, and the art of managing them demands the experience of a man's life." On one bizarre occasion, Marsden witnessed "a country vessel [overturned] in such a manner, that the top of the mast has stuck in the sand, and the lower end made its appearance through her bottom."[113] Often watched by an unfamiliar and possibly dangerous new people on shore, mariners had to navigate the ship safely, "by reckoning," through fraught reefs, shoals, and unwieldy currents. Delano described the experience in his September 1790 voyage in the *Massachusetts* through the Java Sea. As the ship entered the Billington passage, it "filled up with shoals." Avoiding one "most dangerous shoal . . . we continued our course till in latitude 11°00′ north, between north and east, to avoid shoals and sand keys, and never were there more narrow escapes of losing a ship in so short a time."[114] Similarly, Reuban Brumley revealed his fears in the Tonga Islands in May 1807, when he had "a very disagreeable and most anxious night. . . . The weather being thick, and having very limited sea room in which to maneuver the ship, over a bottomless sea, between the islands, as may be judged, when morning came, and gave day light to our aid, it made us sensible of our dangerous situation during the night just past.[115]

Four months later, he had a similar experience as he prepared his ship for departure, when suddenly a lookout "gave the alarm call, that our ship was over discolored water, and on casting my eye over the rail I could plainly see the bottom composed of coral rocks, to appearance about four fathoms of water." Quick action by the officers and crew saved the ship.[116]

The winds and currents of the Great South Sea could be harnessed to push a ship along over thousands of miles of ocean, especially if they could be predicted and even calculated. Yet the same winds and currents could drive a ship ashore. The sight and smell of a coast, the latter often perceived before the former, snapped men into anxious moments, as they strained their eyes for the white foam of hidden shoals and their ears for the pounding of breakers.[117] If they survived, mariners might turn their recollections into navigational guides. So it was in December 1799, when the *Ann & Hope* out of Rhode Island encountered the uncharted Fiji Islands. Ship's surgeon Benjamin Carter later asserted that it was only by God's hand that the crew escaped disaster. He recalled: "The course steered must have precipitated us on the reefs or ashore; but the Deity, who regards the lives of the meanest of his creatures, tempered the winds contrary to our vain wishes; and at dawn, on surveying the dangers we had escaped in the night our sense of his wisdom and goodness was increased. He it was, and not our prudence and foresight, that preserved our barque from a fatal contact with the rocks and shoals which lurked so near us."[118] Aboard the *Franklin* in 1819, Lieutenant John White made notes of the places where reefs would be found:

> These coral reefs and shoals are found in most parts of the world, within the tropics; but the waters of the eastern hemisphere seem to be peculiarly congenial to their production, and, indeed, there appear to be certain spaces or regions in these seas, which are their favourite haunts. Among many others may be mentioned the Mozambique channel, and that tract of ocean, from the eastern coast of Africa, quite across to the coast of Malabar, including the Mahé, Chagas, Maldive and Laccadive archipelagos; the southeastern part of the China sea; the Red sea; the eastern part of the Java sea, between Celebes and Java; the coasts of all the Sunda islands; and various places in the pacific ocean.[119]

To the north, the Philippine Islands extended their own navigational difficulties. Although Spanish forces had established a factory there about 1565 and had built Manila as a global city, the coastlines of 7,641 islands remained to be fully accounted for. Aboard the *Franklin* in 1819, White anticipated that a navigational guide could safeguard East Indies voyagers for years to come, easing the anxieties of generations of mariners. To this end, he summarized the challenges posed by reefs and shoals as he sailed into Manila.[120]

Even when a navigator found reefs and shoals marked on a map, one could not be certain that the map was correct. A good deal of guesswork went into calculations, adding to the anxiety of the voyage. Delano recorded his worries in 1804, writing: "We anchored in a bay on the coast of Peru, which lies in latitude 23°6′ south, and in longitude 70°20′ west. The latitude is correct, but the longitude is taken from a Spanish chart, and I believe can be depended on within a very few miles."[121] Although forced to rely on untrustworthy maps and charts, a vigilant commander and crew could prevent disaster, as Fanning noted in navigating the Tonga islands, recommending, "It is highly important, that a trusty officer, while navigating here, be continually at the mast-head, on a good look-out for those coral reefs, (which seem, as it were, in these seas, to grow up in a night,) and rocks, but which with this caution can be seen at a reasonable distance and avoided, even if under the surface of the water, and no break over them."[122] For the mariner, listening to one's fears could save a ship, cargo, and lives. For those who seldom strayed from their hearth fires, reading Delano and Fanning was a reminder of the elemental dangers that defined this part of the world.

Describing extended passages in unfamiliar waters, maritime historian Judith Fingard employs an adage commonly used to describe war, that it is 98 percent boredom punctuated by 2 percent sheer terror. The travel journals of early American China traders expressed a similar sentiment.[123] A captain sailing beyond Cape Horn or the Cape of Good Hope—beyond hope, as it were—needed every possible advantage as he navigated his vessel, cargo, and crew into seas that were still uncharted. Until the 1840s, few ships carried either reliable chronometers to locate their east-west longitude or accurate maps. Books of celestial navigation, such as Hamilton Moore's *New Practical Navigator* (1800) and Nathaniel Bowditch's *New American Practical Navigator* (1802) provided some reassurance but were useless if left ashore, as Nathaniel Appleton observed in 1799: "I want Hamm. Moore to correct my dead Reckoning for me."[124] Sunken reefs and elusive shoals went unmarked well into the nineteenth century and beyond.[125] Many sites on these "imperfect charts" marked memorable shipwrecks.[126] Approaching the Billington Straits off Java, William Elting recalled the recent loss of Edmund Fanning's ship, the *Ontario* in the same passage. In January 1799, just weeks out from Canton on a return voyage, the *Ontario* struck a reef and "instantly bilged."[127] Elting felt the loss seemed especially unfortunate because the reef lurked beneath calm waters, with "no breakers on any part of it" to alert an oncoming vessel. When the story reached home, American newspapers such as the *Columbian Courier* broadcast an account of the wreck, observing how the obstacle was "not laid down in any charts, though the straits have been much frequented"—a reminder that disaster could strike at any time. Absolving the Ontario's commander of blame, the *Courier* reminded readers of the dangers that Yankee voyagers faced from the dearth of accurate charts, asserting, "The complete knowledge of this shoal is important to our East-India commerce, we hope to publish a more particular account from the journal of Captain Whetten."[128] No traveler could ever feel entirely safe in a place where calamity was so capricious. The men of the *Pallas*, out of Salem, learned that lesson in the autumn monsoons of the South China Sea in October 1799, some months after the *Ontario* tragedy. Only twenty years earlier, the Admiralty of Britain's Royal

Navy had sent three voyages of exploration under Captain James Cook into the Pacific in search of a presumed Terra Australis Incognito, mapping instead East Indies islands such as Borneo. But, along the southern coast of Borneo, Captain Thomas Ward could not know what he would find in these notoriously fraught waters. He dispatched two boats to take soundings; one "which did not venture so far, returned to the Ship with ease," but the other, "with sails and a compass, with the mate, and presuming too much went too far from the Ship with a strong current against them." The maneuver left Ward in a quandary, and he decided at day's end to anchor where he was, "it being squally; and not certain of sufficient depth of Water, in the passage; and the gunner of the Ship said he saw the boat jibe and in so doing upset, it growing dark." In the morning, with no boat to be seen, Ward set a course for China, feverishly scanning the horizons for any sign of his shipmates. This story would have a happy ending: "To the Ship's company great pleasure, on their arrival found them here; they were seven days in an open boat, having nothing to eat but what they forcibly obtained from a Malay praw [prau], and that only about one quart of rice and a little water." The *Pallas* limped into Canton "in such a pitiful situation" that Ward spent much of his time—time he had allocated for trade—overseeing repairs.[129]

In the East Indies, some of the oceans' most dangerous shoals encircled the Indonesian island of Sumatra. They could not be avoided. Not only did Sumatrans grow the world's most sought-after peppercorns, but the island marked the western side of the "notoriously narrow and shallow" Sunda Straits, opposite Java, teeming with drifting logs and eight-foot-long sea snakes, through which a ship must pass to reach the South China Sea.[130] Just north of the Sunda Straits lay the isle of Banka and the Banka Straits. White described the island as "surrounded with shoals in a greater or less degree on every side, though the north east quarter is the most dangerous, where coral reefs extend far out into the sea, and many detached dangers are scattered about in every direction, rendering the navigation of this part of the coast very perilous."[131]

Once past the Sunda Straits, a ship still faced formidable obstacles. On his 1797 cruise to Manila, Bowditch recorded, Captain Henry Prince gingerly maneuvered the *Astrea* through uncharted rocks and shoals and over nauseating anomalies in depths.[132] Amasa Delano recorded his ship's tentative plodding in 1807, remarking: "On the 7th of September, we sailed from Batavia for Canton, crossed over the Java sea, and fell in with an island between Billiton and the Isle of Sal. We attempted to pass between this island and Billiton, found the passage filled up with shoals, tacked ship, head to the southward, tacked again to the northward, and ran through, a little to. . . . We made a most dangerous shoal bearing east." Another time, laying a course toward New Guinea, he recorded this passage into McClure's Inlet, Ambon Island, "The bay was filled with shoals, and we could not advance without sending boats to sound the channels." The passage was made more difficult under the penetrating eyes of marauders: "We had much difficulty to prevent our vessels from getting aground here. The flats were extensive and muddy. We had to use warps from the shore, while at anchor, and when moving, we had to keep boats ahead to tow us. This put us on the watch constantly, lest the natives should attack our men in the boats. The whole navigation of Cut-throat Creek was filled with alarms and mutterings."[133]

In the South Pacific, the Palau Islands set a benchmark for the caution a navigator would have to exercise in encountering even previously marked islands. According Delano's notes, the approach to Onour, which offered the best harbor,

> must be made in the south-west monsoon. A seaman may take his choice to sail
> north or south of it; but if to the north, daylight is necessary as some reefs are
> to be passed in running east and northward for the other islands. A ship ought
> to go well to the south of them all, especially when coming from the westward;
> for if she should keep in the latitude of the mass of the islands, she would fall
> directly upon the reef where Captain Henry Wilson was wrecked in 1783,
> in the *Antelope* packet. This reef lies in the form of a crescent, encompassing
> nearly all the north and west parts of the cluster, so that in attempting to make
> a harbor, it is necessary to sail on the south and east side. It should be remem-
> bered however, that the east side is considerably lined with reefs, although it is
> possible, notwithstanding them, to find a harbor. The south part is most easy of
> access, and yet it is very difficult, in consequence of such innumerable shoals
> of coral rocks. The whole should be sounded with a boat, before any attempt is
> made with a ship. Although I have, been in five or six safe anchoring places,
> formed by the islands and the reefs, I must yet urge great caution upon every
> stranger how he enters among them; and after all, the most minute description
> would be insufficient for his safety.

We can identify within the texts of "voyages round the world," couched in the form of navigational guides, a language of fear, uncertainty, and anxiety. It was revealed, for instance, in Delano's advice on approaching the Formosa (Taiwan) Straits. He wrote, "A ship, sailing through the straits of Formosa, will find it most easy and plain navigation to make Formosa . . . in the daytime; but in the night, it is not very safe to run if the longitude is not known, unless it is a clear night, which is not common in the north east monsoon." He added a note of caution to his advice: "We saw no other danger as we passed within six or seven leagues off it; but I cannot say that other may not exist beyond that distance."[134]

Frequently, a mariner encountered a perfect storm of menacing conditions at once. Approaching the South China Sea through the Formosa Straits, Delano warned of dangerous breakers, hidden shoals, days on end of gale and fog, and strong currents, "which, considering all circumstances, would render it very dangerous to fall in." He concluded, "As this passage is made only in the north east monsoon it is always to be calculated on having excessively bad weather, and a very rough sea, for many degrees to the eastward of Formosa, till entering the bay of Canton."[135] Delano would continue to cruise "round the world" and he would continue to avoid shipwreck—sometimes barely. Edmund Fanning perused Delano's *Narrative* and studied the journals of Cook, Dampier, Rogers, and others, but this did not prevent his own several near-tragedies.

John Richards Child found similar challenges in an 1811 voyage through the South Pacific. Aboard the ship *Hunter*, searching for sandalwood, he coasted along the Fiji Islands, looking for a passage through shoal waters. At one spot, he recorded, "The passage through the reef being narrow and dangerous, we did not succeed." At another, he complained, "It being dangerous to run in we stood off and on between Turtle [Island] and the great group of Feegee." A week later came another frustrating endeavor as "the ship drifting in upon a long island, there was some danger of our getting ashore so that we was oblige to bear down bout and tow her off." A modern reader feels Child's concerns as the log's repetition develops a trope: "We continued running down this passage, which was very dangerous"; "many dangerous shoals"; and in a marginal note in a different hand: "Dangerous sholes [South] of Sand."[136]

In the vision of early American mariners, the Great South Sea extended all the way to the Pacific coast of South America, and the dangers of shoals and reefs continued there, too. Off the coast of Chile in 1806, the presence of seals, penguins, and other shore birds alerted Delano that he was near the coast before he discerned land through the "thick heavy atmosphere" of a gale. With vision limited to less than a mile, he lamented: "The most of this time we considered ourselves in danger of falling in with some islands or rocks, which induced me to give over our search for land. I have not the least doubt but that there are some islands or rocks lying within a short distance of our track."[137]

In chapter XI of his *Adventures and Sufferings*, Samuel Patterson tells his readers about the dangers that the natural world held for those who dared to travel the seas of Oceania. Sailing from the Sandwich Islands (Hawai'i) to Fiji for sandalwood, the brig *Eliza* encountered "heavy gales of wind" that beat hard against the "very bad and leaky" ship, keeping the crew "constantly employed at the pumps, which so were out of repair, to keep her from filling." The dangers of navigating an unfamiliar coast was a conventional theme in this genre, often producing a pivotal moment in a narrative. For Patterson, that moment came off the island of Nirie in the Feegee (Fiji) group about 11 p.m. on June 20, 1808, when the "look out on the forecastle, seeing breakers just ahead, cried out with the greatest vehemence, and gave us alarm." It was too late. The ailing Patterson rushed up on deck just as the ship struck a submerged rock formation. The only thing for the crew to do was to hastily fill a long boat with ship funds, weapons, and supplies. "Our fears were great," he recalled, "that if the vessel went to pieces, went to drift, we should be killed by the Timbers." Two crewmen had lashed canoes to the long boat, but the "violence of the swell and the sea running high, set the canoes a surging"; one man survived, but then died trying to swim to safety. Nine miles away was the island of Nirie, where Patterson would be captured by a cannibal group and held for nearly a year.[138]

The ferocity of the North Atlantic is legendary. Inscribed in poetry, music, and narrative, the " stinging blast," "whooping billow," and " whistling sleet and snow . . . hissing in the brine" have wrecked thousands of vessels.[139] Even so, novice sailors were unprepared for the terror of storms in the South Seas, especially in rounding the southern tips of Africa and South America. Occasionally, they would encounter a ghostly reminder of the perils of a South Sea voyage. In April 1821, for instance, on its voyage home from Calcutta the Salem ship *George* happened upon the *Susannah* of Fredericksburg, abandoned, and "having nothing standing but her bowsprit and jib boom . . . with about two feet of water in her hold. She appeared to have been in this condition a long time."[140] Before he reached the South Pacific, mariner James Oliver claimed that a sailor "prefers the storm itself with all its din and toil and danger, to the tedious monotony of a calm."[141] His assurance disappeared when Oliver's vessel shipwrecked.

"Great are the hardships which sailors usually experience in doubling the southern capes in the winter months," recalled Oliver.[142] Hurricanes, cyclones, and typhoons, along with earthquakes and tsunamis, were the most destructive forces from the East Indies into the South Pacific.[143] The typhoon, known variously as tyfoon, typhong, typhon, or tuffon, observed Osmund Tiffany, "smites with the rapidity and malignancy of Smyrna's plague."[144] Amasa Delano recalled an encounter with a "tuffoon," approaching Canton in 1790 which left his ship's mainsail, foretop sail, and fore-topmast staysail in tatters. Nearby ships suffered more damage. A Dutch vessel sank with her entire crew and as much as $400,000. Other ships were dismasted and required extensive repair. Hundreds of local junks, sampans, and praus "were lost, many torn to pieces in their sails and rigging, and many of them driven on shore."[145] Storms in the South Seas were fearsome; storms along the shoreline were catastrophic. It was often safer to weather a storm in deep water than approach the coast. In 1804, Delano hoped to find a safe harbor along the northern coast of Tasmania, "but the wind was blowing a gale from the west-north-west when we came abreast the port, and caused such a heavy sea that we could not approach the land near enough to see much of the place; but by the appearance of the shore about where the port must be, it seemed to be very unhospitable and dangerous."[146]

The threat of disease in the South Sea was also worsened by distance.[147] A debilitated crew unable to perform the myriad tasks of ascending a masthead, reefing sails, hauling cable, manning pumps, and keeping watch accentuated the ordinary dangers of South Seas voyages and put everyone on edge. If rain did not come, a dehydrated crew survived on a few pints of tainted water and some salted pork, a diet compromising a sailor's immune system, as we know today, but they reckoned only dimly. On the *Glide*'s voyage to the South Seas in 1829, James Oliver complained that the "supply was small for men toiling under the heat of a tropical sun, and subsisting upon salt provisions."[148] Diseases out there were so virulent and medical knowledge so scanty that Americans died in droves. Yankee ships were vulnerable because they rarely carried a trained physician aboard. On the other hand, they were not so congested as on the European East Indiamen, and less crowding lessened the spread of contagion. Still, an able crew was such a rarity that commanders would sometimes note in a ship's log, "My ship's company have been remarkably healthy."[149]

On a long voyage, an ailing crew left a ship vulnerable to a host of dangers. In 1800, as French privateers stalked British and American ships in the East Indies, the captain of the *Magnus* of Philadelphia found himself in a precarious condition when the ship's supercargo fell ill at Bantam and prevented his vessel from joining an East India Company convoy scheduled to return to Atlantic ports. Delano found himself in such a plight at the Galapagos Islands in 1805, in a "weak and helpless condition," his ten-man crew suffering from scurvy, from which one had already died. His sailors were in no position to defend the ship when they encountered the *Henry*, a British privateer commanded by William Watson, "the greatest drunkard, and the most low and mean spirited man, that ever was put in charge of property," who "threatened, with other insults, to take away my men as British Subjects."[150] Often, a vessel had to veer off course to care for a crew laid low. Edmund Fanning redirected the *Betsey*'s course in 1807 to deal with scurvy, writing,

> It would have been a great and very thankful relief to my mind, had we have been permitted to have come at anchor with our ship in the Sound, as I was especially anxious for the relief of our scorbutic patients. Our head cook was this day taken, or reported on the list, with this discouraging and spirit-killing disease, which not only added another to our invalid list, taken off duty, but one with whom it was very inconvenient to dispense. However, our good little ship was now ploughing her way over the surface of Neptune's element, and rapidly advancing on her course before the strong and fair gale.[151]

For a disease such as scurvy, the prospect of a landing offered some hope of recovery. Off Botany Bay in the *Hope* in March 1807, Reuben Brumley "was extremely anxious to get the ship into port. . . . Our sick list with the scurvy had now increased to nine, who were unable to keep the deck, and the number was almost daily increasing."[152] Consequently, many narratives and guides provided detailed directions to anchoring places and water sources. Delano, for instance, advised: "In a voyage to the South Seas, if a ship is very much in want of wood or water, it can be got at Trindade Island, in latitude 20°28′ south, longitude 28°32′ west or if the crew should have the scurvy, it is an excellent place to restore them, as you can get plenty of greens on the southeast part of the island, such as fine purslane and other kinds. These, together with the fine sweet water, soon revive a crew."[153]

The remedy saved men aboard Brumley's *Hope*, as he observed, "The refreshing fragrance from the land, as it came off to the ship with the flaws, had evidently an effect on even the worst of them." But many victims, such as Charles Derby in Hawai'i, were so far gone that it was only a matter of time before they perished. And it was possible to overindulge in the blessings a tropical landfall provided. When the *Panther*'s crew cooled off in the streams of Palau, they exposed themselves to microbes that infected them with tropical fevers. Delano reported: "But we paid too dearly for this pleasure of fresh water bathing. We took it so frequently, and stayed in the stream so long, that we brought on intermittent fevers, and several of our officers died. All would have died, had we not left off this indulgence. Europeans must be always cautious how they bathe in fresh water in hot countries."[154] Tropical fever could attack a ship with remarkable speed. Anchoring off Bencoolen, Sumatra, Delano observed, "Our men began to be sick, and to die, in a most extraordinary manner." Sometimes death followed the sickness of but a single day: "The first symptom of the disease was dizziness in the head; then a violent fever; sometimes the bowels swelled; a lethargy succeeded and the patient died without a groan. We lost nearly twenty men in half the number of days. We were obliged to go out of Pulo-Bay with only one topmast on end in each vessel."[155] Rather than offering relief from illness, some coasts were hot zones of disease. On Sumatra, towns such as Bencoolen, built on "low swampy ground," were frequently and "severely visited by that fatal disease, the jungle fever." Here, too, the "the liver complaint" was endemic.[156]

Yankee mariners often festooned the letters, diaries, and journals that documented their travels with poetry and sketches that proclaimed the beauty and bounty of the South Seas, fostering a mythical sense of paradise found. Yet the Edenic destination that these paeans imagined contrasted with the tedium of the voyage. Mary Wallis was not unusual in complaining that the four-month voyage that carried her to New Zealand in 1844 was relieved only by the "sight of land . . . refreshing to the eye that had grown weary with gazing on sky and water."[157] Beneath the lush greenery and iridescent flowers, however, there lurked further dangers. Threats and perils emerged at a beachhead, from an island's plants and creatures, as well as from the menace of its inhabitants. A crew sent ashore to penetrate jungle streams in search of fresh water commonly found instead "a striking contrast with the reptiles concealed beneath them, among which the traveler was endangered every moment from scorpions, centipedes, guanas, and tarantulas."[158]

Before coal-fueled steamships, sailing vessels required only the wind and currents to propel them to their destinations. But the men who sailed them needed food and water. As they were there to trade, they needed to make contact with the indigenous peoples on shore. Even stepping onto a beachhead required a vigilant watch. When the *Amethyst* arrived at the "small and low" Gowers Island, New Hebrides, in 1802 "for the purpose of procuring water and wood," the ship's first anchorage since departing Boston, Amos Porter found the place nothing like his native Vermont. An anxious landing party of

Porter, the second mate, and four seamen "took our war weapons with us as a means of defense against an enemy." Such was their apprehension of the "dangers near to some of the routes in sailing from Port Jackson to China."[159] But weapons afforded them no protection from the power of the beach itself. Repeated surges of "high surf" pushing their boat onto piercing coral threatened to splinter their sole means of escape and forced them to wade through surf to dry shore. Adding to their vulnerable condition were enormous water snakes and quantities of shellfish "of a frightful" appearance. Once ashore, conditions did not improve. They found coconuts but no other plants "fit for use" and no water.[160]

The island of Pulo Condore approaching the South China Sea offered more, but its residents included renegades from the mainland and a menagerie of troublesome creatures: "The small ones have wings and fly from tree to tree, others which hiss whose sting is mortal. Snakes of a prodigious size and length; centipedes, scorpion, rats, and in short an infinite variety of insects." Rather than a tropical paradise, Pulo Condore was, Porter concluded, "a most wretched abode."[161] Such was John White's experience also. Reaching Pulo Condore in the summer of 1819, he described a virtual mariner's paradise—a beautiful island, "with its lofty summits towering to the clouds," an excellent harbor, and "a fine locked basin, fit for careening." But Pulo Condore's attractions were deceptive, as "the island is very unhealthy and unproductive, abounding in noxious reptiles, and affording no good fresh water."[162]

Ashore, a visitor might be felled by small creatures, such as the poisonous centipede encountered by Amasa Delano, "and unfortunately gave me a most venomous bite upon my throat. It swelled very much, and caused me an extremely painful night . . . The bite of this odious reptile is said to be sometimes mortal, and always as dangerous as that of a scorpion." Moreover, the dangers from insects were not limited to these, as Delano found on New Guinea "immense numbers of snakes on the island, and black scorpions which are most venomous."[163] Americans reported that the slithering creatures were both astonishing and frightening. Pythons and boa constrictors took on enormous proportions in mariner's accounts. "The serpents of Buru are most remarkable," Delano related: "The Resident, or Governor, told us that some of them had swallowed a buffalo. . . . The boa is known to be often about forty feet long, and is said, in books, as I am told, to be much more."[164]

Even in established port cities, such as Batavia, capital of the Dutch East Indies on Java, men lived precariously near crocodiles, yet with remarkable composure. On a voyage to Canton, Charles Tyng's *Cordelia* anchored off Batavia, where he enjoyed music and a hotel and found that

> the city of Batavia lies inward from the shore some distance, and a canal is cut
> from the landing up, and through the city, connecting with others, which like
> streets pass in every direction, on which there are ware houses to receive the
> goods from lighters, that are brought by the shipping. A little ways from the
> landing is a shoal which is the resort of alligators, some very large ones, and
> they come near the boats, which pass in and out of the canal. It is seldom that
> they attack any one. There were some twenty or thirty ships and brigs at
> anchor there, besides several Dutch men of war, three American besides our
> vessel, the others mostly Dutch.[165]

The islands of the Philippines were home to a menagerie of "venomous animals," noted Nathaniel Bowditch on his 1796 visit. He described enormous snakes whose coils could crush a water buffalo, alligators that devoured the women who washed their clothes along riverbanks, and orangutans (imported from Borneo) that were "very vicious," invading domiciles to steal whatever piqued their curiosity and even throwing stones at people who interfered with their thieving.[166] In the Philippines in June 1819, Lieutenant John White described the boa constrictor and "ourang outang, or wild man of the woods." Later the same year, in Cochin China, his crew encountered a boa again, and spent an anxious night ashore guarding a valuable cargo from thieves and themselves from the monster. As they described their ordeal to White,

> They met with no disturbance during the night, but what proceeded from an
> enormous serpent, at least fifteen feet long, as they stated, which came out of
> the river, entered the court, in front of the building, which it crossed, and came
> into the custom house, and glided between the stacks of money, when they lost
> sight of it, nor could their strictest search, with the lamp which they had with
> them, again discover it. From the description of the sailors, I concluded it was
> a *boa constrictor*, and probably had its den in some part of the building, where
> it was retiring to rest, after its nocturnal excursion in search of food. This
> latter conjecture, however, was not at all satisfactory to the sailors, who
> insisted that it must be either the devil in his primitive disguise, or a real
> serpent, which had been trained by the natives, and sent in among them to
> frighten them from their posts, and compel them to leave the treasure unguarded;
> however, whether it were the archenemy himself, a *boa constrictor* returning
> to its den, or a serpent trained by the natives, the tars maintained their posts,
> with great intrepidity.[167]

The world was a dangerous place for Americans, filled with dangerous men and women. In the Ottoman and Chinese empires or in India, the dangers posed by contact with the Other were largely financial, threatening the success of a voyage, or moral and religious, threatening the souls of Christian travelers. Within the bounds of the East Indies and Great South Sea, however, other, more visceral fears defined the region in American consciousness. There was the threat posed by "piratical proas, which infest, more or less, all these straits between the Indian and Pacific oceans and the China sea, who are always on the watch for small or defenseless vessels," observed John White.[168] Cannibal peoples, who reportedly feasted on human flesh, likewise filled the nightmares of Yankee crews. They, too, could not be avoided, according to Captain Benjamin Morrell, who brought cannibals into the public domain in his 1832 study *A Narrative of Four Voyages*, in which he claimed to have identified two previously unknown islands where cannibal peoples unwittingly guarded sites of precious sandalwood and bêche-de-mer.[169]

The first encounter was often informal and spontaneous, as in China and India, where sampans of purveyors and compradors, banyans or dubashes enveloped a ship as it neared port, bartering coconuts and pineapples in Hawai'i and "hogs, fowls and sweet potatoes" in New Zealand (and taking beads, knives, tobacco in exchange) and exchanging in Java "fowls, parrots, monkies, and sometimes pigs, plantains, melons, sweet potatoes, cocoa-nuts, oranges, and green turtles." Beachheads and anchorages were sites where a sailor could collect souvenirs, especially if he anticipated a short stay, and he filled his sea chest with "fine war-spears, canoe-paddles, and shawls." But here, immediately, were sites for conflict to develop. Such had been the experience of Wallis in the *Dolphin* at Tahiti in 1767 and, most famously, of Cook in the *Endeavour* at Hawai'i in 1779.[170] At New Zealand in 1829, James Oliver recalled, "On one occasion, one of the crew being much annoyed by the entreaties of the savages for 'bacco, bacoo,' used this expedient to get rid of them. Taking from his pocket a small piece of the weed, he held it up before them, and then tossed it suddenly into the sea. Instantly, half-a-dozen savages dived after it, like so many dogs. Their search, however, was fruitless, and the last one who rose to the surface bled copiously at the nose, for having been so long under water."[171] Meanness or innocent misunderstanding could brew animosities that would be shared among countrymen and revenged later.

At an isolated atoll, an American crew might find themselves surrounded by hundreds of canoes, paddled with remarkable dexterity, some festooned with spears, severed heads and similar emblems of war, "crowded with natives of both sexes," uncertain whether the reception was for trade, capture, or even both.[172] Many brandished weapons such as clubs "of various sizes, of the hardest wood, and ornamented with sennit and carved wood" and spears, "very long and lancet-shoed, and have barbed fish-bones skillfully affixed to their points."[173] The new arrivals could not be certain what awaited them. On the Northwest coast, Samuel Patterson expressed his dismay, noting: "And on the 2d and 3d of August there came a great number of the natives around the ship with all their war canoes. What their intention was, can only be conjectured; but there cannot remain much doubt but what they had a design upon us, but we received no injury from them."[174] After months at sea, the crew was in desperate need of water and fresh fruit. At Java, they might exchange old clothes, knives, and odds-and-ends for "fowls, parrots, monkeys, and sometimes pigs, plantains, melons, sweet potatoes, cocoa-outs, oranges, and green turtles," as well as Malacca sugarcane.[175] In the Friendly Islands (Tonga), crews that had subsisted on salt pork could not resist the temptations of "tropical fruits and vegetables, as yams, bread-fruit, cocoa-nuts, shaddocks and plantains." In the Fiji archipelago, a plentitude of hogs, coconuts, and plantains could be had for "a pair of scissors or a jackknife."[176]

Other first contacts, too frequently, were attacks. Americans had heard or read accounts from famous explorers, but also more recent tragedies, from "the journals of several English Indiamen, that the natives in this region were hostile to all white people." One example was that of the English ship *Queen Indiaman*, which lost "three boats, with the first, second, and third mates, cut off."[177] These tales made Americans, with their small ships, scant crews, and few cannons, especially nervous. Delano reported: "The natives of New Guinea and of the adjacent islands are negroes, or woolly headed, and are well known to hate white people so much as to reward an individual, by making him a chief, when he will bring them a white man's head. If he will bring three, they will make him a chief of the first rank." Their reputation imbued American crews "with a sense of imminent danger" and primed them to retaliate.[178]

New Guinea was especially notorious, and American mariners passed on a hard-learned lesson. "On most parts of the coast," Delano cautioned, "it is very difficult to procure water, because of danger from the natives." With spears and arrows up to four feet long, and half an inch in diameter, "they were dangerous foes indeed."[179] But it was the Native strategy of ambush—like the "skulking way of war" that infuriated their Puritan forebears—that instilled fear into early American travelers and incited their thirst for revenge. In August 1791, on Manouaran Island approaching the Revenge Straits, Delano was with a landing party fetching water and wood; he was followed by a "gang of natives from New Guinea . . . who appeared hostile in their manners." His crew nervously backed into their boat, but when an unexpected swell capsized it, the New Guineans "brandished their spears, made motions preparatory to throwing them at us, strung their bows, presented their arrows, and stood a moment to observe the effect of this, and to ascertain what advantage they might expect from our condition." Their condition was doubtful, Delano recorded, as their powder and muskets were soaked. Fortunately, the New Guineans did not understand this, and backed off. Their escape "was felt in our hearts with not a few emotions of gratitude mingled with a sense of imminent danger."[180]

Delano's account is representative of how American mariners experienced the fraught nature of first encounters in the East Indies, Oceania, and Northwest coast. In the second voyage of the *Columbia*, John Hoskins shepherded his crew when they went ashore on the Northwest coast in 1791, but knew that others had been attacked for reasons not of their making; it "may have been to revenge some former injuries received from others, or to possess themselves of our clothes and arms."[181] In either case, he described the natives as irrational and unpredictable, qualities that defined a savage people. A voyage gained nothing through conflict with indigenous peoples. Keeping the peace, however, challenged a commander's abilities to contain the crew. As Hoskins wrote in June 1791, "On my landing, I gave positive orders to the boat's crew, not to offer the least umbrage to the natives: and I verily believe they did not, though no doubt it is too often the case that sailors, when no officer is with them; from their ignorance of the language, either miscomprehend the natives, or the natives them; thus each deeming the other insulted, a quarrel ensues, and the officers who are on the shore fall a sacrifice to it. as well in civilized, so in savage governments; from small causes, great evils spring."[182]

Rich in pepper, spices, and other luxury goods and dangerous to the extreme, extending from the South China Seas and through Indonesia, the East Indies lured many Americans to their deaths. Those who survived memorialized the region for generations of readers who grew up on lurid tales of piracy, massacre, and mayhem. Through the news reports and popular books that carried these accounts, Americans at home learned to see the East as a haven for pirates, lurking in the Sunda and Malacca straits, along the Coromandel and Malabar coasts, throughout the South China Sea, and everywhere between. Today, instructors and students can access these archival materials in the classroom and analyze the constellation of fears that American mariners documented as they voyaged through maritime Asia. A well-known example is William Haswell's journal for the bark *Lydia*, which sailed between Manila and Guam in 1801. The entire complement of crew and passengers remained in near-constant apprehension throughout their passage. First mate Haswell recorded their anxiety, fretting: "Now having to pass through dangerous straits.... The pirates are numerous in their prows and we have but eleven in number." As Nathaniel Bowditch sailed for the Indies in the *Putnam* searching for pepper in 1803, he recalled: "Capt. John Gibaut in returning from China through the Straits of Malacca for Bengal was attacked by a number of Prows ... William Brown likewise was attacked there.... [The pirates] have been known to attack vessels even in Manila Bay." Reports had alerted Bowditch to the presence of Malaysian freebooters in the Straits of Malacca, but he had not anticipated so many. His anxiety was heightened after the *Putnam* had passed through the Straits of Banca; "but there our danger was greatest," he reflected. As in the Mediterranean, many local rulers backed local buccaneers, who, Bowditch reported back to Salem, "have been known to attack vessels even in Manilla Bay." Worse, one could never be certain whether a proa might shed its trading guise and and launch a "saucy" assault on a Yankee vessel. At the time Bowditch's *Putnam* lay anchored in Manila, rumors circulated about a Malay prow anchored close by, armed with sixteen guns and ready to pounce on an unsuspecting victim "the moment she is out of port.[183] Such would be conditions until 1824, when the British occupation of Singapore filled the eastern seas with the Union Jack and made piracy almost untenable.[184] Amasa Delano reported his own close calls with pirates, observing: "They have large prows and many of them are well armed. There are frequent instances of vessels having been taken." At the western end of the Indian Ocean, Captain Sandwith Drinker found the Comoros archipelago, "thickly inhabited, the natives, courteous and hospitable, professing the Mahommedan religion, very timid and inoffensive, and frequently suffer from piratical expeditions of the inhabitants of Madagascar, who come over in boats, and prey upon them, laying waste their villages, and carrying off the inhabitants into slavery."[185]

To avoid capture, Yankee vessels tried to arrange sailing in pairs, or "consorts." Yet even friends could not always be trusted. Edmund Fanning had a similar close call. In December 1798, his fully laden *Betsey* had delayed departure for New York to travel with a larger "consort" ship bound for Philadelphia. Rounding a cape, they discovered in the adjoining bay "a fleet of [twenty-nine] piratical proas." At this sight, tthe *Betsey*'s consort instantly fled, leaving Fanning and his crew to fend for themsleves, facing "a set of some of the most hideous animals that ever the light of the sun shone upon," who filled the air with their screams. We know the denouement because the captain abruptly hauled up, changed course, and fired a broadside that so shocked the marauders that the praus swung about in a mass retreat.[186]

Some mariners so feared the horrors of Malay torture that they determined to avoid capture at all costs. Newspaper reports of autumn 1806 confirmed the last-resort strategy in recounting the experience of Captain William Story and the crew of the *Marquis de Sumereulas*. Surprised and overpowered by Malay praus off Sumatra, the crew of the *Marquis* attempted repeatedly to regain the ship. At this point, readers were told, the crew was "rallied and another effort was about to be made. The injunction was given that if they did not succeed, and the Malays took possession of the ship, a match should be applied to the magazine to blow her up." With this, "the natives had retreated, which was immediately discovered by the crew who got on deck with the expectation of a deadly contest."[187]

Readers likewise reveled in John White's depiction, in *Voyage to Cochin China* (1819), of the Banka Straits off Sumatra:

> The coast is inhabited by Malays, who are mostly employed in collecting biches de mer and birds' nests for the China market, in committing depreda-tions upon the unprotected commerce of the Chinese colonists in the neigh-borhood, and in lurking about among the shoals in the adjacent straits of Banka, Gasper and Billiton, watching to take advantage of vessels which pass through these several straits, on their entrance to, and return from, the China sea; here, embarrassed by the numerous reefs, and frequently striking on them, they become an easy prey to these barbarians, who, on these occasions, assemble together in great numbers.[188]

White, in his first encounter with Sumatrans on the morning of May 24, 1819, reminiscent of the assault on Fanning's *Betsey* in 1798, seems to have lacked no doubts about the intentions of the indigenous peoples. Maneuver-ing the *Franklin* through the treacherous Banca Strait off Sumatra, a lookout spotted three prau war canoes lying in wait at the mouth of the Palamban River, each armed with a cannon and propelled by dozens of oarsmen. An un-nerving undulation added to the praus' formidable appearance: the motion of the oars "assumed the appearance of the legs of a centipede in rapid mo-tion." Gossip and published accounts would have alerted the *Franklin*'s crew to what awaited them, and they dreaded the sight, "so shocking to humanity their savage cruelty to their prisoners" (massacring immediately all the Lascars, or Native sailors on board the captured vessels, and putting to death, with the most lingering and agonizing tortures, all the Europeans or whites.) Compounding the Yankees' plight, the pirates used the coastal topography and variable winds to their advantage, watching the *Franklin* drift helplessly against a sand bar. A sudden squall saved the ship, allowing White to steer for the Dutch settlement of Mintow, although his pursuers stayed on his heels. In his account, White followed a common formula of contrasting indigenous "savagery" with European "civility," noting that at Mintow the Dutch official, or resident, supplied the Franklin with powder, ammunition, and wood to repair broken gun carriages.[189]

"Treachery is peculiarly base when it is preceded by this token of peace and confidence," Delano had cause to consider in September 1791. Exploring the Dutch nutmeg colony at Ambon Island, the morning watch spotted a small flotilla coming toward the ship. The telescope revealed "three canoes with about thirty men in each, and eight small ones with each about ten men." Waving a white flag and pouring water over their heads—the usual signs of peace in that part of the world—they brought birds of paradise for trade. Suddenly, "a cloud of arrows now flew at every part of our vessel, at the men in the tops, at those going up, and at all who were upon deck, where it became dangerous to stand." The crew was able to repel the attack, but the treachery left four men wounded, including Delano with an arrow in his chest, the loss of the ship's doctor, and memories that would make them more suspicious in the future.[190]

The pirates of the East Indies were not just numerous. They were notorious for deceit and wanton, almost maniacal cruelty. Employing the trope that came to characterize the East Indies for American readers at home, Delano observed, "The natives [on Sumatra] are Malays, and notoriously treacherous."[191] John White survived an attack in May 1819, and described a Malay vessel he had captured: "The captured proa was about fifty-five feet long, and had twenty-eight oars of a side on two banks. Her gun, which had been dismounted and lay on shore, was an English brass eighteen pounder, with a sliding carriage, and that her barricado was composed of blocks of hewn timber, ten inches square, placed horizontally on each other, (and secured together by trenails,) about six feet high, projecting six feet outside the gunwale on each side, and the front of it covered with plates of iron." It was the prau's crew, however, that White found both fascinating and repulsive, writing, "Her crew, of which only eighteen survived out of about an hundred, had added to the natural ferocity of their temper, by a free use of opium, combined with the juice of a root, called bang; these stimulants, when associated with their Mahometan persuasion of the doctrine of predestination, render them totally exempt from fear, produce the most ungovernable rage and desperation, and stimulate them to deeds of the most savage and diabolical barbarity."[192] Consequently, "so serious have been their depredations upon the commerce of the East of late years, and so shocking to humanity their savage cruelty to their prisoners, that merchant vessels seldom navigate singly those seas."[193]

The sense of dread that permeates these accounts was also reflected in the relief that voyagers felt when they had safely put a notorious cove or bay behind them. Leaving the Banca Straits and entering the Chinese Sea in August 1802, Amos Porter felt "very fortunate in passing through these Piratical Strates."[194] Mariners translated their fears into precautions. Arming the ship was a priority. For defense, there were boarding nets. As the bark *Lydia* sailed between Manila and Guam in 1801, mate William Haswell observed, "Now having to pass through dangerous straits, we went to work to make boarding nettings, and to get our arms in the best order." Yet a sense of fatalism often took over a crew of a dozen or fewer manning a brace of small cannon, and they understood, in Porter's words, "had we been attacked, we should have been taken with ease."[195]

Beyond the East Indies, in Oceania, attacks came at the tip of a Hawai'ian spear or a Fijian club, but often the culprits were their own countrymen or a European crew. Acts of mischief or worse by Western travelers frequently preceded and indeed triggered Native assaults, and such acts of provocation filled the records of the "great age of discovery" and the accounts of renowned explorers such as Magellan, Bougainville, and, most famously, Cook.[196] Even some of his own chroniclers, for instance, had to implicate Captain James Cook's own behavior in his murder on Hawai'i in 1779. As Ruth Scobie writes, "Tension between crew and natives had been building for some time, with a series of thefts and violent incidents building up to this confrontation. The local people possibly resented the huge quantities of food which British sailors had bought or been given, and might also have begun to suspect that the British were planning to settle permanently on the island."[197]

Ingraham, Fanning, and Delano were among the mariners who admitted their own complicity in provoking hostility. One of Fanning's sailors on the *Betsey*'s 1797 cruise even planned to capture an indigenous Patagonian and exhibit him in a traveling freak show, "making a swinging great deal of money by it." For his part, on one voyage Fanning himself held one chief on board against the man's will, excusing the action because he was lost and needed a guide.[198] Delano was more circumspect and more critical of the Western role in East Indies encounters. Coursing the New Guinea Sea in 1791, Delano learned from the logs of several English Indiamen that "the natives in this region were hostile to all white people." The reasons for tension were not one-sided, however, and much of the blame was, "in a great measure, traceable to our own misconduct toward them." As Delano recounted the unhappy history of encounter in the East Indies, "When Europeans first visited New Guinea, the natives manifested no spirit of enmity. But the Europeans seized and carry them away as slaves, in a most treacherous manner. It was common for them to hook the yard tackles of a ship to a canoe, hoist her on deck with all the crew in her, transport them and sell them for slaves. The natives have heard also of the cruelties practiced toward the inhabitants of other islands, and even of the enormities committed by white people against each other at Amboyna, and several places in the vicinity."[199]

After an errant pilot boat from the *Pallas* lost its way back to the ship in Billington Strait, its frantic crew made course for Canton, surviving only on "what they forcibly obtained from a Malay praw [prau].[200] Such acts were often labeled as "mischief," a generous term that encompassed pilferage of vital food supplies, rape, murder, and rioting. When a European or American vessel fled ahead of retribution, leaving the indigenous inhabitants offended and stymied, Native peoples imposed an Oceanic form of justice on the unsuspecting next ship. The unfortunate mariners who faced a "savage" assault consequently produced a narrative in which the Americans were portrayed as innocents, the subjects of unprovoked attacks by irrational, impetuous, and barbarous peoples. Consequently, terms such as "treachery" and "savage" run through the entire East Indies genre.

This truth was just as often difficult for Americans to accept, and the curious logic that purported the innocence of the "civilized" and guilt of the "savage" can be gleaned in a report from diplomat Edmund Roberts in 1832, who had received "the inflicting intelligence that Mr. Knoerle, while on a journey to Palembang, was murdered at the instigation of some of the principal rajahs of Bencoolen." In Roberts's writing, what mattered was the horrific form of execution: "His body was literally cut in pieces, and then burnt with great exultation, by the perpetrators and their friends." When he raised the issue of motivation, Roberts located the cause of "so atrocious and fiend-like an act" in the simple savagery of a barbaric people: "The answer is—*revenge*, which is always deeply seated in the heart of a Malay." Yet the answer was not so simple, and Roberts went on in his narrative to complicate the story. As he wrote, "Mr. Knoerle, imprudently, injured the happiness of many families by his unrestrained passions, and thereby sealed his horrid fate. He should ever have borne in mind that he lived among

> Souls made of fire, and children of the sun,
> With whom revenge is virtue.[201]

In this, Roberts could find no legitimate provocation.

Such was the fate of the *Friendship* at Kuala Batu, Sumatra. In February 1831, the 316-ton Salem Indiaman anchored off the Sumatran village, as Captain Charles Endicott went ashore to barter an exchange for pepper. On the overcast night of February 7, pirates silently rowed out from the village and overwhelmed the *Friendship*'s inattentive crew. Three sailors were killed and another three wounded, but six managed to swim to shore. With the aid of three Yankee ships, which happened to be anchored up the coast, Endicott was able to recover the badly damaged *Friendship*, sailing the vessel into Salem on July 16 and recording $40,000 in losses, five men dead, and six wounded.[202]

Captain Endicott's report was instrumental in framing the popular response as an irrational attack by a savage people on an unsuspecting vessel pursuing an innocent purpose. From the moment of landing at Salem, Endicott appears to have been quite vocal in spreading word of the massacre, eventually producing a lecture titled "Narrative of the Piracy, and Plunder of the Ship Friendship, of Salem, on the West Coast of Sumatra, in February 1831, and the Massacre of Part of her Crew: also, her Recapture Out of the Hands of the Malay Pirates."[203] The first issue he hoped to dispel was that of Yankee complicity contained in reports that "the wrongs they have experienced at our hands have led to their bad faith and perfidy; and that we Americans, are, after all, responsible for it." Almost immediately, questions had arisen about the culpability of American or European crews in provoking retaliation on whatever Western ship should next anchor at Kuala Batu. This was a "base calumny," Endicott insisted. He could not admit a rational cause for the *Friendship* attack because doing so would upset the narrative, and Americans would have to accept some responsibility for provoking the assault. Consequently, Endicott painted the Sumatrans as "the most subtle, crafty and treacherous of all the nations of the East, . . . a people from whom we can never obtain redress for any bad faith or dishonesty; who acknowledge no laws, have no tribunals of justice to which we can appeal for broken faith or violated contracts, and hold themselves bound by no ties of integrity or honor."[204] To bolster his claim that the danger lay in the character of the Achean people, Endicott observed that the Achinese had been interlopers on Sumatra, systematically exterminating the local Malay population and dominating the pepper coast. Endicott drew on the seventeenth-century account of "Commodore Bieuliou's [voyage] to the East Indies in 1619–22" rather than the more recent and authoritative William Marsden, whose *History of Sumatra* would have recast many of Endicott's assertions.[205] In his retelling, Endicott set up a dichotomy: Bieuliou was "universally admired . . . as an officer of distinguished character, both for the integrity of his conduct and the extent of his abilities." In contrast, the Achinese king displayed "savage cruelty in mutilating his subjects upon the most trifling pretext, to which [the Commodore] was a painful eye-witness." Furthermore, "The inhabitants of Acheen are the most vicious of any on the coast. They are proud, perfidious and envious. With an outward show of being strict Mahometans, they are the most consummate hypocrites." Consequently, "we think no candid, liberal and unprejudiced mind will seek far, or look deep, for motives to stimulate such a mercenary people to acts of violence on our ships whenever opportunities offer; and that no other incentives are needed than such as are found inherent in their own breasts, that is, a love of plunder, to deeds of crime and outrage."[206]

The massacre aboard the *Friendship* infuriated President Andrew Jackson and his secretary of the navy, Levi Woodbury, who fretted that the incident could instigate more attacks and ultimately force American merchants to curtail their commerce in Southeast Asia. Ever sensitive to considerations of honor, whether national or personal, Jackson demanded retaliation, and Woodbury complied by rerouting an available warship that was destined for the Pacific. This was the USS *Potomac*, and in command was the same John Downes who had served aboard the *Essex* in 1813 and had participated in the tribal wars on Nuka Hiva. The *Potomac* anchored off Kuala Batu in February 1832, almost exactly a year after the *Friendship* incident. Downes's orders had called for him to survey the scene, identify the culprits, and negotiate restitution for the *Friendship*'s losses. Instead, the impetuous commander ordered a dawn assault on the village and its outlying posts along the coast. Perhaps the intelligence that he had received at Cape Town convinced him of the futility of negotiations; perhaps his experiences serving under Porter in the Marquesas had embittered him. Regardless, by the evening of February 6, one town was in flames, one village plundered, and as many as 150 Sumatrans killed.[207]

Similar recountings of treachery and massacre took place in Oceania. One of the earliest Americans to associate the South Seas with the cannibal concept was the ill-fated Samuel Patterson (b. 1785). Patterson traveled the Pacific on three voyages over six years (1802–1808), stopping at Australia, marooned on Fiji after shipwreck for six months, and raising a family on Hawai'i. Returning from the sea, broken both physically and psychologically, in 1817 he produced *Narrative of the Adventures and Sufferings of Samuel Patterson, Experienced in the Pacific Ocean, and Many other Parts of the World, with an Account of the Feegee, and Sandwich Islands*, a text that influenced a whole genre of American travel writing.[208] Patterson's book is an important example of how ordinary sailors, rather than ships' officers or merchants, constructed the Pacific and its peoples and how these experiences entered the consciousness of Americans to create an imagined world of barbarism populated by cannibal peoples.

In giving his readers "an Account of the Religion, and Customs of the People of Feegee," Patterson focused on what they would find sensationalist and sordid.[209] And, so, he selected the most damning epithet that he knew would lure American readers: "These savages are cannibals, and eat the bodies of their own malefactors, and all those of their prisoners: and as they were continually at war with some of the tribes around them, and the breach of their own laws, in nearly every case was punishable with death, they generally had a supply of human flesh."[210] Patterson painted an image that countered an emerging mythology of Yankee enterprise, energy, and initiative as markers of their "civilized" ways: "When cultivating their lands, and in their other labours, about noon they generally have a hole dug in the ground, heated by a fire made in it; and after they clean out the coals and ashes, they lay in their dead bodies, human, if they have any for eating, if not, hogs, and also potatoes and yams. On these they place a covering of straw, and then bring on the hot ashes and earth. After a few hours they take out the flesh, &c, and each one receives his share."[211] As historian Konstantin Dierks observes, Patterson "came home with reinforced contempt for the sundry 'uncivilized' peoples inhabiting that world."[212] To this end, the erstwhile beachcomber concluded his text with the observation: "How many of our fellow beings, with the exception of speech, scarcely can be said to be before the beasts of the wilderness in improvements:—naked, uncivilized, and preying on their own flesh.

What a change, when the holy principles of the religion of Jesus shall possess the hearts of all men!"

The four-year voyage of the South Sea Exploring Expedition (1838–1842) continued the cannibal trope. Secretary of the Navy James K. Paulding's instructions, dispatched to Lieutenant Charles Wilkes on August 11, 1838, underscored the idea that "the Expedition is not for conquest but discovery" and called for "courtesy and kindness toward the natives." But the legacy of Wilkes's command extended the violence of Manifest Destiny into Oceania. By the time the flotilla departed the South Seas, Wilkes's crews had fired birdshot into crowds of Polynesians to prove the Americans' "prowess and superiority"; arrested a Fijian chief and held others hostage; burned villages, leaving them "a heap of smoking ruins"; and left dozens dead.[213]

Among the world's domains that Americans came to associate with "the treachery of the savages," the most notorious was the Northwest coast. Gazing over a modern map, the Northwest coast of the North American continent might seem a world away from the East Indies or Hawai'i or Polynesia. Images of fat otters cavorting in the rhythmic sway of kelp beds, tall redwoods reaching into the sky upon a rocky, fogbound coast, the "continuous range of high mountains covered with snow," the daily drenching from jostled clouds— all form an impression of an environment dramatically different from that of the steamy jungles of Java or palm-filled coral atolls of Polynesia.[214] The peoples seem different, too—the customs of the Haida, Nootka, and Klingit present a contrast to the Javans, Polynesians, and Marquesans of Oceania. For early American mariners, and the reading public that followed them, however, the lands, waters, and peoples were interconnected parts of the same Great South Sea, and its reach embraced all. This integral vision filled the South Seas books that went through multiple editions across generations. The language that early American mariners used to describe the peoples of this reach conveyed a sense of common danger. Voyagers such as Amasa Delano and John Boit thrilled readers with tales of "sufferings" and "deliverance" and ships "cut off," whether in Fiji and Astoria.[215] Across the expanse of the Great South Sea, their narratives intimated, a traveler encountered "murderous savages" who engaged in "treachery" and "massacres" and mourned innocent seamen "inhumanly butchered."

American traders came to the Northwest coast in 1790, when two Boston vessels, the *Columbia Rediviva* and the *Lady Washington*, sailed around Cape Horn to find otter and seal pelts for the China market. They were following the lead of another Yankee, John Ledyard of Groton, Connecticut, who had sailed as corporal of marines on Captain James Cook's third voyage to Australia, "Owyhee," and the Northwest coast. Ledyard had returned as trade boomed in New York and Philadelphia, having just published his exploits in the first copyrighted book in the new nation, *A Journal of Captain Cook's Last Voyage to the Pacific Ocean*. The vision he promoted in 1783 was an ambitious one: to organize a voyage that would sail around the Cape of Good Hope and then thousands of miles up to Nootka Sound to collect otter furs, then sail the cargo to Canton, stopping at Hawai'i for provisions, then return to the United States with a cargo of tea and porcelain. He had seen how Cook's men had exchanged furs for trinkets from Indians of the Northwest and then sold them for $100 in Canton, and the experiences he described in his reconstructed journal and in person enticed farseeing merchants, such as Robert Morris.[216]

Contested by the British and Spanish in the 1790s, this Pacific enclave was another way station in the Great South Sea, a site where an enterprising mariner could find goods for the China market. But they paid a price, and publications such as Patterson's *Adventures and Sufferings* and Jewitt's *Narrative of the Adventures and Sufferings* (1816) made places such as Nootka Sound famous as killing fields.[217] Like accounts of pirate attacks and bureaucratic corruption in the South China Sea and Indian Ocean, tales of treachery and betrayal on the fierce and isolated Northwest coast or in the warm, shark-filled shoals of West Africa told American readers they were a "new people" in other regards. Along waters that were rich with the pelts of seals and especially sea otter, whose skins fetched as much as $100 on the Canton market, resided peoples whose conventions of property were as unfamiliar as anything Americans would encounter. And it was in this land of the Nootka and the Kwakiutl peoples that treachery, deceit, and sudden death were all too common. Americans quickly came to know it as one of the most dangerous places on earth.

Trading for pelts in Nootka Sound kept a crew in a continuous state of anxiety. Joseph Ingraham of Boston was one early writer who associated the Northwest coast with danger.

Ingraham described the people of Nootka Sound as "more ferocious than any other people I ever saw."[218] The danger was both imagined and real, heard through gossip and experienced. Entries of casualties filled ship's logs and sailors' journals, such as one in Ingraham's journal for August 1793, noting, the "savages" killed three of Captain Gray's men from the *Columbia*.[219] The Northwest peoples observed everything and understood how to leverage the seasonality of the fur trade to their benefit. Consequently, Ingraham warned against staying all winter, despite the financial efficiency of the strategy. For his part, Ingraham wrote, he "made a point never to trust boats away from the vessel after sunset among savages, whatever might be the terms we were upon." Exchanging gifts and sharing dinner might make it seem as if strong bonds had been forged, yet, he cautioned, "it would be doing wrong to trust to these appearances, as will appear . . . where some of our countrymen fell victims to their credulity on the mask of friendship worn by these people."[220]

The cost was a degree of fear that crews experienced and that regaled a public which expressed continued and "considerable interest" in lurid tales of "adventures and sufferings."[221] Ingraham, once again, told the tale, recorded in his journal for July 7, 1791, as his *Hope* was anchored in Magee's Sound along the Northwest coast of America, remarking, "Those who have not witnessed these dreadful situations cannot easily form an adequate idea of the extreme anxiety they occasion, for if the tempest destroys the vessel and the crew escapes with life they have yet everything to fear from a race of savages whose very looks are sufficient to excite horror."[222] The "extreme anxiety" ratcheted up the need for round-the-clock vigilance, stressing the shipboard routines of weary crews who might imagine every wave lapping against the ship to be a canoe filled with warriors, every creak of the ship to be a marauder's footsteps on deck. "To be constantly on guard against the treachery of the savages is as disagreeable a situation as I can conceive of," Ingraham reflected.

By the autumn of 1791, Ingraham had decided against wintering over at Nootka because, as he cautioned his readers, "to have wintered in a port where there were natives, we must have kept our lower mast rigged, lower yards up, boarding nets out, guns mounted, the vessel lumbered up, and a continual watch set which would have ruined the rigging." Ingraham's journal conveyed a salient construction of the Northwest coast to readers in Boston and Philadelphia, familiar with a stadial theory of human development, and they could easily imagine the people of Nootka stagnating at the level of savagery and themselves progressing to the higher reaches of civilization.[223] Recurrent reports of assaults on American vessels satisfied readers that the Northwest coast represented a degree of irrational savagery that would be found in the most primitive hunting-gathering era of their stages of civilization. One notorious incident occurred on the *Columbia*'s second voyage, when Indians killed second officer Joshua Caswell and seamen Joseph Barnes and John Folger as the men were fishing off shore. The site became known to American readers as Murderers' Bay. "In the *Hope* we were generally on our guard, and this unhappy transaction served to convince us how necessary the strictest attention was to guard against the treachery of the savages," Ingraham dryly observed on August 22, 1791.[224]

Consequently, when Ingraham made another voyage to Nootka Sound on the *Hope* in 1791, he knew what precautions he must take. This voyage required wintering over, and foremost in his plans was the need to defend the vessel. Of possibly wintering over in Magee's Sound, he wrote: "But to have wintered in a port where there were natives, we must have kept our lower mast rigged, lower yards ups, boarding nets out, guns mounted, the vessel lumbered up, and a continual watch set which would have ruined the rigging. To be constantly on guard against the treachery of the savages is as disagreeable a situation as I can conceive of."[225]

In this dangerous, disordered world, Americans were weak and on the defensive, and tales of massacred crews and lost ships poured into their public sphere.[226] Three episodes in particular shook the consciousness of the new nation. Perhaps most famous was a different kind of Boston massacre from the one most Americans know, an 1803 tragedy in which the Mowachaht chief Maquinna led his warriors from Yuquot village to attack the merchant ship *Boston*, murdering Captain John Salter and his crew.[227] The massacre employed the essential elements of the characteristic "savage" attack that Americans knew from their frontier wars, involving deception, ambush, spontaneous and coordinated assault, massacre, torture, imprisonment, and the display of trophy body parts.

The story that emerged fascinated and enraged readers. About ten o'clock on the morning of March 22, the chief Maquinna and several of his chiefs and warriors boarded the *Boston*, ostensibly to trade. Captain Salter did not make much of Maquinna's painted body and bear's-head mask, nor the mystical ritual the chief performed before boarding the *Boston*. Salter blithely accepted the chief's suggestion to send half the crew to a cove several miles away to catch salmon. As Salter prepared the *Boston* for departure, Maquinna gave a shout, seized the captain and threw him overboard, where elderly women in the canoes alongside bludgeoned him with their paddles. At a signal from the ship, Mowachaht warriors clubbed, knifed, or shot crewmen aboard the ship and up the coast. To commemorate their victory, they "next proceeded to cut off the heads of all the slain; and threw the bodies overboard. The heads being arranged in order from the Captain to the Cook." The *Boston* went up in flames shortly after.[228] Word reached Boston only in April 1804, when the *Columbian Centennial* printed a brief notice.[229] Three years later, Captain Hill brought the brig *Lydia* into Boston with the news that he had rescued the two survivors and with lurid details of the massacre.[230]

Captains Joseph Ingraham and James McGee knew the emotional environment of the Pacific Northwest well, imagining that the inhabitants took pleasure in "exasperating [mariners] by insulting, plundering, and even killing them on slight grounds." When the two met aboard the *Margaret* in 1792, McGee related a different side of the massacre. In his telling, the *Boston*'s crew had provoked the assault. Unruly crew members had "landed at a village in order to rob the natives and actually cut several skins off the natives' backs. Seeing them gathering to defend themselves, the sailors fired on them, by which they said four [Mowachaht] men were killed."[231] Yuquot villagers had endured a number of such encounters for several years and were determined to seek revenge. The moment for vengeance arose when Captain Salter insulted Maquinna before the chief's people by pushing him roughly and loudly proclaiming him an ungrateful liar. In his ill-considered rashness, Salter unwittingly challenged Maquinna to take action—both to preserve his own standing in the eyes of his people and to finally avenge the abuses inflicted by previous European and American fur traders and explorers.

John Jewitt, one of the two survivors, recounted the assault and his captivity by Maquinna in 1807 in *A Journal Kept at Nootka Sound*, and eight years later in *A Narrative of the Adventures and Sufferings of John R. Jewitt*.[232] The *Narrative* was immensely popular and went through multiple editions. Accompanying the book was an image of the *Boston* under attack, with heads of victims mounted in war canoes.[233] In 1816 and 1841, Richard Alsop recounted Jewitt's adventures in *The Captive of Nootka or the Adventures of John R. Jewitt*, keeping alive Americans' impressions of the Northwest coast as a place of savage danger.[234] Jewitt even starred in a theatrical production of his *Narrative* that opened in Philadelphia in March 1817.[235] And this story, too, became part of Americans' collective consciousness, canonized in high and low publications. It shaped the thinking of the literati of the *North American Review* for May 1816, who learned that "American vessels, in their voyages to and from the North-West Coast of the continent, frequently stop at the Sandwich Islands, for refreshments and repairs, and the restoration of health to their crews, generally impaired by the fatigue incident to the boisterous passage round Cape Horn, and the watchfulness and anxiety necessary in guarding against Indians, inhabiting the North-West coast of America."

Two years after the loss of the *Boston*, Nootka warriors attacked and killed eight members of the crew of the *Atahualpa* on Vancouver Island.[236] In the spring of 1806, newspapers such as the *Aurora General Advertiser* in Philadelphia reported in Ship News, "Arrived Nov. 16. The Atahualpa in June last, on the N. W. coast, was attacked by the natives and an obstinate conflict ensued, by which capt. Porter and nine others were killed, and nine wounded; they defended themselves with great bravery, and with great difficulty brought the ship off." Only five survived. In New York, the *Mercantile Advertiser* led with the headline "Massacre," then laid out the details of each crewman's death: "shot dead"; "daggered, and died immediately"; "daggered, and lived until the ship got out"; "killed . . . with an axe"; "dangerously wounded." Unusual in graphic detail for its time, the report noted, "The crew lost their jack knives, by stabbing the Indians through their skulls, and were unable to draw them out." The report ended on a poignant note: "June 17, deposited the bodies of our deceased shipmates in the deep."[237] The use of "our" was in keeping with the author's style but incidentally underscored the conflict between "our"—the readers'—civilized behavior and their—the "savages'"—deception and violence.[238]

The tragedy of the *Tonquin* in April 1811—the third ship attacked within a six-year span—left a deeper wound on American consciousness and sharpened the idea of the South Sea as a savage place. The bark had sailed from New York on an "enterprising" mission to plant a fur-trading post for John J. Astor. Astor had purchased Fanning's "excellent" ship, a vessel that had proven its mettle in two significant South Sea cruises. A party of thirty-four sailors, officers, company partners, and "clerks" would sail to the Northwest coast to build his visionary Astoria. Astor had chosen a bristly disciplinarian on leave from the navy, Lieutenant Jonathan Thorn, to command the expedition—a decision that foreshadowed the command of the unfortunate United States Exploring Expedition (1838–1842).[239]

By April 12, on the advice of a Nootka chief named Comcomly, Thorn found a site for their trading post (now George Point, Washington). Leaving behind the party of traders and supplies to build Astoria, Thorn set a course for Vancouver Island with twenty-three men, anchoring in Neweatee harbor (Clayoquot Bay). The fate of the *Tonquin* lay with testimony related by the sole survivor of the assault, a Quinault interpreter named Joseachal (or Lamayzie, according to Edmund Fanning). On June 22, 1811, as the ship lay anchored at Clayoquot Bay, Thorn set up an exchange with Tia-o-qui-aht natives. Things took a turn when Thorn insulted Nookamis, a Tia-o-qui-aht elder, slapping him in the face with a pelt, and ordered the ship to depart with some Tia-o-qui-aht still aboard. On June 15, Wickaninnish led an assault on the ship, killing all but four of the crew, who sheltered themselves in the ship's cabin. In the dark of the evening, three of the wounded survivors escaped, leaving the dying purser, James Lewis. In Joseachal's recounting, on June 16, Lewis invited the Tia-o-qui-aht to return to the ship to barter and, with perhaps one hundred people aboard, threw a match into the powder magazine, destroying the ship. Meanwhile, the sailors who had escaped from the *Tonquin* were captured and tortured to death.[240]

Gabriel Franchère was one of the traders left to build the post at Astoria. He related what it felt like to hear rumors of massacre, as others had heard around the Marquesas or Fiji Islands, or New Guinea and Hawai'i. At the end of June, indigenous travelers "bruited . . . that the *Tonquin* had been destroyed on the Coast [but] we did not give creedance to this rumor." As more information sifted in, however, "it did not fail to make a painful impression on our minds and keep us in an excited state of feeling as to the truth of the report." Franchère recalled, "The Indians of the Bay looked fiercer and more warlike than those of our neighborhood; so we doubled our vigilance and performed a daily drill to accustom ourselves to the use of arms."[241] In other parts of the Great South Sea, tales of horror likewise predisposed many travelers to fear the indigenous peoples they encountered. In New Zealand in 1829, James Oliver made a quick leap from gossip to revulsion, recalling: "Among other visitors was a chief, who, as I was informed by an Englishman who came aboard, was supposed to have been concerned in the massacre of the ship *Boyd*'s crew at this island. Some of the particulars of this tragedy were related to me by foreigners resident at New-Zealand. This chief was a man of very powerful frame, and of an exceedingly repulsive appearance."[242] Like Oliver, Franchère had become conditioned to fear the worst.

Consequently, the ways in which Americans reconstructed the "*Tonquin* massacre" broadly contributed to the sense of a dangerous world. The early newspaper accounts, coming in the spring of 1812, just seven months after they advertised tea sales from the previous voyage, were sketchy.[243] *The Connecticut Courant*, on May 12, 1812, and *The Columbian* (New York), on May 13, 1812, printed "a letter . . . dated at Kegharni (in the South Sea) Sept. 5, 1811." This account framed the voyage as an innocent trading cruise. The peaceful scene was shattered when "a great number of Indians went on board [and] suddenly attacked the crew, killed everyone on board, except the captain and one more." The two survivors fled into the powder magazine and, "seeing no possibility of escape, chose to be their own executioners, and . . . blew the ship to pieces, and destroyed many Indians." A boat "on shore for water" was not spared either, as the crew was "instantly shot" as they attempted their escape.[244]

By June, amid another war against Great Britain, news journals across the country continued to bring in accounts of the *Tonquin* affair. *The Daily National Intelligencer* for June 19, 1813, carried a report published a month earlier in the *Missouri Gazette* that promised to "repay the reader [who was] fond of hearing of 'most disastrous chances, of moving accidents by flood and field, of hair-breath 'scapes' that would rival anything from Daniel Boone." Filtering the *Tonquin*'s story down to the sensationalist details that the public craved, the narrative carried also "a particular account of the singular and melancholy fate of the ship Tonquin, the crew of which were destroyed by the savages whilst on a trading voyage on the coast north of the river Columbia, on Vancouver's island." The language drew on that used in Western frontier and East Indies accounts. This framing laid out a tale of "sorrow" and "melancholy." The indigenous people became "a powerful nation," but "ill-disposed"; they practiced deception and violence; they "secreted their knives" and "at a given signal rushed on their prey," who were all "butchered in a few minutes." In contrast, a racist code extolled "the brave resistance of every individual of the whites."

By 1815, after a wartime hiatus of almost three years, newspapers returned to the "Tonquin massacre" and the language incorporated a more nationalist and racist vocabulary. Over the summer of 1815, a number of news journals, including *Poulson's Daily Advertiser*, pulled an article from the *Philosophical Magazine*, headlined it a "Shocking Massacre" (July 15, 1815), and led it with a general racist overview: "The following melancholy account of the massacre of the crew of an American vessel employed in the fur trade, makes us acquainted with a race of savages whose coast it is not unlikely that some British vessels may visit—the information this conveyed may therefore save some valuable lives, which it must prove highly interesting to our readers."[245]

Popular writers also downplayed the provocations by the *Tonquin*'s crew. Authors such as Washington Irving and Edgar Allen Poe memorialized the tragedy, shifting blame from the rational, disciplined work of owner John Jacob Astor and Lieutenant Thorn to the "perfidious" Indians and the "folly" of the agents who unwisely allowed too many Native people aboard the ship.[246] Even Poe noted the efforts of the indigenous guide "who warned Captain Thorn of the perfidious character of the natives. The result was the merciless butchery of the crew."[247]

Fanning's account, published in his popular second book, *Voyages to the South Seas*, with a frontispiece that depicted the *Tonquin* attack, convinced generations of Americans that the Northeast coast was a danger zone. He absolved the martinet, Captain Thorn, with a caution: "Thus, it seems, by placing too much confidence in these wild savages, awfully perished the brave and daring Thorn, and whole of the twenty-two persons under his charge." The author contrasted in this "terrible scene of death" the "gallant and brave" captain and crew with "the savages" with "their horrid war-cry" who "cruelly put to death" four seamen. The deaths were "very lamentable." In his telling, unlike that of Captain Magee, the only innocents were white. Fanning lamented, "They were all put to death by cruel, lingering torture, in the usual horrid manner of savages." As for the perpetrators, they were "those bloody murderers," "these wild murderers," and "these barbarian murderers." The loss of the *Tonquin* and its crew, Fanning concluded, "which happened to be the lot of our first ship, and all on board of her which was sent to the Feejee Islands after sandal wood," drew the connection between the dangers of the East Indies, Polynesia, and the Pacific Northwest.[248]

Lost in the telling, or obscured in the retelling, were the reasons for attacks, as with the *Boston*. However, other sources came forward to depict the assaults as retaliation for violence inflicted first by Yankee mariners. Fur trader Alexander Ross wrote that the Americans had invaded his home, stole furs, and abused Native women. At other times, the Americans had fired on canoes and killed twenty of his Native people.[249] Even Fanning admitted, "The supercargo was very kindly received" on a previous visit, but on Thorn's visit to Clayoquot Bay in 1811 the Natives' demands for higher prices for pelts and lower costs for European goods had "exasperated the captain and induced him to treat the old chief very roughly."[250] Thorn had also "set off a smaller proportion of articles to each otter skin &c. than was usually given by the American traders." A Neweatee elder, an experienced trader, pointedly called out Thorn's charade and ended the exchange. When Thorn threw the elder off his ship, Fanning wrote, the "old savage was rendered by this act wildly mad, and left the ship with terrible threats." For his part, the captain was "in rather a violent passion," and, as always, refused to head the advice of the Native interpreter or the partners. Still, in Fanning's writing, the fault lay with the indigenous people, "knowing the Indian disposition and feelings, that this aged chief would not peaceably put up with such an affront."[251]

Reflections

In an important 2014 article, archaeologist James L. Flexner raised a series of questions about encounters between the West and the Oceanic East: "How do we address the violence of European settlement, especially in the dispossession of native lands? How do we understand colonial culture in light of the great degree of mixing that took place, not only in terms of human gene flows but also in terms of the ecosystems, built landscapes, and material culture that emerged from the recent past?" Flexner's inquiry is predicated on an understanding of colonialism in Oceania, recognizing, "Islander cultures were often used as the foil for those things that defined civilization, simultaneously determining what the West was and what it was not."[252] But even such insights, caution Margaret Jolly and Serge Tcherkézoff, privilege one side of the engagement. The emphasis is understandable from a historiographical point of view. Scholars traditionally have been trained to privilege written and visual documents and to regard oral testimony as fragmentary. But as Bronwen Douglas observes, "Much [Oceanic] scholarship has been imperial in theme and biographical in intent. From an indigenous perspective, such works typically lack ethnographic sensibility and position 'natives' as exotic backdrop to a Eurocentric, often hagiographic agenda which renders indigenous people irrelevant or peripheral. They are either universalized as less advanced versions of 'us' or stereotyped as passive objects or victims of European initiatives and influences whose only agency was a reflex savagery."[253] What has resulted, as I have attempted to show for early American encounters with the peoples of the Great South Sea, is a narrative of "cannibal isles" that is necessarily false by absenting the perspectives of the peoples of the East Indies, Oceania, and the Northwest coast.

Anticipations

For their part, Jolly and Tcherkézoff emphasize the importance of encounter in order "to stress the mutuality inherent in such meetings of bodies, and of minds."[254] More than a metaphor, the beachhead sets the tone for what came next, they suggest, with first impressions influencing, if not determining the relationship between travelers and inhabitants. The nature and results of encounters were malleable, differed depending on conditions, and were subject to the agency and interpretations of inhabitants as well as Yankee travelers. As Bronwen Douglas advises, we might "treat encounters as situated and permeable: not as a generalized clash of incommensurate cultures but as ambiguous intersections of multiple personal agencies, both indigenous and foreign."[255] This emotional context was everything, setting weary, tense, worried travelers against surprised, defensive, concerned inhabitants. The "flux, stress, high emotion and uncertainty of meetings with actual people in the vulnerable settings of voyages under sail" made encounters fraught with a sense of danger, Douglas writes.[256] Often, both sets of participants had heard stories of tragic outcomes and prepared for the worst. The results were stark and permanent. For their part, what Delano, Ingraham, and Fanning wrote formed the basis of an unshakable mythology that would become predicative of future outcomes. As might be expected, when visitors described their encounters as pleasant and productive, they tended to paint indigenous peoples in complimentary terms; when they found the interactions threatening or violent, they wrote about them in a derogatory language.[257]

The voyagers who perceived "savagery" were people whose nerves had been strained by the anxieties of transoceanic travel. As Captain Charles Bernard observed, "Who can describe the feelings of the weather-beaten sailor, and especially one who had endured as much as myself, when he catches upon the distant ocean a view of the light-house and outstretched land, which are his heralds to the haven into which he is shortly entering."[258] Left unwritten in such accounts are details that would have altered the stories that Americans told each other in the early years of the country and, consequently, would revise the stories that have been handed down in the grand narrative that we tell ourselves today. Charles Endicott, commander of the ill-fated *Friendship*, for instance, had heard that the Sumatrans' attack on his vessel was, ironically, a reprisal for the hostile behavior of earlier crews, but refuted the rational explanation for "savage" behavior. Yet some Yankee travelers laid the blame at the feet of Europeans. Delano was one, writing: "It is not therefore a matter of surprise that the natives should encourage and transmit this hatred toward Europeans. The white people have too often, and to their everlasting disgrace, used their arts and force, as members of civilized society, to betray, to kidnap, or to seize openly and violently, the natives for the most selfish and inhuman purposes. They make reprisals upon us, whenever they can, and are peculiarly inveterate against us in their hostility."[259]

Contesting narratives such as those of Endicott, historians Kate Fullagar and Michael McDonald frame the challenge by asking, What would it look like to "write histories of empire with Indigenous people as the *main* subjects?"[260] Gananath Obeyesekere explores similar questions in his pathbreaking study *The Apotheosis of Captain Cook: European Mythmaking in the Pacific*, in which he finds provocations by Europeans, indifferent to or misunderstanding indigenous practices, as the underlying causative force in conflict between different peoples.[261] Together, these scholars call for a need to center the peoples of the East Indies, Oceania, and the Northwest coast in the narrative. Following this guidance, we might query: What did the arrival of the *Friendship*, *Boston*, and *Tonquin* mean to the peoples of Quallah Batoo and Nootka respectively. Who did the Native peoples think the visitors were? Why did they attack?[262] What details, intentionally or inadvertently, were left out of American storytelling? And why has Endicott's perspective, rather than the alternative explanations of Delano and Ingraham, determined the dominant narrative?

Provocations

An inevitable feature of encounters between Americans and the peoples of the Great South Sea were misunderstandings. As I. C. Campbell determined, although there were often layers of resentment that brought about conflict, at heart, "divergent cultural practices, impenetrable assumptions on both sides and the mutual incomprehension of languages inevitably caused confusion and misunderstanding among the participants."[263] Misunderstandings could trigger a chain of tragic incidents. Problems erupted commonly around property, but European mistreatment of Native women also provoked ferocious responses, suggesting how some misunderstanding arose. Sexual mores were famously lax on Polynesian islands such as Tahiti, but, as Ingraham observed on the Northwest coast, "Chastity it would seem is held in great estimation among these people. They never allow one of their own tribe to take the least liberties with their wives—not even to take hold of their hands—and they informed us if a man was known to have connection with another man's wife they were both punished with death and, as they expressed it, their bodies thrown away where the crows would pick out their eyes and the wild beasts devour them."[264]

An integral part of the loss of the *Boston* and other ships like it were the offenses that led to bloodshed. Some mariners asserted, and likely believed, that their ships had been ambushed "without any cause or provocation."[265] Historians such as Anya Zilberstein attribute episodes of violence to "intensifying commercial competition."[266] On the other hand, James Gipson and others attribute increasing episodes of violence to "the imprudent conduct of some of the captains and crews of the ships employed in this [fur] trade." And the record shows another side to the story, the causes of animosity attributed to other traders. Jewitt's recounting of his captivity and the accounts of Ingraham, Patterson, and others point to cultural circumstances, particularly the underlying context of an emotional environment, that conditioned American encounters throughout the Pacific. As Ingraham indelicately put it in his 1791 *Journal*, "Savages seldom forget insults or injuries. It is said of those among us on the east side of the continent that they will never fail to revenge an affront of any kind; for years after the transaction has happened they are apparently on good terms with their advisory—yet only till opportunity presents itself."[267]

Cannibals and Victims

Kelly L. Watson observes that since the time of Herodotus, Western writing has described peoples who inhabited the edges of the "civilized world" as man-eaters, and this has framed "within colonialist literature . . . an assumption that the binary construction of civilization versus savagery and barbarism defines the world." Particularly revealing is her connection between Western assertions of cannibalism and savagery on the one hand and constructions of gender on the other. As she writes:

> Implicit within ideas about barbarism in the early modern world was the inability of barbarians to conform to the established norms of gendered power and sexual practices. Cannibalism, then, existed alongside the perception of inappropriate cultural practices in the writings of European men. The formation of masculine and, later, racist imperial power insisted on the perceived presence of cannibalism. In the early centuries of conquest, cannibalism above all else determined savagery, and savagery established one's place within the hierarchy on which civilization and imperialism rested.[268]

Depicting the cannibal served a useful purpose. As Lisa Lowe writes, in tracing the relationship between the interwoven development of liberal ideas and colonialism, the liberal rhetoric of the early republic depended on oppressing other peoples, both at home and abroad. She investigates the interrelationships, or "intimacies," between continents and between liberalism and colonialism.[269] Lowe urges historians to look at the processes that linked these regions and ideas "intimately." One process was to gain power by claiming victimhood. Consequently, throughout the narratives of voyages to the East Indies and South Seas, the tropes of fear, threats, struggle, and victimhood surface again and again.

It is likely that few American readers subscribed to Michel de Montaigne's famous observation, "Each man calls barbarism whatever is not his own practice . . . for we have no other criterion of reason beyond the . . . opinions and customs of the country we live in." As American mariners reached farther beyond their own shores, authors of a South Seas literature found it useful to inflame readers' imaginations by incorporating encounters with the inhumanity of pirates—the "villains of all nations"—and the debauchery of cannibal peoples. Representing themselves as victims of "cannibal" attacks enabled them to curry sympathy with their audiences. Accounts from mariners such as Patterson (1817), Jewitt (1807), White (1824), and Fanning (1833) adopted the particular language of Native American captivity narratives, insinuating into American consciousness a particular vocabulary of "treachery," "massacre," "savages," "these barbarians," and "cannibals," linking these terms to the people "eastward of Good Hope" and triggering the thirst for retribution.[270]

Watson contends that this language had particular resonance even before Americans traveled beyond Good Hope.[271] The South Seas travelogues continued and enhanced a tradition of captivity narratives that foregrounded the "cannibalism" of Native Americans. Consequently, images such as that of the Polynesian war canoe featured on John Parker's powder horn resonated powerfully within American culture. By examining the concept of the cannibal in colonial America, Watson helps us to interpret South Seas narratives in fresh ways. From this perspective, the language that informs the travelogues of Patterson, Oliver, and Fanning was prepackaged before they ever left American shores. Patterson, for instance, approached his Fiji Islands passages in a curiously understated style: "The food of this country is, yams, potatoes, plantains, cocoanuts, bananas, taros, breadfruit, human flesh, an inferior kind of swine which they raise, &c."[272] Yet a distinct cultural agenda informs his book. Like other Americans, he had been trained by a tradition of Western writing about Native Americans and even Catholics to think about other peoples as lacking the trappings of civilization. Patterson likely expected to have been appalled by cannibalism and the general disorder and lack of discipline he perceived in Fijian villages. As Watson reminds us, travelers do not commonly go into strange lands with open minds; they assume their own cultural superiority and use their own beliefs and practices as benchmarks by which to judge others. Given that his own country was a new and culturally insecure nation, Patterson's *Narrative* offered his readers a sense that they belonged within the community of civilized nations. In doing so, he reinvented canni-balism and savagery for a new generation of Americans.[273]

American accounts tended to incorporate the most sensationalist elements of earlier accounts, contributing to an accumulated mythology that took root in the American consciousness. In time, the idea of the Great South Sea as a haven for violent, backward people who stood in the way of an enlightened, liberal civilization paralleled the mythology of America's western frontier. In the early years of the American nation, words such as "treachery," "ambush," and "cannibal" became associated with dark-skinned people, on the western frontier beyond the Mississippi and on the eastern frontier beyond the Cape of Good Hope.[274] Furthermore, these words triggered a set of responses that became automatic in American culture. As Yankee voyagers translated their experiences into narrative and narrative into national memory, they found these ideas about the world, and the dangers they believed it posed to them, useful.

CHAPTER SIX

Echoes

[The] genuine American . . . neither trembles at the sword, nor blushes at
the plow.
> *Federal Gazette, and Philadelphia Evening Post*, November 12, 1789

The world is a dangerous place.
> Statement from President Donald J. Trump on standing with Saudi
> Arabia, Office of the Press Secretary, November 20, 2019

In his first State of the Union address in 1901, President Theodore Roosevelt
expressed his concerns about the state of the world in words that would have
been familiar to early American travelers. Roosevelt drew attention particularly to dangerous events in the Philippines, an East Indies colony that the
United States had acquired three years earlier in the Spanish-American War.
Among the many regions where the US presence now loomed, Roosevelt
stated, "in the Philippines our problem is larger. They are very rich tropical
islands, inhabited by many varying tribes, representing widely different stages
of progress toward civilization." Beneath the façade of bully president and
confident Rough Rider, the twenty-sixth president employed a language of
fear that Yankee mariners, merchants, and missionaries had employed a hundred years earlier: "We are extremely anxious that the natives shall show the
power of governing themselves. We are anxious, first for their sakes, and next,
because it relieves us of a great burden. There need not be the slightest fear
of our not continuing to give them all the liberty for which they are fit. . . . The
only fear is test in our overanxiety we give them a degree of independence for
which they are unfit, thereby inviting reaction and disaster."

In his performance of benevolent regard and faux expression of "our anxiety for the welfare and progress of the Philippines," Roosevelt echoed the
voices of previous presidents such as Andrew Jackson, as well as the Ottoman
missionary Pliny Fisk, the China trader Robert Bennet Forbes, the India merchant William Augustus Rogers, and the East Indies sea captain Charles Endicott. Yet Roosevelt's concerns foreshadowed the fears that Americans would
feel over the next century. He recalled the real and imagined dangers of a
world past and foreshadowed the threats of a world ahead. Roosevelt had
tapped into a discourse of racial scripts, to appropriate Natalie Molina's term,

that had been employed in maritime narratives published in the period between the Treaty of Paris and the First Opium War and that had been concretized in American consciousness and amplified in American diplomacy in the modern era.[1]

The language of American expansion that we associate with manifest destiny—an "empire of liberty," filibusters, the Monroe and Truman Doctrines, the "opening of Japan," "fire when ready," and the "new world order"—has its roots in the early republic, when Americans imagined the world as a place of disorder and danger.[2] The poets and editorialists of the early republic cast their countrymen as men of unfailing courage, as the editors of Philadelphia's *Federal Gazette* expressed in its November 12, 1789, issue: the "genuine American, who neither trembles at the sword, nor blushes at the plow."[3] Yet, in its relationship with the wider world, the new nation was as much a republic of fear as it was a republic of letters.

The ships' logs that denoted latitude and longitude, weather, winds, currents, and other matters placed a vessel within an East Indies directory, marking imagined "voyages of commerce and discovery" and fostering impressions of enlightened progress. But the private journals, diaries, and correspondence reveal that early overseas travelers described themselves as nervous, terrified, anxious, afraid, and fretful. This disposition influenced how they perceived and recounted how they treated the peoples they encountered. It continues to inform Americans' understanding of the world today. Moreover, Americans' violent responses to these dangers, real and imagined, have followed a trajectory expressed in the warnings of politicians, such as former President Trump, who assert that "The world is a dangerous place" and have in fact contributed to making it so.

This framing of the world as a dangerous place began before Europeans colonized the Americas and increased with America's entry onto the world stage.[4] In describing their early voyages into the world, Yankee mariners articulated their fears of typhoons and tidal bores, tigers and boa constrictors, homesickness and boredom, piratical praus, conniving mandarins, wanton Hindoos, and ferocious cannibals. This imagined world of mayhem framed mariners' responses to the Arab, Indian, Chinese, Polynesian, or Chinook peoples they encountered. They were scared and not prepared to show patience, forbearance, or tolerance. Recognition of the role of fear in early American contacts with other peoples and places in no way mitigates the racist attitudes Yankee mariners carried with them to these lands or their mistreatment of other peoples. To find meanings in their encounters, they developed racial scripts, conventional ways of writing about other peoples, employing particular vocabularies for each region. Another layer of language, drawn from the "scientific" racism of Josiah Clark Nott, Louis Agassiz, and Samuel George Morton augmented these scripts after the 1850s.[5] This language of "debased," "inferior" peoples merged disparagement of the Ottomans, Chinese, Indians, and peoples of the Great South Sea with attacks on African Americans, Native Americans, Hispanic peoples, and Chinese immigrants.

In their own words, overseas travelers fashioned themselves as sophisticated citizens of the world. Yet, as Henk Driessan, Michael Pearson, and Isaac Land have pointed out, it is difficult to characterize these travelers as cosmopolitan.[6] As they settled into Smyrna, Canton, Bombay, and Honolulu, they sought out friends, neighbors, and acquaintances to provide a measure of relief from the monotony and homesickness of an extended journey and to ease the "pain of unbelonging." They traveled the world, observed peoples and places, but did not fit in it. Rather, the arrangements they sought tended toward exclusion. With fewer opportunities to listen to and learn from Indian men and women, these travelers' understanding of the country and its peoples remained necessarily shallow. It became difficult to develop empathy or concern for a people with whom they had few interactions, and these concentrated on matters of trade and profits. This posture of intolerance contributed to a broader phenomenon described by Peter N. Stearns. In his recent study of tolerance in world history, Stearns observes that, although "the early modern period witnessed a marked expansion of the range and intensity of global contacts," this era "did not yield a decisive global trend toward tolerance." As he tells it, even as the West was developing concepts of tolerance, the people it sent abroad were reluctant to apply these to the peoples they encountered: "More commonly, however, new contact patterns challenged tolerance rather than encouraging it."[7] To this extent, Yankee voyagers did not so much encounter the world as create it—or, their version of it, as a world of fear.

From Fear to Force in the Ottoman Empire

When, in 1839, the *North American Review* asserted that "human life has little value, and human faith still" in Islamic societies, the literary magazine was making a claim with which few Americans would have quarreled. Narratives of cruel captivity, false prophets, Turkish tyrannies, plagues, and earthquakes filled bookshelves and libraries throughout the early republic and had prepared the ground for such blanket claims. Yankee visitors continued to describe this imagined East as had John Ledyard—"a scene wretched and interesting beyond any other that I have seen: poverty, rapine, murder, tumult, blind bigotry, cruel persecution, pestilence."[8]

The imagined contours of the Ottoman world as a site of danger and disorder, laid down in the narratives of Barbary captives, opium merchants, and Baptist missionaries, were affirmed and deepened in the national consciousness by later nineteenth-century travelers. Following George English and John L. Stephens, a new breed of Yankee traveler, tourists, boarded ships for the "Near East" ports of Alexandria and Constantinople to luxuriate in packaged tours of "exotic lands." More traveled vicariously, through travelogues, art, lectures, poetry, and novels and novellas that provided "all the advantage of travel without its discomforts and waste of time," fueled partly by the quest for biblical intimacy and the fashionable vogue of Egyptology. The outpouring of literature that flooded the public sphere in the latter part of the nineteenth century, Malini Johar Schueller tells us, further influenced American impressions of the East, especially the Ottoman world.[9]

Most influential in playing on now-familiar tropes was Mark Twain's *Innocents Abroad* (1869). Taking advantage of the novelty of steamship travel, Twain's itinerary of complaint centered around the disordered diversity that Pliny Fisk and John Stephens had lamented. Twain's report of Alexandria as "an eternal circus" where the inhabitants "were thicker than bees, in those narrow streets, and the men were dressed in all the outrageous, outlandish, idolatrous, extravagant, thunder-and-lightning costumes that ever a tailor with the delirium tremens and seven devils could conceive of" seeded a dystopian counterpoint to the virtues of order, godliness, and decorum that his readers imagined in their own communities. His claim that there "was no freak in dress too crazy to be indulged in; no absurdity too absurd to be tolerated; no frenzy in ragged diabolism too fantastic to be attempted" described a society that had breached the bounds of behavior considered proper for civilized people. And his complaint that Turkish shopkeepers "sit cross-legged in [their stalls], and work and trade and smoke long pipes, and smell like—like Turks" resonated with Yankees whose newspapers, chapbooks, and etiquette guides dismissed such cultural practices as "distorted out of all semblance of humanity."

Furthermore, Twain's depictions of sacred sites, where "everywhere was dirt, and dust, and dinginess, and gloom," recalled the sense of decadent ruination conveyed in the travelogues of Fisk, Robinson, Stephens, and Lynch. For Twain's readers, the Mosque of St. Sophia was "the rustiest old barn in heathendom," whose "dirt is much more wonderful than its dome," and even the marble was "battered, ugly and repulsive." Capturing the tourist mentality, Twain complained that the guides "made me take off my boots and walk into the place in my stocking-feet. I caught cold, and got myself so stuck up with a complication of gums, slime and general corruption."[10]

Much of Twain's account recalled recitals of Barbary bagnios and Arabian camps; some of the vocabulary had changed, but the substance remained the same. Similarly, the Ottoman reputation for despotic government continued beyond the nineteenth century. American newspapers and travelogues described cruelties imposed upon the empire's peoples through impoverishing taxation, barbaric justice, and ethnic oppression. As Christian missionaries gained footholds and Muslim influence receded, especially among Armenian populations, Ottoman leaders responded with policies so cruel as to astound American readers. As Jason Goodwin describes, "Massacre became the stock response to threat; the authorities made little effort to check the atrocities; and the frenzied blood-lust of the Turks in retreat is still a delicate subject."[11]

One turn-of-the-century development especially appalled American observers, who drew upon a script that would have been familiar to Thomas Boylston, James Riley, and Pliny Fisk: the Armenian genocide. The success of Christian missions and Russian expansionism had antagonized Ottoman leaders, who initiated pogroms in 1894–1896, 1909, and 1915. There "was little doubt as to American sympathies," as the resulting events horrified Americans and resurrected images of Turkish tyranny.[12] Historians such as Ann Marie Wilson identify a paradigm shift in American perceptions of the world during the 1890s, as Americans expressed a new sense of humanitarian responsibility. "The signal episode in this transformation," Wilson observes, "was the American response to the Armenian massacres of the 1890s."[13] Although President Woodrow Wilson's administration refused to act, the persecution of Christian minorities—killing as many as 1.5 million Armenians out of a total population of about 2.5 million—and the dislodgement of 1 million Greeks and 1.4 million Armenians confirmed long-standing images of cruelty and brought about American philanthropic efforts, such as the American Commission for Armenian and Syrian Relief (1915), the Near East Relief (1919), and the Near East Foundation (1930).[14]

Neologisms as well as imbedded aspersions acquired fresh, horrific meanings and associations. Reporting from the interior, US consuls regularly fed Ambassador Henry Morganthau Sr. accounts of the atrocities, reworking the concept of Turkish "abuses" and introducing into the parlance phrases such as "starving Armenians" and the "Murder of a Nation," reinforcing images of the Ottoman Empire as "a place of horror." For Charlotte Perkins Gilman, writing in 1903, the massacres of 1894–1896, which took the lives of two hundred thousand, could only be associated with terms such as "horror," "atrocities," "massacre," "outrage," "incredible suffering," and "Turkish outrages"—terms that also filled the Barbary and Arabian captivity narratives of a century earlier. Julia Ward Howe referred to the 1890s massacres as "slaughter" in which "this wicked and remorseless power" violated republican "principles of civic and religious liberty." "The spirit of civilization, the sense of Christendom, the heart of humanity" called "for justice" against "barbarous warfare of which the victims are helpless men, tender women and children." For Henry B. Blackwell, the "people in Turkey who are governed are civilized: the government is barbarous."[15] Theodore Roosevelt lamented "the Turkish horror," and the *New York Times* ran 145 articles on the Armenian massacres in 1915 alone, introducing the term "genocide."[16]

When massacre came to US shores, Americans fell back on familiar ways of explaining the horrors. Painful images of attacks on citizens—and even on American soil—were etched into the American consciousness in the latter twentieth and early twenty-first centuries. The 1979 hostage crisis in Iran, the airliner and shipboard hijackings, and the horrific attacks on New York's World Trade Center and the Pentagon on September 11, 2001—all targeting US civilians—have become iconic emblems Americans associate with the region that had been the Ottoman Empire. Brian Michael Jenkins describes the response by writing: "Americans in the post-9/11 era were more inclined to see the world beyond their borders as a source of danger. As in all threatened societies, perimeters had to be defended, new walls built, vigilance increased. The danger had to be kept outside."[17] Again, Americans appropriated an earlier language to describe their own experiences.[18]

The debates over an appropriate response that had characterized the Barbary crisis were replicated during the era of terrorist attacks. Many foreign-policy experts describe the US response as restrained, although the invasion of Iraq and Afghanistan in 2003 garnered much dissent. Mubarak Altwaiji writes, "Although the US government insisted on a 'War of Terror' and not Islam, public opinion was mixed. The threat to 'homeland security' triggered a discourse of neo-Orientalist thought and a return to the idea 'that Islam is a threat to the Western way of life.'"[19] As in the Barbary crisis, many called for all-out war, with one commentator insisting, "It doesn't make any difference who you kill in the process of retaliation against the attacks." Another shrilled,

"This is no time to be precious about locating the exact individuals directly involved in this particular terrorist attack. . . . We should invade their countries, kill their leaders, and convert them to Christianity." The legacy of early encounters in the Ottoman Empire, then, was a posture and language that continued to imagine the region as a haven of "Turkish tyranny" and false prophets.[20]

The intellectual position that posited a "clash of civilizations" was most effectively postulated by scholars Bernard Lewis and Samuel L. Huntington. After publishing the provocative article "The Roots of Muslim Rage" (1990), Lewis poured out a series of books, such as *What Went Wrong? The Clash Between Islam and Modernity in the Middle East* (2002) and *The Crisis of Islam: Holy War and Unholy Terror* (2003), arguing that supposedly immutable differences based on civilizations form the primary source of conflict.[21] Huntington took Lewis's argument further, asserting, "The great divisions among humankind and the dominating source of conflict will be cultural. . . . The principal conflicts of global politics will occur between nations and groups of different civilizations. The clash of civilizations will dominate global politics.[22] This neoconservative interpretation incorporated the language, consciously or not, of John L. Stephens, James Leander Cathcart, and James Riley, depicting what was now called the Arab world, as Abdullah al-Ahsan and others observe, as a site of an "irrational but surely historic reaction of an ancient rival against our Judeo-Christian heritage, our secular present, and the worldwide expansion of both."[23]

Alongside of the "clash of civilizations" literature that swamped American consciousness, a competing postcolonial interpretation emerged, anchored in Edward Said's *Orientalism* (1978) and extended in the work of John Esposito and others. Said's criticism of Lewis resonated in the present with postcolonial scholars and with the past in recalling the language of captivity narratives that had proclaimed that "Islam is an irrational herd or mass phenomenon ruling Muslims by passions, instincts, and unreflecting hatred. The whole point of his exposition is to frighten his audience, to make it never yield an inch to Islam. . . . Islam does not develop, and neither do Muslims; they merely are and they are to be watched."[24]

From Fear to Force in China

The first sixty years of contact in the Old China trade had insinuated a set of tropes in the American consciousness that imagined an empire stained by corruption and an ossified bureaucratic regimen, perennially on the brink of famine, flood, and revolution. By the latter nineteenth century, the conventional wisdom about China drew from an accumulation of records of reenacted encounters by merchants and missionaries such as Thomas Ward, William Elting, and Harriet Low. Ward condemned Chinese "impositions"; John Boit implicated "the *Rasscles* of the Chinese"; and Samuel Dorr complained, "the Chinamen will lye," and these impressions of corruption and malfeasance on the docks and in the factories of Canton, Whampoa, and Macao framed Americans' understanding of China. In Ward's memorable phrasing, "There is no villainy that they will not be guilty of if possible."[25]

Impressions laid down in the early narratives imprinted later American thought when the direction was reversed and substantial numbers of Chinese emigrated to the United States after 1870.[26] The tropes, with a vocabulary particular to the Old China trade, were taken up as a regular feature of anti-Chinese propaganda into the twenty-first century. Seaport cities such as San Francisco on the West Coast and New York on the East Coast were points of entry for anti-Chinese racist ideas. As ports developed their distinctive Chinatowns, such as San Francisco's "tenement ghetto of gambling and opium dens, tong wars, and an army of allegedly exotic prostitutes," social reformers complained that the corruption of Chinese culture prostituted its women and made its men "sexual predators who lured white women into their 'dens of vice and depravity.'"[27] In New York, the words of Ward, Elting, and other China traders found their way into the polemics of 1870s labor activists and editorialists such as John Swinton, who framed immigration from the East as the "Chinese Question," and politicians such as San Francisco mayor James D. Phelan and public intellectual Edward A. Ross extended this fear of Chinese corruption to the Japanese and other members of the "Mongolian race."[28] By 1901, Arthur Judson Brown could follow an embedded racial script that posited "this fossilized conservatism" as a "lower" civilization.[29] As John Kuo Wei Tchen and Judy Yung describe, "coolie" labor was yet a different face of an established danger, aimed directly at American workers on their home shores, yet described in a familiar language that castigated a "depraved and debased" race.[30] Increasingly conceived of as an American social problem, the racial noise found its way into the Chinese Exclusion Act of 1882, which initially prohibited the entry of Chinese laborers for ten years.[31] In 1929, even scholars used terms such as "Chinaman," "yellow men," "the Mongolian," and "the yellow race."[32]

The new China that emerged in 1949 featured a Communist bureaucracy reminiscent of the old mandarin structure, and three incidents in the South

China Sea reminded Americans that the region remained dangerous. On a torpid August day, a US-flagged vessel cruised the South China Sea, not far from where Lieutenant John White had sailed the *Franklin* in 1819. Suddenly, a flotilla of prau-like boats appeared and surrounded the vessel. In a performative rendition of Amasa Delano and Edmund Fanning, Captain John J. Herrick ordered his vessel to face the attackers and fire a broadside. The year was 1964, the ship was the US destroyer *Maddox*, and the Gulf of Tonkin incident provoked Congress to pass the resolution that led the country into the Indochina War. All had been scripted and choreographed over a century earlier. In fact, the Johnson administration had set the whole thing up.

Four years later, in another distant part of the world, a modest civilian research ship engaged in a "voyage of commerce and discovery" met a worse fate. Just north of the site of the Maddox's engagement, the *Pueblo* was assaulted and overtaken by coastal patrol boats. Surrounded and overwhelmed by superior forces, Captain Lloyd Bucher saw no recourse but to surrender the ship and its eighty-three crew members. Captured and hauled into port, the *Pueblo*'s crew were imprisoned and tortured for eleven months. The moment was January 23, 1968, and this time President Lyndon Johnson chose to negotiate with the North Korean captors. Few Americans at the time understood that this incident, too, had been played out before in the losses of the *Boston* (1803), the *Tonquin* (1805), and the *Friendship* (1831).

Six years after the capture of the *Pueblo*, another US-flagged vessel strayed into dangerous waters. Another merchant ship was captured and its crew imprisoned under grueling conditions. As in the efforts of the *Intrepid* to recover the USS *Philadelphia* in 1804, marines again attempted a rescue, but, unlike the heroics of Lieutenant Stephen Decatur in the *Intrepid*, this attempt failed. Three marines left behind were executed by the tyrannical state. In May 1975, the SS *Mayaguez* remained in the hands of Khmer Rouge forces on the island of Koh Tang, in the Communist state of Kampuchea (Cambodia).

The language used in business journals and on talk shows to describe China today, emphasizing corruption and obscure regulations, would resonate with Samuel Dorr and John Ward with a particular twist: "China is not infrequently mentioned as the major potential (or actual) threat to the US" in American business and political circles.[33] After asking, "What kind of superpower will China be [in the twenty-first century?]," Michael Schuman points to "clear patterns of a consistent worldview" that go back into early dynasties in which the "Chinese would also police their system in other, coercive ways—by, for instance, denying proper trading rights to unruly foreigners"—a sentiment that could have been uttered by Robert Bennet Forbes or William C. Hunter.[34] Influential business magazines such as *Forbes* cudgel what they see as China's innate corruption, another bête noire that emerged as early as Samuel Shaw's description in the 1780s.[35] A recent report from the Carnegie Foundation continues the trope, asserting that "endemic corruption among Chinese officials poses one of the most serious threats to the nation's future economic and political stability."[36] The *Wall Street Journal* even asks if "a certain degree of corruption might actually have been essential to China's growth model."[37] Generally, however, politicians continue to incorporate the corpus of early prejudices into current debates. On an Asian tour in October 2020, for instance, Secretary of State Mike Pompeo made a point of warning of "threats posed by the Chinese Communist Party"—not of military domination but of flouting international rules against pollution, overfishing, and consumption of illegal goods. For Pompeo, China remains a danger: he warned that it is "more critical now than ever that we collaborate to protect our people and partners from the CCP's exploitation, corruption and coercion." Echoing Hunter and Harriet Low on the mandarins' mishandling of floods and subsequent famines, Pompeo stated, the "pandemic that came from Wuhan" was "made infinitely worse by the Chinese Communist Party's cover-up."[38]

From Fear to Force in India

The accounts of early travelers to India differed from those describing the Ottoman Empire, China, or the South Seas, yet the Yankee mariners and missionaries who journeyed to the subcontinent represented it as similarly disordered and dangerous, although in other ways. Reports appearing after the Civil War appropriated the language and impressions of William Augustus Rogers, Dudley Pickman, Ann Hasseltine Judson, Harriet Newell, and others, and conveyed a set of stock tropes into the next century. Some mirrored sentiments found in Rogers's journals, for whom the subcontinent was a site of cultural contamination and religious pollution. Others lamented the Hindu rituals that Pickman found revolting for their "pride," "self-satisfaction," and festivity. Virtually all later commentators described, as had Judson and Newell, "poor benighted creatures" occupying a "land of darkness." In the jungles, a traveler encountered "a savage underbrush" inhabited by people "even more savage then the rude wilds in which they dwell." In the ports, Benjamin Carpenter found himself dependent on "artful men," who, John Crowninshield warned, "will make money out of you"; and the supercargo of the *General Washington* complained, "The whole life and study of the Indians is to cheat you." In this "land of idolatry," William Rogers feared for his profits during Hindu religious festivals, when "everything gives way to debauchery and drunkenness." Adventurer Josiah Harlan, whose accounts of Afghanistan were published in 1842 as *A Memoir of India and Avghanistaun*, portrayed an inverted world: "Let no Christian be deceived. . . . Amongst the customs of the Orientals, we meet with strange perversions of our commonest received principles."[39]

US trade with the subcontinent expanded after 1840, as "Americans imbued news from India with real significance." The *Princeton Review* and *Knickerbocker* signaled the importance of India in the American imaginary as the 1857 Sepoy Mutiny shook the foundations of the Raj and was "arresting the current thoughts of all readers." Political and social activists appropriated this "news from the East" to evoke comparisons with filibustering, slavery, slave rebellions, women's rights, the treatment of Native Americans, and other domestic developments.[40] For Mary Boykin Chestnut, for instance, the mutiny had provided a way to explore her anxieties over slave rebellions.[41] Ulysses S. Grant found his 1877 tour of India a useful means of critiquing the Raj, even after using his two terms as president to expropriate Native American lands. Even a consul to India (1905–1912), William Michaels, dismissed the humanity of its people and opposed their immigration to the United States.[42]

In the antebellum era, for those interested in moral regeneration, Transcendentalism had embraced filtered forms of Eastern mysticism, and this fascination with Eastern mysticism continued after the Civil War. Postbellum writers, few of whom actually traveled to the subcontinent, mitigated the harsh tones of earlier accounts somewhat, as the 1870s opened a revived "American awareness of the world of Asian thought." Yet, Nikhil Bilwakesh observes that the conventional view was "a depiction with very little deviation, of an exotic seat of mystical apathy spiced with hints of hideous barbarism, where men act faithfully in accordance to what Emerson calls 'the idea of a deaf, implorable, immense fate.'"[43] Most prominent were James Freeman Clarke, offering his *Ten Great Religions* in 1871, with its "strange mixture of admiration and distaste in his analysis"; Samuel Johnson, publishing the first volume of his *Oriental Religions* in 1872 and asserting that "the cardinal virtues and beliefs belong not to one religion, but to all religions"; and Moncure Conway, whose capacious American edition of his *Sacred Anthology* appeared in 1874, and who did travel to India to leave "behind Anglo-Saxonism cruel, ambitious, canting, aggressive to mingle with people who knew 'the blessedness of being little.'"[44] Yet many Americans were not enlightened by these intellectual exercises, and fears of Hinduism as an "eccentric cult seeking to fasten itself upon a superior Christianity" that threatened to corrupt American virtues continued into the twentieth century.[45] By the 1930s, W. Norman Brown could summarize American attitudes as, "A large number of Americans . . . have a picture of India as a land of meditating omphalopsychites, hypnotic swamis, naked ascetics, bejewelled princes of fabulous wealth and incomparable harems, gross superstition, bare-skinned, poverty-stricken, famine-ridden masses, where everyone is a beggar and caste is more important than life, the countryside terrifying with Bengal tigers, the houses and fields infested with hooded serpents, a land where disease and depravity are rampant."[46]

The strategy of playing on humanitarian themes, such as relief for epidemics and famine or support for women's education, to extract funds for missionary work continued into the twentieth century. Regular accounts of famine likewise filled American newspapers and circulated throughout the country.[47] Some of this was appropriation to push a political agenda, as when, in January 1897, the editors of the *Parsons Weekly Blade* (Kansas) used the "ravages of poverty in India" to lash out at Populists, who "should thank the stars that they are possessed of something of which they can be robbed."[48] For its part, the *Cherokee Advocate* (Oklahoma), in 1889, described India as a place of rampant poverty due to wages of fifty cents per week, a wage on which "an American or German would starve."[49] In 1900, the *Biloxi Daily Herald* told its readers in a front-page report that India was "a worn-out country" and "in spite of all of [the government's] exertions," inveterate poverty and sterile soil "due to the neglect of the illiterate peasants" were "proverbial."[50] Reporting on the "Extent of Poverty in India," newspapers such as the *Wichita Searchlight*, in August 1908, counted over one million people "dependent on state aid."[51]

American women such as Grace Thompson-Seton, Katherine Mayo, Gertrude Emerson, and Nilla Cram Cook, in particular, lifted the veil off gender relations. They differed on assigning blame for the rampant poverty, disease, and lack of public education they observed in the subcontinent: Thompson-Seton and Mayo asserted that the causes were deeply rooted within Indian cultures and that British "civilizing" rule was necessary; Emerson and Mayo accused the British occupation of holding India back. Yet all continued the trope of India's backwardness and social degradation, especially in gender relations.[52] As Frederic Carpenter was to observe later, "The qualities which made *Mother India* a best seller in 1928 were emphasized by the writers and reviewers of 1818."

Observers locate one source of danger in India's perceived disorder. The "the danger of chaos, disease and poverty engulfing the Indian subcontinent and other Third World countries certainly permeates current American opinion," a sentiment of which earlier commentators would have approved.[53] India's diversity and apparent disorder, as well as the perception of a dangerous instability, continue to be American concerns. As Surjit Mansingh observes, "Most Americans are bewildered, if not confounded, that such a multiplicity of community, faith, cast and language can coexist in One India. They find ethnic conflict and/or religious political self-identification there more comprehensible and worthy of comment then the unity of the Indian state or the longevity of Indian civilization."[54]

From Fear to Force in the Great South Sea

Encounters that occurred "eastward of Good Hope" after the Opium Wars left Americans with conflicting visions of the Great South Sea. Some of these dominated in narratives of "cannibal isles"; others sat in the recesses of national consciousness, to be dredged up when useful to support economic or strategic interests or to entertain mass audiences. The accounts of Herman Melville and his ilk had painted word pictures of paradise, beauty and bounty, and natural innocence, inviting readers to be vicariously "refreshed and delighted by the fragrance from off the beautiful green foliage" of the islands and to view the "perpetual spring" of groves of "cocoa-nut trees . . . growing in great luxuriance upon the high lands, and rice in the valleys, . . . with useful and ornamental fruits and flowers . . . eminently beautiful, and perhaps unrivalled."[55] Samuel Patterson, Charles Wilkes, Charles Endicott, and many more added their own versions of the cannibal tale. For John Richards Child, "the natives are said to be cannibals, very wild and savage"; for James Oliver, New Zealand "had ever been associated in our minds with all that is barbarous and inhuman in savage life"; Mary Wallis brought her readers to the "abominations of cannibal Feejee"; and Amasa Delano described the "hostility of the natives of New Guinea" and the "treachery of the Malays."

By the end of the century, however, the peoples of the East Indies, the Pacific, and and the American continent's Northwest coast had been reduced in numbers and power. Contact with the West had contributed to the devastation of the islands and disruption of viable lifeways. On the Marquesas Islands, for instance, an estimated population of 6,000 at the time of Melville's month-long sojourn in 1842 had fallen to 682 by 1900. Guam's Chamorro population had fallen to just over 11,000 in 1910. Of the Philippine Islands' nearly

8 million inhabitants, 20,000 insurgents died, while estimates of civilian casualties range from 200,000 to 1.5 million; American newspapers dwelt on the 4,000 American combat casualties, however.[56]

As the American navy incorporated the technologies of empire, the temptation to use force in the East Indies and South Pacific came easily. The philosophy that had guided the Jackson administration in 1832 in responding to the "daring outrage having been committed in those seas" on the *Friendship* and the subsequent impulse to demand "immediate satisfaction for the injury and indemnity to the sufferers" underlay the nation's imperialist program after 1870.[57]

By the turn of the century, President William McKinley and a "yellow press" had brought the country to war against Spain, adding resources and labor to the country's industrial might. Ironically, in the age of the Chinese Exclusion Act (1882) and *Plessy v. Ferguson* (1896), many Americans feared the ramifications of colonial conquest, particularly the prospect of tens of thousands of dark-skinned people coming to their shores. Some Americans who opposed the war and the subsequent seizure of Hawaiʻi in 1898, for instance, objected to "the racial character of the Hawaiʻian population that would become eligible for US citizenship." Thus, the Great South Sea continued to represent a site of perilous venture, but with a twist.[58] Where earlier in the century, mariners expressed their dread of contact with "savages" who could eat their bodies or corrupt their souls, similar to the danger of "turning Turk" in the Ottoman world, many now feared that annexation could bring similar contagion home to the entirety of American society. The result was that both political parties sought to exclude the suffrage from all nonwhite peoples.

While Cuba remained independent, the United States acquired the remaining Spanish territories of the Philippines, Guam, and Puerto Rico. However, acquiring territories proved controversial for the once-colonial nation. In 1901, the US Supreme Court augmented the racist language in the Insular Cases as it decided the status of US territories and their peoples acquired during the Spanish-American War. The court determined that the Constitution did not necessarily follow the flag and that "the inhabitants of the territories conquered during the Spanish-American War were not entitled to the full protection of the Constitution."[59] The conquered peoples were "savage tribes."[60] In 1901, the Supreme Court asserted thar Guam's "alien race" couldn't comprehend "Anglo-Saxon principles." Consequently, Justice Brown noted that "differences of race, habits, laws and customs of the people, and from differences of soil, climate and production" required Congress to take a stewardship role over the indigenous people.[61] Indeed, the court decided that the full Constitution did not apply to the acquired territory. In twenty-four subsequent cases adjudicated throughout the twentieth century, the court reaffirmed its racism in both their deliberations and language.

Powerful voices created an echo chamber of imperialist thought. On the surface, they were divided between imperialists and anti-imperialists, but the underlying assumption of "cannibal isles" remained. William Howard Taft, colonial administrator of the Philippines, 1900–1904, and future president and chief justice of the Supreme Court, asserted that the Filipino people were "in many respects nothing but grown up children." It would take, Taft predicted, a century of probation before they understood the principles of Anglo-Saxon government. Anything before then would be premature independence, resulting in disorder and corruption.[62] His predecessor as president expressed similar concerns. Theodore Roosevelt's first State of the Union message in 1901 was a litany of doubt about the ability of people of the East Indies to catch up to that of his own "masterful race":

> What has taken us thirty generations to achieve, we cannot expect to have another race accomplish out of hand, especially when large portions of that race start very far behind the point which our ancestors had reached even thirty generations ago. In dealing with the Philippine people we must show both patience and strength, forbearance and steadfast resolution. Our aim is high. We do not desire to do for the islanders merely what has elsewhere been done for tropic peoples by even the best foreign governments. We hope to do for them what has never before been done for any people of the tropics—to make them fit for self-government after the fashion of the really free nations.

The twentieth century saw a softer, if not less ruthless exploitation, as American leaders confiscated the islands for global war and atomic testing, leaving behind an "archaeology of brutal encounter."[63]

Modern America in a Dangerous World

Would Thomas Boylston be able to recognize the contours of his country or the wider world today? Would the essential fault lines of nation and race be at all familiar to Amasa Delano or Pliny Fisk or Ann Judson or Harriet Low? Could they discern continuities in the relationship between America and the world in their times and ours? Would they perceive the same kinds of threats to Americans and to their culture and interests across the globe?[64] It seems likely that they could trace these connections, and certainly they would find similarities in the language through which we convey our sense of a dangerous, chaotic world.

In his memoir of his years spent in reporting from the Middle East, *Eastward to Tartary*, journalist Robert D. Kaplan identifies "a question often asked in crisis situations": "Should we intervene?"[65] Our response to global crises that threaten to rage out of control, or to come too near to our shores, has been rooted in the accounts of an imagined East described in this book. Before the antebellum era, when the rest of the world seemed so distant, Americans were content to furrow their brows, shake their heads, and leave the world to itself. By the 1830s, however, in the wake of grisly assaults on their countrymen's ships and lives, Americans came to believe that the peoples of the world were too threatening and benighted to govern their own affairs.

Kaplan's question brings us back to the inquiries that began this study: When did Americans become afraid of the world? Why did Americans come to see that reordering the lives of people who inhabited distant places "eastward of Good Hope" was their responsibility?

The answers certainly do not make the United States exceptional. America is not so much unique as it is frightened. We remain suspicious of the same things that have always alarmed us—assimilation with "inferior" peoples, threats from rogue states, attacks on our economic interests, and competition with our gods. Whether our interventions in the world have taken the form of building walls, bombing capitals, or setting tariffs, we seek boundaries to separate us from the dangerous peoples of the world. These have been manifestations of our fears rather than testimony to our power.

Preface

1. *The Balance, and Columbian Repository* (Hudson, New York), November 4, 1806; *Hampshire Federalist* (Springfield, MA), November 4, 1806; *American Mercury* (Hartford, CT), November 6, 1806; *Republican Advocate* (Frederick, Maryland), October 31, 1806; *Mercantile Advertiser*, October 29, 1806; and *Providence Phoenix* (Providence, RI), November 1, 1806, among many others.

2. Throughout the book, I will be using "the East," "the great South Seas," or "the South Seas" in "the extended sense of [their] early nineteenth-century inventors," following current usage. See, for instance, Bronwen Douglas and Chris Ballard, "Race, Place and Civilisation: Colonial Encounters and Governance in Greater Oceania," *Journal of Pacific History*, 47, no. 3 (September 2012), 247.

3. European scholars have also begun to explore the role of fear, anxiety, and other negative emotions in the formation of colonial empires. Harald Fischer-Tiné, ed., *Anxieties, Fear, and Panic in Colonial Settings: Empires on the Verge of a Nervous Breakdown* (Houndmills, UK: Palgrave Macmillan, 2016); Jonathan Bergman, "Disaster: A Useful Category of Historical Analysis," *History Compass*, 6, no. 3 (2008): 934–946.

4. Beth Fowkes Tobin, *Picturing Imperial Power: Colonial Subjects in Eighteenth-Century British Painting* (Durham, NC: Duke University Pres, 1999), 10.

5. Bronwen Douglas, "Voyages, Encounters, and Agency in Oceania: Captain Cook and Indigenous People," *History Compass*, 6, no. 3 (2008): 712–737.

6. Kathleen Donegan, *Seasons of Misery: Catastrophe and Colonial Settlement in Early America* (Philadelphia: University of Pennsylvania Press, 2015); Peter Silver, *Our Savage Neighbors: How Indian War Transformed Early America* (New York: W. W. Norton, 2008); Linda Colley, *Captives: Britain, Empire, and the World, 1600–1850* (New York: Random House, 2002); Lauric Henneton and L. H. Roper, *Fear and the Shaping of Early American Societies* (New York: Brill, 2016); Alan Taylor, *The Civil War of 1812: American Citizens, British Subjects, Irish Rebels, and Indian Allies* (New York: Vintage, 2011); Holger Hoock, *Scars of Independence: America's Violent Birth* (New York: Random House, 2017).

7. Sunil S. Amrith, *Crossing the Bay of Bengal: The Furies of Nature and the Fortunes of Migrants* (Cambridge: Harvard University Press, 2013), 5.

8. Amy Greenberg, *Manifest Manhood and the Antebellum American Empire* (New York: Cambridge University Press, 2005).

Chapter 1 • Coffeehouse Chatter

1. Upon the death of Thomas Boylston in 1739, Nicholas and Thomas Jr. inherited much of their father's estate, leveraging their capital to make enormous profits during the French and Indian War (1754–1763) and in opening trade with Russia during the 1760s. Norman E. Saul, "The Beginnings of American-Russian Trade, 1763–1766," *William and Mary Quarterly*, 26, no. 4 (October 1969): 596–600.

2. This was the second of three portraits that Copley produced of Boylston. Boylston purchased the house in 1761, with profits from the French and Indian War. William Bentinck-Smith, "Nicholas Boylston and His Harvard Chair," *Proceedings of the Massachusetts Historical Society*, 3rd series, 93 (1981): 17–39, www.mfa.org /collections/object/nicholas-boylston-32060.

3. The banyan originated in India, corrupted from a Gujarati term, *Banya*, the preeminent caste of village or town trader. Another kind of headpiece was known as a *braul* or *turbant*, described in the *Encyclopedia Britannica* for 1768 as a blue-and-white striped Indian cloth. Phyllis Whitman Hunter, *Purchasing Identity in the Atlantic World: Massachusetts Merchants, 1670–1780* (Ithaca, NY: Cornell University Press, 2001), 208n4; Ifran Habib, "Merchant Communities in Precolonial India," in *The Rise of Merchant Empires: Long-Distance Trade in the Early Modern World, 1350–1750*, ed. James D. Tracy (New York: Cambridge University Press, 1990): 371–399; K. N. Chaudhuri, *The Trading World of Asia and the English East India Company, 1660–1760* (New York: Cambridge University Press, 1978), 137, 335.

4. Isabel Breskin, "'On the Periphery of a Greater World': John Singleton Copley's 'Turquerie' Portraits," *Winterthur Portfolio*, 36, no. 2/3 (Summer–Autumn 2001): 97–123; John Singleton Copley, *Thomas Boylston II (1721–1798)*, ca. 1767–1769, Harvard University Art Galleries, accessed May 30, 2017, www.harvardartmuseums.org/art/299946; Carol Troyen, "A Choice Gallery of Harvard Tories: John Singleton Copley's Portraits Memorialize a Vanquished Way of Life," *Harvard Magazine*, 99 (March 1997–April 1997): 55–60. As Harvard Art Museum notes, "In 1766, Boylston hired Copley to paint six portraits (of himself, his younger brother Thomas, their three sisters, and their mother) to grace the hall of the magnificent family mansion in School Street." The Boylston's partnership seems to have been separate from the longer-standing arrangement of Green and Boylston, which purveyed transatlantic goods throughout the 1760s. John Singleton Copley, *Portrait of Rebecca Boylston Gill*, ca. 1773, Rhode Island School of Design Museum, accessed July 10, 2017, http://risdmuseum.org/art_design/objects/667 _portrait_of_rebecca_boylston_gill.

5. With the exception of business documents, such as daybooks and ledgers, few documents from Nicholas and Thomas Boylston have survived, virtually none of them the kind of correspondence that would fill out this story. As the Massachusetts Historical Society observes of nephew Ward Nicholas Boylston, "The historical record is often fragmentary and misleading, and we may never know the truth behind Bentham's claims. Unfortunately, the Boylston collection contains very little personal correspondence between the family members directly involved." Susan Martin, "A Boylston Family Mystery," *The Beehive* (blog), May 30, 2012, www.masshist.org/blog/749; Saul, *"Beginnings,"* 596–597.

6. Jane Kamensky, *A Revolution in Color: The World of John Singleton Copley* (New York: W. W. Norton, 2016), 191; Susan Rather, "Carpenter, Tailor, Shoemaker,

Artist: Copley and Portrait Painting around 1770," *The Art Bulletin*, 79, no. 2 (June 1997): 269–290.

7. On the "calico craze" and other aspects of the British American fascination with Asian goods, see Hunter, *Purchasing Identity*, 77, 100–101; Jonathan Eacott, *Selling Empire: India in the Making of Britain and America, 1600–1830* (Chapel Hill: University of North Carolina Press, 2016).

8. Robert J. Allison, *The Crescent Obscured: The United States and the Muslim World, 1776–1815* (New York: Oxford University Press, 1995); Lawrence A. Peskin, *Captives and Countrymen: Barbary Slavery and the American Public, 1785–1816* (Baltimore, MD: Johns Hopkins University Press, 2009).

9. *Letters of the Right Honourable Lady M--y W-----y M------e: written, during her travels in Europe, Asia and Africa, to persons of distinction, men of letters, &c. in different parts of Europe. Which contain, among other curious relations, accounts of the policy and manners of the Turks; drawn from sources that have been inaccessible to other travellers,* 4th ed. (Providence, RI: Sarah Goddard, 1766).

10. "Turquerie," *The Metropolitan Museum of Art Bulletin*, new series, 26, no. 5 (January 1968): 225–239; Eve R. Meyer, "Turquerie and Eighteenth-Century Music," *Eighteenth-Century Studies*, 7, no. 4 (Summer 1974): 474–488; Perrin Stein, "Amédée Van Loo's *Costume turc*: The French Sultana," *The Art Bulletin*, 78, no. 3 (September 1996): 417–438; Isabel Breskin, "'On the Periphery of a Greater World': John Singleton Copley's 'Turquerie' Portraits," *Winterthur Portfolio*, 36, no. 2/3 (Summer–Autumn, 2001): 97–123; Suraiya Faroqhi, *The Ottoman Empire and the World Around It* (London: I. B. Tauris, 2004); Jennifer Tonkovich, "Claude Gillot's Costume Designs for the Paris Opéra: Some New Sources," *The Burlington Magazine*, 147, no. 1225, French Art and Artists (April 2005): 248–252; Florence Clarke D'hardemare, "The Follies of a King-Duke," *Garden History*, 37, no. 1 (Summer 2009): 56–67; Nebahat Avcioğlu and Finbarr Barry Flood, "Introduction: Globalizing Cultures: Art and Mobility in the Eighteenth Century," *Ars Orientalis*, 39 (2010): 15; Lale Babaoğlu Balkiş, "Defining the Turk: Construction of Meaning in Operatic Orientalism," *International Review of the Aesthetics and Sociology of Music*, 41, no. 2 (December 2010): 185–193.

11. Yet established minimalists such as William Hogarth decried the appropriation of Oriental styles in European art and even complained in 1753 that Chinese painting represented a "mean taste," unworthy of influence or imitation. Avcioğlu and Flood, "Introduction," 16–17.

12. *Massachusetts Gazette and Boston News-Letter*, September 1, 1763.

13. Charles M. Andrews, *The Colonial Period of American History* (New Haven: Yale University Press, 1964), I: 385; Mukhtar Ali Isani, "Cotton Mather and the Orient," *The New England Quarterly*, 43, no. 1 (March 1970), 47.

14. Adam Smith, *An Inquiry into the Nature and Causes of the Wealth of Nations*, book 4, chap. 2 (London, 1776).

15. Mukhtar Ali Isani, "Cotton Mather," 46–58; John Kuo Wei Tchen, *New York before Chinatown: Orientalism and the Shaping of American Culture, 1776–1882* (Baltimore, MD: Johns Hopkins University Press, 1999), xv; Caroline Frank, *Objectifying China, Imagining America: Chinese Commodities in Early America* (Chicago: University of Chicago Press, 2011), 61.

16.   There is an extensive literature on fear of the unknown. See, for example, Barbara Dawson, *In the Eye of the Beholder: What Six Nineteenth-century Women Tell Us about Indigenous Authority and Identity* (Canberra, A.C.T.: ANU Press, 2014); Robin Clifton, "The Popular Fear of Catholics during the English Revolution," *Past & Present*, no. 52 (August 1971): 23–55; Robert M. Gordon, "Fear," *The Philosophical Review*, 89, no. 4 (October 1980): 560–578; Karen Ordahl Kupperman, "Fear of Hot Climates in the Anglo-American Colonial Experience," *The William and Mary Quarterly*, 41, no. 2 (April 1984): 213–240; Edna Bradlow, "The 'Great Fear' at the Cape of Good Hope, 1851–52," *The International Journal of African Historical Studies*, 22, no. 3 (1989): 401–421; Joanna Bourke, "Fear and Anxiety: Writing about Emotion in Modern History," *History Workshop Journal*, no. 55 (Spring 2003): 111–133; Matthew Sparke, "Forum: Geopolitical Fears, Geoeconomic Hopes, and the Responsibilities of Geography," *Annals of the Association of American Geographers*, 97, no. 2 (June 2007): 338–349; Victoria Lawson, "Forum: Introduction: Geographies of Fear and Hope," *Annals of the Association of American Geographers*, 97, no. 2 (June 2007): 335–337; Brian Klinkenberg, "Forum: Geospatial Technologies and the Geographies of Hope and Fear," *Annals of the Association of American Geographers*, 97, no. 2 (June 2007): 350–360; Aviva Briefel, "Hands of Beauty, Hands of Horror: Fear and Egyptian Art at the Fin de Siècle," *Victorian Studies*, 50, no. 2, Papers and Responses from the Fifth Annual Conference of the North American Victorian Studies Association, Held Jointly with the Victorian Studies Association of Western Canada (Winter 2008): 263–271.

17.   Nicholas Boylston purchased the School Street structure from Jacob Wendell in 1764. Invited to dinner at the Boylston's opulent Mansion House on January 16, 1766, John Adams observed: "An elegant Dinner indeed! Went over the House to view the Furniture, which alone costs a thousand Pounds sterling. A Seat it is for a noble Man, a Prince. The Turkey Carpets, the painted Hangings, the Marble Tables, the rich Beds with crimson Damask Curtains and Counterpins, the beautiful Chimny Clock, the Spacious Garden, are the most magnificent of any Thing I have ever seen." John Adams, *Diary of John Adams*, I, January 15, 1766, *Adams Family Papers: An Electronic Archive*, www.masshist.org/digitaladams/archive/diary; Annie Haven Thwing, *The Crooked and Narrow Streets of Boston, 1630–1822* (Boston: Marshall Jones, 1920), 109; Hunter, *Purchasing Identity*, 148.

18.   This chapter follows an inspiring introduction to Gary Nash's *The Urban Crucible: The Northern Seaports and the Origins of the American Revolution*, titled "The Web of Seaport Life" (Cambridge: Harvard University Press, 1979). Frank, *Objectifying China*, 59.

19.   Daniela Bleichmar and Peter C. Mancall, "Collecting across Cultures: Material Exchanges in the Early Modern Atlantic World," *Journal of World History*, 24, no. 4 (December 2013): 883–887.

20.   Mechal Sobel, *Teach Me Dreams: The Search for Self in the Revolutionary Era* (Princeton, NJ: Princeton University Press, 2000); Alan Taylor, "Midnight Ramblers," in *Writing Early American History* (Philadelphia: University of Pennsylvanis Press, 2005), 90–96.

21.   Mark A. Peterson, "Life on the Margins: Boston's Anxieties of Influence in the Atlantic World," in *The Atlantic World: Essays on Slavery, Migration, and Imagination*, ed. Wim Klooster and Alfred Padula (Upper Saddle River, NJ: Pearson Prentice-Hall,

2005), 45–59. Peterson attributes the "anxieties" that characterized colonial Boston as a Puritan seaport on the peripheries of the Atlantic community as a result of internal contradictions: Puritan leaders sought to provide a "model of Christian charity" for the world, yet reject its commercial and material influences. Setting Boston and other colonial towns within a global context underscores how this sense of anxiety derived from fears of non-Western Others.

22. *New-York Mercury,* March 1, 1756; *New-England Weekly Journal,* October 10, 1727.

23. *New-England Weekly Journal,* October 10, 1727.

24. See William Price, "A new plan of ye great town of Boston in New England in America with the many additionall buildings & new streets, to the year, 1769," Library of Congress Geography and Map Division, accessed May 12, 2017, www.loc.gov/item /73691791.

25. Kamensky, *Revolution in Color,* 94.

26. Emanuel Timonius's essay (1714) described the procedure used in Constantinople; Jacob Pylarinus's piece (1716) explained its use in Smyrna. Zabdiel Boylston, *An Historical Account of the Small-pox Inoculated in New England* (London: S. Chandler, 1726).

27. Kathleen Donegan, *Seasons of Misery: Catastrophe and Colonial Settlement in Early America* (Philadelphia: University of Pennsylvania Press, 2013).

28. Peterson, "Life on the Margins," 56–59; John B. Blake, *Public Health in the Town of Boston, 1630–1822* (Cambridge: Harvard University Press, 1959); Ola Elizabeth Winslow, *A Destroying Angel: The Conquest of Smallpox in Colonial Boston* (Boston: Houghton Mifflin, 1974); Kenneth Silverman, *The Life and Times of Cotton Mather* (New York: Columbia University Press, 1985): 336–363.

29. *Providence Gazette,* June 30, 1770.

30. Abigail Adams wrote, "A number of females, some say a hundred, some say more, assembled with a cart and trucks, marched down to the warehouse, and demanded the keys, which he refused to deliver." Letter from Abigail Adams to John Adams, July 30–31, 1777 [electronic edition], Adams Family Papers: An Electronic Archive, Massachusetts Historical Society, www.masshist.org/digitaladams. Boylston joined merchant Andrew Belcher and others as targets of food riots. Barbara Clark Smith, "Food Rioters and the American Revolution," *Libcom.org* (blog), January 24, 2012, https://libcom.org/history/food-rioters-american-revolution-barbara-clark -smith. Mark A. Peterson, *The Price of Redemption: The Spiritual Economy of Puritan New England* (Stanford, CA: Stanford University Press, 1997).

31. *General Advertiser* (London), April 27, 1778, quoted in Kamensky, *Revolution in Color,* 287.

32. Peter Silver, *Our Savage Neighbors: How Indian War Transformed Early America* (New York: W. W. Norton and Company, 2008), xvii–xviii.

33. Donegan, *Seasons of Misery,* 36, 56, 155.

34. Jack P. Greene, *Evaluating Empire and Confronting Colonialism in Eighteenth-Century Britain* (New York: Cambridge University Press, 2013), xii–xiii. In documenting various discourses of empire, Greene identifies in particular a language of alterity that dehumanized the Other, but he includes Britons outside the metropolitan sphere and who were participants in the work of colonization and settlement.

35. Samuel Pepys, *The Diary of Samuel Pepys*, vol. 1, part 2, trans. Edward Griffin (repr., New York: Norwood Press, 1900).

36. Douglas, "Voyages," 712–737.

37. The South Pacific region was known as the Great South Sea and would be known as the South Seas as late as Robert Louis Stevenson's day. *Robert Louis Stevenson: In the South Seas*, biographical edit. (New York, 1966), 168, quoted in S. Whittemore Boggs, "American Contributions to Geographical Knowledge of the Central Pacific," *Geographical Review*, 28, no. 2 (April 1938): 177–192.

38. Edwin Wolf, 2nd, "The Dispersal of the Library of William Byrd of Westover," *Proceedings of the American Antiquarian Society*, 68 (1958): 19–106; Edwin Wolf, 2nd, "More Books from the Library of the Byrds of Westover," *Proceedings of the American Antiquarian Society*, 88 (April 1978): 51–82.

39. Bookshop ads did not always produce titles accurately. Robert Wood's *The Ruins of Athens, Balbec, Palmyra* described in one advertisement actually referred to two titles by the Georgian-era antiquarian Robert Wood: *The Ruins of Palmyra* (1753) and *The Ruins of Balbec* (1757).

40. On the development of these scholarly magazines that appealed to the genteel audiences of British America, see Dorothy Foster, "The Earliest Precursor of Our Present-Day Monthly Miscellanies," *PMLA*, 32, no. 1 (1917): 22–58; Norman S. Fiering, "The Transatlantic Republic of Letters: A Note on the Circulation of Learned Periodicals to Early Eighteenth-Century America," *The William and Mary Quarterly*, 33, no. 4 (October 1976): 642–660; and Edwin Wolf, "The Reconstruction of Benjamin Franklin's Library," *Papers of the Bibliographical Society of America*, 6 (1962): 3, 7.

41. Henry Moore's *Travels* remained popular beyond the colonial era, as observed in Ralph Earl's 1789 portrait of Connecticut merchant Elijah Boardman, depicted holding a copy of Moore's travelogue, along with copies of Shakespeare's plays, Milton's *Paradise Lost*, Johnson's *Dictionary*, and a 1786 issue of the *London Magazine, or Gentleman's Monthly Intelligencer* (Metropolitan Museum of Art, accession number 1979.395.

42. Rubiés and Ollé find evidence of interest in travelogues in both Europe and Ming China during this time. Joan-Pau Rubiés and Manel Ollé, "The Comparative History of a Genre: The Production and Circulation of Books on Travel and Ethnographies in Early Modern Europe and China," *Modern Asian Studies* (August 2015): 1–51, https://doi.org/10.1017/S0026749X15000086.

43. British American ideology situated this capacity for ordering the world within a Protestant imperative. Michael Walzer, *The Revolution of the Saints: A Study in the Origins of Radical Politics* (Cambridge: Harvard University Press, 1982); David D. Hall, *A Reforming People: Puritanism and the Transformation of Public Life in New England* (New York: Knopf, 2011); Owen Stanwood, "The Protestant Moment: Antipopery, the Revolution of 1688–1689, and the Making of an Anglo-American Empire," *Journal of British Studies*, 46, no. 3 (July 2007): 481–508; Brendan McConville, *The King's Three Faces: The Rise and Fall of Royal America, 1688–1776* (Chapel Hill: University of North Carolina Press, 2007), chap. 3.

44. Bronwen Douglas and Chris Ballard, "Race, Place, and Civilisation: Colonial Encounters and Governance in Greater Oceania," *The Journal of Pacific History*, 47, no. 3 (September 2012), 247.

45. Captain John Smith, *The True Travels, Adventures, and Observations of Captaine John Smith; in Europe, Asia, Affrica, and America* (London, 1630). For more on Smith's prejudices, see Eacott, *Selling Empire*, 14–15. Image of four stages of the supposed evolutionary stages of civilization—Barbarous, Savage, Half-Civilized, and Civilized & Enlightened—from Roswell Chamberlain Smith, *Geography of the Productive System*, Cady & Burgess, 1848, Osher Map Library, accessed April 23, 2017, www.oshermaps.org /map/7646.001. Douglas and Ballard, "Race, Place, and Civilisation," 251–252.

46. The various kinds of tea originate from a common plant, *Camellia sinensis*, "and the difference between kinds of tea reflects growing conditions and manufacturing process. For darker teas, the leaves are allowed to oxidize before being cured or roasted." Markman Ellis, "A Nation of Tea-Drinkers," *Spitalfields Life* (blog), June 11, 2016, https://spitalfieldslife.com/2016/06/11/a-nation-of-tea-drinkers; Steven C. Bullock, *Tea Sets and Tyranny: The Politics of Politeness in Early America* (Philadelphia: University of Pennsylvania Press, 2016).

47. Frank, *Objectifying China*, 79.

48. Frank identifies a umber of possibly coromandel screens in early eighteenth-century inventories. Frank, *Objectifying China*, 60–67, 82.

49. Frank notes that many merchant inventories include coromandel screens. Frank, *Objectifying China*, 82.

50. Frank, *Objectifying China*, 83–85.

51. James Walvin, *Fruits of Empire: Exotic Produce and British Trade, 1660–1800* (New York: Palgrave Macmillan, 1997), 26–27; Frank, *Objectifying China*, 99; Jonathan P. Eacott, "Making an Imperial Compromise: The Calico Acts, the Atlantic Colonies, and the Structure of the British Empire," *The William and Mary Quarterly*, 69, no. 4 (October 2012): 731–762.

52. A robust literature describes the Atlantic community. See, for example, Bernard Bailyn, *Atlantic History: Concept and Contours* (Cambridge: Harvard University Press, 2005); Thomas Benjamin, Timothy Hall, and David Rutherford, *The Atlantic World in the Age of Empire* (Boston: Houghton Mifflin, 2001); Rainer F. Buschmann, *Oceans in World History* (Boston: McGraw Hill, 2007); Wim Klooster and Alfred Padula, *The Atlantic World: Essays on Slavery, Migration, and Imagination* (Upper Saddle River, NJ: Pearson Prentice-Hall, 2005); and Sarah M. Pearsall, *Atlantic Families: Lives and Letters in the Later Eighteenth Century* (New York: Oxford University Press, 2008).

53. *Boston Post-Boy*, March 17, 1711.

54. Henry Popple, *A Map of the British Empire in America* (1733), David Rumsey Map Collection, accessed May 17, 2017, www.davidrumsey.com/maps1901.html.

55. Jonathan D. Spence, *The Chan's Great Continent: China in Western Minds* (New York: W. W. Norton, 1998), 17; Frank, *Objectifying China*, 83.

56. See Kamensky, *Revolution in Color*, 65.

57. Benjamin Breen, "Drugs and Early Modernity," *History Compass*, 15, no. 4 (April 2017): https://onlinelibrary.wiley.com/doi/abs/10.1111/hic3.12376.

58. See also Walvin, *Fruits of Empire*; Ken Albala, *Eating Right in the Renaissance* (Oakland: University of California Press, 2002); Mary Lindemann, *Medicine and Society in Early Modern Europe* (New York: Cambridge University Press, 2010); and David Gentilcore, *Food and Health in Early Modern Europe: Diet, Medicine, and Society, 1450–1800* (London: Bloomsbury Academic, 2015).

59. Benjamin Breen, "Drugs and Early Modernity," 1–2.

60. David R. Shields, *Civil Tongues and Polite Letters in British America* (Chapel Hill: University of North Carolina Press, 1997), 56; Bentinck-Smith, "Nicholas Boylston," 22–23. Comparable numbers reveal the fantasies underlying Western mythologies of "cities of gold" and the subsequent racism: about the time of Copley's portraits, Boston had a population of fifteen thousand; New York held thirteen thousand. In comparison, historians believe that Beijing and Guangzhou held nearly a million each; Constantinople held half a million; London and Paris held nearly a million.

61. In colonies such as Massachusetts Bay, it was necessary to procure a license to sell tea, coffee, and china wares from a court or justice of the peace. Francis Bernard, "A List of Instruments," in *The Papers of Francis Bernard: Governor of Colonial Massachusetts, 1760–1769*, vol. 2, ed. Colin Nicholson (Boston: Colonial Society of Massachusetts, 2012): 169–170; Emİnegül Karababa and Gülİz Ger, "Early Modern Ottoman Coffeehouse Culture and the Formation of the Consumer Subject," *Journal of Consumer Research*, 37, no. 5 (February 2011): 737–760.

62. London counted 550 coffeehouses by 1740. Walvin, *Fruits of Empire*, 32.

63. Nancy Um, *Shipped but Not Sold: Material Culture and the Social Protocols of Trade during Yemen's Age of Coffee* (Honolulu: University of Hawai'i Press, 2017), 2.

64. Shields, *Civil Tongues*, chap. 3; Avcioğlu and Flood make an important point about another trend, noting, "Modernity is often seen both as an idiosyncratically European phenomenon and as sui generis, many of its characteristic features are neither unique to Europe, nor inseparable from more extensive (and not always peaceful) histories of transregional contact and circulation." Avcioğlu and Flood, "Introduction," 31.

65. Walvin, *Fruits of Empire*, 32.

66. Walvin, 14–23; Shields, *Civil Tongues*, 56–60. The global nature of luxuries, becoming commodities over the eighteenth century, is explored in Christopher M. Parsons, "The Natural History of Colonial Science: Joseph-François Lafitau's Discovery of Ginseng and Its Afterlives," *The William and Mary Quarterly*, 73, no. 1 (January 2016): 37–72.

67. Kamensky, *Revolution in Color*, 187.

68. Quoted in Walvin, *Fruits of Empire*, 32. Coffee's career exemplifies the course of global trade, originating in Ethiopia, transplanted to Arabia, and thriving in Yemen.

69. Walvin, 14.

70. Walvin, 10–11, 12–16, 32–40; Erik Gilbert and Jonathan Reynolds, *Trading Tastes: Commodity and Cultural Exchange to 1750* (Upper Saddle River, NJ: Pearson Prentice-Hall, 2006). Gentile Bellini's portrait of Mehmett II is held by the National Gallery, London.

71. Frank, *Objectifying China*, 119.

72. Frank, 102–103.

73. Kamensky, *Revolution in Color*, 196.

74. Hunter, *Purchasing Identity*, 3.

75. *Boston Gazette*, August 12, 1728.

76. *Boston News-Letter*, October 10, 1727.

77. Avcioğlu and Flood, "Introduction," 30. See also Said Amir Arjomand, "Coffeehouses, Guilds, and Oriental Despotism: Government and Civil Society in Late 17th to

Early 18th Century Istanbul and Isfahan, and as seen from Paris and London," *European Journal of Sociology*, 45, no. 1 (2004): 23–42; Ralph S. Hattox, *Coffee and Coffeehouses: The Origins of a Social Beverage in the Medieval Near East* (Seattle: University of Washington Press, 1985); and Nancy Um, *The Merchant Houses of Mocha: Trade and Architecture in an Indian Ocean Port* (Seattle: University of Washington Press, 2009).

78. Andrew Pettigrew, *The Invention of News: How the World Came to Know about Itself* (New Haven, CT: Yale University Press, 2014), 1–2, 13; Karen A. Weyler, *Empowering Words: Outsiders and Authorship in Early America* (Athens: University of Georgia Press, 2013), 2, 9.

79. Kathleen Wilson, "The Good, the Bad, and the Impotent: Imperialism and the Politics of Identity in Georgian England," in *The Consumption of Culture 1600–1800: Image, Object, Text,* ed. Ann Bermingham and John Brewer (London: Routledge, 1997): 237–262; Benedict Anderson, *Imagined Communities: Reflections on the Origins and Spread of Nationalism.* (London: Verso, 1991).

80. Nat Cutter, "Turks, Moors, Deys and Kingdoms: North African Diversity in English Periodical News before 1700," *Melbourne Historical Journal*, 46, no. 1 (December 2018): 61–84.

81. Clark and Wetherell, for instance, categorize the content of the *Pennsylvania Gazette* by "news from the remotest location and working toward reports from the closer European points; news from England outside the metropolis; news from London and Westminster; and advertisements." Charles E. Clark and Charles Wetherell, "The Measure of Maturity: The *Pennsylvania Gazette*, 1728–1765," *The William and Mary Quarterly*, 46, no. 2 (April 1989): 282.

82. Tamara Plakins Thornton, *Nathaniel Bowditch and the Power of Numbers: How a Nineteenth-Century Man of Business, Science, and the Sea Changed American Life* (Chapel Hill: University of North Carolina Press, 2016), 34.

83. Silver, *Our Savage Neighbors*, xvii–xviii.

84. *Boston Evening-Post*, August 20, 1764.

85. *New-York Mercury*, February 6, 1764.

86. *New-York Mercury*, March 1, 1756; Peterson, "Life on the Margins," 54–55.

87. Gordon M. Sayre, "Communion in Captivity: Torture, Maytyrdom, and Gender in New France and New England," in *Finding Colonial America: Essays Honoring J. A. Leo Lemay,* ed. Carla Mulford and David S. Shields (Newark: University of Delaware Press, 2001), 50.

88. Marcus Rediker, "The Pirate and the Gallows: An Atlantic Theater of Terror and Resistance," in *Seascapes: Maritime Histories, Littoral Cultures, and Transoceanic Exchanges,* Jerry H. Bentley, Renate Bridenthal, and Kären Wigen (Honolulu: University of Hawai'i Press, 2007): 239–250; Gregory N. Flemming, *At the Point of a Cutlass: The Pirate Capture, Bold Escape, and Lonely Exile of Philip Ashton* (Hanover, NH: ForeEdge, 2015).

89. Frank, *Objectifying China*, 4; Marcus Rediker, *Villains of All Nations, Atlantic Pirates in the Golden Age* (Boston: Beacon Press, 2004); Sonja Schillings, *Enemies of All Humankind: Fictions of Legitimate Violence* (Hanover, NH: Dartmouth College Press, 2017); Robert C. Ritchie, *Captain Kidd and the War against the Pirates* (Cambridge, MA: Harvard University Press, 1986); Benjamin Schmidt, "The Purpose of Pirates, or Assimilating New Worlds in the Renaissance," in *The Atlantic World: Essays on Slavery,*

Migration, and Imagination, ed. Wim Klooster and Alfred Padula (Upper Saddle River, NJ: Pearson Prentice-Hall, 2005), 161–176.

90. Mark G. Hanna, *Pirate Nests and the Rise of the British Empire, 1570–1740* (Chapel Hill: University of North Carolina Press, 2015), 1.

91. Hanna, *Pirate Nests*, 58.

92. Hunter, *Purchasing Identity*, 82.

93. Rubiés and Ollé, "Comparative History," 1–51.

94. Shields, *Civil Tongues*, 57.

95. *Pennsylvania Gazette*, August 19, 1742.

96. George Abbot, *A Briefe Description of the Whole World Wherein is particularly described all the monarchies, empires, and kingdomes of the same, with their academies. Newly augmented and enlarged; with their severall titles and scituations thereunto adjoyning* ("At London: Printed [by Thomas Snodham] for John Browne, and are to be sold at his shoppe in Saint Dunstans churchyard in Fleet-streete, 1617.")

97. Comprehensive studies of the European reception of China can be found in Donald F. Lach, *Asia in the Making of Europe*, vols. 1–4 (Chicago: University of Chicago Press, 1965); Virgile Pinot, *La Chine et la formation de l'Esprit Philosophique en France, 1640–1740* (Paris: Librairie Orientaliste, 1932); and Porter, *Ideographia: The Chinese Cipher in Early Modern Europe* (Stanford: Stanford University Press, 2001),

98. *American Weekly Mercury*, October 19, 1727.

99. *Rivington's New-York Gazetteer*, October 12, 1775. Rivington had emigrated from England and, by 1762, opened the London Book Store in Boston, where he advertised in the *Boston Post-Boy* (December 3, 1762), the *Boston News-Letter* (December 9, 1763), and the *New-Hampshire Gazette* (February 19, 1762) before moving on to New York.

100. Clark and Wetherall assert, "The world the *Gazette* presented to its readers in the middle part of the eighteenth century was thus predominantly a European rather than an American one (293)," privileging matters of war and diplomacy; however, news from non-Western parts of the world were regular features of colonial newspapers, at times bringing four or five reports per issue. Clark and Wetherell, "Measure of Maturity," 279–303.

101. Michael A. Verney, "An Eye for Prices, an Eye for Souls: Americans in the Indian Subcontinent, 1784–1838," *Journal of the Early Republic*, 33, no. 3 (Fall 2013): 401–402.

102. *Boston News-Letter*, June 9–13, 1720.

103. *New-England Weekly Journal*, March 2, 1730.

104. Kamensky, *Revolution in Color*, 50.

105. See Kamensky, 51n29.

106. G. A. Starr, "Defoe and China," *Eighteenth-Century Studies*, 43, no. 4 (2010), 438.

107. Frank, *Objectifying China*, 103–104.

108. Caroline Frank estimates some 1,325 unique advertisements for porcelain in the northern colonies from 1766 through 1768. Frank, 119, 148.

109. Frank, 107.

110. Linda Colley, *Captives: Britain, Empire, and the World, 1600–1850* (New York: Anchor, 2002), 143; Patrick M. Malone, *The Skulking Way of War: Technology and Tactics among the Indians of New England* (Lanham, MD: Madison, 1991).

111. Claudio Saunt, *West of the Revolution: An Uncommon History of 1776* (New York: W. W. Norton, 2014), passim; *Newport Mercury*, September 5, 1763.

112. Colley, *Captives,* 147.

113. Verney, "Eye for Prices," 402.

114. *Boston Gazette,* October 20, 1741

115. *New-York Evening Post,* December 17, 1744.

116. *New-York Evening Post,* December 17, 1744.

117. *New-York Mercury,* February 6, 1764.

118. *Boston Weekly News-Letter,* December 31, 1730.

119. Fariba Zarinebaf, *Crime and Punishment in Istanbul: 1700–1800* (Berkeley: University of California Press, 2010).

120. *Pennsylvania Gazette,* January 19, 1774.

121. The Atlas mountain range in the Maghreb desert was inhabited by roaming Berber peoples. *New-York Mercury,* February 6, 1764.

122. *New-York Gazette,* June 18, 1770.

123. *Boston Chronicle,* September 14, 1769.

124. In Philadelphia, cockfighting and bullbaiting were among the diversions proscribed by the government. Shields, *Civil Tongues,* 63.

125. In the autumn of 1741, newspapers reported from Galway, "The Fever rages so in this Town, that Physicians say 'tis more like a Plague." *Boston Gazette,* October 20, 1741; Nükhet Varlik, "From 'Bête Noire' to 'le Mal de Constantinople': Plagues, Medicine, and the Early Modern Ottoman State," *Journal of World History,* 24, no. 4 (December 2013): 741–770; Katherine Arner, "Making Global Commerce into International Health Diplomacy: Consuls and Disease Control in the Age of Revolutions," *Journal of World History,* 24, no. 4 (December 2013): 771–796.

126. *American Weekly Mercury,* January 30, 1733.

127. Pennsylvania Gazette, January 19, 1774.

128. Cervantes's five years in captivity, 1575–1680, produced materials for works such as *Don Quixote, El trato de Argel* (*Life in Algiers*), and *Los baños de Argel.* Miguel de Cervantes, *"The Bagnios of Algiers" and "The Great Sultana": Two Plays of Captivity,* trans. Barbara Fuchs and Aaron J. Ilika (Philadelphia: University of Pennsylvania Press, 2012), xiii–xiv.

129. Quoted in Ralph D. Paine, *The Ships and Sailors of Old Salem: The Record of a Brilliant Era of Achievement* (New York: Outing, 1908), 22; David Watters, ed., "A Letter from Samuel Sewall to his Father," *New England Quarterly,* 58, no. 4 (December 1985): 598–601. Robert Allison observes earlier encounters, citing Morocco's capture of an American vessel in 1625; the successful resistance by a vessel from Cambridge, Massachusetts, against Algerian corsairs in the 1640s; and the capture of a New York vessel in 1673. Allison, *Crescent Obscured,* xiv–xv.

130. *Boston Weekly News-Letter,* February 17, 1737.

131. *Boston Gazette,* August 12, 1728.

132. *Boston Weekly News-Letter,* December 31, 1730.

133. *New-York Mercury,* March 1, 1756.

134. *New-London Gazette,* October 25, 1765.

135. "Cape St. Mary, on VV. coast of Africa. Lon. 16. 35. VV. Lat. 13. 20. N.," [Joseph Emerson] Worcester, *A Geographical Dictionary, or, Universal Gazetteer, Ancient and Modern,* 2nd ed. (Boston: Cummings & Hilliard, 1823), 321.

136. *New-London Gazette*, January 27, 1764; *Boston Post-Boy*, January 23, 1764; *New-York Mercury*, February 6, 1764.

137. Stefan Gaarsmand Jacobsen, "Chinese Influences or Images? Fluctuating Histories of How Enlightenment Europe Read China," *Journal of World History*, 24, no. 3 (September 2013): 623–660.; Jennifer L. Gaynor, "Ages of Sail, Ocean Basins, and Southeast Asia," *Journal of World History*, 24, no. 2 (June 2013): 309–333; Adam Clulow, "Like Lambs in Japan and Devils outside Their Land: Diplomacy, Violence, and Japanese Merchants in Southeast Asia," *Journal of World History*, 24, no. 2 (June 2013): 335–358.

138. *American Weekly Mercury*, January 30, 1733.

139. *Weekly Rehearsal* [Boston], February 28, 1732.

140. *Boston Gazette*, October 20, 1741.

141. *New-York Gazette*, April 20, 1767; *Providence Gazette*, May 2, 1767.

142. On the Atlantic slave trade, see Toby Green, *The Rise of the Trans-Atlantic Slave Trade in Western Africa, 1300–1589* (Cambridge: Cambridge University Press, 2012); Patrick Manning, *The African Diaspora: A History through Culture* (New York: Columbia University Press, 2009).

143. Jonathan Swift, *On Poetry* (London, 1733), quoted in John O. Hunwick, "A Region of the Mind: Medieval Arab Views of African Geography and Ethnography and their Legacy," *Sudanic Africa*, 16 (2005): 104.

144. *Virginia Gazette*, June 27, 1766.

145. *Newport Mercury*, September 5, 1763.

146. *New-York Evening Post*, December 17, 1744.

147. *Pennsylvania Gazette*, March 2, 1758.

148. The story was a parable of the uncertainties of global trade: Although the survivors recaptured the vessel and brought her into Puerto Rico, Spanish officials there confiscated both ship and cargo. *Boston Evening-Post*, August 20, 1764.

149. *New-York Gazette*, June 18, 1770; *Providence Gazette*, June 30, 1770;

150. Printed also in *Newport Mercury*, July 9, 1770; *New-York Gazette*, July 2, 1770; *Providence Gazette*, June 30, 1770.

151. *Pennsylvania Chronicle*, December 19, 1768.

152. Pemberton's collection included the two volumes of Harris's *Voyages* (16), Rolfe's *History* (83), Raleigh's *History* (82), and Basnage's *History of the Jews* (54), as well.

153. *Massachusetts Spy*, December 12–19, 1771.

154. Franklin advertised books, which introduced exotic fables, for sale in the *Pennsylvania Gazette*, August 19, 1742.

155. "Books just imported from London, and to be sold by William Bradford, at his shop, adjoining the London Coffee-House in Market-Street." Early American Imprints, series 1, no. 7368.

156. In the *Pennsylvania Gazette* for June 9, 1743, Franklin advertised Bibles, "lettered for Gentlemen's Libraries," sermons, prayer books "neatly printed and bound in Morocco and Turkey [cloth]," philosophies, theological pieces, chemistry, mathematics, and medical texts, navigation and surveying guides, as well as histories and classical studies; also suitable for gentlemen's libraries were the *Turkish Spy, Persian Tales*, and *Chinese Tales*.

157. Many printers also sold books. In the town of Williamsburg in the 1760s, when this catalog was published, two printers—Joseph Royle and then Alexander Purdie—held the commission to serve as postmaster. Rebecca Onion, "The Books Virginia Colonists Were Buying in the Decade Before the Revolution," *Slate* (website), April 24, 2015, www.slate.com/blogs/the_vault/2015/04/24.

158. Onion, "Books Virginia Colonists Were Buying."

159. *New Hampshire Gazette*, May 8, 1767.

160. Norman S. Fiering, "The Transatlantic Republic of Letters: A Note on the Circulation of Learned Periodicals to Early Eighteenth-Century America," *The William and Mary Quarterly*, 33, no. 4 (October 1976): 642–660.

161. Alexander Hamilton, *The History of the Ancient and Honorable Tuesday Club*, ed. Robert Micklus (Chapel Hill: University of North Carolina Press, 1990), 1:xvii.

162. *Newport Mercury*, September 5, 1763.

163. *New-England Weekly Journal*, October 10, 1727.

164. *Boston Gazette*, January 3, 1732.

165. From Kamensky, *Revolution in Color*, 258.

166. *Boston Weekly News-Letter*, June 14, 1744.

167. *Boston Evening-Post*, August 13, 1744.

168. *London Magazine, or Gentleman's Monthly Intelligencer*, 29 (February 1760), 29.

169. *London Magazine, or Gentleman's Monthly Intelligencer*, 29 (February 1760), 65.

170. For eighteenth-century discussions and debates about the empire, see Abigail L. Swingen, *Competing Visions of Empire: Labor, Slavery, and the Origins of the British Atlantic Empire* (New Haven, CT: Yale University Press, 2015).

171. Greene, *Evaluating Empire*, chap. 4.

172. *New-York Weekly Journal*, January 28, 1733.

173. *New-York Weekly Journal*, January 28, 1733, and December 31, 1733.

174. Hamilton, *History*, 1:8, 29; 8:167.

175. *New-York Weekly Journal*, January 19, 1735.

176. Greene, *Evaluating Empire*, 34.

177. *New-York Weekly Journal*, January 19, 1735.

178. *New-York Weekly Journal*, August 21, 1738.

179. *Boston Post-Boy*, May 14, 753.

180. *Boston Gazette*, October 2, 1721.

181. *Boston Gazette*, November 7, 1768.

182. Selections of *The London Merchant* were published in the *New-England Weekly Journal* (February 14, 1732), which also reported on the celebrities who attended the production in London (*New-England Weekly Journal*, March 6, 1732). The play was performed in the theater at John Street in New York during the winter of 1768 (*New-York Gazette*, February 4, 1768) and an advertisement was printed in Philadelphia (*Dunlap's Pennsylvania Packet*, December 5, 1774). Even in Massachusetts, where theater was prohibited until the 1790s, patriot printer Isaiah Thomas published and sold *The London Merchant* through his newspaper, the *Massachusetts Spy* (March 4, 1783).

183. *American Weekly Mercury*, January 14, 1723. The fear and hatred of Islam and its Prophet were ingrained in the colonial consciousness, forming a core rationale in Britons' ideology of overseas expansion, featured in such popular and influential texts as Samuel

Purchas, *Hakluutus Posthumus; or, Purchas, His Pilgrimes* (London, 1625) and Captain John Smith's *The True Travels, Adventures, and Observations of Captaine John Smith; in Europe, Asia, Affrica, and America* [. . .] (London, 1630). Eacott, *Selling Empire*, 14–16.

184. *Boston Gazette,* October 20, 1741.

185. *New-York Weekly Journal,* January 19, 1735.

186. *Boston Post-Boy,* September 29, 1760.

187. Mather quoted the mystic Algazal in the *Egyptian History* by the historian Murtadi (Abû-Hâmid ibn Muhammed, al-Ghazzâlî) and one "Arabian commentary upon the Alchoran," among others remarks. See Isani, "Cotton Mather," 48; Alison Games, *The Web of Empire: English Cosmopolitans in an Age of Expansion, 1560–1660* (New York: Oxford University Press, 2008), 39–46.

188. Here, I mean a supposed connection between Old Testament Hebrews and the Wampanoag people that was asserted by Puritan divines such as John Eliot, the Mathers, and others, rather than the documented geological land bridge that surfaced intermittently during successive ice ages. Dane Morrison, *A Praying People: Massachusett Acculturation and the Failure of the Puritan Mission, 1600–1690* (New York: Peter Lang, 1995); Cotton Mather, *Magnalia Christi Americana* (Hartford, 1853), 1:44–45, 249; 2:594; Cotton Mather, *India Christiana* (Boston, 1721).

189. Cited in Mel Yazawa, ed., *The Diary and Life of Samuel Sewell* (Boston: Bedford, 1998), 31. See also Watters, "Letter from Samuel Sewall," 598–601.

190. Thomas S. Kidd, "'Let Hell and Rome Do Their Worst': World News, Anti-Catholicism, and International Protestantism in Early-Eighteenth-Century Boston," *New England Quarterly,* 2 (June 2003), 270.

191. Quoted in David D. Hall, *A Reforming People: Puritanism and the Transformation of Public Life in New England* (New York: Knopf Doubleday, 2011), 83.

192. Cotton Mather, *Memorable Providences, Relating to Witchcrafts and Possessions. A Faithful Account of many Wonderful and Surprising Things, that have befallen several Bewitched and Possessed Persons in New-England. Particularly, A Narrative of the marvelous Trouble and Relief Experienced by a pious Family in Boston, very lately and sadly molested with Evil Spirits.* (Boston: Joseph Brunning, 1689); David Armitage, *The Ideological Origins of the British Empire* (Cambridge: Cambridge University Press, 2000); Thomas Cogswell, *The Blessed Revolution: English Politics and the Coming of War, 1621–1624* (Cambridge: Cambridge University Press, 1989); Thomas Cogswell, "England and the Spanish Match," in *Conflict in Early Stuart England: Studies in Religion and Politics, 1603–1642,* ed. Richard Cust and Ann Hughes (London: Routledge, 1989); Eacott, *Selling Empire,* 17, 19.

193. *A sermon wherein is shewed that it is the duty and should be the care of believers on Christ, to live in the constant exercise of grace,* by Nathanael Mather Pastor of a church at Dublin in Ireland (1684), 51.

194. Mather, *Memorable,* 4.

195. John Davenport, "Another essay for investigation of the truth, in answer to two questions, concerning I. The subject of baptism. II. The consociation of churches" (Cambridge, 1663), 8.

196. Richard Mather, *A defence of the answer and arguments of the Synod met at Boston in the year 1662. Concerning the subject of baptism, and consociation of churches. Against the reply made thereto, by the Reverend Mr. John Davenport, Pastor of the church*

at New-Haven, in his treatise entituled, Another essay for investigation of the truth, &c. Together with an answer to the apologetical preface set before that essay. By some of the elders who were members of the synod above-mentioned (Cambridge, 1664), 12.

197. Thomas Shepard, *Wine for Gospel Wantons* (Cambridge, 1668), 9.

198. Phillip H. Round, *By Nature and Custom Cursed: Transatlantic Discourse and New England Cultural Production, 1620–1660* (Hanover, NH: University Press of New England, 1999); Kristina Bross, *Dry Bones and Indian Sermons: Praying Indians in Colonial America* (Ithaca, NY: Cornell University Press, 2004).

199. Eugenia Zuroski, *A Taste for China: English Subjectivity and the Prehistory of Orientalism* (New York: Oxford University Press, 2013); Eacott, *Selling Empire*; Bullock, *Tea Sets*.

200. Hamilton, *Tuesday Club*, 8:167.

201. Richard Bland, "An Inquiry into the Rights of the British Colonies," in *American Political Writing during the Founding Era, 1760–1805*, ed. Charles S. Hyneman and Donald S. Lutz (Indianapolis, IN: Liberty Fund, 1983), 1:83; *Boston Gazette*, October 19, 1772; *Essex Gazette*, October 20, 1772.

202. Alexander Hamilton, "A full vindication of the measures of the Congress" (New York: James Rivington, 1774; Massachusetts Historical Society Collections).

203. Quoted in T. H. Breen, *The Marketplace of Revolution: How Consumer Politics Shaped American Independence* (New York: Oxford University Press, 2014), 2–3.

204. This reference to an imagined Jewish oppression was a curious digression from the conventional trope of Asian despotism.

205. *Connecticut Courant*, July 3, 1776.

206. Samuel West, "On the Right to Rebel Against Governors," and William Whiting, "An Address to the Inhabitants of Berkshire County, Mass.," in Hyneman and Lutz, *American Political Writing*, 465, 438.

207. Jeremiah Atwater, "A Sermon"; John Leland, "The Connecticut Dissenters' Strong Box: No. 1"; Noah Webster, "An Oration on the Anniversary of the Declaration of Independence"; and Fischer Ames, "The Dangers of American Liberty," in Hyneman and Lutz, *American Political Writing*, 2:1173, 1190, 1199, 1227, 1341.

208. *Diary and Autobiography of John Adams*, 2 (92), quoted in Kamensky, *Revolution in Color*, 216.

209. Quoted in Greene, *Evaluating Empire*, 137.

210. Sheldon S. Cohen, "The Turkish Tyranny," *The William and Mary Quarterly*, 47 (December 1974): 567.

211. Lorgia García-Peña, *The Borders of Dominicanidad: Race, Nation, and Archives of Contradiction* (Durham, NC: Duke University Press, 2016), L.

212. Douglas, "Voyages," 712.

213. See Echang, "Brief Account of the English Character" in Research: *Fan quai* folder, Massachusetts Historical Society.

Chapter 2 • Unholy Lands

1. John Ledyard to Thomas Jefferson, August 15, 1788, *Founders Online* (website), National Archives, July 12, 2016, https://founders.archives.gov/documents/Jefferson /01-13-02-0395 [original source: *The Papers of Thomas Jefferson*, vol. 27, *1 September–31 December 1793*, ed. John Catanzariti (Princeton, NJ: Princeton University Press, 1997),

764–765]; John Ledyard, *The Last Voyage of Captain Cook: The Collected Writings of John Ledyard*, ed. James Zug (Washington, DC: National Geographic, 2005), 245–254; Edward C. Gray, *The Making of John Ledyard: Empire and Ambition in the Life of an Early American Traveler* (New Haven, CT: Yale University Press 2007), 181; James R. Durand, *The Life and Adventures of James R. Durand . . . 1820* (Sandwich, MA: Chapman Billies, 1995), 29.

2. "To Thomas Jefferson from John Ledyard, 10 September 1788," *Founders Online* (website), National Archives, http://founders.archives.gov/documents/Jefferson/01-13 -02-0469 [original source: *The Papers of Thomas Jefferson*, vol. 13, *March–7 October 1788*, ed. Julian P. Boyd (Princeton, NJ: Princeton University Press, 1956), 594–597]. Claude-Étienne Savary, *Lettres sur l'Égypte, où l'on offre le parallèle des mœurs anciennes & modernes de ses habitans, où l'on décrit l'état, le commerce, l'agriculture, le gouvernement du pays*, 3 vols. (Paris, 1785–1786) was acquired by T.J. from Froullé on June 27, 1787 (Sowerby, no. 3949). Savary also died in 1788 and was just Ledyard's age; he was in Egypt from 1776 to 1779.

3. John Ledyard to Thomas Jefferson, August 15, 1788, Founders Online (website), National Archives, https://founders.archives.gov/documents/Jefferson/01-14-02-0056 [original source: *The Papers of Thomas Jefferson*, vol. 13, *March–7 October 1788*, ed. Julian P. Boyd (Princeton, NJ: Princeton University Press, 1956), 594–597].

4. John Ledyard to Thomas Jefferson, Cairo, November 15, 1788. National Archives, https://founders.archives.gov/documents/Jefferson/01-14-02-0056. Ledyard's views may have been influential as well as representative, as seen newspapers such as Matthew Carey's *United States' Recorder* for April 1, 1798, which promoted a forthcoming volume of Ledyard's *Interesting Travels* in a half-column advertisement.

5. As early as the sixteenth century, Europeans such as Martin Luther inaccurately identified all Muslims as "Turks." Sean Foley, "Muslims and Social Change in the Atlantic Basin," *Journal of World History*, 20, no. 3 (September 2009), 382.

6. There is a copious history of English encounters with the Ottoman Empire, especially the "Barbary," or North African Coast, produced by scholars such as Nabil Matar, *Islam in Britain* (Cambridge: Cambridge University Press, 1998) and *Turks, Moors, and Englishmen in the Age of Discovery* (New York: Columbia University Press, 1999); Linda Colley, *Captives: Britain, Empire, and the World, 1600–1850* (London: Jonathan Cape, 2002); Robert C. Davis, *Christian Slaves, Muslim Masters* (Houndmills, UK: Palgrave Macmillan, 2003); Richmond Barbour, *Before Orientalism* (Cambridge: Cambridge University Press, 2003); Daniel Vitkus, *Turning Turk* (Houndmills, UK: Palgrave Macmillan, 2003); Gerald Maclean, *The Rise of Oriental Travel* (Houndmills, UK: Palgrave Macmillan, 2004); Ros Ballaster, *Fables of the East* (Oxford: Oxford University Press, 2005); Gerald Maclean, *Looking East* (Houndmills, UK: Palgrave Macmillan, 2007); Emily C. Bartels, *Speaking of the Moor* (Philadelphia: University of Pennsylvania Press, 2008); Gerald MacLean and Nabil Matar, *Britain and the Islamic World* (Oxford: Oxford University Press, 2011); John Tolan, Henry Laurens, and Gilles Veinstein, *Europe and the Islamic World: A History* (Princeton, NJ: Princeton University Press, 2013); and Nat Cutter, "Turks, Moors, Deys, and Kingdoms: North African Diversity in English News before 1700," *Melbourne Historical Journal*, 46 (2018): 61–84.

7. For similar examinations of the relationship between print culture and the formation of national identity in other states, see Partha Chatterjee, *The Nation and Its*

Fragments: Colonial and Postcolonial Histories (Princeton, NJ: Princeton University Press, 1993); Linda Colley, *Britons: Forging the Nation 1707–1837* (New Haven, CT: Yale University Press, 1992); and Colley, *Captives*.

8. Albert Hourani, *A History of the Arab Peoples* (Cambridge, MA: Belknap Press of Harvard University Press, 1991), 1; Foley, "Muslims and Social Change," 377–398; Durand, *Life*, 5, 23, 29, 31, 32, 37; William F. Lynch, *Narrative of the Expedition to the River Jordan and the Dead Sea* (London, 1860), 37; Timothy Roberts, "Commercial Philanthropy: American Missionaries and the American Opium Trade in Izmir during the First Part of the Nineteenth Century," *Journal of Mediterranean Studies* (January 2010), 372–373.

9. A. Owen Aldridge, "Natural Religion and Deism in America before Ethan Allen and Thomas Paine," *William and Mary Quarterly*, 54, no. 4, Religion in Early America (October 1997): 835–848.

10. Christine Leigh Heyrman, *American Apostles: When Evangelicals Entered the World of Islam* (New York: Hill and Wang, 2015), 8; Alvan Bond, *Memoir of the Rev. Pliny Fisk, A.M.: Late Missionary to Palestine* (Boston, 1828), 4; Emily Conroy-Krutz, *Christian Imperialism: Converting the World in the Early American Republic* (Ithaca, NY: Cornell University Press, 2015), 38–40.

11. Bond, *Memoir*, iii; Conroy-Kurtz, *Christian Imperialism*, 39; Heyrman, *American Apostles*, 130.

12. Conroy-Krutz, *Christian Imperialism*, xv–xvi. 5, 75–76; Michael A. Verney, "An Eye for Prices, an Eye for Souls: Americans in the Indian Subcontinent, 1784–1838," *Journal of the Early Republic*, 33, no. 3 (Fall 2013), 421–422.

13. John Lloyd Stephens, *Incidents of Travel in Egypt, Arabia, Petraea, and the Holy Land*, 2nd ed. (New York, 1837), iv.

14. Edward Robinson, *Biblical Researches in Palestine and the Adjacent Regions: A Journal of Travels in the Year 1838* (London: 1840), xi, 31.

15. Robinson, *Biblical Researches*, vi.

16. Lynch, *Narrative*, 29; Bruce A. Harvey, *American Geographics: U.S. National Narratives and the Representation of the Non-European World, 1830–1865* (Stanford, CA: Stanford University Press, 2001), 29; Robert Irwin, *For Lust of Knowing: The Orientalists and Their Enemies* (London: Penguin, 2006); Milette Shamir, "'Interesting' Expedition to the Dead Sea," *Journal of the Early Republic*, 38, no. 3 (Fall 2018): 475–499.

17. *A Catalogue of the Books Belonging to the Library Company of Philadelphia*, 2 vols. (Philadelphia: C. Sherman, 1835); Lawrence A. Peskin, *Captives and Countrymen: Barbary Slavery and the American Public, 1785–1816* (Baltimore, MD: Johns Hopkins University Press, 2009); Cutter, "Turks, Moors, Deys, and Kingdoms," 62–64.

18. Isaac Hinckley, "Journal of a Voyage of the Brig, Reaper, 1809–1810," in Glenn Stine Gordinier, "A Case Study of Early American Trade with India: The Voyage of the Reaper, 1809–1810" (master's thesis, Lehigh University, 1981), 96; Glenn Stein Gordinier, "Early American Trade with India: Taking an Observation" *American Neptune*, 45, no. 3 (Summer 1985): 155; Sandwith Drinker, *A Private Journal of Events and Scenes at Sea and in India* (Boston: N. pub., 1990), 59–60.

19. Robert M. Gordon, "Fear," *Philosophical Review*, 89, no. 4 (October 1980): 560–578; Jodi Dean, "Virtual Fears," *Signs*, 24, no. 4, Institutions, Regulation, and Social Control

(Summer 1999): 1069–1078; Joanna Bourke, "Fear and Anxiety: Writing about Emotion in Modern History," *History Workshop Journal*, 55 (Spring 2003): 111–133; Melanie Perrault, "To Fear and to Love Us: Intercultural Violence in the English Atlantic," *Journal of World History*, 17, no. 1 (March 2006): 71–93; Matthew Sparke, Forum: "Geopolitical Fears, Geoeconomic Hopes, and the Responsibilities of Geography," *Annals of the Association of American Geographers*, 97, no. 2 (June 2007): 338–349; Darren M. McMahon, "Fear and Trembling: Strangers and Strange Lands," *Daedalus*, 137, no. 3 (Summer 2008): 5–17.

20. Drinker, *Private Journal*, 53–54, 57, 62; Susan J. Matt, "You Can't Go Home Again: Homesickness and Nostalgia in U. S. History," *Journal of American History*, 94, no. 2 (September 2007): 469–497.

21. Durand, *Life*, 24.

22. Durand, 24; Robinson, *Biblical Researches*, 2.

23. Amasa Delano, *A Narrative of Voyages and Travels in the Northern and Southern Hemispheres* (Boston, 1817), 308–309.

24. Drinker, *Private Journal*; Delano, *Narrative*, 210–211, 308–309; Richard Jeffry Cleveland, *Voyages and Commercial Enterprises of the Sons of New England* (New York: Burt Franklin, 1857), 218–219; Alexander McKee, *Wreck of the Medusa: The Tragic Story of the Death Raft* (New York: Penguin, 1975).

25. Stephens, *Incidents*, 13; William Bainbridge to the Secretary of the Navy, November 1, 1803, in "Capture of the Frigate USS *Philadelphia*, 31 October 1803: Selected Naval Documents," Naval History and Heritage Command, www.history.navy .mil/research/library/online-reading-room/title-list-alphabetically/c/capture-of-the -frigate-uss-philadelphia.html; Allison, *Crescent Obscured*; Peskin, *Captives*, 153–157; Robert J. Antony, *Pirates in the Age of Sail* (New York: W. W. Norton, 2007), 29; George Bethune English, *A Narrative of the Expedition to Dongola and Sennaar* (London, 1822), 16–18, 39.

26. Stephens, *Incidents*; Robinson, *Biblical Researches*, 2–3.

27. Nancy Um, *Shipped but Not Sold: Material Culture and the Social Protocols of Trade during Yemen's Age of Coffee* (Honolulu: University of Hawai'i Press, 2017).

28. A sampling of the corpus of work on the American experience with North African corsairs includes H. G. Barnby, *The Prisoners of Algiers: An Account of the Forgotten American Algerian War, 1785–1797* (New York, Oxford University Press, 1966); Donald Barr Chidsey, *The Wars in Barbary: Arab Piracy and the Birth of the United States Navy* (New York: Crown, 1971); Allison, *Crescent Obscured*; Michael Kitzen, "Money Bags or Cannon Balls: The Origins of the Tripolitan War, 1795–1801," *Journal of the Early Republic*, 16, no. 4 (Winter 1996): 601–624; Paul Baepler, *White Slaves, African Masters: An Anthology of American Barbary Captivity Narratives* (Chicago: University of Chicago Press, 1999); Davis, *Christian Slaves*; Hester Blum, "Pirated Tars, Piratical Texts: Barbary Captivity and American Sea Narratives," *Early American Studies* 1 (Fall 2003): 133–158; Martha Elena Rojas, "Insults Unpunished: Barbary Captives, American Slaves, and the Negotiation of Liberty," *Early American Studies* 1 (Fall 2003): 159–186; Frank Lambert, *The Barbary Wars: American Independence in the Atlantic World* (New York: Hill and Wang, 2005); Peskin, *Captives and Countrymen*; Angela Sutton, "Atlantic Orientalism: How Language in Jefferson's America Defeated the Barbary Pirates," *Dark Matter in the Ruins of Imperial Culture* (December 20, 2009), www.darkmatter101.org

/site/2009/12/20/atlantic-orientalism-how-language-in-jefferson's-america-defeated
-the-barbary-pirates.

29. Antony, *Pirates*; Allison, *Crescent Obscured*, 9–10; Lambert, *Barbary Wars*,
59–60; Barnby, *Prisoners of Algiers*, 1–2; Gardner W. Allen, *Our Naval War with France*
(Boston: Houghton Mifflin, 1909), 41. The xebec was a three-masted lateen-rigged
vessel that featured a bow and stern that projected well off the hull.

30. Although Morocco had returned the *Betsey* in March, the haphazard nature of
news dissemination conflated events for American readers, and it is likely that many
heard of the captures but not the releases. James Leander Cathcart, *The Captives* (La
Porte, IN: Herald, 1899), 5; Allison, *Crescent Obscured*, 9–10; Lambert, *Barbary Wars*,
59–60.

31. The literature on North African captivity is extensive and seems to grow almost
weekly. For a survey of the sources on European, especially British, captivity, see Colley,
Captives. For US materials, see Barnby, *Prisoners of Algiers*; Lambert, *Barbary Wars*;
Peskin, *Captives*; Baepler, *White Slaves*; Chidsey, *Wars in Barbary*; Davis, *Christian Slaves*;
Blum, "Pirated Tars," 133–158; Rojas, "Insults Unpunished," 159–186; and Sutton,
"Atlantic Orientalism."

32. Rojas, "Insults Unpunished," 165; Hanna, *Pirate Nests*, 60.

33. Kenneth J. Hagan, *This People's Navy: The Making of American Sea Power* (New
York: Simon and Schuster, 1992), 22; Gordinier, "Case Study," 101.

34. Cited in Richard E. Winslow, *"Wealth and Honour": Portsmouth During the
Golden Age of Privateering, 1775–1815* (Portsmouth, NH: Portsmouth Marine Society,
1988), 78; *New Hampshire Gazette*, March 15, 1794.

35. Blum, "Pirated Tars," 139; Paul Michel Baepler, "The Barbary Captivity
Narrative in American Culture," *Early American Literature*, 39, no. 2 (2004): 217–246;
Baepler, *White Slaves*, 159; Allison, *Crescent Obscured*, 109; Peskin, *Captives*, viii.

36. John Foss, *A Journal, of the Captivity and Sufferings of John Foss* (Newburyport,
MA, 1795), 10–11.

37. Foss, *Journal*, 9–10.

38. *Oracle of the Day*, March 22, 1794.

39. Cathcart, *Captives*, 6.

40. Foss, *Journal*, 11–12.

41. Sowande' M. Mustakeem, *Slavery at Sea: Terror, Sex, and Sickness in the Middle
Passage* (Champaign: University of Illinois Press, 2016), 19–36; Cathcart, *Captives*, 7;
Foss, *Journal*, 11–13; William Ray, *Horrors of Slavery: or, The American Tars in Tripoli*
(Troy, 1808), 85; Baepler, *White Slaves*, 103.

42. James Riley, *An Authentic Narrative of the Loss of the American Brig, Commerce,
on the Western Coast of Africa, in 1815; with an Account of the Sufferings of her Surviving
Officers and Crew: and Observations Historical and Geographical* (3rd ed., 1818); Archibald
Robbins, *A Journal, Comprising an Account of the Loss of the Brig Commerce, James
Riley, Master, upon the Western Coast of Africa; also of the Slavery and Sufferings of the
Author, and the Rest of the Crew, upon the Desert of Zahara, in the Years 1815, 1817* (1817),
v; Peskin, *Captives*, chap. 5; Allison, *Crescent Obscured*, 107.

43. Ray, *Horrors of Slavery*, 85; Foss, *Journal*, 22–23; Cathcart, *Captives*, 10.

44. *New Hampshire Gazette*, January 4, March 15, and August 5, 1794; *Portsmouth
Oracle*, November 16, 1796, cited in Winslow, *"Wealth and Honour,"* 79.

45. Foss, *Journal*, 21–24.

46. *New Hampshire Gazette*, March 15, 1794; Ray, *Horrors of Slavery*, 85; Cathcart, *Captives*, 9–10.

47. Cathcart, *Captives*, 10; *New Hampshire Gazette*, August 5, 1794; Peskin, *Captives*, 31, 37, 40, 47–48, 130.

48. Ray, *Horrors of Slavery*, 85, 90; Foss, *Journal*, 24–25.

49. J. L. Tomlin, "'As Arbitrary as the Grand Turke:' Religious Othering and the First American Revolution," *Age of Revolutions* (website), October 14, 2019, https://ageofrevolutions.com/2019/10/14/as-arbitrary-as-the-grand-turke-religious-othering-and-the-first-american-revolution.

50. *Freeman's Journal, or The North-American Intelligencer*, June 22, 1785.

51. *Worcester (Massachusetts) Magazine . . . Containing Politicks, Miscellanies, Poetry, and News,* May 15, 1787. Actually, Lamb arrived in Algiers on March 25, 1786, and stayed briefly, having failed to reach an agreement with the Dey. Peskin, *Captives*, 31; Richard Norton Smith, *Patriarch: George Washington and the New American Nation* (Boston: Houghton Mifflin, 1993), 276; *Georgia Gazette*, June 18, 1801.

52. [Frederick C. Fischer], *Experienced and Conquered: Frederick C. Fischer, Musician, U.S. Navy aboard USS Constitution, 1844–1846,* ed. Annabell F. Fischer, trans. Noah G. Good (Westminster, MD: Peach, 1996); Samuel Patterson, *Narrative of the Adventures and Sufferings of Samuel Patterson, Who made three voyages to the North West Coast of America, and who sailed to the Sandwich islands, and to many other parts of This World before being shipwrecked on the Feegee Islands* (1817; reprint Fairfield, WAS: Ye Galleon, 1967), 20–29; Ira Dye, *The Fatal Cruise of the Argus: Two Captains in the War of 1812* (Annapolis, MD: Naval Institute Press, 1994), 5–26; Allison, *Crescent Obscured*, 175–176; Chidsey, *Wars in Barbary*, 62–63; Hanna, *Pirate Nests*, 61.

53. Antony, *Pirates*, 15–17; Cathryn J. Pearce, *Cornish Wrecking, 1700–1860: Reality and Popular Myth* (Martlesham, UK: Boydell & Brewer, 2010).

54. Daniel Saunders, *A Journal of the Travels and Sufferings of Daniel Saunders, jun. A Mariner on board the Ship Commerce, of Boston, Samuel Johnson, Commander, which was cast away Cape Morebet, on the Coast of Arabia, July 10, 1792* (Salem: Thomas C. Cushing, 1794), 5–9, 10–21. Years later, Amasa Delano met Captain Johnson and found "it difficult to reconcile this story with the idea, that he possessed proper qualifications for a ship-master on foreign voyages." Delano, *Narrative*, 210.

55. Riley, *Authentic Narrative*; Dean King, *Skeletons on the Zahara: A True Story of Survival* (New York: Little, Brown, 2004); Robbins, *Journal*, Riley's treatment was reputedly a favorite book of Abraham Lincoln.

56. "Early American Interactions with the Barbary States," William L. Clements Library, University of Michigan, https://clements.umich.edu/exhibit/barbary-wars/early-barbary-interactions; George Nichols, quoted in Charles E. Trow, *The Old Shipmasters of Salem* (New York: G. P. Putnam's Sons, 1905), 191; Delano, *Narrative*, 544.

57. Drinker, *Private Journal*, 59–60; "Philadelphia Quaker, Soldier of Fortune: The Story of Sandwith Drinker," *Hong Kong's First* (July 2014), http://hongkongsfirst.blogspot.com/2012/02/philadelphia-quaker-soldier-of-fortune.html.

58. Drinker, *Private Journal*, 62–63.

59. Drinker, 88–89.

60. Drinker, 97–98.

61. Drinker, 97–99.

62. Ibram X. Kendi, *Stamped from the Beginning: The Definitive History of Racist Ideas in America* (New York: Nation, 2016), 96–98.

63. English, *Narrative of the Expedition*, 53; Eric R. Dursteler, "Fearing the 'Turk' and Feeling the Spirit: Emotion and Conversion in the Early Modern Mediterranean," *Journal of Religious History*, 39, no. 4 (December 2015): 484–505; Heyrman, *American Apostles*, 147–150.

64. Seth Low to Harriet Low, May 17, 1829, in *The China Trade Post-Bag of the Low Family of Salem and New York, 1829–1873*, ed. Elma Loines (Manchester, ME: Falmouth Publishing House, 1953), 19–21; Durand, *Life*, 30.

65. Lisa Lowe, *Critical Terrains: French and British Orientalisms* (Ithaca, NY: Cornell University Press, 1991), 31; Jedidiah Morse, *Geography Made Easy* (Boston: Thomas & Andrews, 1790), 308; Durand, *Life*, 26.

66. Durand, *Life*, 26; Jason Goodwin, *Lords of the Horizons: A History of the Ottoman Empire* (New York: Henry Holt, 1998); 252.

67. Nükhet Varlik, "From 'Bête Noire' to 'le Mal de Constantinople': Plagues, Medicine, and the Early Modern Ottoman State," *Journal of World History*, 24, no. 4 (December 2013), 741–770; Nükhet Varlik, *Plague and Contagion in the Islamic Mediterranean* (Kalamazoo, MI: ARC Humanities, 2017).

68. Hourani, *History of the Arab Peoples*, 211.

69. Durand, *Life*, 26; Goodwin, *Lords of the Horizons*, 138, 252; Varlik, "Bête Noire," 741–770; Varlik, *Plague*; Hourani, *History of the Arab Peoples*, 211; Jacob Saphir, *Iben Safir*, 2 vols. (Lyck, 1866).

70. Arthur William Kinglake, *Eothen: Traces of Travel Brought Home from the East* (Reprint, London, 1844; New York: Cosimo, 2010), 1–2; Robinson, *Biblical Researches*, 3, 13–15, 23–25; Hourani, *History of the Arab Peoples*, 268; *Salem Gazette*, March 11, 1788; Barnby, *Prisoners of Algiers*, 303; Varlik, *Plague*, passim; Peskin, *Captives*, 31–32; English, *Narrative of the Expedition*, 3, 53; Durand, *Life*, 20; Stephens, *Incidents*, 14–15; James Alexander Dun, *Dangerous Neighbors: Making the Haitian Revolution in Early America* (Philadelphia: University of Pennsylvania Press, 2016), 86–87, 128–129.

71. Heyrman, *American Apostles*, 130; Bond, *Memoir*, 3.

72. Charles Tyng, *Before the Wind: The Memoir of an American Sea Captain, 1808–1833*, ed. Susan Fels (New York: Viking, 1999), 84; Robinson, *Biblical Researches*, 4; Stephens, *Incidents*, 14.

73. Goodwin, *Lords of the Horizons*, 115–117; Maria Rosa Menocal, *The Ornament of the World: How Muslims, Jews, and Christians Created a Culture of Tolerance in Medieval Spain* (New York: Little, Brown, 1992); Riley, *Authentic Narrative*, iv; Foley, "Muslims and Social Change," 378.

74. Complicating our understanding of Ottoman identity and what early Americans knew of it, Isom-Verhaaren observes, as well, "While modern scholars find the term 'Ottoman' useful, this word was rarely used." Christine Isom-Verhaaren, "Was There Room in Rum for Corsairs? Who Was an Ottoman in the Naval Forces of the Ottoman Empire in the 15th and 16th Centuries?" *Osmanlı Araştırmaları / The Journal of Ottoman Studies*, XLIV (2014): 237.

75. Isom-Verhaaren, "Was There Room in Rum," 237; Roberts, "Commercial Philanthropy," 372; James Field, *America and the Mediterranean World 1776–1882* (Princeton,

NJ: Princeton University Press, 1969); Daniel Goffman and Bruce Masters, *The Ottoman City between East and West: Aleppo, Izmir, and Istanbul* (New York: Cambridge University Press, 1999); Abraham Marcus, *Middle East on the Eve of Modernity: Aleppo in the Eighteenth Century* (New York: Columbia University Press, 1989); Felipe Fernández-Armesto, *Pathfinders: A Global History of Exploration* (New York: W. W. Norton, 2006), 275–278; Isom-Verhaaren, "Was There Room in Rum," 238; Suraiya Faroqhi, The *Ottoman Empire and the World around It* (London: I.B. Tauris, 2004), 2–3.

76. Gordinier, "Case Study," 102.

77. Durand, *Life*, 28, 36; Jennifer L. Morgan, "'Some Could Suckle over Their Shoulder': Male Travelers, Female Bodies, and the Gendering of Racial Ideology, 1500–1770," *William and Mary Quarterly*, 54, no. 1 (January 1997): 167–192; Robinson, *Biblical Researches*, 14; Lynch, *Narrative*, 52.

78. Robinson, *Biblical Researches*, 24, 29; Lynch, *Narrative*, 51.

79. Roberts, "Commercial Philanthropy," 372; Robinson, *Biblical Researches*, 15.

80. Roberts, "Commercial Philanthropy," 372.

81. Quoted in Cutter, "Turks, Moors, Deys, and Kingdoms," 61–84; Nabil Matar, "Introduction: England and Mediterranean Captivity, 1577–1704," in *Piracy, Slavery, and Redemption*, ed. Daniel J. Vitkus (New York: Columbia University Press, 2001), 1–54; Nabil Matar, *Britain and Barbary* (Gainesville: University of Florida Press, 2005); Katie Sisneros, "'The Abhorred Name of Turk': Muslims and the Politics of Identity in Seventeenth-Century English Broadside Ballads" (PhD diss., University of Minnesota, 2016).

82. Cutter, "Turks, Moors, Deys, and Kingdoms," 61–84; Nabil Matar, "Introduction: England and Mediterranean Captivity, 1577–1704," 1–54; Matar, *Britain and Barbary*; Sisneros, "Abhorred Name," 22–25; Baepler, *White Slaves*, 160.

83. Jürgen Osterhammel, *Unfabling the East: The Enlightenment's Encounter with Asia*, trans. Robert Savage (Princeton, NJ: Princeton University Press, 2018), 290.

84. Kinglake, *Eothen*, xxiii; Durand, *Life*, 31; Robinson, *Biblical Researches*, 15–18.

85. Bond, *Memoir*, 122

86. Bond, 122.

87. Bond, 126, 142.

88. Bond, 126.

89. Bond, 123, 127.

90. Heyrman, *American Apostles*, 5, 8–20.

91. English, *Narrative of the Expedition*, 99.

92. Stephens, *Incidents*; William Carlsen, *Jungle of Stone: The Extraordinary Journey of John L. Stephens and Frederick Catherwood and the Discovery of the Lost Civilization of the Maya* (New York: William Morrow, 2016).

93. Stephens, *Incidents*, 14.

94. Stephens, 16.

95. Stephens, 14–16, 22.

96. Stephens, 14–15.

97. Stephens, 19–20

98. Robinson, *Biblical Researches*, 5, 6; Henry B. Smith and Roswell D. Hitchcock, *The Life, Writings and Character of Edward Robinson* (New York, 1863); Julius A. Bewer, "Edward Robinson as a Biblical Scholar," *Journal of Biblical Literature*, 58, no. 4 (December 1939): 355–363.

99. Robinson, *Biblical Researches*, 15.

100. Robinson, 18–19.

101. Samuel Taylor Coleridge, "Ozymandias," *The Examiner*, 524 (January 11, 1818), 24; William Freedman, "Postponement and Perspectives in Shelley's 'Ozymandias,'" *Studies in Romanticism*, 25, no. 1 (Spring 1986): 63–73; R. S. Edgecombe, "Displaced Christian Images in Shelley's 'Ozymandias,'" *Keats Shelley Review*, 14 (2000): 95–99; Robinson, *Biblical Researches*, 20–26.

102. Robinson, 28–30.

103. Lynch, *Narrative*; Andrew C. A. Jampoler, *Sailors in the Holy Land: The 1848 American Expedition to the Dead Sea and the Search for Sodom and Gomorrah* (Annapolis, MD: Naval Institute Press, 2005); David Haward Bain, *Bitter Waters: America's Forgotten Naval Mission to the Dead Sea* (New York: Overlook Press, 2011); Milette Shamir, "On the Uselessness of Knowledge: William F. Lynch's "'Interesting' Expedition to the Dead Sea," *Journal of the Early Republic*, 38, no. 3 (Fall 2018): 475–499; Shamir, "Interesting Expedition," 478.

104. Shamir, "Interesting Expedition," 477; Lynch, *Narrative*, 35, 36, 40

105. Lynch, *Narrative*, 38.

106. Lynch, 45, 48, 49, 58.

107. Lynch, 51.

108. Heyrman, *American Apostles*, 147–149.

109. Morrison, *True Yankees*, 8, 47.

110. Allison, *Crescent Obscured*; Peskin, *Captives*; Blum, "Barbary"; Gordon M. Sayre, "Renegades from Barbary: The Transnational Turn in Captivity Studies," *American Literary History*, 22, no. 2 (Summer 2010): 348; Pauline Turner Strong, *Captive Selves, Captivating Others: The Politics and Poetics of Colonial American Captivity Narratives* (Boulder, CO: Westview, 1999).

111. Allison, *Crescent Obscured*; Peskin, *Captives*; Malini Johar Schueller, *U. S. Orientalisms: Race, Nation, and Gender in Literature, 1790–1890* (Ann Arbor: University of Michigan Press, 1998).

112. Sayre, "Renegades," 348–349; Lisa Voigt, *Writing Captivity in the Early Modern Atlantic: Circulations of Knowledge and Authority in the Iberian and English Imperial Worlds* (Chapel Hill: University of North Carolina Press, 2009).

113. Andrew W. Drummond, "Thomas Muntzer and the Fear of Man," *Sixteenth Century Journal*, 10, no. 2 (Summer 1979): 63–71; Victoria Lawson, "Introduction: Geographies of Fear and Hope," *Annals of the Association of American Geographers*, 97, no. 2 (June 2007): 335–337; Dursteler, "Fearing the 'Turk,'" 484–505.

114. Adam Shatz, "'Orientalism,' Then and Now," *New York Review of Books* (blog), May 20, 2019, www.nybooks.com/daily/2019/05/20/orientalism-then-and-now; Susan Muaddi Darraj, "Orientalism and Empire in the United States" (review of Malini Johar Schueller, *U. S. Orientalisms: Race, Nation, and Gender in Literature, 1790–1890*), *Jouvert: A Journal of Postcolonial Studies*, 7, no. 1 (Autumn 2002), https://legacy.chass.ncsu.edu /jouvert/v7is1/darraj.htm.

115. *Freeman's Journal*, June 4, 1788; *New Haven Gazette*, June 12, 1788.

116. Lowe, Critical Terrains, 30–31. As Billie Melman observes, from the Mediterranean to India was considered part of the "European room"; a border area in Western imagination, "It was of the West, yet outside it, familiar, yet alien." Billie Melman, "The

Middle East/Arabia: 'The Cradle of Islam,'" in Peter Hulme and Tim Youngs, eds., The Cambridge Companion to Travel Writing (Cambridge, ENG: Cambridge University Press, 2002), 105; Fabio López Lázaro, "The Rise and Global Significance of the First 'West': The Medieval Islamic Maghrib," Journal of World History, 24, no. 2 (June 2013): 259–307.

117. Colley, *Captives*, 102–103, 132–133; Alison Games, *Web*; MacLean, *Rise*.

118. Lowe, *Critical Terrains*, 31; Matar, "Introduction: England and Mediterranean Captivity, 1577–1704," 51–54; Matar, *Britain and Barbary*; Ros Ballaster, *Fabulous Orients: Fictions of the East in England, 1662–1785* (New York: Oxford University Press, 2005); Brotton, *Orient Isle*; Sisneros, "Abhored Name"; Cutter, "Turks, Moors, Deys, and Kingdoms," 61–84.

119. *The Examiner*, January 11, 1818. A companion piece by Smith appeared on February 1, 1818; Edward Chaney, "Egypt in England and America: The Cultural Memorials of Religion, Royalty and Revolution," in *Sites of Exchange: European Crossroads and Faultlines*, ed. Maurizio Ascari and Adriana Corrado (Amsterdam: Rodopi, 2006), 39–74.

Chapter 3 • "Unfeeling Mandarins" in Canton and Macao

1. William Bentinck-Smith, "Nicholas Boylston and His Harvard Chair," *Proceedings of the Massachusetts Historical Society*, 3rd series, 93 (1981): 17, 29, 33; Abigail Adams to John Adams, July 31, 1777, Adams Papers, Massachusetts Historical Society, Boston; Kimberly S. Alexander, *Treasures Afoot: Shoe Stories in the Georgian Era* (Baltimore, MD: Johns Hopkins University Press, 2018); Steven C. Bullock, *Tea Sets and Tyranny: The Politics of Politeness in Early America* (Philadelphia: University of Pennsylvania Press, 2016); *Boston Evening-Post*, November 27, 1769.

2. Others would have read this excerpt from Young's book in *Pennsylvania Chronicle* (Philadelphia), August 22, 1772; *Connecticut Journal, and the New Haven Post-Boy* (New Haven), September 4, 1772; *Essex Gazette* (Salem, Massachusetts), September 15, 1772; *New-Hampshire Gazette, and Historical Chronicle* (Portsmouth), September 18, 1772; *Newport Mercury* (Rhode Island), September 21, 1772. "The Annotated Newspapers of Harbottle Dorr, Jr.," Massachusetts Historical Society, www.masshist.org/dorr.

3. Paul A. Van Dyke, ed., *Americans and Macao: Trade, Smuggling, and Diplomacy on the South China Coast* (Aberdeen: Hong Kong University Press, 2012); Paul A. Van Dyke, *Merchants of Canton and Macao: Politics and Strategies in Eighteenth-Century Chinese Trade* (Sakyo, Kyoto: Kyoto University Press, 2011).

4. Pedro Machado, *Ocean of Trade: South Asian Merchants, Africa and the Indian Ocean, c. 1750–1850* (Cambridge, UK: Cambridge University Press, 2014), 5–7.

5. Joseph Ingraham, *Joseph Ingraham's Journal of the Brigantine Hope on a Voyage to the Northwest Coast of North America, 1790–92* (Barre, MA: Imprint Society, 1971), 40; Douglas R. Egerton, Alison Games, Jane G. Landers, Kris Lane, and Donald R. Wright, *The Atlantic World: A History, 1400–1888* (Malden, MA: Wiley-Blackwell, 2007), 13; Peter Booth Wiley, *Yankees in the Land of the Gods: Commodore Perry and the Opening of Japan* (New York: Penguin, 1990), 129; Huw Lewis-Jones, *The Sea Journal: Seafarers' Sketchbooks* (London: Thames & Hudson, 2019), 11–12.

6. We can find some wonderful examinations in Robert Foulke's *The Sea Voyage Narrative* (New York: Routledge, 2001) and Margaret Creighton's *Rites and Passages: The Experience of American Whaling, 1830–1870* (New York: Cambridge University Press, 1995), but far less attention is given in other important works, such as Paul Gilje, *To Swear like a Sailor: Maritime Culture in America, 1750–1850* (New York: Cambridge University Press, 2016); Daniel Vickers and Vince Walsh, *Young Men and the Sea: Yankee Seafarers in the Age of Sail* (New Haven, CT: Yale University Press, 2007); Marcus Rediker, *Between the Devil and the Deep Blue Sea: Merchant Seamen, Pirates, and the Anglo-American Maritime World, 1700–1750* (New York: Cambridge University Press, 1989); Hester Blum, *The View from the Masthead: Maritime Imagination and Antebellum American Sea Narratives* (Durham, NC: University of North Carolina Press, 2008); Nathan Perl-Rosenthal, *Citizen Sailors: Becoming American in the Age of Revolution* (Cambridge: Harvard University Press, 2015).

7. Charles Oscar Paullin, *American Voyages to the Orient, 1690–1865* (Annapolis, MD: United States Naval Institute, 1971), 11; Tamara Plakins Thornton, *Nathaniel Bowditch and the Power of Numbers: How a Nineteenth-Century Man of Business, Science, and the Sea Changed American Life* (Chapel Hill: University of North Carolina Press, 2016), 36–37.

8. The earliest use of the term in print may have come in William Bolt's 1772 book, *Considerations upon Indian Affairs*: "How many *lacks* shall I put in my pocket?" See Jack P. Greene, *Evaluating Empire and Confronting Colonialism in Eighteenth-Century Britain* (New York: Cambridge University Press, 2013), 136.

9. In 1790, Captain Benjamin Carpenter of the *Ruby* observed the "universal use of umbrellas in China. Susan S. Bean, *Yankee India: American Commercial and Cultural Encounters with India in the Age of Sail, 1784–1860* (Salem, MA: Peabody Essex Museum, 2001), 54; Charles Tyng, *Before the Wind: The Memoir of an American Sea Captain, 1808–1833*, ed. Susan Fels (New York: Viking, 1999).

10. Sullivan Dorr to Ebenezer Dorr, Canton, September 17, 1799, "Letters of Sullivan Dorr," *Proceedings of the Massachusetts Historical Society*, 3rd series, 67 (October 1941): 182; Robert Bennet Forbes, *Letters from China: The Canton-Boston Correspondence of Robert Bennet Forbes, 1838–1840*, comp. and ed. Phyllis Forbes Kerr (Mystic, CT: Mystic Seaport Museum, 1996), 68–69; Charles H. Barnard, *A Narrative of the Sufferings and Adventures of Capt. Charles H. Barnard, in a Recent Voyage Round the World, Including an Account of his Residence for Two Years on an Uninhabited Island* (New York: J. P. Callender, 1836), 245.

11. Richard Jeffry Cleveland, *Voyages and Commercial Enterprises of the Sons of New England* (New York: Burt Franklin, 1857), 296–297.

12. Cleveland, *Voyages*, 238–239.

13. Robert Bennet Forbes to Rose Forbes, April 14, 1839, quoted in Forbes, *Letters from China*, 118.

14. Frederick D. Grant Jr., "Hong Merchant Litigation in the American Courts," *Proceedings of the Massachusetts Historical Society*, 3rd series, 99 (1987): 243.

15. Ralph D. Paine, *The Ships and Sailors of Old Salem* (Cambridge, UK: Cambridge University Press, 1985), 144.

16. Delano, *Narrative*, 529.

17. Ingraham, *Joseph Ingraham's Journal*, 192.

18. William P. Elting, *Notebook, 1797–1803*, Massachusetts Historical Society; Ingraham, *Journal*, 178, 247–248; Edmund Fanning, *Voyages Round the World; with Selected Sketches of Voyages to the South Seas, North and South Pacific Oceans, China, etc.* (New York: Collins and Hannay, 1833), 299; Delano, *Narrative*, 161.

19. Delano, *Narrative*, 161; Robert E. Peabody, *The Logs of the Grand Turks* (Boston: Houghton Mifflin, 1926), 56, 99–100, 103; Fanning, *Voyages*, 313.

20. William C. Hunter, *The 'Fan Kwae' at Canton before Treaty Days, 1825–1844* (Taipei: Ch'eng-Wen, 1965), 1; British Library India Office Records, L/MAR/C/27A, Minutes of the Committee of Shippin fo. 12r entry, 19 August 1685, courtesy of Mark Williams; Drinker, *Private Journal*, 3.

21. Harriet Low to Seth Low, March 16, 1829, in *The China Trade Post-Bag of the Low Family of Salem and New York, 1829–1873*, ed. Elma Loines (Manchester, ME: Falmouth, 1953), 19; Seth Low to Harriet Low, New York, May 17, 1829, in Loines, 20.

22. Fanning, *Voyages*, 280.

23. Rediker, *Devil*, 3–4; Sullivan Dorr to Ebenezer Dorr, Canton, September 10, 1799, "Letters of Sullivan Dorr," ed. Howard Corning, *Proceedings of the Massachusetts Historical Society*, 67 (October 1941–May 1944): 180.

24. Harriet Low, *Journal*, August 11, 1829, Low-Mills Family Papers, Library of Congress.

25. Amos Porter, *The China Journal of Amos Porter, 1802–1803* (Greensboro, VT: Greensboro Historical Society, 1984), 45.

26. "Nathaniel Appleton's Journal of the Voyage of the Ship Concord Around the World October 1799 to July 1802," ed. James Duncan Phillips, *Essex Institute Historical Collections*, 83 (1947): 151.

27. Samuel Shaw, *The Journals of Major Samuel Shaw, the First American Consul at Canton*, ed. Josiah Quincy (Taipei: Ch'eng-Wen, 1968), 319.

28. John S. Sewall, *The Logbook of the Captain's Clerk: Adventures in the China Seas* (Bangor, ME: Charles H. Glass, 1905), 40; Thornton, *Bowditch*, 38; Sullivan Dorr to Ebenezer Dorr, Canton, September 10, 1799, "Letters of Sullivan Dorr," 180; Sullivan Dorr to Joseph Dorr and John Dorr, Canton, November 1, 1799, "Letters of Sullivan Dorr," 188.

29. Tyng, *Before the Wind*, 27–28, 99.

30. As the *Sailors' Magazine* observed in 1847, "A sailor's calling is one in which he must struggle for life or death against winds, waters, rocks, & lightnings. . . . This makes him a man of great activity, vigor and energy of action, thought, feeling & language"; John Richards Child Child, "Journal of a Voyage from Boston to the South Seas & Canton by John Child" (1811), John Richards Child Papers, Massachusetts Historical Society; Rediker, *Deep Blue Sea*, 1–3.

31. Tyng, *Before the Wind*, 99; Forbes, *Letters*, 56; John B. Sewell, *The Logbook of the Captain's Clerk*, ed. Arthur Powell Dudden (Chicago: Lakeside, 1995), 59, 62, 75.

32. Ingraham, *Journal*, 19.

33. Charles H. Barnard, *A Narrative of the Sufferings and Adventures of Capt. Charles H. Barnard in a Recent Voyage Round the World* (New York: J. P. Callender, 1836), 251.

34. Delano, *Narrative*, 39; "Nathaniel Appleton's Journal," 148–149; Sewall, *Logbook*, 54–57.

35. Barnard, *Narrative*, 252.

36. Sullivan Dorr to Ebenezer Dorr, Canton, October 1, 1799, "Letters of Sullivan Dorr," 183. When William C. Hunter arrived aboard the *Citizen* "out of season" at Canton in February 1825, he found the "regular tea season" was over. Hunter, *Fan Kwae*, 13.

37. Elting, "Notebook."

38. Sullivan Dorr to Joseph and John Dorr, Canton, October 7, 1799, "Letters of Sullivan Dorr," 188, 197.

39. Ingraham, *Journal*, 7–8; Robert Bennet Forbes to Rose Forbes, August 12, 1839, in Forbes, *Letters*, 157; Forbes to Rose Forbes, October 5, 1838, in Forbes, *Letters*, 56; Joseph Conrad, "Typhoon," *Pall Mall Magazine* (January–March, 1902).

40. Nathaniel Bowditch, *Early American Philippine Trade: The Journal of Nathaniel Bowditch in Manila, 1796*, ed. Thomas R. McHale and Mary C. McHale (New Haven, CT: Yale University/Cellar Bookshop, 1962), 55; Felipe Fernández-Armesto, *Pathfinders: A Global History of Exploration* (New York: W. W. Norton, 2006), 112–113; Shih-Shan Henry Tsai, *Maritime Taiwan: Historical Encounters with the East and the West* (London: M. E. Sharpe, 2009), 47–54; Sewall, *Logbook*, 59; Charles Corn, *The Scents of Eden: A Narrative of the Spice Trade* (New York: Kodansha International, 1998).

41. Elting, "Notebook," 73; Tyng, *Before the Wind*, 92; Sewell, *Logbook*, 59; Wiley, *Yankees*, 129.

42. Leonard Blussé describes the period 1790–1810 as one in which pirates and smugglers ravaged the coasts of Guangdong and Guangxi provinces to an unprecedented extent. Leonard Blussé, *Visible Cities: Canton, Nagasaki, and Batavia and the Coming of the Americans* (Cambridge: Harvard University Press, 2008). 64.

43. David Armitage, *The Declaration of Independence: A Global History* (Cambridge: Harvard University Press, 2008); Eliga H. Gould, *Among the Powers of the Earth: The American Revolution and the Making of a New World Empire* (Cambridge: Harvard University Press, 2013).

44. Richard J. Grace, *Opium and Empire: The Lives and Careers of William Jardine and James Matheson* (Montreal: McGill-Queen's University Press, 2014), 59–60; Michael Laver, "Neither Here nor There: Trade, Piracy, and the 'Space Between' in Early Modern East Asia," in *Sea Rovers, Silver, and Samurai: Maritime East Asia in Global History, 1550–1700*, ed. Tonio Andrade and Xing Hang (Honolulu: University of Hawai'i, 2016): 28–37; Tsai, *Maritime Taiwan*, 106–107.

45. Sonja Schillings, *Enemies of All Humankind: Fictions of Legitimate Violence* (Hanover, NH: Dartmouth College Press, 2017).

46. Sewell, *Logbook*, 97; Paul A. Van Dyke, "Smuggling Networks of the Pearl River Delta before 1842," in *Americans and Macao: Trade, Smuggling, and Diplomacy on the South China Coast*, ed. Paul A. Van Dyke (Aberdeen: Hong Kong University Press, 2012), 58.

47. Laver, "Neither Here nor There," 28–37.

48. Charles C. Mann, *1493: Uncovering the New World Columbus Created* (New York: Vintage, 2011), 163.

49. Robert J. Antony, "Trade, Piracy, and Resistance in the Gulf of Tonkin in the Seventeenth Century," in Andrade and Hang, *Sea Rovers, Silver, and Samurai*, 47–56, 312–334; Dian Murray, "Commerce, Crisis, Coercion: The Role of Piracy in Late Eighteenth and Early Nineteenth Century Sino-Western Relations," *American Neptune*, 48, no. 4 (Fall 1988): 237.

50. Murray, "Commerce, Crisis, Coercion," 237; Porter, *China Journal*, 25, 29–30.

51. *Salem Gazette* (Massachusetts), January 30, 1810.

52. Stephen R. Platt, *Imperial Twilight: The Opium War and the End of China's Last Golden Age* (New York: Alfred A. Knopf, 2018), 110–111, 115–116.

53. John Turner, *A Narrative of the Captivity and Sufferings, of John Turner, First Officer of the ship John Jay, of Bombay, among the Ladrones of Pirates* (New York: Largin & Thompson, 1814), 22, 33. Readers could find Turner's book prominently advertised in the *Baltimore Patriot & Evening Advertiser* for May 7, 1814, by Waite's bookshop. Enlarged were the phrases "Captivity and Sufferings" and "Ladrones of Pirates." The cost of Turner's pamphlet was twenty-five cents. *National Advocate* (New York), March 5, 1814.

54. This may have been the same vessel that was attacked in June 1805 on the Northwest Coast, leaving ten dead, including the captain, and nine wounded. *Aurora General Advertiser* (Philadelphia), April 9, 1806; *Freeman's Weekly Museum* (Walpole, NH), April 11, 1806; *Mercantile Advertiser* (New York), April 12, 1806; *The Reporter* (Brattleboro, Vermont), April 12, 1806. The Atahualpa had cleared Boston for Canton and the Northwest Coast by October 23, 1806. *People's Friend & Daily Advertiser* (New York), October 10–28, 1806.

55. The *St. Albans* was captained by Francis Austen, brother of the British novelist Jane Austen.

56. *Federal Republican* (Baltimore), January 29, 1810; *Mercantile Advertiser*, January 25, 1810; *Salem Gazette*, January 30, 1810. By 1810, the imperial government quelled the Ladrone's assaults through a policy of amnesty and embargoing supplies. The British and Americans employed the same mantra of insults against the imperial government: "arbitrary"; "oppressive"; "corrupt." Platt, *Twilight*, 120–122, 268.

57. Paradoxically, many of these self-styled protectors of liberty had found their own smuggling and slaving as legitimate business practices. *Gazette of the United States*, May 1789.

58. Dorothy Shurman Hawes, "To the Farthest Gulf. Outline of the Old China Trade," *Essex Institute Historical Collections*, 77, no. 2 (April 1941): 101–142. Her articles were later brought together and republished as *To the Farthest Gulf: The Story of the American China Trade* (Ipswich, MA: Ipswich Press, 1990. See also Paine, *Ships*; Peabody, *Logs*; James Duncan Phillips, *Pepper and Pirates: Adventures in the Sumatra Pepper Trade of Salem* (Boston: Houghton Mifflin, 1949); Charles E. Trow, *The Old Shipmasters of Salem* (New York: G. P. Putnam's Sons, 1905).

59. Felipe Fernández-Armesto, *The World: A History* (Upper Saddle River, NJ: Pearson, 2007), 368, 570.

60. Sullivan Dorr to Ebenezer Dorr, Canton, September 17, 1799, "Letters of Sullivan Dorr," 182.

61. Brian Fagan, *The Little Ice Age: How Climate Made History 1300–1850* (New York: Basic, 2001; William K. Klingaman and Nicholas P. Klingaman, *The Year without Summer: 1816 and the Volcano That Darkened the World and Changed History* (New

York: St. Martin's Griffin, 2014; Sam White, *A Cold Welcome: The Little Ice Age and Europe's Encounter with North America* (Cambridge, MA: Harvard University Press, 2017.

62. William C. Hunter, *Bits of Old China* (London, 1885), 30, 35; John White, *A Voyage to Cochin China* (London, 1824), 20; C. Toogood Downing, *The Fan-Qui in China in 1636–1637* [1838], 3 vols. (New York: Barnes & Noble, 1972), 1:103, 187.

63. Downing, *Fan-Qui*, 1:196; Sullivan Dorr to Ebenezer Dorr, Canton, September 17, 1799, "Letters of Sullivan Dorr,"182; Tyng, *Before the Wind*, 94.

64. Fernández-Arnesto, *World*, 368; Osterhammel, *Unfabling*, 164; Rebecca Kinsman Munroe, "The Daily Life of Mrs. Nathaniel Kinsman in China, 1846," *The Essex Institute Historical Collections*, 88 (January 1952): 49.

65. Conroy-Krutz, Christian *Imperialism*, 94; Shaw, *Journals*, 221–225, 235; Jonathan Tucker, "The First Voyage to India from Salem, 1786–1787; Written by Jonathan Tucker, Grandson of Captain John Tucker, about 1868," *Essex Institute Historical Collections*, 75, no. 1 (January 1939): 46–47.

66. Harriett Low, Journal, September 9, 1833; January 17 and 19, 1834; February 27, 1834, March 12, 15, and 30, 1834; and April 30, 1834, Phillips Library, Peabody Essex Museum; *South African Commercial Advertiser*, March 26, 1834; Forbes, *Letters from China*, 67; Downing, *Fan-Qui*, 1:196.

67. Charles Bernard added the flux (dysentery) to the list of woes a crew encountered. Barnard, *Narrative*, 248–249, 258; Child, "Journal," June 2, 1813; Delano, *Narrative*, 26, 35; Thornton, *Bowditch*, 38.

68. Downing, *Fan-Qui*, 1:187–188.

69. Tyng, *Before the Wind*, 221.

70. Hunter, *Bits of Old China*, 16–17.

71. Jacques M. Downs, *The Golden Ghetto: The American Commercial Community at Canton and the Shaping of American China Policy, 1784–1844* (Bethlehem, PA: Lehigh University Press, 1997), 19.

72. Elting, "Notebook," 72; Van Dyke, "Smuggling Networks," 56.

73. Elting, "Notebook," 72; Barnard, *Narrative*, 245–246. "[illegible]" has been used for indecipherable words in original source material.

74. Fanning, *Voyages*, 183–184, 189, 225; Downing, *Fan-Qui*, 1:2–3; Robinson, *Biblical Researches*, 31.

75. Sewall, *Logbook*, 177; Low, *Journal*, 56.

76. Ingraham, *Journal*, 178; Hawes, "To the Farthest Gulf," 110; Downs, *Golden Ghetto*, 19; Forbes, *Letters*, 72; Barnard, *Narrative*, 244–245.

77. The Bocca Tigris (a Portuguese term) was also known as the Bogue. Downs, *Golden Ghetto*, 19; Carl L. Crossman, *The Decorative Arts of the China Trade: Paintings, Furnishings and Exotic Curiosities* (Woodbridge, UK: Antique Collectors' Club, 1997), 29; Tyng, *Before the Wind*, 28.

78. Downing, *Fan-Qui*, 1:103.

79. Hunter, *Fan Kwae*, 1; Tyng, *Before the Wind*, 28.

80. Downs, *Golden Ghetto*, 19, 24, Barnard, *Narrative*, 246.

81. Elting, "Notebook, 72–73; Drinker, *Journal*, 13–14.

82. Forbes, *Letters*, 58.

83. Peabody, *Logs*, 81–83; Van Dyke, *Americans and Macao*; Van Dyke, *Merchants*; Van Dyke, *The Canton Trade: Life and Enterprise on the China Coast, 1700–1845*

(Aberdeen: Hong Kong University Press, 2015); Tyng, *Before the Wind*, 29. Tyng recalled these events from his ca. 1815 voyage in the *Cordelia*.

84. Peabody, *Logs*, 80–85; Thornton, *Bowditch*, 46–47. For comparison, Nathaniel Bowditch found the port fees in Manila in 1796 reasonable. Bowditch, *Journal*, 38, 46–47.

85. Exorbitant fees and incidental costs were not limited to the Chinese at Canton; Nathaniel Bowditch complained that the fees for hiring a boat were "very high" at Spanish Cavite (Manila harbor). Bowditch, *Journal*, 27; Crossman, *Decorative Arts*, 29; Elting, "Notebook," 75, 108; Walter Muir Whitehill, ed., "Remarks on the Canton Trade and the Manner of Transacting Business," *Essex Institute Historical Collections*, 73, no. 4 (October 1937): 307; Barnard, *Narrative*, 247.

86. Crossman, *Decorative Arts*, 29; Tyng, *Before the Wind*, 29; Robinson, *Biblical Researches*, 15–16; Peabody, *Logs*, 81.

87. Fanning, *Voyages*, 263–264; Whitehill, "Remarks," 307.

88. Boit described "the Art of Thieving" as a universal trait of the common people, but distinguished the "lower order" from "Chinese Gentlemen," who "stood upon the nicest Etiquette" and showed "polite attention . . . to strangers at Canton." John Boit, "Boit's Log of the *Columbia*, 1790–1792," *Proceedings of the Massachusetts Historical Society*, 3rd series, 53 (October 1919–June 1920): 265.

89. Whitehill, "Remarks," 305.

90. Peabody, *Logs*, 81; Crossman, *Decorative Arts*, 29; Van Dyke, "Smuggling Networks," 56.

91. Hunter, *Fan Kwae*, 50; Peabody, *Logs*, 81.

92. Sullivan Dorr to Ebenezer Dorr, Canton, October 7 and 29, 1799, "Letters of Sullivan Dorr," 184.

93. Whitehill, "Remarks," 306

94. Platt, *Twilight*, 74–75.

95. Van Dyke, "Smuggling Networks," 49–72.

96. Anna Farrow, Joel Lang, and Jenifer Frank, *Complicity: How the North Promoted, Prolonged, and Profited from Slavery* (New York: Ballantine, 2006).

97. Drinker, *Journal*, 12. Drinker made this trip on August 15, 1838.

98. Tyng, *Before the Wind*, 99.

99. Downing, *Fan-Qui*, 1:204.

100. Gordinier, "Early American Trade with India," 27.

101. Tyng, *Before the Wind*, 31. By "pangui," perhaps the Chinese meant, "Yankee."

102. Tyng, *Before the Wind*, 31–32; Downs, *Golden Ghetto*, 27; Egerton et al., *Atlantic World*, 168–169; Robinson, *Biblical Researches*, 15–16; Hunter, *Bits of Old China*, 13; Fanning, *Voyages*, 263; Shaw, *Journals*, 178–179.

103. Downing, *Fan-Qui*, 1:39.

104. Bowditch, *Journal*, 40.

105. Downs, *Golden Ghetto*, 73; Hawes, "To the Farthest Gulf," 111; Shaw, *Journals*, 184.

106. Sullivan Dorr to Joseph Dorr and John Dorr, Canton, November 1, 1799, "Letters of Sullivan Dorr," 188–189.

107. Porter, *China Journal*, 29.

108. Low, *Journal*, October 10, 1829; Forbes, *Letters*, 63.

109. Forbes, *Letters*, 68.

110. Elting, "Notebook," 73.

111. Quoted in John W. Foster, *American Diplomacy in the Orient* (Boston: Houghton Mifflin, 1904), 34–35; Thornton, *Bowditch*, 34, 46; Sullivan Dorr to Ebenezer Dorr, Canton, October 28, 1799, "Letters of Sullivan Dorr," 186; Sullivan Dorr to Ebenezer Dorr, September 10, 1799, "Letters of Sullivan Dorr," 180–181; Sullivan Dorr to Joseph Dorr and John Dorr, Canton, November 12, 1799, "Letters of Sullivan Dorr," 193; Sullivan Dorr to Joseph Dorr and John Dorr, Canton, November 30, 1799, "Letters "Letters of Sullivan Dorr," 199–201; Sullivan Dorr to Ebenezer Dorr, Canton, November 2, 1799, "Letters of Sullivan Dorr," 191.

112. Crossman, *Decorative Arts*, 29–30.

113. Whitehill, "Remarks," 307.

114. Elting, "Notebook," 75.

115. Foster, *American Diplomacy*, 7; Porter, *China Journal*, 26–28; Sullivan Dorr to Joseph Dorr and John Dorr, Canton, November 6, 1799, "Letters of Sullivan Dorr," 190.

116. Robinson, *Biblical Researches*, 29.

117. Fanning, *Voyages*, 259.

118. Porter, *China Journal*, 29.

119. Tomlin, "Arbitrary."

120. Robinson, *Biblical Researches*, 29.

121. Fanning, *Voyages*, 259.

122. Robert Bennet Forbes, Personal *Reminiscences* (Boston: Little, Brown, 1878), 141, 89–90; Robert Bennet Forbes to Rose Forbes, August 12, 1839, *Letters*, 157, 67.

123. Isabel Morais, "Henrietta Hall Shuck: Engendering Faith, Education and Culture in Nineteenth Century Macao," in Van Dyke, *Americans and Macao*, 111; Henrietta Shuck, *Scenes, or, Sketches of the Country, Religion, and Customs of the Chinese* (Phildelphia, 1851), 130.

124. Shaw, *Journals*, 184.

125. Fanning, *Voyages*, 256.

126. Downs, *Golden Ghetto*, 61.

127. Fanning, *Voyages*, 275–276; *Other Merchants and Sea Captains of Old Boston* (Boston: State Street Trust Company), 191; Timothy Brook, Jérôme Bourgon, and Gregory Blue, *Death by a Thousand Cuts* (Cambridge: Harvard University Press, 2008).

128. Robert Bennet Forbes to Rose Forbes, February 27, 1839, in Forbes, *Letters*, 98–99.

129. Li Chen, "Law as the Decoding Machine and Cultural Translation for Colonial Control: Staunton's *Ta Tsing Leu Lee* and Its Historical Legacy." American Association for Chinese Studies, www.google.com/search?client=safari&rls=en&q=Chen,+%22Law +as+the+Decoding+Machine%22&ie=UTF-8&oe=UTF-8, 13–14; Benjamin H. Williams, "The Protection of American Citizens in China: Extraterritoriality," *American Journal of International Law*, 16, no. 1 (January 1922), 43.

130. Shaw, *Journals*, 235; Li Chen, "Law, Empire, and Historiography of Modern Sino-Western Relations: A Case Study of the 'Lady Hughes' Controversy in 1784," *Law and History Review*, 27, no. 1 (Spring 2009): 1–53.

131. Teemu Ruskola, "Canton Is Not Boston: The Invention of American Imperial Sovereignty," *American Quarterly*, 57, no. 3 (September 2005): 859–884.

132. Foster, *American Diplomacy*, 40; H. B. Morse, *Britain and the China Trade, 1635–1842* (London: Routledge, 1940), 4:11–12; [Anon.], "Execution of an Italian at Canton," *North American Review*, 40, no. 86 (January 1835): 58–59.

133. Fanning, *Voyages*, 252–253.

134. The Wabash Affair in 1817 confirmed the "servile" nature of the American position. Earl Swisher, "Extraterritoriality and the Wabash Case," *American Journal of International Law*, 45, no. 3 (July 1951): 564–571.

135. Foster, *American Diplomacy*, 40–41; John Francis Davis, *The Chinese: A General Description of the Empire of China and Its Inhabitants*. 2 vols. (London, 1836); Samuel Wells Williams and Frederick Wells Williams, *A History of China, being the Historical Chapters from "The Middle Kingdom"* (London, 1897); Karl Friedrich Gützlaff, *A Sketch of Chinese History, Ancient and Modern Comprising a Retrospect of the Foreign Intercourse and Trade with China* (London, 1834), 2:267; *Congressional Globe*, December 17, 1840, 9–52.

136. Ruskola, "Canton Is Not Boston," 866.

137. S. Wells Williams and Frederick Wells Williams, *A History of China* (London: Sampson Low, Marston, 1897), 108.

138. "Relations between the United States of America and China: consuls at Canton; narrative of the Empress, the first American ship which visited this port; trial of Terranova; treatment of national ships," *Chinese Repository* (Canton, 1837): 218–231.

139. "Execution of an Italian at Canton," 59–63. See n133.

140. Jonathan Goldstein, "A Clash of Civilizations in the Pearl River Delta: Stephen Girard's Trade with China—1787–1824," in Van Dyke, *Americans and Macao*, 25–26, 29.

141. Ruskola, "Canton Is Not Boston," 866.

142. Marisa J. Fuentes, *Dispossessed Lives: Enslaved Women, Violence, and the Archive* (Philadelphia: University of Pennsylvania Press, 2016).

143. Fuentes, *Dispossessed Lives*; Michel-Rolph Trouillot, *Silencing the Past: Power and the Production of History* (Boston: Beacon, 2015); Lisa Lowe, *The Intimacies of Four Continents* (Durham, NC: Duke University Press, 2015).

144. Rebecca Solnit, foreword to *Call Them by Their True Names: American Crises* (Chicago: Haymarket, 2018).

145. Munroe, "Daily Life," 126, 133.

146. Munroe, "Daily Life," 133.

147. Natalia Molina, *How Race Is Made in America: Immigration, Citizenship, and the Historical Power of Racial Scripts* (Berkeley: University of California Press, 2014), 6, 22.

148. Rev. of Etsuko Taketani, *U.S. Women Writers and the Discourses of Colonialism, 1825–1861* (Knoxville: University of Tennessee Press, 2003) by Jeanne Boydston, *Journal of American History*, 91, no. 2 (September 2004): 623–624.

149. Henk Driessen, "Mediterranean Port Cities: Cosmopolitanism Reconsidered," *History and Anthropology*, 16, no. 1 (March 2005), 130–134.

150. Isaac Land, "Antagonistic Tolerance and Other Port Town Paradoxes," *Forum Navale*, 72 (2016): 83.

Chapter 4 • Hindoos and Fakirs in India

1. Charles Storrow, *Journal*, 98–99, Storrow Family Papers, Massachusetts Historical Society (MHS), Boston.

2. *Orient* was a term originally intended to designate what we call the Middle East, but geographers and travelers extended it to include the Indian Ocean and beyond.

3. Osterhammel, *Unfabling the Orient*, 196–197.

4. Sugata Bose, *A Hundred Horizons: The Indian Ocean in the Age of Global Empire* (Cambridge: Harvard University Press, 2006), 15.

5. Bean, *Yankee India*, 268; Verney, "Souls," 402, 408; Ditz, "Shipwrecked," 51–80; Hannah to son Thomas Smith, 24 [January?] 1816, Smith Papers, MHS.

6. G. Bhagat, *Americans in India, 1784–1860* (New York: New York University Press. 1970), 5, 28; Bean, *Yankee India*, 17; *Salem Gazette*, June 2, 1789.

7. Giancarlo Casale, "The Ottoman 'Discovery' of the Indian Ocean in the Sixteenth Century," in *Seascapes: Maritime Histories, Littoral Cultures, and Transoceanic Exchanges*, ed. Jerry H. Bentley, Renate Bridenthal, and Karen Wigen (Honolulu: University of Hawai'i Press, 2007); I. C. Campbell, *A History of the Pacific Islands* (Berkeley: University of California Press, 1989), 7; Sunil S. Amrith, *Crossing the Bay of Bengal: The Furies of Nature and the Fortunes of Migrants* (Cambridge: Harvard University Press, 2013), 18–24; William Milburn, *Oriental Commerce; containing a Geographical Description of the Principal Places in the East Indies, China, and Japan* (London, 1811), 1:157, 329.

8. Gordinier, "Case Study," 101; Thornton, *Bowditch*, 36–41.

9. As Gordinier observes, "In fact, this pattern of carrying specie to India was so strong that for every dollar's worth of merchandise shipped to India, American merchants shipped six dollars' worth of specie between 1802 and 1806. Gordinier, "Taking an Observation," 155; Delano, *Narrative*, 221; Elting, "Notebook."

10. Benjamin Carpenter, "Journal of a Voyage in the Ship HERCULES: Commanded by Capt. Benjamin Carpenter," in Paine, *Ships and Sailors of Old Salem*, 417.

11. Delano, *Narrative*, 221.

12. Carpenter, "Journal" [ca. May 14, 1792]; Bean, *Yankee India*, 143–144.

13. Delano, *Narrative*, 15–16.

14. Bean, *Yankee India*, 93.

15. William Augustus Rogers, "Journal containing Remarks & Observations during a Voyage to INDIA A.D. 1817–18," M656 1817T4, Phillips Library, Peabody Essex Museum, Salem, MA; Bean, *Yankee India*, 144.

16. Bean, *Yankee India*, 156.

17. Rediker, *Devil*, passim; Marcus Rediker and Peter Linbaugh, *The Many-Headed Hydra: Sailors, Slaves, Commoners, and the Hidden History of the Revolutionary Atlantic* (Boston: Beacon Press, 2000); Marcus Rediker, "A Motley Crew for our Times? Multiracial Mobs, History from Below and the Memory of Struggle," *Radical Philosophy*, 2, no. 7 (Spring 2020), www.radicalphilosophy.com/interview/a-motley-crew-for-our-times.

18. Thomas Farel Heffernan, *Mutiny on the Globe: The Fatal Voyage of Samuel Comstock* (New York: Penguin, 2002); Paul A. Gilje, *Liberty on the Waterfront: American Maritime Culture in the Age of Revolution* (Philadelphia: University of Pennsylvania, 2004), 86–92; Hester Blum, *The View from the Masthead: Maritime Imagination and Antebellum American Sea Narratives* (Chapel Hill: University of North Carolina Press, 2008), 34–35; Rediker, *Devil*, 227–229.

19. Thomas N. Layton, *The Voyage of the 'Frolic': New England Merchants and the Opium Trade* (Stanford, CA: Stanford University Press, 1997), 137.

20. Sullivan Dorr to Joseph Dorr and John Dorr, Canton, December 12, 1799, "Letters from Sullivan Dorr," 201; Thornton, *Bowditch*, 52; W. Jeffrey Bolster, *Black Jacks: African American Seamen in the Age of Sail* (Cambridge: Harvard University Press, 1997).

21. Drinker, Private *Journal*, 59–60; [Anon.], "Philadelphia Quaker, Soldier of Fortune."

22. Drinker, *Journal* 68.

23. Drinker, 67.

24. Drinker, 67.

25. Drinker, 66.

26. Drinker, 63.

27. William Marsden, *The History of Sumatra*, 2nd ed. (London, 1784), 19.

28. Bean, *Yankee India*, 157.

29. Layton, *Voyage*, 80.

30. George W. Johnson, *The Stranger in India; or, Three Years in Calcutta* (London: Henry Colburn, 1843), 1:5.

31. Bean, *Yankee India*, 110.

32. White, *Voyage*, 213.

33. Harriett Low, *Lights and Shadows of a Macao Life: The Journal of Harriett Low, Travelling Spinster*, ed. Nan Hodges and Arthur William Hummel (Woodinville, WA: History Bank, 2002), 45.

34. Fanning, *Voyages*, 277.

35. William Augustus Rogers, "Journal of the *Tartar*, from Boston to Bombay," January 31, 1818, Log 935, Ship *Tartar*, Phillips Library, Peabody Essex Museum, Rowley, MA.

36. Rogers, June 3, 1818.

37. Rogers, January 23, 1818.

38. Storrow, *Journal*, September 15, 1861.

39. Lawrence Waters Jenkins, *Bryant Parrott Tilden of Salem, at a Chinese Dinner Party, Canton: 1819* (Princeton, NJ: Princeton University Press, 1944), 9.

40. Delano, *Narrative*, 100.

41. Bean, *Yankee India*, 157; Milburn, *Oriental Commerce*, 1:169.

42. Milburn, *Oriental Commerce*, 1:321

43. Bean, *Yankee India*, 145.

44. Milburn, *Oriental Commerce*, 1:366.

45. White, *Voyage* 32.

46. Marsden, *History of Sumatra*, 19.

47. Johnson, *Stranger in India*, 27.

48. William Scollay, "Travel Journal, 1811–1812," November 14, 1811, Jacob Bigelow papers, ms. N-1841, Massachusetts Historical Society; Karen Ordahl Kupperman, "Fear of Hot Climates in the Anglo-American Colonial Experience," *William and Mary Quarterly*, 41, no. 2 (April 1984): 213–240.

49. Carpenter, "Journal," August 17, 1793.

50. Bhagat, *Americans in India*, 4.

51. Bean, *Yankee India*, 51.

52. Storrow, *Journal*, September 9–10, 1861, 96. Fears of "intemperate climates" and their role in disease and death had been longstanding within colonial America culture. See, for instance, Kupperman, "Fear," 213–240.

53. Bean, *Yankee India*, 100.

54. Verney, "Souls," 415.

55. George Granville Putnam, *Salem Vessels and Their Voyages* (Salem: Essex Institute, 1924), ser. 2, 10.

56. Delano, *Narrative*, 231.

57. John Crowninshield, "Journal of Capt. John Crowninshield at Calcutta, 1797–1798, When Master of the Ship "Belisarius," *Essex Institute Historical Collections*, 81, no. 18 (1945): 363.

58. Rediker, *Devil*, 41.

59. Johnson, *Stranger in India*, 70–73, 79.

60. Bean, *Yankee India*, 113–114.

61. Delano, *Narrative*, 215.

62. Amrith, *Crossing the Bay of Bengal*, 5, 8, 10, 13. *Monsoon* derives from the word *mawsim*, the Arabian term for season.

63. James D. Knowles, *Memoir of Mrs. Ann H. Judson* (London, 1849), 45, 53.

64. Bean, *Yankee India*, 109; Gordinier, "Reaper,"155.

65. Bean, *Yankee India*, 109; Gordinier, "Early American Trade," 155.

66. Delano, *Narrative*, 235.

67. Knowles, *Memoir of Mrs. Ann H. Judson*, 53.

68. Johnson, *Stranger in India*, 23.

69. Gordinier, "Early American Trade," 155.

70. Gordinier, 159.

71. Putnam, *Salem Vessels*, series 2, 10.

72. [Artist Unknown], "*Surf Boat Landing European Passengers at Madras [Chennai]*, ca. 1800, Royal Museums Greenwich; Thomas and William Daniell, *South East View of Fort St. George, Madras*, 1797, The British Library; William Daniell, *Madras, or Fort St. George, in the Bay of Bengal—A Squall Passing Off*, 1833, Yale Center for British Art.

73. Bean, *Yankee India*, 100.

74. Bean, 231.

75. Johnson, *Stranger in India*, 24.

76. Thornton, *Bowditch*, 42–43.

77. Crowninshield, "Journal," 255.

78. Scollay, "Travel Journal," November 17, 1811, 11–16.

79. Storrow, *Journal*, 92–93.

80. Bean, *Yankee India*, 231.

81. Verney, "Souls," 425.

82. Scollay, "Travel Journal," November 21, 1811.

83. Scollay, November 21, 1811.

84. Scollay, November 21, 1811.

85. Verney, "Souls," 425.

86. See also Bean, *Yankee India*, 156.

87. Called also *Sri Pada* in Singhalese. Rogers, "Journal of the *Tartar*," January 23, 1818; Milburn, *Oriental Commerce*, 1:336.

88. Johnson, *Stranger in India*, 51.

89. Knowles, *Memoir of Mrs. Ann H. Judson*, 55.

90. See also Bean, *Yankee India*, 156.

91. See also Bean, 156.

92. Storrow, *Journal*, September 15, 1861, 99.

93. Storrow, September 18, 1861, 103.

94. Bean, *Yankee India*, 52.

95. Bean, 49.

96. In 1843, Johnson was defining *dinghy* as "a native boat or canoe" for his English readers. Johnson, *Stranger in India*, 28; Milburn, *Oriental Commerce*, 1:329.

97. Carpenter, "Journal," June 7, 1793.

98. Carpenter, "Journal," July 10 and August 13, 1793.

99. Johnson, *Stranger in India*, 32.

100. Rogers, "Journal of the *Tartar*," January 23, 1818.

101. Scollay, "Travel Journal," November 17, 1811. That we do not know what the people of Nicobar thought of Scollay and his cohort illustrates the problem of the archives described by Marisa J. Fuentes in *Dispossessed Lives: Enslaved Women, Violence, and the Archive* (Philadelphia: University of Pennsylvania Press, 2016). The selective nature of collecting papers, privileging one point of view, prevents us from developing a balanced and authentic sense of early American encounters in the East.

102. Scollay, "Travel Journal," November 15, 1811.

103. Johnson, *Stranger in India*, 31–32.

104. Scollay, "Travel Journal," November 18, 1811.

105. His efforts to find these officials were, at least, more succesful than were his efforts to make contact with the banian at the port of Aden some months earlier. Gordinier, "Case Study," 102; Bean, *Yankee India*, 51.

106. Bean, *Yankee India*, 156.

107. Bean, 99.

108. John Crowninshield, "Journal at Calcutta, 1797–1798," ed. Edward Daland Lovejoy, *Essex Institute Historical Collections*, 81 (October 1945), 355.

109. Cleveland, 118.

110. Gordinier, "Reaper," 102.

111. Carpenter, in Bean, *Yankee India*, 51.

112. Sheila Collingwood-Whittick, ed., *The Pain of Unbelonging: Alienation and Identity in Australasian Literature* (Amsterdam: Rodopi, 2007), xiii–xliii.

113. Captain Dudley Pickman, *Belisarius*, 1799–1800, in Bean, *Yankee India*, 102.

114. Collingwood-Whittick, *Pain of Unbelonging*, xiii–xliii; Peter Jackson, "The Cultural Politics of Masculinity: Towards a Social Geography," *Transactions of the Institute of British Geographers*, 16, no. 2 (1991): 199–213; Michael Pearson, *The Indian Ocean* (London: Routledge, 2003), 32; Henk Driessen, "Mediterranean Port Cities: Cosmopolitanism Reconsidered," *History and Anthropology*, 16, no. 1 (March 2005), 130, 131, 134; Land, "Tolerance," 78–101.

115. Scollay, "Travel Journal," November 24, 1811. Ann Judson shared Scollay's experience, writing, "It was with considerable fear I rode, as the streets were full of natives and English carriages." Knowles, *Memoir of Mrs. Ann H. Judson*, 53.

116. A few Yankee expatriates did comment on the wrenching poverty they found in India but showed no inclination to address it. See, for instance, Delano, *Narrative*, 239. Ann Laura Stoler and Frederick Cooper, "Liberal Strategies of Exclusion," *Tensions of Empire: Colonial Cultures in a Bourgeois World*, ed. Frederick Cooper and Ann Laura Stoler (Berkeley: University of California Press, 1997: 59–86.

117. Bhagat, *Americans in India*, 6–8.

118. Gordinier, "Reaper," 156.

119. Bean, *Yankee India*, 11, 50–59.

120. Bean, 89.

121. Gordinier, "Reaper," 157.

122. Delano, *Narrative*, 211, 248.

123. Bhagat, *Americans in India*, viii–x; K. N. Chaudhury, *The Trading World of Asia and the English East India Company, 1660–1760* (New York: Cambridge University Press, 1978); Walvin, *Fruits of Empire*; Bean, *Yankee India*; P. J. Marshall, *The Making and Unmaking of Empires: Britain, India, and America, c. 1750–1783* (New York: Oxford University Press, 2005); Emily Erikson and Peter Bearman, "Malfeasance and the Foundations for Global Trade: The Structure of English Trade in the East Indies, 1601–1833," *American Journal of Sociology*, 112, no. 1 (July 2006): 195–230; Stanley Wolpert, *A New History of India*, 8th ed. (New York: Oxford University Press, 2009); Benjamin L. Carp, *Defiance of the Patriots: The Boston Tea Party and the Making of America* (New Haven, CT: Yale University Press, 2010); Greene, *Evaluating Empire*; Margaret R. Hunt and Phillip J. Stern, eds., *The English East India Company at the Height of Mughal Expansion: A Soldier's Diary of the 1689 Siege of Bombay, with Related Documents* (New York: Bedford/St. Martin's, 2016); William Dalrymple, *The Anarchy: The East India Company, Corporate Violence, and the Pillage of an Empire* (London: Bloomsbury, 2019).

124. Dalrymple, *Anarchy*, 216.

125. Bean, *Yankee India*, 128; Bhagat, *Americans in India*, 115.

126. Marshall, *Making and Unmaking of Empires*, 228–230.

127. Bean, *Yankee India*, 61.

128. Gordinier, "Reaper," 157.

129. Gordinier, 156; Verney, "Souls," 408.

130. Bean, *Yankee India*, 51.

131. Bean, 111–112.

132. Bean, 102.

133. Crowninshield, "Journal," 356, 359.

134. Bean, *Yankee India*, 51.

135. Bean, 72, quoted in Verney, "Souls," 409.

136. Crowninshield, "Journal," 372.

137. Bean, *Yankee India*, 268.

138. Robert G. Albion, William A. Baker, and Benjamin W. Labaree, *New England and the Sea* (Mystic, CT: Mystic Seaport Museum, 1972), 59; Bhagat, *Americans in India*, 9.

139. Bean, *Yankee India*, 99.

140. Bean, 166.

141. Bean, 102.

142. Kendi, *Stamped*, 94–95, 98–99.

143. Bean, *Yankee India*, 51–52.

144. Bean, 106.

145. Dorothy B. Jones, *The Portrayal of China and India on the American Screen, 1896–1955* (Cambridge, MA: MIT Press, 1955); Anand A. Yang, "Images of Asia: A Passage through Fiction and Film," *History Teacher*, 13, no. 3 (May 1980): 351–369; R. P. Peerenboom, "The Rational American and the Inscrutable Oriental as Seen from the Perspective of a Puzzled European: A Review (And Response) in Three Stereotypes: A Reply to Carine Defoort," *Philosophy East and West*, 44, no. 2 (April 1994): 368–379; Kiara Szmańko, *Invisibility in African American and Asian American Literature: A Comparative Study* (Jefferson, NC: McFarland, 2008), 96.

146. Johnson, *Stranger in India*, 13; Verney, "Souls," 425.

147. Porter, *Journal*, 25.

148. Bruce Scates, "'We Are Not . . . [A]boriginal . . . We Are Australian'": William Lane, Racism, and the Construction of Aboriginality," *Labour History*, 72 (May 1997): 35–49; Leith Mullings, "Interrogating Racism: Toward an Antiracist Anthropology," *Annual Review of Anthropology*, 34 (2005): 667–693; Vijay Mishra, "Race, Speight, and the Crisis In Fiji, in *Coup: Reflections on the Political Crisis in Fiji*, ed. Brij V. Lal, and Michael Pretes (Canberra, Australia: ANU E Press, 2008).

149. Bean, *Yankee India*, 53.

150. Bean, 52.

151. Regarding currency exhanges in India, Gordinier observes, "In fact, this pattern of carrying specie to India was so strong that for every dollar's worth of merchandise shipped to India, American merchants shipped six dollars' worth of specie between 1802 and 1806." Gordinier, "Reaper," 155.

152. Bean, *Yankee India*, 164.

153. Crowninshield, "Journal," 356.

154. Thornton, *Bowditch*, 38.

155. Carpenter, "Journal," May 5 and June 7, 1793; Bean, *Yankee India*, 51.

156. Bean, *Yankee India*, 97.

157. Jason E. Pierce, *Making the White Man's West: Whiteness and the Creation of the American West* (Boulder: University Press of Colorado, 2016), 51–52; Bean, *Yankee India*, 228.

158. Joseph J. Ondishko Jr., "A View of Anxiety, Fear and Panic," *Military Affairs*, 36, no. 2 (April 1972): 58–60.

159. Bean, *Yankee India*, 164–165.

160. Bean, 117, 268; Michael J. Altman, *Heathen, Hindoo, Hindu: American Representations of India, 1721–1893* (New York: Oxford University Press, 2017).

161. Verney, "Souls," 422.

162. Bean, *Yankee India*, 189.

163. Bean, 190.

164. Bean, 115–116.

165. Bean, 164–165.

166. Bean, 165.

167. Bean, *Yankee India*, 165.

168. Bean, 165.

169. Merchants such as Crowninshield had little use for the India missions. Bhagat, *Americans in India*, 115–116.

170. Samuel Newell, *Memoirs of Mrs. Harriet Newell: Wife of the Rev. Samuel Newell, Missionary to India, who Died at the Isle of France, Nov. 30, 1812, Aged 19 Years* (1814). Reverand Newell died in 1821 of cholera contracted at Tannah.

171. Conroy-Krutz, Christian *Imperialism*, 4.

172. The British EIC held "strong prejudices" against missionaries of any nationality or sect, and famously refused passage to China in 1806 for Robert Morrison, who had to board a ship in New York; even when he arrived in Canton in September 1897, he was refused residence in the British factory. Platt, *Twilight*, 90–91.

173. Conroy-Krutz, Christian *Imperialism*, xiv, 61; Verney, "Souls," 421.

174. Verney, "Souls," 424, 401; Conroy-Krutz, Christian *Imperialism*, xiv, 4, 32.

175. Verney, "Souls," 397–431.

176. Conroy-Krutz, Christian *Imperialism*, 22.

177. Ann Hasseltine Judson, "Address to Females in America Relative to the Situation of Heathen Females of the East," in *Baptist Magazine for 1840*, ser. 4, vol. 3, no. 32 (1840), 39.

178. Verney, "Souls," 324.

179. Knowles, *Memoir of Mrs. Ann H. Judson*, 54.

180. Knowles, 54; Verney, "Souls," 324.

181. Knowles, *Memoir of Mrs. Ann H. Judson*, 55.

182. Verney "Souls," 422.

183. Knowles, *Memoir of Mrs. Ann H. Judson*, 53.

184. Conroy-Krutz, Christian *Imperialism*, 80.

185. Conroy- Krutz, Christian *Imperialism*, 81.

186. Conroy-Krutz, 81.

187. Kate Teltsher, "India/Calcutta: City of Palaces and Dreadful Night," in *The Cambridge Companion to Travel Writing*, ed. Peter Hulme and Tim Youngs (Cambridge, UK: Cambridge University Press, 2002), 191.

188. Bean, *Yankee India*, 145–146.

189. Mary Louise Pratt, *Imperial Eyes: Travel Writing and Transculturation* (London: Routledge, 1992), 7.

190. Dalrymple, *Anarchy*, xxix.

191. John Quincy Adams Diary Digital Project, December 23, 1817, MHS, www.mass hist.org/publications/jqadiaries/index.php.

192. Richard J[effry] Cleveland, *A Narrative of Voyages and Commercial Enterprises* (Cambridge: John Owen, 1842), 1:108–112.

193. Bean, *Yankee India*, 165.

194. Bidisha Chakraborty, "Construction of Drains for a Healthier City," in *Calcutta in the Nineteenth Century: An Archival Exploration*, ed. Bidisha Chakraborty and Sarmistha De (New Delhi: Niyogi, 2014), 238–247; Bidisha Chakraborty, "Pollution of the Circular Canal," in Chakraborty and De *Calcutta in the Nineteenth Century*, 265–269.

195. Peter A. Carmichael, "The Sense of Ugliness," *Journal of Aesthetics and Art Criticism*. 30, no. 4 (Summer 1972), 496.

196. Quoted in McMahon, "Fear," 5–6.

197. Amina Marzouk Chouchene, review of Harald Fischer-Tiné, *Anxieties, Fear, and Panic in Colonial Settings: Empires on the Verge of a Nervous Breakdown* (Houndmills, UK: Palgrave Macmillan, 2016), in *Imperial and Global Forum* (blog of the Centre for Imperial and Global History at the University of Exeter), August 28, 2019, https://imperialglobalexeter.com/2019/08/28/anxieties-fear-and-panic-in-colonial -settings.

198. *Captain Cook's Three Voyages* (Boston, 1797), 218.

199. Molina, How *Race is Made*, 1–6; Chouchene, review of *Anxieties, Fear, and Panic.*

200. Stephen S. Bush, "Horribly Wrong: Moral Disgust and Killing," *Journal of Religious Ethics*, 41, no. 4 (December 2013): 585–600.

201. Jeffrey Stout, "Abominations," *Soundings: An Interdisciplinary Journal*, 66, no. 1 (Spring 1983), 8.

202. Stout, "Abominations," 5.

203. Strout, 10.

Chapter 5 • Cannibal Isles

1. The indigenous peoples who participated in the Deerfield raid included Kanienkehaka (Mohawk), Wendat (Huron) and Wôbanaki warriors. Colin Calloway, ed., *After King Philip's War: Presence and Persistence in Indian New England* (Hanover, NH: University Press of New England, 1997); Evan Haefeli and Kevin Sweeney, *Captors and Captives: The 1704 French and Indian Raid on Deerfield* (Amherst, MA: University of Massachusetts Press, 2003). The original plate of "a war-canoe of the savages in the South Seas" appeared in the *Gentleman's Magazine*, September 1773, 432, and included a drawing of a branch of a breadfruit tree. Caroline Frank, "New England and the World," *Historic Deerfield*, 17 (Autumn 2018): 6.

2. Thank you to curator Anne Bentley at the Massachusetts Historical Society for bringing this artifact to my attention. A rich literature in maritime World History undergirds the "exotic" material culture of the South Seas, including Tonio Andrade and Xing Hang, eds., *Sea Rovers, Silver, and Samurai: Maritime East Asia in Global History, 1550–1700* (Honolulu: University of Hawai'i Press, 2016); Jerry H. Bentley, Renate Bridenthal, and Karen Wigen, *Seascapes: Maritime Histories, Littoral Cultures, and Transoceanic Exchanges* (Honolulu: University of Hawai'i Press, 2007); Campbell, *History of the Pacific Islands*; Ryan Dominic Crewe, "Pacific Purgatory: Spanish Dominicans, Chinese Sangleys, and the Entanglement of Mission and Commerce in Manila, 1580–1620," *Journal of Early Modern History*, 19 (2015): 337–365; Ernest S. Dodge, *Europe and the World in the Age of Expansion*, vol. 7., *Islands and Empires: Western Impact on the Pacific and East Asia* (Minneapolis: University of Minnesota Press, 1976); Fernández-Armesto, *Pathfinders*; Anna Jackson and Amin Jaffer, eds., *Encounters: The Meeting of Asia and Europe, 1500–1800* (London: V & A, 2004); Brian Rouleau, *With Sails Whitening Every Sea: Mariners and the Making of an American Maritime Empire* (Ithaca, NY: Cornell University Press, 2014); Paulo Jorge de Sousa Pinto, "Manila, Macao and Chinese Networks in South China Sea: Adaptive Strategies of Cooperation and Survival (Sixteenth-to-Seventeenth Centuries)," *Anais de História de Além-Mar*, 15 (2014): 79–100; and Joan-Pau Rubiés and Manel Ollé, "The Comparative History of a Genre: The Production and Circulation of Books on Travel and Ethnog-

raphies in Early Modern Europe and China," *Modern Asian Studies* (August 2015): 1–51.

3. Edmund Roberts wrote of Sumatra as a "part of India." Edmund Roberts, *Embassy to the Eastern Courts of Cochin-China, Siam, and Muscat; in the U.S. Sloop-of-War Peacock . . . during the Years 1832-3-4* (New York: Harper, 1337), 37.

4. Margaret Jolly and Serge Tcherkézoff, "Oceanic Encounters: A Prelude," in *Oceanic Encounters: Exchange, Desire, Violence,* ed. Margaret Jolly, Serge Tcherkézoff, and Darrell Tryon (Canberra: Australian National University E Press, 2009), 3.

5. Bhagat, *Americans in India,* 42–43.

6. For background, see Anne Salmond, *The Trial of the Cannibal Dog: Captain Cook in the South Seas* (London: Penguin, 2003); Anne Salmond, *Aphrodite's Island: The European Discovery of Tahiti;* and Anne Salmond, *Tears of Rangi: Experiments Across Worlds* (Auckland, NZ: University of Auckland Press, 2017).

7. Steven Hooper identifies objects that carry more currency within Fijian society—barkcloth and whale teeth. Steven Hooper, *Fiji: Art & Life in the Pacific* (Norwich, UK: Sainsbury, 2016), 17.

8. Delano, *Narrative,* 394.

9. Cited in Hooper, *Fiji,* 19.

10. John Richards Child, *Journal,* April 1811.

11. Nathaniel Philbrick, *The Heart of the Sea* (New York: Penguin, 2001), 95–97.

12. [James Oliver], *Wreck of the Glide, with Recollections of the Fijis, and of Wallis Island* (New York: Wiley & Putnam, 1848), 17.

13. Christina Thompson, *Sea Peoples: The Puzzle of Polynesia* (New York: Harper-Collins, 2019), 11.

14. William B. Ardiff, "The Ship *Putnam,*" *Essex Institute Historical Collections,* 96, no. 25 (1960): 126–130.

15. Oceanic peoples employed a variety of names to identify Western explorers and traders, including *haole, papalangi, popa´ a, waet* man, and *salsaliri.* Jolly and Tcherkézoff, "Oceanic Encounters," 17.

16. John B. Williams, *The New Zealand Journal, 1842–1844, of John B. Williams,* ed. Robert W. Kenny (Salem, MA: Peabody Museum of Salem, 1956), 32.

17. I. C. Campbell, *"Gone Native" in Polynesia* (Westport, CT: Greenwood, 1998); Caroline Ralston, *Grass Huts and Warehouses: Pacific Beach Communities of the Nineteenth Century* (St. Lucia, Australia: University of Queensland Press, 2014).

18. On the porous boundaries between fictional and authentic Pacific Ocean travelogues, see Jolly and Tcherkézoff, "Oceanic Encounters," 4–9.

19. Bronwen Douglas and Chris Ballard, "Race, Place and Civilisation: Colonial Encounters and Governance in Greater Oceania," *Journal of Pacific History,* 47, no. 3, Race, Place and Governance in Greater Oceania (September 2012), 247.

20. Library Company, *Catalogue.*

21. Mary Wallis, *Life in Feejee, or, Five Years among the Cannibals* (Boston, 1851), iv.

22. Several news journals, as well as Salem diarist William Bentley, recorded Derby's death: *The Diary of William Bentley* (Salem, MA: Essex Institute, 1911), 3:17; Amos Porter, *The China Journal of Amos Porter, 1802–1803* (Greensboro, VT: Greensboro Historical Society, 1984), 27; and Samuel Eliot Morison, "Boston Traders in the Hawaiian Islands," *Proceedings of the Massachusetts Historical Society* (1920): 170n12.

23. William C. Hunter, *The 'Fan Kwae' before Treaty Days, 1825–1844* (London, 1882), 13.

24. Bean, Yankee *India*, 141.

25. Delano, *Narrative*, 26, 35; R. Michael Feener, "'Abd al-Samad in Arabia: The Yemeni Years of a Shaykh from Sumatra," *Southeast Asian Studies*, 4 (August 2015): 259–277.

26. Nathaniel Bowditch, *Early American Philippines Trade: The Journal of Nathaniel Bowditch in Manila, 1796*, ed. Thomas R. McHale and Mary C. McHale, Southeast Asia Studies, monograph series no. 2 (New Haven, CT: Yale University, 1962), 26.

27. Personal communication, Dr. Michael Feener, July 17, 2009. See also Daniel Abdrew Birchok, "Sojourning on Mecca's Verandah: Place, Temporality, and Islam in an Indonesian Province" (PhD diss., University of Michigan, 2013), 95–96.

28. C. Toogood Downing, *The Fan-Qui in China in 1636–1637* (New York: Barnes & Noble, 1972), 1:188–189.

29. Low, *Journal*, Wednesday, August 26, 1829.

30. Bowditch, *Journal*, 41; Tamara Plakins Thornton, *Nathaniel Bowditch and the Power of Numbers: How a Nineteenth-Century Man of Business, Science, and the Sea Changed American Life* (Chapel Hill: University of North Carolina Press, 2016), 45, 52.

31. A sampling of seminal studies that examine motivations for and the nature of overseas encounters in world history would include Bentley, *Seascapes*; Sebastian Conrad, *What Is Global History?* (Princeton, NJ: Princeton University Press, 2016); Alan Karras and Laura J. Mitchell, *Encounters Old and New in World History: Essays Inspired by Jerry H. Bentley* (Honolulu: University of Hawai'i Press, 2017); Huw Lewis-Jones and Kari Herbert, *Explorers' Sketchbooks: The Art of Discovery & Adventure* (London: Thames & Hudson, 2016); Lowe, *Intimacies*; P. J. Marshall and Glyn Williams, *The Great Map of Mankind: Perceptions of New Worlds in the Age of Enlightenment* (Cambridge: Harvard University Press, 1982); Mary Louise Pratt, *Imperial Eyes: Travel Writing and Transculturation* (London: Routledge, 1992); Sonja Schillings, *Enemies of All Humankind: Fictions of Legitimate Violence* (Hanover, NH: Dartmouth College Press, 2017); Benjamin Schmidt, *Inventing Exoticism: Geography, Globalism, and Europe's Early Modern World* (Philadelphia: University of Pennsylvania Press, 2015); and Larry Stewart, "Global Pillage: Science, Commerce, and Empire," in *The Cambridge History of Science*, vol. 4, *Eighteenth-Century Science*, ed. Roy Porter (Cambridge: Cambridge University Press, 2003), 825–44.

32. Delano, *Narrative*, 421–422.

33. Phillips, *Pepper and Pirates*, chap. 1; Corn, *Scents of Eden*, 231–241.

34. Delano, *Narrative*, 83.

35. Jedidiah Morse, *Geography Made Easy* (New Haven, CT: Meigs, Bowen, 1784), 201.

36. As Amasa Delano fashioned himself on an 1803 cruise "to the South Sea." Delano, *Narrative*, 423.

37. Margaret E. Schotte, *Sailing School: Navigating Science and Skill, 1550–1800* (Baltimore, MD: Johns Hopkins University Press, 2019), 6–9.

38. Delano, *Narrative*, 421–422.

39. As Katrina Gulliver observes, "Littered with wrecks, the Southern Ocean contains the point on the globe farthest from any land rescue." The South Seas, to the

north, proved just as intimidating in the age of sail. Katrina Gulliver, "The Wildest Waters in the World," review of Joy McCann, *Wild Sea: A History of the Southern Ocean* (Chicago: University of Chicago Press, 2019), in *The Spectator*, June 8, 2019, www .spectator.com.au/2019/06/the-wildest-waters-in-the-world.

40. Thornton, *Bowditch*, 44.

41. Edmund Fanning, for instance, owned a copy of Delano's *Narrative*. On early debates over the location of Pacific islands, see Jolly and Tcherkézoff, "Oceanic Encounters," 4.

42. Thornton, *Bowditch*, 44.

43. William Barker, "A Chart of the World, according to Mercators Projection, shewing the latest Discoveries of Capt. Cook" (Philadelphia: Mathew Carey, 1796), 1978, folio 150, Beinecke Rare Book and Manuscript Library, Yale University Library.

44. William Herbert and Samuel Dunn, *A New Directory for the East Indies: Containing, I. The First Discoveries made in the East-Indies by European Voyagers with Directions for Sailing to and from the East-Indies*, 6th ed. (London: Gilbert and Wright, 1791).

45. H. M. Elmore, *The British mariner's directory and guide to the trade and navigation of the Indian and China seas. Containing Instructions for Navigating from Europe to India and China, and from Port to Port in those Regions, and Parts Adjacent: With an Account of the Trade, Mercantile Habits, Manners, and Customs of the Natives* (London, T. Bensley, 1802).

46. James Horsburgh, *Memoirs: Comprising the Navigation to and from China, by the China Sea, and through the various Straits and Channels in the Indian Archipelago; also, the Navigation of Bombay Harbour* (London: C. Mercier, 1805).

47. W. Spotswood and J. Nancrede published the first edition in Boston in 1797. John Malham, *The Naval Gazetteer: or, Seaman's Complete Guide. Containing a Full And Accurate Account, Alphabetically Arranged, of The Several Coasts of All the Countries and Islands in the Known World* (Boston, 1797), 1:76. On racial scripts, see Molina, *How Race Is Made*; and Natalia Molina, "Understanding Race as a Relational Concept," *Modern American History*, 1, no. 1 (March 2018): 100–105.

48. Milburn *Oriental Commerce*.

49. Bhagat, *India*, 39; Hawes, *Gulf*, 117.

50. Ingraham, *Journal*.

51. Tyng, *Before the Wind*, 14–16.

52. Delano, *Narrative*, 253–255.

53. A number of writers took pains to explain the origins of Eastern place names, but in ways that heightened the mystery and intrigue they sought to instill. Delano observed, "The island Tierra del Fuego takes its name from its formerly having been very noted for volcanoes, and I believe they burn on some part of it at this time." Delano, *Narrative*, 219.

54. Delano, 36–37.

55. Delano advised carrying two, one a check on the other, and Roberts found on one East Indies voyage, "our chronometers being useless." Delano, *Narrative*, 37; Roberts, *Embassy*, 46. Even officers of the British navy had to buy their own maps and charts in the 1800s. Michael T. Bravo, "Precision and Curiosity in Scientific Travel: James Rennell and the Orientalist Geography of the New Imperial Age (1760–1830),"

in Jaś Elsner and Joan-Paul Rubiés, eds., *Voyages & Visions: Towards a Cultural History of Travel* (London: Reaktion, 1999), 175.

56. Delano, *Narrative*, 37; Thompson, *Sea Peoples*, 10.

57. Peabody, *Logs*, 60–61.

58. Thornton, *Bowditch*, 45.

59. Delano, *Narrative*, 420–421.

60. Delano, 421.

61. Gabriel Franchère, *A Voyage to the Northwest Coast of America*, ed. Milo Milton Quaife (Chicago: Lakeside, 1954), 10–11.

62. Drinker, Private *Journal*, 3, 59–60.

63. Dodge, *Europe and the World*, 7; Paul W. Blank and Fred Spier, introduction to *Defining the Pacific: Opportunities and Constraints*, vol. 1 of *The Pacific World: Lands, Peoples, and History of the Pacific, 1500–1900*, ed. Paul W. Blank and Fred Spier (Aldershot, UK: Ashgate, 2002), xv; Matt K. Matsuda, *Pacific Worlds: A History of Seas, Peoples, and Cultures* (Cambridge: Cambridge University Press, 2012); John Gilbert, "Charting the Vast Pacific," in *The Encyclopedia of Discovery and Exploration: Pacific Voyages* (Garden City, NY: Doubleday, 1971), 169–202.

64. Ernest S. Dodge, *New England and the South Seas* (Cambridge, MA: Harvard University Press, 1965), 1–10.

65. Campbell, *Pacific Islands*, 11; Fernandez-Arnesto, *World*, 388.

66. Anthropologists, archaeologists, linguists, and others have made great contributions in revealing the prehistory of the peoples of the Pacific Ocean. See Ernest S. Dodge, "The American Sources for Pacific Ethnohistory Research," *Ethnohistory*, 15, no. 1 (Winter 1968): 1–10; Francis X. Hezel, "The Beginnings of Foreign Contact with Truk," *Journal of Pacific History*, 8 (1973): 51–73; Jolly and Tcherkézoff, "Oceanic Encounters," 1–2; Thompson, *Sea Peoples*.

67. Campbell, *Pacific Islands*, 34–39; Dodge, *Europe and the World*; Darrell Tryon, "Linguistic Encounter and Responses in the South Pacific," in Jolly and Tcherkézoff, "Oceanic Encounters," 37–55.

68. Alexander G, Ioannidis, Javier Blanco-Portillo, Karla Sandoval, Erika Hagelber, et al., "Native American Gene Flow into Polynesia Predating Easter Island Settlement," *Nature*, July 8, 2020.

69. Campbell, *Pacific Islands*, 28–29; Fernández-Armesto, *Pathfinders*, 43–46; Thompson, *Sea Peoples*, 8–9, 17–18.

70. Campbell, *Pacific Islands*, 41.

71. Thompson, *Sea Peoples*, 17.

72. Delano, *Narrative*, 70, 71, 82, 98, 312, 434.

73. Edmund Fanning, *Voyages to the South Seas, Indian and Pacific Oceans* (New York, 1838), 33, 42.

74. Fanning, *South Seas*, 37, 47.

75. Gulliver, "Wildest Waters."

76. Child, *Journal*, September 9 and October 6, 1811; Rediker, *Devil*, 1–3.

77. Drinker, *Journal*, April 27, 1838, 3–4.

78. Thomas Suárez, *Early Mapping of the Pacific: The Epic Story of Seafarers, Adventurers, and Catographers Who Mapped the Earth's Greatest Ocean* (Singapore: Periplus,, 2004).

79. Thompson, *Sea Peoples*, 42–43.

80. Fanning, *Voyages*, 228–236. Fanning had incautiously maneuvered his ship through a "route so entirely new and untraversed"; following the escape, he returned the ship to "the usual track of the Spanish manilla ships . . . a path so often sailed over, we were not in any probability likely to make any farther discoveries while on this passage."

81. Fanning, *Voyages*, 219–220.

82. Thompson, *Sea People*, 70.

83. Fanning, *Voyages*, 153.

84. Michael Block, "The Importance of the China Trade in American Exploration and Conquest of the Pacific, 1830–1850," in *Americans and Macao: Trade, Smuggling, and Diplomacy on the South China Coast*, ed. Paul A. Van Dyke (Aberdeen: Hong Kong University Press, 2012): 95–104.

85. Delano, *Narrative*, 58.

86. Delano, 102.

87. Delano, 430.

88. Oliver, *Wreck of the Glide*, 26–27.

89. Oliver, 27.

90. Barnard, *Narrative*, 256, 258.

91. David Wilma, "Graveyard of the Pacific: Shipwrecks on the Washington Coast," September 12, 2006, HistoryLink (website), www.historylink.org/File/7936.

92. As one survivor, ship's carpenter John Weeks, described: "After you had passed our boat, the breakers caused by the meeting of the wind roll and the ebb-tide became a great deal heavier than when we entered the river with the flood. The boat, for want of a rudder, became very hard to manage, and we let her drift at the mercy of the tide till, after having escaped several surges, one struck us midship and capsized." Franchère, *Voyage*, xx, 59; Fanning, *Voyages*; Alexander Ross, *Adventures of the First Settlers on the Oregon or Columbia River* (London: Smith, Elder, 1849); Alexander Begg, *History of British Columbia from Its Earliest Discovery to the Present Time* (Toronto: William Briggs, 1894); Magdalen Coughlin, "Commercial Foundations of Political Interest in the Opening Pacific, 1789–1829," *California Historical Quarterly*, 50, no. 1 (March 1971), 19.

93. Washington Irving, *Astoria; or, Anecdotes of an Enterprise Beyond the Rocky Mountains* (Philadelphia, 1836).

94. Even Thorn's defenders could not describe his assault on the Columbia bar as well-advised, as he had rejected repeated admonitions for caution. Franchère, *Voyage*, xxvii.

95. Franchère, 53.

96. Franchère, 55.

97. "Some natives visited us this day, bringing with them beaver skins; but the inquietude caused in our minds by the loss of two boats' crews, for whom we wished to make search, did not permit us to think of traffic." Franchère, 58.

98. Franchère, 62.

99. Delano, *Narrative*, 152.

100. Delano, 429.

101. Fanning, *Voyages*, 153.

102. Delano, *Narrative*, 97.

103. Delano, *Narrative*, 486.

104. Oliver, *Wreck of the Glide*, 27.

105. Marsden, *Sumatra*, 13–15.

106. Delano, *Narrative*, 58.

107. Delano, 101.

108. White, *Voyage*, 29–30, 57–58, 96, 114, 311–312.

109. William H. Goetzmann, *New Lands, New Men: America and the Second Great Age of Discovery* (New York: Viking, 1986); Helen M. Rozwadowski, *Fathoming the Ocean: The Discovery and Exploration of the Deep Sea* (Cambridge, MA: Harvard University Press, 2005).

110. Bravo, "Precision," 162–183.

111. Fanning, *Voyages*, 67.

112. White, *Voyage*, 29–30.

113. Marsden, *Sumatra*, 29.

114. Delano, *Narrative*, 39.

115. Fanning, *Voyages*, 39.

116. Fanning, 64–65.

117. Hunter, *Fan Kwae*, 9.

118. R. Gerard Ward, "The First Chart of Southwest Fiji, 1799," *Journal of Pacific History*, 42, no. 1 (June 2007): 99.

119. White, *Voyage*, 102–103. White described the formation of reefs as productions of "zoophytes, that compound of animal and vegetable life, whose incessant and rapid labours, and, as we are told by naturalists, whose polypus-like powers of receiving perfect form and vitality into numberless dismembered portions of their bodies, have long excited much curiosity and admiration." He was still a US Navy lieutenant in 1832 aboard the USS *Peacock*, his health apparently debilitated by East India service and drinking, but the vessel's captain was reluctant to relieve him of service because of his "great experience in the Indian Ocean and China Seas." Andrew C. A. Jampoler, *Embassy to the Eastern Courts: America's Secret First Pivot toward Asia, 1832–37* (Annapolis, MD: Naval Institute Press, 2015), 52.

120. White, *Voyage*, 98.

121. Delano, *Narrative*, 477. In fact, modern GPS places the site well inland.

122. It is not always clear in Fanning's book, *Voyages to the South Seas, Indian and Pacific Oceans*, whose words are being used. Fanning, *Voyages*, 34.

123. Judith Fingard, *Jack in Port: Sailortowns of Eastern Canada* (Toronto: University of Toronto Press, 1982.

124. Appleton, "Journal," 151; Charles H. Cotter, "Forum: John Hamilton Moore and Nathaniel Bowditch," *Journal of Navigation*, 30, no. 2 (May 1977): 323–326; Tamara Plakins Thornton, "The 'Intelligent Mariner': Nathaniel Bowditch, the Science of Navigation, and the Art of Upward Mobility in the Maritime World," *New England Quarterly*, 79, no. 4 (2006): 609–635. Sandwith Drinker purchased for his African servant, Juma, "an edition of Bowditch's Navigator, which is generally used by Americans, (in fact the English prefer it to their own publications, as being more correct)." Drinker, *Journal*, 67.

125. Lewis-Jones, *Explorers' Sketchbooks*, 12. Even with advanced navigational technology, the challenge of hidden shoals remains, seen in the loss of the minesweeper USS *Guardian* in the Philippines in 2013. Jason Smith, *To Master the Boundless Sea:*

The U.S. Navy, the Marine Environment, and the Cartography of Empire (Durham, NC: University of North Carolina Press, 2018), i.

126. John B. Sewell, *The Logbook of the Captain's Clerk*, edited by Arthur Powell Dudden (Chicago: Lakeside, 1995), 62.

127. Elting, *Notebook*.

128. *The Columbian Courier* (June 19, 1799) was one of many newspapers that carried the story.

129. Sullivan Dorr to Ebenezer Dorr, October 7, 1799.

130. Thornton, *Bowditch*, 44.

131. White, *Voyage*, 22–23.

132. Thornton, *Bowditch*, 45.

133. Delano, *Narrative*, 38–39, 97–98.

134. Delano, 58, 405–406.

135. Delano, 406–407

136. Child, *Journal*, April 27, 1811; May 8 and 16, 1811.

137. Delano, *Narrative*, 477.

138. Patterson, *Narrative*, 82; Thomas Bargatzky, "Beachcombers and Castaways as Innovators," *Journal of Pacific History*, 15, no. 2 (April 1980): 93–102.

139. Henry Wadsworth Longfellow, "The Wreck of the Hesperus," in *Ballads and Other Poems*, 1842.

140. Putnam, *Vessels*, 10.

141. Oliver, *Wreck of the Glide*, 15.

142. Oliver, 16.

143. Bowditch, *Journal*, 41.

144. Osmund Tiffany Jr., *The Canton Chinese, or, the American's Sojourn in the Celestial Empire* (Boston, 1849), 13; Bowditch, *Journal*, 39.

145. Delano, *Narrative*, 39.

146. Delano, 430.

147. Schotte, *Sailing School*, 7.

148. Oliver, *Wreck of the Glide*, 15.

149. Paullin, *American Voyages*, 15.

150. Delano, *Narrative*, 373–374; Paullin, *American Voyages*, 15.

151. Fanning, *Voyages*, 25.

152. Fanning, 26–27.

153. Delano, *Narrative*, 68, 311.

154. Delano, 107.

155. Delano, 153–154. Tropical fevers could also strike at inconvenient times and endanger a voyage entirely. Such a threat befell the *Magus* of Philadelphia, when her supercargo fell ill at Bantam, and prevented her from joining a convoy home as French privateers stalked the Indies. Paullin, *American Voyages*, 15.

156. Roberts, *Embassy*, 35–36.

157. Mary Wallis, *Life in Feejee*, 17.

158. Delano, *Narrative*, 51.

159. Porter, *China Journal*, 14; W. H. Allen, *India Directory, Or, Directions for Sailing to and from the East Indies* (London, 1836), 696–697.

160. Porter, *China Journal*, 14.

161. Porter, 145.

162. White, *Voyage*, 30.

163. Delano, *Narrative*, 99.

164. Delano, 87.

165. Tyng, *Before the Wind*, 92–93.

166. Bowditch, *Philippine Trade,*, 29.

167. White, *Voyage*, 148, 291–292.

168. White, 13.

169. James Fairhead, *The Captain and "the Cannibal"* (New Haven, CT: Yale University Press, 2015); Block, "Importance of the China Trade," 100

170. Thompson, *Sea Peoples*, 71–76.

171. Delano, *Narrative*, 37; Oliver, *Wreck of the Glide*, 18; Hunter, *Fan Kwei*, 9.

172. Delano, *Narrative*, 58; Oliver, *Wreck of the Glide*, 25.

173. Oliver, *Wreck of the Glide*, 24.

174. Patterson, *Narrative*, 61.

175. Delano, *Narrative*, 37.

176. Oliver, *Wreck of the Glide*, 23, 25.

177. Delano, *Narrative*, 80.

178. Delano, 83.

179. Delano, 95.

180. Delano, 79.

181. John Hoskins, "Narrative of the Second Voyage of the 'Columbia,'" in F. W. Howay, *Voyages of the Columbia to the Northwest Coast, 1787–1790 and 1790–1793* (Portland: Oregon Historical Society, 1990), 192.

182. Hoskins, "Narrative," 192.

183. As a measure if the uncertainties of the East Indies, the rumors did not stop Bowditch from trading for the prau's cargo of pepper. Bowditch, *Philippine Trade*, 39.

184. Bowditch, 38.

185. William Haswell, "Remarks on a Voyage in 1801 to the Island of Guam," *Essex Institute Historical Collections*, 53, no. 3 (July 1917): 193–214; Bowditch, *Philippine Trade*, 38–39; Trow, *Old Shipmasters*, 192; Drinker, *Journal*, 92–93.

186. Fanning, *Voyages*, 195–198.

187. Paine, *Ships and Sailors*, 185.

188. White, *Voyage*, 22–23.

189. White, 13–16.

190. Delano, *Narrative*, 93–94.

191. Delano, 157.

192. White, *Voyage*, 18–19.

193. White, *Journal*, quoted in Trow, *Old Shipmasters*, 223.

194. Porter, *China Journal*, 15.

195. Paine, *Ships and Sailors*, 242–243.

196. Delano, *Narrative*, 85.

197. Ruth Scobie, "The Many Deaths of Captain Cook: A Study in Metropolitan Mass Culture, 1780–1810" (PhD diss., York University, April 2013), 6.

198. Fanning, *Voyages*, 160–161.

199. Delano, *Narrative*, 80–81, 85.

200. Sullivan Dorr to Ebenezer Dorr, Canton, October 7, 1799, "Letters," *Proceedings of the Massachusetts Historical Society*, 183–184.

201. Roberts, *Embassy*, 37–38.

202. Charles M. Endicott, "Narrative of the Piracy, and Plunder of the Ship Friendship, of Salem, on the West Coast of Sumatra, in February 1831, and the Massacre of Part of her Crew: also, her Recapture Out of the Hands of the Malay Pirates," *Essex Institute Historical Collections*, 1, no. 1 (April 1859), 15–16.

203. Endicott, "Narrative," 15–16.

204. Endicott, "Narrative," 15.

205. Endicott, 16–17; Marsden, *Sumatra*, 280–282.

206. Endicott, "Narrative," 15–16.

207. David F. Long, "'Martial Thunder': The First Official American Armed Intervention in Asia," *Pacific Historical Review*, 42, no. 2 (May 1973): 148–149; Benjamin Armstrong, "'Immediate Redress': USS Potomac and the Pirates of Quallah Batoo," *Small Wars & Insurgencies*, 24, no. 1 (2013): 171–193.

208. It is likely that Patterson's book was an example of social writing, perhaps disctated to his minister who then edited the whole. We see hints in the Biblical epigrams to each chapter, such as "With melting heart and weeping eyes, / My trembling soul in anguish lies."

209. Patterson's *Eliza* wrecked on Nairai Island in June 1808.

210. Patterson, *Narrative*, 88.

211. Patterson, 87–88.

212. *Globalization of the United States, 1789–1861* (online exhibit), curated by Konstantin Dierks, Lilly Library, Indiana University, Bloomington, https://globalamerica.indiana.edu.

213. William Reynolds, *The Private Journal of William Reynolds, United States Exploring Expedition, 1838–1842*, ed. Nathaniel Philbrick & Thomas Philbrick (New York: Penguin, 2004), 122–124, 129; Herman J. Viola and Carolyn Margolis, eds., *Magnificent Voyagers: The U.S. Exploring Expedition, 1838–1842* (Washington, DC: Smithsonian Institution Press, 1985); 200, 206, 217–218; Charles S. Wilkes, *Voyage Round the World, embracing the Principal Events of the Narrative of the United States Exploring Expedition* (Philadelphia, 1849), 450.

214. Franchère, *Voyage*, 56

215. Versions of Jewitt's *Narrative of Adventures and Sufferings* went through eleven printings before 1860. F. W. Howay, "An Early Account of the Loss of the Boston, 1803," *Washington Historical Quarterly*, 17, no. 4 (October 1926), 287–288.

216. *A Journal of Captain Cook's Last Voyage to the Pacific Ocean, and in Pursuit of a North-west Passage, between Asia and America; Performed in the Years 1776, 1777, 1778, and 1779* (Hartford, CT: Nathaniel Patten, 1783); Gray, *Ledyard*, 98, 129–130; Bill Gifford, *Ledyard: In Search of the First American Explorer* (New York: Harcourt, 2007); James Zug, *The Last Voyage of Captain Cook: The Collected Writings of John Ledyard* (Washington, DC: National Geographic, 2005); James Zug, *American Traveler: The Life and Adventures of John Ledyard, the Man Who Dreamed of Walking The World* (New York: Basic, 2005); Goetzmann, *New Lands*, 231; Sydney Greenbie and Marjorie Barstow Greenbie, *Gold of Ophir: The China Trade in the Making of America* (New

York: Wilson-Erickson, 1937), 28; Hawes, *Gulf,* 113–116; Jared Sparks, *Life of John Ledyard, the American* (Cambridge, 1828).

217. What Americans made of these tales changed across generations. As the event receded in time and the eastern and western frontiers were "tamed," we see different treatments. For instance, in his 1926 article, Howay asserts that Jewitt's tale "has appealed strongly to all lovers of adventure since 1815." Howay, "Early Account," 280.

218. Ingraham, *Journal,* 156.

219. Ingraham, 139.

220. Ingraham, 103–104.

221. *The American Register* for 1807 noted, for instance, "There is likewise considerable interest in J. R. Jewett's Journal of Transactions at Nootka Sound. Mr. J. was one of the surviving crew of a ship whose commander was murdered in that place"; *American Register: or General Repository of History, Politics, and Science,* vol. 2, 157.

222. Ingraham, *Journal,* 104.

223. Joseph R. Ellis, *After the Revolution: Profiles of Early American Culture* (New York: W. W. Norton, 1979), 194–195.

224. Ingraham, *Journal,* 97

225. Ingraham, 47, 97.

226. Franchere, *Voyage,* 77.

227. Dodge, *New England;* James R. Gibson, *Otter Skins, Boston Ships, and China Goods: The Maritime Fur Trade of the Northwest Coast, 1785–1841* (Seattle: University of Washington Press, 1992); Anya Zilberstein, "Objects of Distant Exchange: The Northwest Coast, Early America, and the Global Imagination," *William and Mary Quarterly,* 3rd series, 64, no. 3 (July 2007): 591–620.

228. Howay, "Account," 285–287.

229. *Columbian Centennial,* April 25, 1804.

230. *Independent Chronicle* (Boston), May 14, 1807.

231. Ingraham, *Journal,* 225.

232. John R. Jewitt, *A Journal, Kept at Nootka Sound . . . Interspersed with Some Account of the Natives, Their Manners and Customs* (Boston, 1807); Jewitt, *A Narrative of the Adventures and Sufferings, of John R. Jewitt; Only Survivor of the Ship Boston, During a Captivity of Nearly Three Years among the Savages of Nootka Sound: With an Account of the Manners, Mode of Living, and Religious Opinions of the Natives* (Middletown, CT, 1815). Richard Alsop had popularized Jewitt's *Journal* in the more thrilling *A Narrative of the Adventures and Sufferings,* drawing on English travelogues and Defoe's *Robinson Crusoe.* Samuel Patterson's 1817 book chronicled his *Adventures and Sufferings* around the world, including a stint on the Northwest coast. After a miserable passage of ten months in a leaky ship with short supplies of food and water, his ship "was wrecked by drifting, and being hove by the billowed sea, in a calm and current on the coral reef, and every soul on board of her, save the Tonga native pilot, perished, or were massacred by the savages, as each individual obtained, through the breakers and surf, a foothold on the rocks."

233. John R. Jewitt, *Narrative of the Adventures and Sufferings of John R. Jewitt* (Ithaca, NY: Mack, Andrus, 1849).

234. *North American Review,* 3, no. 7 (May 1816): 42.

235. Zilberstein, "Objects," 593n2.

236. This was the same vessel that was attacked by sixteen pirate junks in the South China Sea some years later. *Aurora General Advertiser* (Philadelphia), April 9, 1806; *Freeman's Weekly Museum* (Walpole, NH), April 11, 1806; *Mercantile Advertiser* (New York), April 12, 1806; *The Reporter* (Brattleboro, VT), April 12, 1806. The *Atahualpa* had cleared Boston for Canton and the Northwest coast by October 23, 1806. *People's Friend & Daily Advertiser* (New York), October 10–28, 1806.

237. *Aurora General Advertiser* (Philadelphia), April 9, 1806.

238. F. W. Howay, "The Trading Voyages of the Atahualpa," *Washington Historical Quarterly,* 19, no. 1 (January 1928), 5–6. "Later that account was in substance published in the form of a chap-book by Champante & Whitrow, Jewry Street, Aldgate, London, and sold for sixpence."

239. During the voyge, Thorn had tried to abandon a party from the *Tonquin* in the Falkland Islands, an attempt prevented only when partner Robert Stuart threatened to shoot him. Fanning, *Voyages,* 139–150.

240. F. W. Howay. "The Loss of the 'Tonquin,'" *Washington Historical Quarterly*, 13, no. 2 (April 1922): 83–92; Robert F. Jones, "The Identity of the Tonquin's Interpreter," *Oregon Historical Quarterly*, 98, no. 3 (Fall 1997): 296–314.

241. Franchère, *Voyage,* 87.

242. Oliver, *Wreck of the Glide,* 20.

243. *New-York Gazette & General Advertiser*, October 19, 1811.

244. Also carrying the report were the *Massachusetts Spy* (published as *Thomas's Massachusetts Spy, or Worcester Gazette*), May 13, 1812; *Poulson's American Daily Advertiser*, May 13, 1812; *Windham Herald* (CT), May 14, 1812; and *The Reporter* (Brattleboro, VT), May 16, 1812; the *Alexandria Herald* (Alexandria, VA), May 18, 1812; the *Federal Republican* (Baltimore, MD), May 19, 1812; and two dozen or more other papers, from New Hampshire to South Carolina.

245. *Philosophical Magazine*, 61: 314–316, The report appeared also in the *Federal Republican for the Country*, July 21, 1815

246. Terms such as "regular" and "well regulated" distinguish European and American enterprise from that of the "savages."

247. Edgar Alan Poe, "Review of *Astoria*" (reprint), in *The Works of Edgar Allan Poe* (1856), 4:410–447.

248. Fanning, *Voyages,* 137, 146–150, 166.

249. Arrell Morgan Gibson, *Yankees in Paradise: The Pacific Basin Frontier* (Alberquerque: University of New Mexico Press, 1993), 112.

250. Fanning, *Voyages,* 139–140.

251. Fanning, 140–141.

252. James L. Flexner, "Historical Archaeology, Contact, and Colonialism in Oceania," *Journal of Archaeological Research*, 22, no. 1 (March 2014): 43–87.

253. Douglas, "Voyages," 714.

254. Jolly and Tcherkézoff, "Oceanic Encounters," 1.

255. Douglas, "Voyages," 712.

256. Douglas, 713.

257. Douglas, 720.

258. Barnard, *Narrative,* 260.

259. Delano, *Narrative*, 80–81.

260. Kate Fullagar and Michael A. McDonnell, eds., *Facing Empire: Indigenous Experiences in a Revolutionary Age* (Baltimore, MD: Johns Hopkins University Press, 2018), 4.

261. Gananath Obeyesekere, *The Apotheosis of Captain Cook: European Mythmaking in the Pacific* (Princeton, NJ: Princeton University Press, 1992).

262. Fullagar and McDonnell, *Facing Empire*, 4.

263. I. C. Campbell, "European-Polynesian Encounters: A Critique of the Pearson Thesis," *Journal of Pacific History*, 29, no. 2 (December 1994), 222.

264. Mark D. Kaplanoff, "Nootka Sound in 1789: Joseph Ingraham's Account," *Pacific Northwest Quarterly*, 65, no. 4 (October 1974), 162; Serge Tcherkézoff, "A Reconsideration of the Role of Polynesian Women in Early Encounters with Europeans: Supplement to Marshall Sahlins' Voyage around the Islands of History," in Jolly and Tcherkézoff, "Oceanic Encounters," 113–159.

265. Imgraham, *Journal*, 224.

266. Zilberstein, "Objects," 598–605.

267. Ingraham, *Journal*, 179–180.

268. Kelly L. Watson, *Insatiable Appetites: Imperial Encounters with Cannibals in the North Atlantic World* (New York: NYU Press, 2016), 7, 26. Watson is interested in the evolving concept, rather than the practice, of the cannibal. There is much more to Watson's study—particularly her ability to situate the construction of barbarism with ideas of gender. See also Jared Staller, *Converging on Cannibals: Terrors of Slaving in Atlantic Africa, 1509–1670* (Athens: Ohio University Press, 2019).

269. Lowe, *Intimacies*.

270. This title is drawn from George Fitzhugh's 1857 proslavery tract, *Cannibals All! Or, Slaves without Masters*. Fitzhugh maintained that the capitalism of the Northern states fostered a kind of "moral cannibalism," a metaphor for management's exploitation of workers. Like most early Americans, Fitzhugh used the term "cannibal" rather cavalierly to suggest conditions of anarchy or savagery. White, *Voyage*, 14.

271. Watson, *Insatiable Appetites*, 7–9.

272. Patterson, *Narrative*, 87.

273. Watson, *Insatiable Appetites*, 1–5.

274. Rouleau, especially, has demonstrated how American mariners appropriated terms associated with Native Americans and imposed them upon a Pacific Ocean setting. Rouleau, *Sails*.

Chapter 6 • Echoes

1. Molina, *How Race Is Made*, 1–6.

2. Greenberg, *Manhood*, 9–17.

3. *Federal Gazette, and Philadelphia Evening Post*, November 12, 1789.

4. Richard Slotkin, *Regeneration through Violence: The Mythology of the American Frontier, 1600–1860* (Middletown, CT: Wesleyan University Press, 1973); Richard Drinnon, *Facing West: The Metaphysics of Indian Hating and Empire Building* (Minneapolis: University of Minnesota Press, 1980); Alan Taylor, *The Civil War of 1812: American Citizens, British Subjects, Irish Rebels, & Indian Allies* (New York:

Alfred A. Knopf, 2010); Donegan, *Seasons*; Holger Hoock, *Scars of Independence: America's Violent Birth* (New York: Random House, 2017).

5. Reginald Horsman, *Race and Manifest Destiny: The Origins of American Racial Anglo-Saxonism* (Cambridge: Harvard University Press, 1981), 129–157.

6. Collingwood-Whittick, *Pain*, xiii–xliii; Jackson, "Masculinity," 199–213; Pearson, *Ocean*, 32; Driessen, "Mediterranean," 130, 131, 134; Land, "Tolerance," 78–101.

7. Peter N. Stearns, *Tolerance in World History* (London: Routledge, 2017), 97–98.

8. Elizabeth Kelly Gray, "Whisper to Him the Word 'India': Trans-Atlantic Critics and American Slavery, 1830–1860," *Journal of the Early Republic*, 28, no. 3 (Fall 2008): 388.

9. Schueller, *Orientalisms*, 76–78.

10. Mark Twain, *Innocents Abroad; or, the New Pilgrims' Progress* (Hartford, 1869; Digireads.com Publishing, 2018), 211–214.

11. Goodwin, *Horizons*, 313–315.

12. David Fromkin, *A Piece to End All Peace: The Fall of the Ottoman Empire and the Creation of the Modern Middle East* (New York: Avon, 1989), 211–212; Ann Marie Wilson, "In the Name of God, Civilization, and Humanity: The United States and the Armenian Massacres of the 1890s," *Le Mouvement Social*, 227 (April–June 2009): 27–44; Harry N. Howard, "The Bicentennial in American-Turkish Relations," *Middle East Journal*, 30, no. 3 (Summer 1976), 298.

13. Wilson, "In the Name of God," 27.

14. Howard, "Bicentennial," 299; Stephan Astourian," The Armenian Genocide: An Interpretation," *History Teacher*, 23, no. 2 (February 1990), 114.

15. Balakian, *The Burning Tigris: The Armenian Genocide and America's Response* (New York: Harper, 2004), 20.

16. Balakian, xviii, 10, 19–20; Astourian, 113; Wilson, "In the Name of God," 28.

17. Brian Michael Jenkins, "The Land of the Fearful, or the Home of the Brave?" in *The Long Shadow of 9/11: America's Response to Terrorism,* ed. Brian Michael Jenkins and John Paul Godges (Santa Monica, CA: RAND, 2011), 195–208.

18. Oren, *Power*, 582–585.

19. Mubarak Altwaiji, "Neo-Orientalism and the Neo-Imperialism Thesis: Post-9/11 US and Arab World Relationship," *Arab Studies Quarterly*, 36, no. 4 (Fall 2014): 313.

20. Carol Fadda-Conrey, "Arab American Citizenship in Crisis: Destabilizing Representations of Arabs and Muslims in the US after 9/11," *Modern Fiction Studies*, 57, no. 3 (Fall 2011): 532–555; Heather Hurlburt, "The Only Thing We Have to Fear Is Fear-Based Politics," *Democracy Beyond COVID-19* (April 2020): 20–23.

21. Mohammed Ayoob, "Was Huntington Right? Revisiting the Clash of Civilizations," *Insight Turkey*, 14, no. 4 (Fall 2012): 3.

22. Quoted in Ayoob, "Was Huntington Right?," 3.

23. Abdullah al-Ahsan, "The Clash of Civilizations Thesis and Muslims: The Search for an Alternative Paradigm," *Islamic Studies*, 48, no. 2 (Summer 2009): 189–217; Eric Neumayer and Thomas Plümper, "International Terrorism and the Clash of Civilizations," *British Journal of Political Science*, 39, no. 4 (October 2009): 713.

24. M. A. Muqtedar Khan, "Post-Orientalism and Geopolitics," *Insight Turkey*, 22, no. 2 (Spring 2020): 128–133.

25. Whitehill, "Remarks," 306

26. Kendall A. Johnson, *The New Middle Kingdom: China and the Early American Romance of Free Trade* (Baltimore, MD: Johns Hopkins University Press, 2017).

27. Fred H. Matthews, "White Community and 'Yellow Peril,'" *Mississippi Valley Historical Review*, 50, no. 4 (March 1964): 613; Judy Yung, *The Chinese Exclusion Act and Angel Island: A Brief History with Documents* (New York: Bedford St. Martins, 2018).

28. Matthews, "White Community," 614–615.

29. Michael C. Coleman, "Presbyterian Missionary Attitudes Toward China and the Chinese, 1837–1900," *Journal of Presbyterian History*, 56, no. 3 (Fall 1978), 186–187.

30. John Kuo Wei Tchen, *New York before Chinatown: Orientalism and the Shaping of American Culture, 1776–1882* (Baltimore, MD: Johns Hopkins University Press, 1999), chap. 1; Judy Yung, *The Chinese Exclusion Act and Angel Island: A Brief History with Documents* (New York: Bedford St. Martins, 2018), 5–14.

31. Yung, *Chinese Exclusion Act*, 5–14.

32. B. P. Wilcox, "Anti-Chinese Riots in Washington," *Washington Historical Quarterly*, 20, no. 3 (July 1929): 204–212.

33. Nonhistorians look to the past to inform the idea of China as a bugaboo but are selective in their use of history. See, for instance, Surjit Mansingh, "How the US Perceives China and India," *World Affairs: The Journal of International Issues*, 1, no. 4 (October–December 1997): 126–142.

34. Michael Schuman, "What Happens When China Leads the World," *The Atlantic*, October 5, 2020.

35. Ralph Jennings, "Bad For Business? China's Corruption Isn't Getting Any Better Despite Government Crackdowns," *Forbes*, May 15, 2018.

36. Minxin Pei, "Corruption Threatens China's Future," *Carnegie Endowment for International Peace Policy Brief*, 55 (October 2007): 1–7, https://carnegieendowment.org/files/pb55-pei_china_corruption_final.pdf.

37. Nathaniel Taplin, "China's Corruption Paradox," *Wall Street Journal*, November 1, 2019.

38. Anthony Kuhn, "Pompeo Rails against China at 'Quad' Meeting with Foreign Ministers in Tokyo," NPR (website), October 6, 2020, www.npr.org/2020/10/06/920683263/pompeo-rails-against-china-at-quad-meeting-with-foreign-ministers-in-tokyo; Humeyra Pamuk and Sakura Murakami, "Pompeo Uses Tokyo Visit to Slam China, Seek Asian Allies' Support," Reuters (website), October 5, 2020, www.reuters.com/article/usa-asia-pompeo/pompeo-uses-tokyo-visit-to-slam-china-seek-asian-allies-support-idUSKBN26Q2E6.

39. Josiah Harlan, *A Memoir of India and Avghanistaun* (Philadelphia: J. Dobson, 1842); Josiah Harlan, *Central Asia: Personal Narrative of Josiah Harlan, 1823–1841*, ed. Frank E. Ross (London: Luzac, 1939), 10; Mukhtar Ali Isani, "Melville and the 'Bloody Battle in Affghanistan,'" *American Quarterly*, 20, no. 3 (Autumn 1968): 645–649.

40. Gray, "Whisper to Him," 384–396.

41. Nikhil Bilwakesh, "'Their Faces Were Like So Many of the Same Sort at Home': American Responses to the Indian Rebellion of 1857," *American Periodicals*, 21, no. 1 (2011): 1.

42. Sujit Mukherjee, "Early American Images of India," *India Quarterly*, 20, no. 1 (January–March 1964), 44.

43. Nikhil Bilwakesh, "Their Faces Were Like So Many of the Same Sort at Home": American Responses to the Indian Rebellion of 1857," *American Periodicals*, 21, no. 1 (2011), 1.

44. Frederic Carpenter, *Emerson and Asia* (Cambridge, MA: Harvard University Press, 1930); Arthur Christy, *The Orient in American Transcendentalism: A Study of Emerson, Thoreau, and Alcott* (New York: Columbia University Press, 1932); Carl T. Jackson, "The Orient in Post-Bellum American Thought: Three Pioneer Popularizers," *American Quarterly*, 22, no. 1 (Spring 1970): 67–81; James Freeman Clarke, *Ten Great Religions: An Essay in Comparative Theology* (Boston, 1871); Samuel Johnson, *Oriental Religions and their Relation to Universal Religion* (Boston, 1872); Jackson, "Orient in Post-Bellum American Thought," 70, 74, 80

45. Quoted in Mukherjee, "Early American Images of India," 48.

46. Quoted in Mukherjee, 50.

47. See, for instance, the *San Antonio Express*, May 10, 1902; the *Bee* (Washington, DC), November 28, 1908; the *Appeal* (St. Paul, MN), September 7, 1917; and the *Pueblo Chieftain* (Colorado), May 2, 1919.

48. *Parsons Weekly Blade* (Kansas), January 16, 1897.

49. *Cherokee Advocate* (Oklahoma), July 17, 1889.

50. *Biloxi Daily Herald* (Mississippi), May 4, 1900.

51. *Wichita Searchlight* (Kansas), August 1, 1908.

52. Katherine Mayo, *Mother India* (New York: Harcourt Brace, 1927); Grace Thompson-Seton, *Yes, Lady Saheb: A Woman's Adventurings with Mysterious India* (New York: Harper, 1925); Gertrude Emerson, *Voiceless India* (New York: Doubleday, Doran, 1930); Nilla Cram Cook, *My Road to India* (New York: Lee Furman, 1938); Grace Campbell, "Interlopers in India: American Women Travelers 1919–1939" (MA thesis, Salem State University, 2019).

53. Mansingh, "How the US Perceives China and India," 128.

54. Mansingh, 135.

55. Fanning, *Voyages*, 224; Delano, *Narrative*, 185–186.

56. Neil Rennie, *Far-Fetched Facts: The Literature of Travel and the Idea of the South Seas* (New York: Oxford University Press, 1995), 186; Juan R. Torruella, "Ruling America's Colonies: The 'Insular Cases,'" *Yale Law & Policy Review*, 32, no. 1 (Fall 2013): 63–64.

57. Andrew Jackson, Third Annual Message, December 6, 1831, The American Presidency Project, www.presidency.ucsb.edu/documents/third-annual-message-3; Andrew Jackson, Fourth Annual Message, December 4, 1832, The American Presidency Project, www.presidency.ucsb.edu/documents/fourth-annual-message-3.

58. Piero Gleijeses, "1898: The Opposition to the Spanish-American War," *Journal of Latin American Studies*, 35, no. 4 (November 2003): 681–719; Lauren L. Basson, "Fit for Annexation but Unfit to Vote? Debating Hawaiian Suffrage Qualifications at the Turn of the Twentieth Century," *Social Science History*, 29, no. 4 (Winter 2005): 575–598.

59. Lisa M. Kömives, "Enfranchising a Discrete and Insular Minority: Extending Federal Voting Rights to American Citizens Living in United States Territories," *University of Miami Inter-American Law Review*, 36, no. 1 (Fall 2004), 115–138; Eric Schepard, "The Great Dissenter's Greatest Dissents: The First Justice Harlan, the

'Color-Blind' Constitution and the Meaning of His Dissents in the 'Insular Cases' for the War on Terror," *American Journal of Legal History*, 48, no. 2 (April 2006): 119–146; Torruella, "Ruling America's Colonies," 57–95.

60. Torruella, "Ruling America's Colonies," 69.

61. Schepard, "Great Dissenter's Greatest Dissents," 134.

62. Schepard, 133; Adam D. Burns, "Retentionist in Chief: William Howard Taft and the Question of Philippine Independence, 1912–1916," *Philippine Studies: Historical & Ethnographic Viewpoints*, 61, no. 2 (June 2013): 163–192.

63. Steve Brown, "Archaeology of Brutal Encounter: Heritage and Bomb Testing on Bikini Atoll, Republic of the Marshall Islands," *Archaeology in Oceania*, 48, no. 1 (April 2013): 26–39; Jeffrey Sasha Davis, "Representing Place: 'Deserted Isles' and the Reproduction of Bikini Atoll," *Annals of the Association of American Geographers*, 95, no. 3 (September 2005): 607–625.

64. Fischer-Tiné, *Anxieties*; Bergman, "Disaster," 934–946.

65. Robert D. Kaplan, *Eastward to Tartary* (New York: Vintage, 2014), xiii.